A Cognitive Appro
Language Learning

Peter Skehan

Oxford University Press   1998

Oxford University Press
Great Clarendon Street, Oxford OX2 6DP

Oxford New York
Athens Auckland Bangkok Bogota Bombay
Buenos Aires Calcutta Cape Town Dar es Salaam
Delhi Florence Hong Kong Istanbul Karachi
Kuala Lumpur Madras Madrid Melbourne
Mexico City Nairobi Paris Singapore
Taipei Tokyo Toronto Warsaw

and associated companies in
Berlin Ibadan

Oxford and *Oxford English* are trade marks of
Oxford University Press

ISBN 0 19 437217 0

Typeset by Oxford University Press

Printed in Hong Kong

Contents

Acknowledgements

It is a pleasure to thank the many people who have helped in the preparation of this book. I must first mention the Centre for Applied Linguistic Research (CALR) at Thames Valley University who have been consistently supportive of the project to complete the book, and whose funds have been very much appreciated. Within the Centre I must thank my colleague Pauline Foster who, with CALR and Economic and Social Research Council (ESRC) financial support, has been so important in collaborating in the research reported as part of Chapters 3 and 5. I am grateful also to Uta Mehnert on whose research some of the discussion is based.

A number of people have been wonderfully helpful in providing material for the book, as well as reading and commenting on parts of it. I would very much like to thank Martin Bygate, Carol Chapelle, Bill Grabe, Jeannette Littlemore, Tim McNamara, Peter Robinson, Richard Schmidt, Merrill Swain, Jill Wigglesworth, and Dave and Jane Willis. I would also like to thank the anonymous reviewers (two of whom were Paul Meara and Tom Scovel), as well as my editor at Oxford University Press, for constructive suggestions throughout. My thanks go also to Henry Widdowson, for encouragement all along the way, as well as good comments on the manuscript. Finally, I would like to thank my family, once again, for patience during my extended preoccupation.

The author and publisher are grateful to the following for permission to reproduce extracts and figures from copyright material:

Academic Press Inc. for a figure from J.S. Johnson and E. Newport: 'Critical period effects in second language learning: the influence of maturational state on the acquisition of English as a second language' in *Cognitive Psychology* 21 (1989)

Addison Wesley Longman Ltd. for permission to adapt a table from J. Willis: *A Framework for Task-Based Learning* (Longman, 1996)

Lyle F. Bachman for two tables from *Fundamental Considerations in Language Testing* (Oxford University Press, 1990)

Cambridge University Press for a table from G.A. Brown *et al.*: *Teaching Talk: Strategies for Production and Assessment* (Cambridge University Press, 1984)

Oxford University Press for permission to adapt a figure from 'Modelling performance: Opening Pandora's box' in *Applied Linguistics* 16 (1995) by T. McNamara

Despite every effort to trace and contact copyright holders before publication, this has not always been possible. If notified, the publisher will be pleased to rectify any errors or omissions at the earliest opportunity.

For Anna

Preface

This book represents a personal view of second language acquisition from a processing perspective. It attempts to relate two of my interests: second language acquisition, with its emphasis on universal processes, and the study of individual differences, with its clear concern for how people are different when they learn second languages. I attempt to relate them through the underlying approach which is used—to investigate second language learning through the cognitive abilities of the learner and the processing problems that the learner has to confront.

As a result, there are many areas which are neglected. Sociolinguistic influences barely get a mention. Nor is there explicit concern with the nature of the language system *per se*. Even within the scope of individual differences there are many areas of omission—affective influences being the major one of these. It is not that I consider any of these areas unimportant. It is, rather, that I restrict myself to trying to unify issues on second language learning within a cognitive perspective, pushing this explanatory approach as far as it will go, in the hope that it will be illuminating. There is also an implicit claim that much research in second language acquisition and the study of language learning has emphasized relatively unrewarding areas. So in this book there is little concern with universal grammar, or with interaction-based accounts. In each case I consider that these areas, although interesting and each the starting point for an impressive research tradition, are not effective in accounting for much variance in second language learning.

This book was written to sketch out an alternative account which redresses some of these imbalances. It seems to me that there has been a shift towards the acceptance of a processing perspective within the field of second language learning, and that if such a perspective gathers pace, it will have a beneficial influence on the way research concerns and pedagogic practice come together more closely. I would like to try to encourage such a development.

Introduction

Issues and themes: universalist and differential accounts of second language learning and performance

The fields of second language acquisition and language pedagogy have seen large numbers of publications in recent years, and so the appearance of another book requires some justification. Of course, there is always the argument that developments occur through research and publication and that these need consolidation periodically in book form to make them more accessible, to bring them together, and to organize the claims that are made. But this argument is effectively neutralized by the relatively recent publication of, for example, Larsen-Freeman and Long's (1991) *An Introduction to Second Language Acquisition Research*, and especially Ellis's (1994) *The Study of Second Language Acquisition*, which, at more than 800 pages, represents a milestone for the profession, providing comprehensive coverage of the entire field.

The present book does not attempt to provide complete or even-handed coverage of second language acquisition (SLA) and pedagogy. Rather it tries to argue more narrowly for particular viewpoints which I feel have been under-represented in recent years. In that respect, it tries to redress what I see as misplaced emphases, thus bringing back into prominence certain influences upon second language learning which, often for historical reasons, have been neglected. Stating three underlying problems helps to clarify these claims:

1 Psycholinguistics, the study of the psychological processes underlying language learning and use, has been insufficiently influential on our profession as a foundation discipline, losing out in importance to linguistics and sociolinguistics.
2 There is an unfortunate division between universalist accounts, which focus on common structures and processes in all second language learning, and differential accounts, which focus on differences between learners.
3 Theory and pedagogy have an uneasy relationship with one another: frequently pedagogic applications derived from theoretical approaches have only a perfunctory quality, rather than being properly rooted in theory.

The influence of psycholinguistics

The relative lack of influence of psycholinguistics, the first theme of this book, is becoming more apparent as continued progress is made in this 'feeder' discipline. It is, of course, understandable that the language teaching profession should be sceptical of the discipline which bequeathed it audiolingualism, pattern practice, and the like. Such scepticism has undoubtedly been a factor in the way in which it is linguistics which has been seen as the parent discipline for language teaching. Structural linguistics, especially in North America, has had an immense influence, either through figures such as Bloomfield and Fries, with audiolingual applications, or through Chomsky, and generative grammar, with its assumptions about Language Acquisition Devices (LADs) and the engagement of naturalistic learning processes. In either case, the nature of the linguistic material which is the target for learning has shaped our understanding of how learning itself takes place. Sociolinguistics has also grown in influence in the last twenty-five years through the work of such people as Hymes, Labov, and Tarone, who have demonstrated more clearly the importance of the social contexts in which languages are learned, and the way they influence the meanings which are expressed.

I am not arguing that linguistics and sociolinguistics are not relevant for second language learning and use, but rather that their attractions have rather diverted attention from the role of psycholinguistics. Of course, there are many who would argue that psycholinguistic analyses have been all too important (Bourne 1986). Such critics could draw our attention to the enormous increase in importance of second language acquisition as an independent discipline, with the implicit claim that if SLA is not psycholinguistics, then what else could be! But I want to argue that indeed SLA has itself been overly influenced by linguistics and sociolinguistics, and has not, until recently, drawn effectively on contemporary cognitive psychology. There has been a widespread assumption that language is special, and that if a language acquisition module exists in humans, our views of second language acquisition too will be constrained by this basic endowment. As a result, an interpretation of psycholinguistics which emphasizes information processing and cognitive abilities, two of the major objectives of contemporary cognitive psychology, has been of secondary importance to linguistically-motivated universals and sociolinguistic generalizations.

I argue that two general assumptions for language learning as a cognitive activity justify an increased scope for the operation of psycholinguistic factors. First, there is the old chestnut of whether there is a critical period for language learning. The contrasting positions on this question each have long antecedents. It will be argued in this book (principally in Chapter 9) that the balance of evidence now is in favour of the existence of such a temporary predisposition for language learning amongst humans. Before the end of the critical period, language acquisition is indeed qualitatively different from other learning, but that after the period is over, language learning is constrained by similar structures and processes to other learning. If, as a result, we have to regard second language learning as cognitive in orientation, then we need to take more seriously what psychologists tell us generally about how humans learn.

The second underlying assumption is less biological and more social and psychological. It is that *meaning* takes priority for older learners, and that the *form* of language has secondary importance. This claim relates to both comprehension and production. Regarding comprehension, the resources to extract meaning that humans possess increase in effectiveness as we get older. We become more adept at using strategies of communication, at exploiting schematic knowledge so that we say less but mean more, because we can exploit the collaborative construction of meaning that becomes increasingly possible. We also deliberately engage in more elliptical communication to avoid accusations of pedantry and to ensure that conversations proceed purposefully. Corder (1974) gives the example of an exchange between an airline passenger (on an early morning flight), and a steward, holding a coffee jug and clearly about to return to the front of the cabin:

Passenger: '*I say!*'
Steward: '*Empty.*'

The exchange lacks for nothing, given that the context, including the passenger's obvious fear of caffeine deprival, renders the need for complete sentences irrelevant.

As a result, we can often bypass a pivotal role for form in conversations since meaning can be extracted without exhaustive analyses of the structural aspects of language—we only need to understand enough for the communicative encounter we are in to proceed. Even if there were no critical period, these factors would give a LAD a more difficult task to accomplish in the case of the older learner of a second language. In many communicative interactions, the LAD would not be needed to extract meaning, and so the quality of the new material which would be input to the acquisition processes would be impoverished.

Moving to production as language users, we develop effective means of coping with one of the greatest problems of all: how to keep speaking at normal rates in real time. We do this in a number of ways (as we will see in succeeding chapters), but one of the most important (in itself as well as for language learning) is that, as native speakers, we draw upon lexical modes of communication. In other words, rather than construct each utterance 'mint fresh' (as Bolinger has characterized it), and so require considerable computational power, we economize by stitching together language chunks which free processing resources during communication so that planning for the form and content of future utterances can proceed more smoothly.

This claim, simply put, is far-reaching in its consequences. It recasts our views of what language is, and it changes definitively the relationship between competence and performance. It also implies the existence of a dual-coding approach to language performance and to language learning. The dual coding requires us to account for the use of a rule-based system in economical and parsimonious performance and a memory-based system which provides fast access. An account is also needed of the coexistence of these two systems.

When we turn to learning and change, the analysis becomes even more intriguing. The argument so far has been that meaning is primary, and that a range of factors (for example, elliptical, strategic communication; lexically-based performance) takes attention away from form. But if that is the case, how can learning proceed? Such learning requires, in some way, the development of an underlying and evolving interlanguage system which becomes progressively more complex and closer to the target language system in question. But to trigger such a process, methods of contriving a focus on form are needed which capture learners' attention, so that they may incorporate newly-noticed forms into their developing language systems. Discussions of consciousness, and above all, noticing (Schmidt 1990), are relevant here, and profitably shift the discussion to the factors which make noticing more likely to occur.

Task-based instruction and language testing

Following from such general discussion of psycholinguistic influences on performance and learning, two major practical applications are offered: towards task-based instruction and towards language testing. Much foreign language instruction is based on form-focused language presentation, followed by controlled practice. Only then is some degree of free production used. A task-based approach, in contrast, gives learners tasks to transact in the expectation that doing such tasks, for example comparing one another's family trees, will drive forward language development. Given that language is learned for communication, and that meaning is primary, the attraction of a task-based approach to instruction is that it enables each of these to operate fairly directly. But of course the disadvantage is that engaging meaning and enabling communication might de-emphasize form even further than might be the case otherwise. So the challenge of task-based instruction is to contrive sufficient focus on form to enable interlanguage development to proceed without compromising the naturalness of the communication that tasks can generate. Three issues are fundamental to such pedagogic aspirations:

– how tasks are selected to maximize the chances of a focus on form;
– how tasks are implemented, through pre- and post-task activities, as well as task adaptation;
– how performance on tasks can best be conceptualized and evaluated.

The discussion of the selection and implementation of tasks will explore how a form–content balance can be struck, and how learners can be induced to take risks in their language performance and push for change, when this is appropriate, as well as focus on conservatism, consolidation, control, and accuracy, at other times. This discussion links with the ways in which task-based performance is evaluated, since a three-way distinction will be made between fluency (often achieved through memorized and integrated language elements); accuracy (when learners try to use an interlanguage system of a particular level to produce correct, but possibly limited, language); and complexity (a willingness to take risks, to try out new forms even though they may not be completely correct). We will see that these three aspects of performance are somewhat independent of one another and that the influences upon each of them are rather different—a claim which has important implications for how task-based instruction can best be organized.

The second practical implication of an information-processing perspective is for testing. If it is accepted that language performance is based on a dual-coding system and that coping with real-time performance means developing effective modes of coexistence between form- and lexis-based systems, the manner in which testing is carried out has to change. It is no longer feasible to use tests to sample performance to gain an indirect insight into underlying competence and the structure of abilities. Instead, it is important to have systematic ways of approaching performance itself, and how processing factors influence it. This leads to the need to use a task-based approach to testing also, coupled with more effective ways of capturing different aspects of test performance. Once again, the distinction between fluency, accuracy, and complexity is relevant, and suggests that we need to draw upon cognitive psychology to shape how we make test-based generalizations about real-world performances.

Learner similarities and differences

So far we have been concerned with the usefulness of psycholinguistic approaches to general issues in language learning and processing. Now we can return to the second major theme which underlies the book: the contrast between a focus on learner similarities and a focus on learner differences. The most natural way to do this is through the discussion of foreign language aptitude, the construct which accounts for the variation in language-learning ability. A starting point for this discussion is the claim that aptitude has a componential structure, and that it is more appropriate to think of aptitude profiles, conveying the idea that rather than think of individual learners as more or less talented, one should think of them having strengths and weaknesses. Profiles can also be the basis for a reconceptualization of aptitude in information-processing terms. The fundamental claim of this argument is that one can make more sense of aptitude if one distinguishes between the three information-processing stages of input, central processing, and output. The three stages of information processing then provide a foundation for the different components of aptitude, since the three-component structure which is proposed can be linked to the three stages. The first, phonemic coding ability, can be linked to input processing. The second, language analytic ability, is more relevant to central processing, while the third, memory, goes beyond initial learning of new material, and also concerns retrieval of material and fluency in output. In tabular form, this can be represented as follows:

Processing Stage	Aptitude Component
input	phonemic coding ability
central processing	language analytic ability
output	memory

Looking at aptitude in this way is interesting in itself. But beyond that, other fruitful issues can be explored. The analysis enables a more interesting account to be given of the language–cognition relationship. It also allows us to explore the nature of exceptional learners, and to relate such learners to what might be termed the 'normally very talented' learners. It also allows a more productive discussion of the critical period evidence. And finally it allows us to re-examine the concept of learning style and to relate this to an information-processing viewpoint. As a result, some of the controversies within the literature on cognitive style are given a new perspective, and it will be argued that there is still considerable potential for research in this area.

These new analyses of the nature of learner difference lead, in turn, to a new set of pedagogic applications. The applications outlined earlier (task-based instruction and testing) made the assumption that everyone is the same and that no adaptation in teaching is necessary to take account of differences between learners. But the analysis of aptitude and cognitive style suggests that a profile approach to characterizing learners is more productive. The profiles of different sorts of learner are relatively small in number, with the result that one can envisage useful adaptations of instructional approaches which fall far short of the nightmare of a different set of materials for every different learner.

Two general sets of application are discussed. First, a contrast is made between analytic and memory-based learners, and it is argued that one can think of implementing materials, such as those for task-based instruction, to exploit learners' strengths, and to help learners to compensate for their weaknesses. This sort of application moderates the general conclusions that would follow from universalist perspectives alone. The second set of applications is more concerned with newer approaches to second language instruction which highlight the learner as an independent agent in the language-learning process. I argue that such approaches (process syllabuses, project work, for example) make a number of implicit assumptions about learners which are not often met. That is, there is often a gulf between what the learner is capable of doing and what the freedom of the new approach assumes can be done. Thus, there is a strong role for finding ways to equip the learner to assume the independence that is thought to be desirable. Research into learner differences, in both aptitude and style as well as in the area of learner strategies, can provide considerable guidance as to how pedagogic intervention can be carried out more effectively, and so Chapter 11 of the book explores how individuality can be conceptualized within approaches which encourage learner independence.

An outline of the book

The organization of the book follows from the above discussion. The first half of the book has four chapters on fundamental concepts in psycholinguistics, followed by Chapters 4–7, applications to instruction and testing based on these concepts. In the second half of the book, Chapters 8–11 cover basic issues in the study of learner differences followed, once again, by applications. The final chapter then attempts to bring these different threads together, the general and the variationist, the theoretical and the practical, to provide a more unified picture of second language learning. Looking at the outline in more detail, Chapter 1 examines the role of comprehension and production strategies in language learning. It explores early comprehension-based accounts, as well as the role of comprehension strategies. It moves on to look at the attacks that were mounted on comprehension-based accounts of language development, and the role proposed for the Comprehensible Output Hypothesis (Swain 1985). A discussion of communication strategies leads to the claim that the output hypothesis, too, is limited in its explanatory power, and that more complex approaches are necessary to do justice to the relationship between form and meaning in second language learning.

From this first chapter emerges the theme that language users are adept at coping with the pressures of real-time communication. Chapter 2 discusses one way in which this is done in greater depth—by drawing upon memorized language. This area has been much more active in recent years and the chapter reviews some of the major themes found in the literature. It suggests that earlier claims, by Bolinger, for example, that memory-based language is more important than universalist accounts propose have been corroborated through contemporary corpus-based linguistics. The chapter then explores the consequences for psycholinguistics and processing of the existence of dual-mode systems, one relying on structure and rule, and the other on chunk-based language and idiom. The former holds the key to continued interlanguage development, while the latter is more serviceable for real-time expression of meanings. The chapter ends by considering the way a tension between the two systems has importance for second language use and development.

Chapter 3 sketches out a psycholinguistic model of second language performance. It relates the stages of information processing (input, central processing, and output) to progressively more complex models of memory in second language performance and learning. Following researchers such as Schmidt (1990) and Gass (1988), the chapter argues for the central importance of noticing as a trigger for interlanguage change. Then the chapter examines evidence on the coexistence of rule- and exemplar-based representational systems before looking at an instance-based account of fluency. The chapter concludes with an extensive review of relevant empirical work in the area of second language performance.

In Chapter 4 some models of second language learning are discussed. The intention here is not to be comprehensive, but to look at what relevant models have to say to account for processing perspectives in second language research. Universal Grammar and the Multidimensional Model are covered relatively briefly, and then Bialystok's (1990) analysis-control model is discussed in a little more detail. In the final part of the chapter I present a more developed version of a dual-mode model and how it could be expected to contribute to our understanding of both second language performance and second language development.

Chapter 5 presents a rationale for the use of task-based instruction as the most effective means currently available to deal with the tensions that have been discussed in earlier chapters between:

– form and meaning
– rule and memory
– fluency, accuracy, and complexity.

I review the extensive research which is now available in this area, in an attempt to establish generalizations which allow us to understand how task choices affect performance and how different methods of implementing tasks also have impact. The chapter concludes with a summary of the most dependable findings which have emerged from task-based research.

This summary provides the entry point to Chapter 6, which is concerned with pedagogic application. This chapter discusses goals in task-based instruction and the ways in which we need principles which guide how tasks are chosen and are used. Five such principles are proposed, and then a pedagogic model is presented which tries to guide teachers in working with tasks in such a way that the benefits of this approach are realized, while its dangers are minimized. In effect, the chapter provides (yet another) justification for *balance* in foreign language teaching, and an avoidance of excessive prioritization on any one of the goals of fluency, accuracy, and complexity for extended periods.

Chapter 7 is also concerned with the application of an information-processing perspective, but this time to the field of language testing. Its basic thesis is that most current approaches to testing (such as Bachman 1990) use the starting point of a search for the structure of language abilities. I argue in this chapter that an abilities-based approach is too limited. Testing needs to develop an account of processing, showing how, based on the existence of a dual-mode system, abilities are mobilized in actual performance. Drawing on the discussion and research from the earlier chapters, I argue for a task-based approach to oral testing, and outline a model which tries to capture the range of influences on language test scores.

The remaining chapters in the book develop the contrasting theme of individual differences. Chapter 8 examines the nature of language aptitude. It updates the concept of aptitude and relates it to current work in cognitive psychology. As a starting point, a number of assumptions underlying aptitude research are proposed, as well as some of the criticisms that have been levelled against the concept of aptitude and its relevance. Several research areas within aptitude are reviewed, which show that the assumptions are, in the main, justified, and that the concept of aptitude is relevant to a wide variety of learning contexts, that it can be used profitably within acquisitional research, and above all, that the components of aptitude can be usefully related to an information-processing framework.

Chapter 9 takes the research into the information-processing interpretation of aptitude as a starting-point. The main themes of the chapter, though, are the grander issues of modularity and the critical period for language learning. These are approached through the study of aptitude structure, and particularly, of exceptional learners and users, especially as such people relate to aptitude. After examining theory and evidence on the critical period, the chapter argues that there is modularity in first and second language learning, but that the nature of the modularity changes at around the time that a critical period for language learning comes to a close.

Chapter 10 discusses concepts of learner style, and reinterprets them in more cognitive terms. After a review of early applications and debates arising from Witkin's (1962) proposals concerning field dependence/independence constructs, several more recent proposals are considered which characterize learning style in terms of two dimensions. It is proposed that the various proposals, with different approaches to the two dimensions in each case, can be reconciled within the superordinate categories of representation and processing, categories which are easily interpretable in information-processing terms.

Finally, drawing on Chapters 8 to 10, which all focus on learner differences, Chapter 11 tries to take these earlier discussions of differences into account, and explore what implications they have for instruction. After an initial discursion into the reasons for the neglect of the learner in language teaching and applied linguistics, applications of aptitudinal differences and processing style preferences are made to traditional instruction and procedural syllabuses. Then the final applications concern the scope that process syllabuses and project work have to develop learner strategies; and the potential there is to adapt instruction to different learner styles.

1 Comprehension and production strategies in language learning

In an influential paper which discusses differences between first and second language learning, Bley-Vroman (1989) draws attention to the extent to which second language (L2) learning often does not lead to success while first language learning, except in unusual cases, does. Faced with such an unsettling vote of no confidence, it is hardly surprising that the language teaching profession has explored many alternatives in the search to find more effective methods (Larsen-Freeman 1986). And it is equally unsurprising that one of the responses the profession has made is to see whether approaches to second language teaching which connect with *first* language acquisition hold out any promise.

This chapter will review two such instructional approaches. The first is broadly concerned with comprehension-driven learning, regarding second language development as likely to proceed, under the right conditions, simply as a result of exposure to meaningful input. The second, which in some ways arose out of dissatisfaction with the first, proposes that engaging in interaction and producing output will be sufficient to drive second language development forward. In each case, clearly, interlanguage development is seen to be the by-product of engaging in meaning-processing—in the first case through comprehension, and in the second through production. As a broader aim, the chapter develops the claim that instructional activities that emphasize meaning, whether comprehension or production-based, may induce learners to rely on strategies for communication which result in a bypassing of the form of language.

The place of comprehension in language learning

The clearest example of a comprehension-based account of second language development derives from Krashen (1985). He proposed that comprehensible input is the driving force for interlanguage development and change, and that the effects of such change carry over to influence production—that is, one learns to speak by listening, a claim which is interesting because of its counter-intuitive nature. Krashen argues that the predictability of the context makes what is said function as a commentary on what is already understood. The result is that it is more likely that the interlanguage system will be extended by the context-to-language mapping involved.

Krashen articulates a rationale for comprehension-based instruction. He draws attention to the success that various listening-based methodologies can claim, such as Total Physical Response (Asher 1977), as well as more experimental research in its support (Winitz 1978; Postovsky 1977). Most of all, though, he is enthusiastic about the achievements of immersion education, in which content-based learning 'drags' language learning with it parasitically. The features of immersion education, such as a learning environment which is supportive, and where bilingual teachers provide ample content-based input while allowing learners to produce language at their own pace, are seen as consistent with Krashen's position. Many evaluations of such an approach to foreign language education (Swain and Lapkin 1982) have shown that immersion-educated children reach much higher levels of achievement than do children educated by traditional 'core' methods, and in some areas perform at levels comparable to those of native-speaker children. And this is achieved without compromising content-based learning in areas such as geography, mathematics, science, and so on.

Krashen's views have been influential within second language education and have had considerable impact on the nature of pedagogic provision. Not surprisingly, therefore, they have been subjected to searching criticism, and it would now seem that the claims that were made cannot be substantiated. General criticisms of the theoretical status of Krashen's Monitor Model can be found in McLaughlin (1987), Gregg (1984), Spolsky (1985) and Skehan (1984a). The present discussion will be confined to analyses of the functioning of comprehension, and the ways that comprehension-driven learning may (or may not) occur.

Perhaps first of all, however, it is worth returning to the Canadian immersion programmes. Earlier evaluations were generally favourable, and suggested that such an approach to language provision might be worth adapting in other contexts. However, more recently the limitations of immersion approaches have also become apparent. In particular, attention is now increasingly drawn to the contrast in achievement between receptive and productive skills. Although the children concerned perform at levels of comprehension close to native speakers, the same cannot be said of their production abilities. Harley and Swain (1984) and Swain (1985) report that immersion-educated children, after many years of instruction, still make persistent errors when speaking and writing, suggesting that the automatic transfer between comprehension and production that Krashen argues for does not occur with any certainty.

This sort of evaluation demonstrates that an unqualified interpretation of the benefits of comprehension-based methodologies is not justified. In retrospect, it is difficult to see how comprehension-based approaches could have been so readily accepted, since they offered only rudimentary accounts of the mechanisms and processes by which comprehension was supposed to influence underlying interlanguage and generalize to production. Consequently, the next section will examine comprehension processes in more detail to try to account for the immersion evaluation findings.

Comprehension strategies

The findings become much more understandable if one examines the relevance of native-speaker comprehension models for the process of second language learning. Looking at comprehension in more 'micro' terms, Clark and Clark (1977) have argued that native-speaker listeners typically draw upon a range of comprehension strategies when they are listening. They focus on how syntactic and semantic strategies may be used to recover the meaning of what is heard in a rather improvisatory manner (ibid. 57–85). Examples of syntactic strategies that they discuss are:

1 Whenever you find a determiner (a, an, the) or quantifier (some, all, many, two, six, etc.) begin a new noun phrase.
2 Whenever you find a co-ordinating conjunction (and, or, but, nor) begin a new constituent similar to the one you just completed.
3 Try to attach each new word to the constituent that came just before.

(ibid.: 66)

They illustrate this last strategy through an advertising campaign run by a London evening paper with posters such as 'Zoo keeper finds Jaguar queuing for underground ticket', and 'Butler finds new station between Piccadilly and Oxford Street'. The paper wanted more people to realize how useful its small advertisements section was and to attract their attention to posters they would normally glance at only briefly while passing. So they exploited the 'double-take' that readers were led into by using the third of the above micro-strategies. Readers then had to recognize the improbability of their first interpretation of 'queuing' being attached to 'Jaguar' and 'new station' to 'between Piccadilly and Oxford Street', and move the link to the first noun in each sentence.

Clark and Clark (ibid.: 72–79) also discuss semantic strategies, such as:

4 Using content words alone, build propositions that make sense and parse the sentence into constituents accordingly.

Fillenbaum (1971) illustrates the operation of this strategy by showing that when people were asked to paraphrase 'perverse' sentences like 'John dressed and had a bath', they normalized them, with more than half of his subjects even asserting there was 'not a shred of difference' between the paraphrase and the original.

Clark and Clark are, in effect, arguing that native-speaker comprehension is probabilistic in nature, and does not follow any sort of deterministic model which would rely on an exhaustive parsing of the utterance concerned. Instead, listeners use a variety of means to maximize the chances that they will be able to recover the intended meaning of what is being said to them. They are not, in other words, using some linguistic model to retrieve meaning comprehensively and unambiguously. Instead, they cope with the problem of having to process language in real time by employing a variety of strategies which will probably combine to be effective, even though there is no guarantee that this will be the case. Presumably if a comprehension difficulty arises during ongoing processing, the listener can shift to a different mode of meaning extraction, as perhaps in the case of the zoo keeper and the Jaguar (as was intended by the authors of the poster). But this is not done routinely: the primary strategy is to achieve effectiveness in very fast language processing. Most listeners, in their native language, prefer to make a best-guess and keep up, rather than be accused of being slow-witted but accurate pedants (although we can all bring to mind some members of this species).

These 'micro' issues discussed by Clark and Clark (1977) can be located within a wider model of comprehension, which has a more macro perspective. The following table is adapted from Anderson and Lynch (1988: 13), who suggest that comprehension (again, for the moment, native-speaker comprehension) is dependent on three main sources of knowledge:

Schematic knowledge
    background knowledge
      – factual
      – sociocultural
    procedural knowledge
      – how knowledge is used in discourse

Contextual knowledge
    knowledge of situation
      – physical setting, participants, etc.
    knowledge of co-text
      – what has been, will be said

Systemic knowledge
    syntactic
    semantic
    morphological

These knowledge sources are drawn on, interactively, to achieve comprehension. Micro approaches (compare Clark and Clark 1977) are largely concerned with the operation of systemic knowledge which allows effective guesses to be made as to the meaning of what is being said. But

Anderson and Lynch are proposing that listeners build meanings by drawing on a wider range of resources, including both schematic and contextual knowledge. This implies that we are not exclusively dependent on the nature of the sounds addressed to us to achieve meaning. If we can relate what is being said to previous knowledge that we have, then we may be able to make very effective inferences about the messages concerned. Similarly, if we relate the message to the probable things that are likely to be said given the nature of the situational context, for example the bus queue, or what has been said previously, we are cutting down the range of possible meanings that we encounter, and making our guesses about meaning more likely to work. In this respect, listeners are behaving in exactly the same way as skilled readers do when they sample the printed material in front of them, rather than poring over every letter. Comprehension, in other words, is a mixture of bottom–up and top–down processes (Eskey 1988), with the more effective use of top–down processes reducing the extent of the dependence on the acoustic or visual stimulus involved.

What all this implies is that the comprehension process can be partly detached from the underlying syntactic system and from production. If comprehension draws on effective strategy use and on a capacity to relate input to context, then it may partly be an autonomous skill, whose development does not transfer automatically to other areas. A good comprehender may be an effective and appropriate strategy user, rather than someone who necessarily extracts useful syntactic inferences from the language which is being processed (Swain 1985). Effective comprehension may leave the underlying interlanguage system untouched and unscathed.

These arguments apply particularly forcefully to the second or foreign language learner. In such cases, we are dealing with people who do not lack schematic knowledge, but who do have limited systemic knowledge. Such learners, when confronted by comprehension problems, are likely to exploit what they are best at—mobilizing relevant schematic and contextual knowledge to overcome their systemic limitations. As a result, the need for the interlanguage system to be engaged, and to have the chance to change and grow, is reduced. To put this as directly as possible, it would seem that, after all, learning to speak a second language, at least for most people, is not accomplished simply by listening to it.

From comprehension to production

Krashen's proposal (1985), that comprehensible input drives forward language development and generalizes to speaking was attractive. Claiming that we learn through exposure to meaningful material may not be very startling—we are unlikely to learn from material we do not understand, after all. But claiming that interlanguage change arises in a receptive modality and later becomes available to production was by no means self-evident—hence the attraction of the argument.

We have seen, though, that the evidence reported from evaluations of immersion was not supportive of the original claim and so we have to accept that speaking does not come 'for free' simply through listening to comprehensible input. In this respect, Long (1985) makes a three-level distinction between conditions for second language learning. He suggests that it is valuable to consider whether factors such as input are:

1 necessary
2 sufficient
3 efficient

Logically, an influence might operate at level 1, 2, or 3, with 3 efficiency constituting the most searching criterion, that an influence is not just causative (necessary and sufficient), but is also likely to produce successful language learning most quickly. At the other extreme, level 1, necessary, an influence would have to be present, but would not be enough, in itself to produce successful learning (let alone accomplish this rapidly) since it could act simply as a precondition. Krashen's proposal was that input is necessary, sufficient, and efficient, while the preceding pages have argued against this.

Roles for output

Swain (1985; Swain and Lapkin 1982), an important contributor of immersion-based evidence, was led to consider whether other factors besides input might take us further in meeting the three levels of condition proposed by Long, and account for how language development might be driven forward. In particular, she proposed the Comprehensible Output Hypothesis, that to learn to speak we have to actually speak! Drawing on her specific suggestions (Swain 1985), as well as on other sources, several roles for output can be identified that are relevant to language learning. The first two of the proposed roles still have a connection with input, but rework this relationship in some way. The remaining roles for output are more specifically targeted on the productive modality itself.

A   To generate better input

Paradoxically, one needs to start by drawing attention to the way in which one could only get good quality input by using output (speaking) to give one's interlocutor feedback, so that the input directed to the listener is more finely tuned to the listener's current competence (Long 1985). In this view, output is important as a signalling device to negotiate better input: input would still be the major explanatory construct, but output would be necessary to generate it most effectively. Simply listening would not ensure that good quality input would be received, since one would have to rely on good luck or the sensitivity of one's interlocutor, neither of which is very.dependable. The strongest form of this account concerns the 'negotiation for meaning' literature (Pica 1994). This proposes that engaging in meaning negotiation, as indexed by the use of, for example, clarification requests, confirmation checks, and comprehension checks, evidences efficient signalling of miscomprehension and the clear engagement of a malleable interlanguage system which is more likely, as a result, to develop productively. In such cases, better input should be received, but in addition the attempt to engage in conversation will trigger support at very important points for interlanguage development.

B   *To force syntactic processing*

Swain (1985) argues that knowing that one will need to speak makes one more likely to attend to syntax when one is listening. She suggests that if listeners are aware that it is not enough simply to extract meaning from input, but that they may also need to pay attention to the means by which meanings are expressed in order to use such knowledge as the basis for their own production later, they will be more likely to pay attention to the syntax underlying speech. It is similar to watching a top-class tennis player, say, and making a distinction between simply observing and admiring a stroke, on the one hand, and observing and analysing the stroke so that it can be emulated later, on the other. So once again, we are dealing here with output having an indirect effect in that it causes input and listening to be used more effectively for interlanguage development.

C   *To test hypotheses*

To accept the input hypothesis is to be dependent on what is said by others. If this is enlightening, given the learner's current state of interlanguage grammar, then progress may result. But one is extremely unlikely to be so fortunate as to receive relevant information for specific points of interlanguage development relevant to the areas where one is framing hypotheses at exactly the right time. Speaking, in contrast, allows the speaker to control the agenda and to take risks and look for feedback on the points of uncertainty in a developing grammar (Swain 1985; 1995). This is likely to make learning more efficient, since the speaker can control what is going on and engineer feedback that is likely to be most revealing.

D   *To develop automaticity*

To be effective in the use of a language, one needs to be able to use the language with some ease and speed. Earlier, in the section on comprehension, the 'real time' problem was mentioned, according to which it is important to posit mechanisms of comprehension which have some chance of explaining listening in real time. The same basically applies to speaking, the only way in which learners can go beyond carefully constructed utterances and achieve some level of natural speed and rhythm. To obtain the automaticity that this involves requires frequent opportunity to link together the components of utterances so that they can be produced without undue effort, so that what will be important will be the meanings underlying the speech rather than the speech itself. In this respect, there is an aspect of speaking which makes it an example of skilled behaviour, like driving a car, or, probably more relevantly, like playing a musical instrument. Only by frequent use is the fluency side of speech likely to be improved.

This applies to all speech, but it is likely to apply even more forcefully to some aspects than others. It may affect morphology vitally, but hardly affect word order. Hence the opportunity to practise speech in languages where morphology plays a more prominent role may be all the more important.

E   To develop discourse skills

The previous arguments for the importance of output have not challenged the view that language learning is essentially the development of a sentence-based interlanguage system. But it has been claimed (Brown and Yule 1983) that much ELT work focuses excessively on 'short turns', and that as a result learners' capacities to take part in extended discourse are not stretched. Certainly, current developments in discourse analysis suggest that there is a lot to be learned if one is to become an effective communicator. Discourse management (Bygate 1987), turn-taking skills, and a range of similar capacities which underlie the negotiation of meaning in ongoing discourse (Cook 1989), can only be achieved by actually participating in discourse. If meaning-making is a jointly collaborative activity, then we cannot read about these skills, or even acquire them passively, but instead have to take part in discourse and realize how our resources are put to work to build conversations and negotiate meaning. Extensive speaking practice is therefore unavoidable.

F   To develop a personal voice

A learner who is completely dependent on what others say, is unlikely to be able to develop a personal manner of speaking. Such a learner will be dependent on the sorts of meanings that he or she has been exposed to, and will not able to exert an influence on conversational topics. This implies a strange, passive view of what language is used for, and how personal concerns are manifested by it. It seems inevitable that if one wants to say things that are important, one must have, during language learning, the opportunity to steer conversations along routes of interest to the speaker, and to find ways of expressing individual meanings. A role for output here seems unavoidable.

The importance of output

These six reasons for the importance of output provide yet another argument against the sufficiency of a comprehension-based approach. They detail the inadequacy of simply listening, and show that output too is a necessary condition for successful language learning. But the next question is to consider whether output, in turn, is sufficient and efficient as a condition for language learning.

The six roles for output listed above might suggest that it is. The first such use, obtaining better input (see p.16), will not be pursued here since it is only a more sensitive form of Krashen's views. The last two roles, acquiring discourse skills and developing a personal voice (see p.18), are more concerned with the construct of communicative competence, and will be considered in Chapter 7. The central roles for output in promoting interlanguage development are forcing syntactic processing, testing hypotheses, and developing automaticity. The first two of these central roles focus on form while the third is more concerned with performance and fluency.

The contrast implied here, between attention to form and attention to performance, suggests a question which is susceptible to empirical investigation. We need to devise studies which can establish whether actual output favours form or emphasizes fluency at the expense of form. Although output may generally be a good thing, the roles it serves in specific situations may not be so beneficial. It then becomes important to establish, through research, the conditions and constraints under which output promotes a focus on form.

In the literature, two general accounts of the role of communication in language development have been proposed: language development through the negotiation of meaning (Pica 1994, for example); and development through the operation of strategic competence (such as Bialystok 1990). We will examine each of them in turn to assess whether they can clarify whether output and interaction have a positive influence, and if so, what that influence might be.

Negotiation of meaning

Advocates of the negotiation of meaning approach (Gass and Varonis 1994 and Pica 1994, for example) suggest that the ongoing identification of difficulties in interactive encounters stimulates learners to overcome such difficulties. In so doing, it is hypothesized that modifications which are made to speech in the service of repairing conversational breakdown have beneficial spin-off effects on underlying interlanguage. Conversation is then seen as the ideal supportive mechanism to:

a identify areas where interlanguage is limited and needs extension;
b provide scaffolding and feedback at precisely the point when it will be most useful since the learner will be particularly sensitive to the cues provided to enable new meanings to be encoded.

Conversational moves such as comprehension checks, clarification requests, and the like will reflect how conversation leads to engagement with an underlying interlanguage system when it is made unusually malleable. To link back with the roles for output discussed above, such negotiation of meaning provides ideal opportunities for hypotheses to be tested and a syntactic mode of processing to be highlighted.

There are, however, problems here. Aston (1986), for example, has questioned the desirability of contriving interactions intended to generate extensive negotiation of meaning, and whose value is judged according to how well this is achieved. He proposes, in fact, that such interactions can be irritating for students, and unrepresentative as far as natural discourse is concerned. The wider issue, essentially, is that it is one thing for successful negotiation to take place, but quite another for this to have beneficial consequences for interlanguage development. Far from scaffolding interlanguage development, negotiation sequences may distract the learners and overload the processing systems they are using, with the result that even when successful scaffolded negotiations occur which produce more complex language, these may not have an impact upon underlying change because there is no time to consolidate them.

In any case, there is also the possibility that such studies may have overestimated the empirical importance of negotiation for meaning. Foster (1998) demonstrates that although one can, indeed, point to differences between interaction types and participation patterns as far as negotiation of meaning indices are concerned, global figures disguise the true state of affairs. In fact, unusually active students account for significant differences between groups, but most individual students, whatever the task or participation pattern, engage in the same amount of negotiation of meaning—nil. As a result, we have to conclude that for most students this aspect of output does not have a definite impact on interlanguage change and development.

Strategic competence

The situation is not particularly different with respect to the operation of strategic competence and communication strategies, the other more general framework which might provide a rationale for output-led interlanguage development. This literature (Tarone 1981; Færch and Kasper 1983; Bialystok 1990) has examined the ways in which the strategies that learners adopt when faced by communication problems can be described clearly and classified. Many categorization systems have been proposed, such as Færch and Kasper's (1983) distinction between achievement and avoidance strategies, and Bialystok's (1990) contrast between linguistic and cognitive factors. One attraction of such systems is that they account for the range of strategies which are used as parsimoniously and yet as comprehensively as possible. In addition, it is useful if they can be grounded in related fields, as is the case with Færch and Kasper's (1983) appeal to general psycholinguistic models.

However, a central issue is whether the operation of such strategies of communication at a particular time to solve particular problems has any implications for interlanguage change and development over time.[1] One could ask, for example, whether achievement strategies (that is, retain the original intention of meaning, and use resources creatively to solve a communication problem) are more likely to lead to development than avoidance strategies (that is, do not extend one's linguistic repertoire, but instead change the message to be communicated so that it comes within available resources). Similarly, one could ask whether there are different implications from the use of linguistic strategies compared with cognitive ones.

A different way of examining essentially the same point is to consider the relationship between communication strategies and the Canale and Swain (1980) model of communicative competence. This contains three (Canale and Swain 1980) or four (Canale 1983) competences: linguistic, sociolinguistic, discourse, and strategic (discourse being the added fourth competence: see the discussion in McNamara 1995). Linguistic, sociolinguistic, and discourse competences are, in a sense, more basic, since they represent areas of coherent competence in relation to different aspects of communication. Strategic competence, in this formulation, has a less integrated quality in that it is meant to function in an improvisatory manner when problems are encountered because other competences are lacking. (See Bachman (1990) and the discussion in Chapter 7 for an account of how strategic competence can be differently viewed.) Presumably the capacity to negotiate meaning would be part of a more general strategic competence.

A weak interpretation of what is happening would be that such strategies have no other function than to solve some sort of communicative breakdown in order that conversation can proceed. With this interpretation, all that happens when a problem is encountered is that some degree of resourcefulness is drawn on, and the problem in question may or may not be solved. In this view, it is not assumed that there is much *trace* from the activity of solving the problem in question. Although the 'solution' may enable further interaction to take place (which is, of course, not a bad thing), its details are regarded as transitory and unimportant.

However, a stronger interpretation is that when communication strategies are used, they have implications for longer-term language development. There are three requirements for this to happen. First, it is necessary that solving current communicative problems leaves some sort of trace. In other words, what is initially an improvisation to convey one's meaning when resources are limited is noticed and becomes more than a transitory but evanescent success; there must be something about the interaction which is sufficiently salient, and/or the processing capacity available allows such attention. Second, the improvisation which has become a solution must be useful to future problems—it must have some transfer or generalizing power. Such an outcome would reflect the way the interaction itself has led to useful hypothesis generation or to syntactic processing (Swain 1985; 1995). Third, the communicative solution needs to become proceduralized, either because it is so striking during *one* occurrence (Logan 1988), or because its strength is built up more gradually through repeated related solutions to essentially the same communicative problem (Anderson 1992). In any case, it becomes available as part of one's communicative repertoire on subsequent occasions when problems similar to the original one are encountered. If all these conditions are met, and interlanguage development occurs, then we do indeed have a case of learning to talk by talking. In this case solving communicative problems engages a language learning capacity directly, since solving problems is what puts pressure on the communicative system to change.

Problems with communication strategies

There are a number of problems with such an interpretation of how communication strategies function beneficially over time. Of course, what would be ideal, in this regard, would be longitudinal studies of the impact of different patterns of communication strategy use on interlanguage development, since such studies would chart the nature of interlanguage change, for relevant learners, relating interaction patterns and strategic language use to the underlying system change which occurs. Unfortunately, such studies are in short supply and isolated case studies have to be relied upon to an excessive degree. (The thrust of most such research has been to establish classification schemes or analytic frameworks which have little to say about longer-term change.) Even so, there is some information available.

Empirically-motivated concerns

Schmidt (1983) reports the case of Wes, a Japanese learner of English in

Hawaii. Schmidt studied Wes over an extended period, gathering data on his language performance in informal settings over two years. Schmidt used as a guiding theoretical framework the Canale and Swain (1980) model of communicative competence mentioned earlier. He also drew attention to Wes's attitude to learning and using English, since Wes was quite clear that he was uninterested in instruction or correctness, and was more concerned with achieving effective communication with those people he wanted to talk to. In this he was successful, since in the period of the study he went from being regarded as a minimal English speaker to being taken as a worthwhile interlocutor by native speakers who clearly reacted to him, at the end of the period of study, as a conversational equal.

The most interesting aspect of the study, however, is that when Wes's improvement over the period was charted in terms of the Canale and Swain framework, it was apparent that while his strategic and discourse competence changed markedly for the better, his improvement in terms of linguistic competence was minimal (and his syntax was as fractured at the end of the period as it was at the beginning) while in the sociolinguistic area the change was not very great. In this case, then, Wes's reliance on strategic capabilities to achieve communication was spectacularly successful when judged in terms of conveying meanings and being acceptable as a conversational partner, but very unsuccessful when judged in terms of development in his underlying interlanguage system. Reliance on communication strategies, that is, seemed to be harmful to his linguistic health, a point that evidently did not disturb Wes, since he had achieved the goals he had set for himself as far as communication was concerned.

A similar conclusion arises from work done at the Foreign Service Institute (Higgs and Clifford 1982), which is also of a longitudinal nature. The Foreign Service Institute (FSI) training programme emphasizes the acquisition of oral skills, and is accompanied by the administration of the FSI-ILR (Interagency Language Roundtable) oral interview test (Lowe 1982). This test enables both a global and an analytic view of the competence of the personnel being trained to be obtained. The former is based on a five-step scale on which global proficiency can be estimated (supplemented by plus scores for each numerical category). The latter gives separate ratings for syntax, vocabulary, fluency, and other skill areas. In this way, the longitudinal development of the learners can be monitored through an examination of the profiles generated by the analytic marking scheme over several points in time.

Higgs and Clifford (1982) report that profiles of students at earlier points of instruction can be used predictively to estimate the likely later gain of the candidates in question. Given the basic five-step scale, candidates whose grammar ratings were above or equal to their ratings in vocabulary or fluency tended to continue to progress and reach higher performance levels as they received more instruction. In other words, balanced analytic ratings or higher grammar predicted continued gain and capacity to profit from instruction. In contrast, students whose earlier profiles showed stronger fluency and vocabulary skills did not manifest the same degree of sustained improvement. Higgs and Clifford (1982) called these learners 'terminal 2s', (from the five-step scale), suggesting that the earlier profile was associated with a probable plateauing in achievement at around Level 2. It seemed as though the earlier fluency and vocabulary gains compromised continued development, and may have been associated with fossilization. These learners corresponded, in some ways, to Schmidt's Wes, since earlier communicative effectiveness (and the higher fluency and vocabulary scores earlier in instruction might be connected with a communicative orientation on the part of such learners) represented a short-term advantage which proved expensive in the longer run since it was associated with an interlanguage system which became less permeable. Once again, the suggestion is that unless there is direct involvement of the underlying language system in communication, it need not develop, even though communicative effectiveness does change.

Theoretically-based concerns

In addition to these empirically motivated concerns over the usefulness of communication strategies, there are some more theoretically-based worries. First of all, there are what might be termed logical criticisms of the viewpoint. For example, it is difficult to imagine exactly how such strategies can leave a trace. It is likely that interesting operations will occur when achievement strategies are used to cope with communicative problems whose solution will require some adaptation of the underlying system. But in such cases the need to solve unforeseen problems will ensure that the lion's share of cognitive resources will be directed to conveying meanings. As a result, it is not easy to see how memory of what exactly has worked can be effectively retained for the next occasion when the strategy may be useful, since this outcome would require the spare capacity to fumble towards such a solution *and* simultaneously to monitor its nature and its effect. It seems unlikely that the conflicting calls on limited resources will allow this with any dependability. VanPatten (1990) makes a similar point in relation to comprehension, where he demonstrates that syntactic and semantic processing seem to conflict as far as attentional resources are concerned, and that attention span is too limited to allow both to be emphasized simultaneously. One can only assume that speaking, as part of the interaction, will pose significantly greater problems for learning.

More generally, for the use of communication strategies to work to foster progress systematically, it would be necessary to show not simply that they leave a trace, but also that the use of such strategies has some cumulative building potential. For if SLA research has demonstrated anything, it is that developmental sequences have considerable importance. It would be necessary, therefore, to show that the progressive improvisations which solve communication problems build upon one another, and are not isolated chance manipulations of language elements in one restricted area, but have system-developing potential, and push the interlanguage system in some consistent direction. Unfortunately, this argument seems hard to envisage. Communication strategies seem much easier to imagine as unplanned resourceful solutions rather than as cumulative building blocks. It would seem that researchers in this area have devoted much more effort to debating the relative merits of different classification systems for strategies than to examining the developmental potential of the different strategy types that have been classified. When one examines the literature on types of strategy used, things are distinctly unpromising. First of all, a research bias in this area often leads investigators to provoke the need for strategy use by requiring subjects to focus on vocabulary problems. As a result, the area we know most about is probably the least relevant for interlanguage development. Further, when one looks at examples of strategies, (for example, approximation, word coinage, circumlocution, literal translation, avoidance, and so on, (Bialystok 1990)), one can hardly see how they can help make a sustained contribution to language development. Similarly, negotiation of meaning sequences (Pica 1994; Lyster and Ranta 1997) show little evidence of useful modifications to interlanguage being made, or of the incorporation of scaffolded supports for more complex language. So, once again, a *potential* way in which interaction could drive forward interlanguage development reveals itself to be implausible.

Even more generally there is the point that much of communication is elliptical, a joint creation by the participants in conversation who each spend their time working out what the other knows. In other words, if Grice's maxims are being followed, speakers will judge their contributions to conversation so that they are relevant and brief. Such people, native speakers or learners, are going to place great emphasis on communicating meanings, but may not necessarily worry about the exact form that they use (Kess 1992). In this respect, Grice (1975) has made it clear that maxims for conversation make for a considerable processing burden because of what is *not* said. To spell everything out in complete and well-formed sentences would soon empty rooms, and get one classified as a boring pedant. Much adult conversation is elliptical and incomplete in surface form, heavy in the assumptions that it makes about background knowledge which enables inferences about intended meaning, speaker attitudes, and so on (Widdowson 1989). Recall the early morning flight example of the steward–passenger exchange: 'I say! Empty!' given in the Introduction, where passenger needs and rights are not disputed as the steward goes directly to the central condition that needs to be satisfied—there must be coffee in the pot. It goes against the grain, in other words, to do more than use form as one element or pressure in native-speaker communication, where the major emphasis will be on the satisfactoriness of the flow of the conversation, not the correctness, or completeness, (or the usefulness for interlanguage development amongst learners) of what is said.

So speakers will generally, or at least often, say only what needs to be said, confident that their interlocutors will engage in whatever conversational implicature is necessary to recover the intended meaning (or will say something that will enable the first speaker to correct any misinterpretation that will occur). Learning to participate in such conversations will therefore not be learning to use complete and well-formed sentences, but instead learning how to make well-judged interventions which one's conversational partners will judge as furthering the conversation. And just as with comprehension, the problem from a language learner's point of view is that mature language users are just *too good* at grasping the full meaning of utterances which are elliptical. The knowledge sources covered earlier from Anderson and Lynch (1988) in relation to comprehension (schematic, contextual, and systemic) are just as relevant in the case of production, since the speaker is framing what is said with the comprehension abilities of the listener in mind. In this respect we have a clear difference between the mature and the child language learner. The mature language learner is able to draw on vastly greater stores of schematic and contextual knowledge, and is not (particularly) egocentric in orientation (although we can all quickly think of exceptions amongst our acquaintances). Consequently he or she is able to bypass syntax for a great deal of the time. Since it is meanings which are primary, as long as the speaker feels that communication is proceeding satisfactorily, the need for precise syntax is diminished. This contrasts very clearly with the younger language learner who has much less schematic and contextual knowledge available personally, and who is also much less able to imagine what his or her interlocutor has by way of knowledge in each of these areas. As a result, the child has much less scope to take syntactic liberties and short cuts.

We are now facing quite a changed picture regarding the usefulness (or lack of it) of conversation for language development. There is less need, for the older learner, to produce complete and well-formed utterances, because most interactions require collaborative construction of meaning rather than solipsistic party pieces. Further, when communicative problems occur, the strategies second language learners adopt are not likely to push forward underlying system change in any cumulative way. Finally, there is the issue that, even if conversation were by means of complete, well-formed utterances, *and* attempts to cope with communicative problems were useful, there is still the likelihood that attempts to cope with ongoing processing demands would not allow the learner to capitalize upon such a temporary breakthrough, establish a memory trace of it, and use it in the future.

Conclusion

The central theme of this chapter has been that syntax has fragile properties. Normal communication is pervaded by the pressures of processing language in real time. We comprehend and produce language not by exhaustively analysing and computing (although we can do these things if we have to, for reasons of creativity or precision) but instead by drawing shamelessly on probabilistic strategies which work effectively enough (given the support and potential for retrieval of miscommunication that discourse provides) at considerable speed of processing. We rely on time-creating devices, context, prediction skills, elliptical language, and a range of similar performance factors to reduce the processing load that we have to deal with during conversation. And the older we become (up to a point) the more adept we can be at exploiting these resources.

The central point is that language use, in itself, does not lead to the development of an analytic knowledge system since meaning distracts attention from form. But clearly communication does proceed, so one can infer that speakers draw upon other non-analytic knowledge systems which, one assumes, have qualities relevant to real-time communication. Increasingly it is argued that there is a parallel knowledge system which is primarily lexical in nature and which is more attuned to the hurly-burly of actual language use (Bolinger 1975; Widdowson 1989). That is the subject of the next chapter.

Note

1   In one sense, of course, this point is addressed through the distinction between communication and learning strategies. The former emphasizes solutions to immediate communication problems, while the latter are concerned with activities which are intended by the learner to lead to longer-term development. In some cases this distinction is clear, as when, for example, a communication strategy deals with (say) how to express an idea when a lexical item is missing (and has no lasting effect) or when a learner deliberately organizes a list of words for memorization, not attempting to use these words immediately, but instead working towards the extension of an underlying vocabulary. But the central issue is that one can also regard the operation of many communication strategies as containing learning potential, for example when a useful communication strategy becomes proceduralized and so reusable. It is precisely this type of communication strategy that is relevant in this section.

2 The role of memory and lexical learning

What we have looked at so far tacitly assumes that, while conversation may be the main channel for much communication, the system that it draws upon to achieve meaning is syntactic. There may be times when this syntactic system is bypassed, or not exploited to the full, but the system has been portrayed as fundamental and pervasive. The resulting problem, as far as interlanguage development is concerned, is the decoupling or the lack of engagement with syntax, as though a potentially powerful system is spurned in favour of lower-power improvisation. But there is an alternative perspective, which suggests that language is much more lexical than is usually accepted, particularly when real-time processing is involved. The implications of such a contrasting perspective require a general review of the area before we relate lexical processing to second language learning as part of the dual-coding model outlined in Chapters 3 and, particularly, 4. Accordingly, the first half of this chapter reviews linguistic analyses which claim a more extended role for lexis in language, while the second half of the chapter focuses on lexical factors in language processing.

Limits on analytic approaches: the pervasive nature of formulaic learning

To the extent that linguistic models are relevant for language use, some sort of processing system has to be assumed, even if it is not central for the linguistic model itself (for example those of a generative grammar type). In a typical linguistic model processing system, rules have primary importance, and language is produced by 'filling out' these rules with lexical exponents since the priority is to construct sentences which conform to the grammar (rule system) of the language in question. The approach allows the elegance, parsimony, and generality of the underlying model of grammar to be connected to the actual processing of language, to relate competence to performance.

Unfortunately, it does have some drawbacks as far as actual use is concerned. Above all, it requires a considerable degree of on-line computation during language production. For the sake of argument, one can identify (at least) the following:

- structures have to be constructed for the meanings which are to be expressed;
- planning has to take place some distance in advance;
- appropriate 'slotting in' of open-class elements has to be accomplished.

It is not clear how these different factors would interact, i.e. how often appropriate 'slotting in' of open-class elements (nouns, verbs, and so on) would have to occur: every clause? and every sentence? Whatever is meant to happen, there is likely to be a degree of computation involved to handle the various processing demands that are involved (Levelt 1989).

Advantages of a rule-based system

Still, there are meant to be advantages to viewing language in this way. First of all, it enables maximum creativity and flexibility in what is said. There is no constraint on the production of new combinations of meanings, since it is assumed that a rule-based system is operating 'anew' for the production of each utterance, and so constructions can be accomplished in total freedom. Second, since the 'slotting in' phase is, in a sense, subservient to the rule-governed phase, the implications for an underlying memory system and the 'units' it contains seem attractive. For example, it is a goal of the linguistic approach that parsimony should be an important criterion for evaluating the worth of different proposed grammatical models, and so accounts with fewer and more elegant rules are preferable, making even fewer demands on memory storage. Similarly, the units or lexical elements which clothe the structures will not need to be represented in memory more than once, since they only need to be well organized so that they can be 'looked up' wherever they are kept. As a result, the storage system which is meant to underlie the processing system can be as small as possible, rather as if the problem were to design a programme to fit into the limited memory space typical of earlier computers.

Such a self-contained, syntactic view of language leads to a very clear framework for the assessment of the quality of theories, and for academic advancement: it is up to the ambitious linguist to provide a convincingly powerful but compact description of language which also has explanatory power as far as linguistic structures are concerned. Compare with this the relative poverty, for professional advancement, of having to say about lexis that there is very little evidence of system, and lexical elements are best considered as isolated individual units where enumeration is the most practical activity that can be engaged in. Small wonder, in view of this, that students of lexical 'organization' have tended to be shunted to academic backwaters.

The psychological assumptions of such a rule-based approach are that

- computation is 'cheap' and fast;
- memory systems should be compact, and organized efficiently and non-redundantly.

Yet, as we have seen in Chapter 1, neither assumption is self-evidently valid. Computation, i.e. operating such a rule system, may be expensive in psychological resources, and quite possibly inadequate for the demands of real-time language processing. Similarly, there is no convincing reason why properties of the human memory system need to be efficiently organized and avoid duplication in storage.

Alternative theories

Rejection of these two assumptions changes significantly how we should look at the contrast between analyst's and user's models, and so it is useful to explore alternatives to such a neatly generative viewpoint. In the first instance, one can consider the sorts of 'time-creating devices' discussed in Bygate (1987). These, such as fillers, hesitations, rephrasings, and so on, buy the native speaker time while using language, by reducing the density of information packed into speech. They have the effect, linguistically, of 'slowing down' time. In this way, they would ease the operation of a computationally driven model, and make it more feasible to operate. There would be no basic change in orientation, but a significant change in implementation.

However, it has been argued that such a 'tinkering' approach to how language is actually used would not adequately address the scale of the problem and that a more radical solution is needed. In some ways, the most uncompromising position was taken by Bolinger (1975) who proposed that language itself is much more memory-based than has been generally considered. He suggested that much of language consists of lexical elements, and that, on occasion, these may not even be easily described by rules. He gave the example of expressions with 'else', like 'somewhere else', 'somebody else', but not '*sometime else'. Pawley and Syder (1983) similarly give the examples of 'horror', 'horrid', 'horrify'; 'terror', *'terrid', 'terrify'; 'candour', 'candid', *'candify' . All the examples cry out for completion of a rule-based system, and consistency, but this expectation is unfulfilled. Both Bolinger and Pawley and Syder use such examples to argue that a rule-based approach to language is an imposition of the linguist, and may not always be justified.

Bolinger, particularly, argued that the rule-governed basis of language itself may have been over-emphasized, and that, in reality, instances of language use are much more based on lexical elements, of varying sizes, than used to be thought. But he went on to make even more powerful claims. First of all, we saw that a rule-based approach to language facilitates the expression of new meanings, and enables the generation of utterances which have never been produced before. What Bolinger (1975) questioned is whether this portrayal of language use is characteristic of what language users do most of the time. Bolinger proposed instead that much of language use is, in fact, repetitive, and not particularly creative. While not denying the potential for creativity and novelty, he suggested that most of the speech we produce is likely to have been produced before, probably by the speaker. We do not typically, he argued, deal in originality: much interaction is of a spectacularly non-creative type, being more concerned with mundane and fairly predictable matters.

In many ways it could not be otherwise since one might well find a diet of creative language, encoding new meanings, rather difficult to handle, and even, possibly, a little threatening. One of the functions of literature, perhaps, is to institutionalize the areas where creative and original language use can be found and responded to with the intensity it requires.

An additional perspective on these claims comes from an examination of the empirical methods that are used to validate claims. Of course, very impressive work has been done to demonstrate the rule-based nature of much of language. But the point is that the 'evidence' against which this is accountable is generally that of linguists' intuitions. Now, it is not being argued that such intuitions are not empirical or not valid. Rather, the problem is that such evidence is likely to be selective, and not representative of larger corpora of material (Stubbs 1996). As a result, it is likely to be biased towards the discovery of regularity and rule, rather than to turn up exceptions. It is likely that the growing existence of large corpora of texts (Sinclair 1988) together with the existence of increasingly sophisticated text analytic software (Murison-Bowie 1993; Scott 1996), will for the first time reveal the ways in which there is lack of regularity and rule much more of the time than was previously thought.

Biber (1988) and Biber, Conrad, and Rippen (1994) demonstrate that use of semi-automatic analysis methods with large corpora can reveal aspects of regularity missed or downplayed by descriptive and pedagogic grammars. They show how grammar entries for post-modification, for example, do not capture regularity which is present in language, and even mislead in the descriptions that they offer of this area. Carter and McCarthy (1995) demonstrate essentially the same point with a much smaller corpus of spoken English, which they show is sufficient to demonstrate the inadequacy of a number of grammatical accounts. Biber *et al.* (1994) also offer interesting analyses of sub-corpora of different registers. They show that many generalizations about regularity have limited domains of application. Working closer to the lexical level, Stubbs (1995) shows that the meanings of lexical items, as used, are often not captured by dictionary definitions. The word 'cause', for example, usually defined in terms of logical relations, in fact, almost invariably co-occurs with unpleasant things—pleasant things indeed may be caused, but they are not described in this way.

Similarly, Sinclair (1991) argues that while grammar enables endless combinatorial possibilities, in practice most such possibilities are ignored, and particular combinations of lexical elements occur again and again. He proposes two principles to account for this—the open-choice principle and the idiom principle. The open-choice principle is grammaticality restated—the capacity to use (and understand) unconstrained combinations of words. The idiom principle makes three interlocking claims. First, it suggests that co-occurrences of words are limited, and that the use of one word markedly changes the probability that other words will collocate (compare Stubbs's (1995) example of 'cause' increasing the likelihood that words like 'problem', 'damage', 'death', 'disease', and 'concern' will occur). Second, Sinclair argues that many frequent words become delexicalized since they enter into frequent collocations and phrases, and they lose meaning to the collocation or phrase as a whole. Third, he proposes that the idiom principle takes precedence, arguing, 'The open-choice analysis could be imagined as an analytic process which goes on in principle all the time, but whose results are only intermittently called for' (1991: 114). In other words, it is natural to communicate by lexical means, and we only relinquish this preferred mode if we have to.

Tannen (1989) extends this analysis to the general area of conversation, focusing on both formulaic language in general and repetition in particular. The formulaic nature of language often has importance in the way we manage conversations. This has the processing implication that we have noted already: repetition in what we hear means that the discourse we have to process is less dense; repetition in the language we produce provides more time to engage in micro and macro conversational planning. In acquisitional terms, repetition in conversation can serve to consolidate what is being learned, since the conversation may act as an unobtrusive but effective scaffold for what is causing learning difficulty. Needless to say, this is not something that is often or easily provided for learners of a language.

There are, however, discourse implications as well for how we communicate. Formulaic language can create a frame to highlight the new information we are presenting. In this way we can make it more likely that our interlocutor will attend to what we want to be attended to, and not get distracted by other elements in what we are saying. We are guiding our interlocutor in terms of what meanings should be listened to. But even more, we can use repetition in conversation (Tannen 1989) to indicate involvement. Repeating what has been said to us can function as a back-channel response to encourage the speaker, and at the same time indicate involvement in the conversation that is proceeding. As Tannen (1989: 52) says:

'Repeating the words, phrases, or sentences of other speakers (a) accomplishes a conversation, (b) shows one's response to another's utterance, (c) shows acceptance of others' utterances, their participation, and them, and (d) gives evidence of one's own participation.

And, one should add, the converse. If repetition indicates all these things, and it is *not* provided, the speaker's intention will be clear, and the conversation hardly carried forward. At the most general level, Tannen argues that 'current' conversations contain comforting echoes of previous conversations, and that we judge current conversations using easy access to many such conversations in the past. She proposes that this is the case for both transactional as well as interactional conversations, and suggests that much of the effectiveness of speech derives from the resonances which it strikes with previous conversations (sadly, an insight which politicians are fully aware of). There are limits to the newness of the language and to the propositions that we can cope with: repetition serves to reduce the processing load, facilitate conversational development, and also make things less threatening.

Lexical influences on language performance

These analyses require that we review the assumptions made earlier by generative accounts of language; that is (a) little computational overhead, and (b) a compact, efficiently organized memory system. In Bolinger's (1975) approach to language and performance, we see a specific questioning of the view of memory that generative grammarians assume. First of all, Bolinger proposes that memory is not particularly compact, and that one should, instead, characterize it as capacious, and not necessarily organized to occupy as little space (or nodes, or connections, or whatever) as possible. Bolinger assumes, in fact, that the memory system is extremely large. Further, he does not assume that it has to be efficiently organized, in the sense of containing only one entry per item in order to minimize size. Bolinger prefers to assume redundancy in memory, with dual, and indeed multiple representations of items and what will be termed, for the moment, item-bundles. That is, the same word may well be stored more than once. Presumably the reference item stored in memory is the basic word, in the form in which it can take part in generatively produced 'first principles' utterances. But the other representations of a given word are likely to be combinations of that base word with other words to form ready-made expressions, which can then be accessed as wholes. In this way, the memory system is organized not for efficient compactness, but for ease of use.

Bolinger's ideas, then, have a stronger and a weaker form. The stronger form asserts that it is a misrepresentation to regard language purely as a rule-driven system, since there are too many exceptions to such a viewpoint (compare Sinclair 1991 on this issue). The weaker form takes a processing perspective, and claims only that computation is demanding. Longer-term memory capacity and parsimonious storage are not the crucial issue, and so a greater capacity to access memorized chunks compensates for limitations in processing speed in the human brain (Peters 1983). Or, as Bolinger (1961: 371), says, 'Speakers do at least as much remembering as they do putting together', and, quoting Robert Louis Stevenson,

> the business of life is carried on not by words, but in set phrases, each with a special and almost a slang signification.

and most memorably of all,

> Many scholars ... have pointed out that idioms are where reductionist theories of language break down. But what we are now in a position to recognise is that idiomaticity is a vastly more pervasive phenomenon than we ever imagined, and vastly harder to separate from the pure freedom of syntax, if indeed any such fiery zone as pure syntax exists. (ibid.: 3)

We can relate this view on lexicality to the earlier proposal, following Bygate (1987), that 'time-creating devices' permeate native-speaker conversations, where we saw that such devices would free up capacity to use language based on rule generation. Now, in addition to such conversational strategies, it is being proposed that much of language production is based on a redundantly organized memory system, and that speakers frequently avoid having to engage in clause-internal processing (demanding as this is in real time), through the use of memorized chunks of language. In view of this, it is important to survey the ways in which memorized language has been investigated.

Investigations of memorized language

Native-like fluency

Pawley and Syder (1983) talk about the use of lexicalized sentence stems to achieve native-like fluency (one of the two 'puzzles' they propose for linguistic theory). As they say:

> ... what makes an expression a lexical item, what makes it part of the speech community's common dictionary, is, firstly that the meaning of the expression is not (totally) predictable from its form, second, that it behaves as a minimal unit for certain syntactic purposes, and third, that it is a social institution. (ibid.: 209)

They exemplify lexicalized sentence stems (LSS) with the following expressions:

I'm sorry to keep you waiting.
I'm so sorry to have kept you waiting.
Mr X is sorry to keep you waiting all this time.

All of these are derived from the 'base' LSS of:

NP be-TENSE sorry to keep-TENSE you waiting

We see, in this example, how there is a nucleus of lexicalized elements, how this nucleus may be varied, while at the same time leaving what Dechert (1983) has called 'islands of reliability', and how, certainly in this case, the LSS has become conventionalized as a social phrase.

The average native speaker, Pawley and Syder (1983) suggest, knows hundreds of thousands of such lexicalized sentence stems, and these are then available as a repertoire of elements which may be used in ongoing conversation to achieve the degree of real-time fluency which we take for granted, and which would not be attainable otherwise. In addition, Pawley and Syder propose that the planning unit for speech is not very long. They advance the 'one clause at a time' hypothesis, to suggest that we only plan ahead this length of time to avoid having to engage in extensive structural planning while speaking. Instead, we work on the assumption that we will sort out the problems from the next clause when we get closer to it.

Nattinger and DeCarrico (1992) present a fairly similar analysis of what they call lexical phrases. They talk about four such phrase types:

- polywords
- institutionalized expressions
- phrasal constraints
- sentence builders

with these phrase types increasing in the likelihood of variability and discontinuity, or to put this another way, to allow some variation in a way similar to that shown by the 'sorry to keep you waiting' example taken from Pawley and Syder (1983). Other researchers have similarly discussed types of lexicalized language use, occupying some middle ground between purely syntactic language and pure lexis. Lyons (1968), for example, talks about 'phrase schemata' and 'sentence schemata', while Ellis (1984) discusses the use of 'scripts', both in similar ways to what has been discussed in this section.

It has been proposed that there are neurolinguistic implications for the dual representation system that is implied here. Van Lancker (1987) suggests that rule-based, propositional, temporal-order processing is specialized to the left hemisphere of the brain while holistic, non-propositional processing tends to be associated with the right hemisphere. (Interestingly, aspects of intonation, especially those associated with how propositions are expressed, and who expresses them, variables that are implicated often in sociolinguistic studies, are right hemisphere based, while other aspects of intonation and pitch, such as those associated with meaning differences in tone-based languages, are associated with the left hemisphere.) These issues will be taken up again in the section of Chapter 9 on exceptional language learners.

Social linkage of lexical items

We can now take a different perspective on the production of speech to take into account the proposals made by researchers such as Bolinger, Pawley and Syder, and Nattinger and DeCarrico. Producing speech seems to be much more a case of improvising on a clause-by-clause basis, using lexical elements (lexicalized sentence stems, or lexical phrases) wherever possible, to minimize processing demands. Then, as ends-of-clauses are approached, improvisation skills allow us to tack one clause on to the next (usually, but not always) because we have a wide repertoire of lexicalized sentence stems which can 'fit' given the syntactic constraints that have been set up by our previous lexically-based improvisations. And, in any case, as a last resort we can 'push down' to first-principled approaches and produce language generated from rules if we have to, because a satisfactory 'bespoke' ready-made lexicalized sentence stem has not presented itself (Sinclair 1991). In this way, speech continues, and keeps up with real time, with the account presented here being more consistent with the subjective impression one has of what is going on during speech execution—of a dual representation system being used to satisfy a number of competing demands.

There is in the account presented here a slight change of emphasis from the discussion by Pawley and Syder (1983) and Nattinger and DeCarrico (1992). Both of these publications emphasize the social linkage of lexicalized sentence stems or lexical phrases, indicating that there are important form–meaning relationships to consider, and that the conventionalized meanings that these lexicalized elements convey have some sort of social warrant or consensual interpretation (a viewpoint also shared by Cowie 1988). Such lexical elements are used, therefore, to pick one's way amongst agreed meanings, while minimizing the need for extensive ongoing speech planning.

The viewpoint argued here, though, emphasizes this social-meaning interpretation much less, and is more concerned with psycholinguistic aspects of speech planning. It is assumed that the propositions which are being expressed may be novel, but the means to express these propositions, it is argued, is often lexical, and based on lexical frames which only need to be adapted minimally. In other words, there is no disagreement about the elements which are being used, but it is proposed here that such collections of relatively fixed phrases can be adapted to convey different meanings on different occasions of use.

The emphasis, therefore, is on the individual rather than the group. The implication of this, incidentally, is that individuals have the capacity to expand their repertoire of lexicalized phrases very considerably, and that it is possible that such individual repertoires have their own unique stamp, since they reflect the meanings that any particular individual is most likely to express. Obviously, there will be an overlap between the meanings that are expressed and the conventionalized means for doing so in any speech community, but one can talk about 'lexicalized idiolects' which are typical of any individual speaker.

Everything so far has emphasized the way in which speakers can ease the processing burden while composing speech. But of course, hearers also have a processing burden, and as we saw in Chapter 1, are likely to engage in strategies of comprehension to make their task more feasible. In that respect, the use of lexical phrases is double edged. If a phrase is recognized as lexical, then it can be processed accordingly, since the corresponding phrase can be accessed in the hearer's language repertoire. In other words, there is no need for the hearer to analyse language exhaustively. In this case, incoming language can be processed more by a 'matching' strategy than by extensive (and computationally demanding) analysis. As a result, *all* the participants in a conversation will have their task eased.

Of course, this suggests that there may sometimes be a mismatch between the individual and the interactional. The speaker may be using phrases that are a familiar part of his or her lexical idiolect, while these same phrases may not be part of the listener's idiolect. The result is likely to be a relatively greater processing burden for the listener. This, perhaps, connects with the emphasis placed by Pawley and Syder (1983) and Nattinger and DeCarrico (1992) on the social dimension of conventionalized language. If such language is not partly socially accepted, it may create more problems than it solves. Still, it is assumed here that the processing problems of listening are less severe than those of producing language, and for that reason the speaker is 'allowed' more scope to create idiolectal speech repertoires.

Native-like selection

Earlier it was mentioned that in their 1983 article Pawley and Syder posed two puzzles for linguistic theory, yet so far the emphasis here has been on just one of these: the puzzle of native-like fluency. They also discuss the puzzle of native-like selection, the capacity to sound idiomatic, and to say the sort of things in a second language that a native speaker of that language would say. They propose that many learners achieve native-like fluency without achieving native-like selection, in that they can produce the target language at a rate not particularly different from that produced by native speakers, but they are still not taken as native speakers (accent notwithstanding) because their choice of language makes it clear that they are operating a different system. They may, in other words, produce grammatical and fluent utterances, but still sound foreign. This relates to the fourth of Hymes's parameters for language: that something should be done (Aston 1995)—the other parameters being that language should be well-formed, appropriate, and feasible. Such learners are making choices which are effective in many ways, but these choices are recognized as not being the choices that a native speaker would make. Or, to put this another way, the language system may allow an enormous number of choices to be made, only some of which are actually realized. Native speakers, then, are sensitive to the choices which are currently being made within a speech community.

A lexical view of language poses problems for any account of language learning, and, as Pawley and Syder (1983) say, for linguistic theory, too. In effect, if the 'conventional' problem of internalizing a well-organized system seemed daunting enough, to achieve grammatical and fluent control over the second language, then to accept the importance of Hymes's fourth parameter is truly a vicious example of goalpost moving. For it suggests that to be accepted as a native speaker one has to acquire an enormous repertoire of lexicalized sentence stems; these stems have to be accessible, and an appropriate selection has to be made.

Clearly there are social and lexical dimensions here. The social dimensions, which are close to the sense discussed earlier, imply that what is *done* has a reassuring quality for the native speaker, since it indicates familiarity, and also implies easier language processing. The lexical dimension is that many of the choices that need to be made to achieve acceptability as a native speaker are choices of lexical phrases. Learners need to make the choice from a range of grammatically acceptable utterances that would be used by native speakers. As we have seen, native speakers make choices which are lexically based. Learners who restrict themselves to item-and-rule approaches to language will be for ever marked as non-members of the speech community they aspire to. To achieve that acceptability, to satisfy Hymes's requirement of using language which is 'done', they will have to become more lexical in their mode of communication, and correspondingly in the repertoire of language knowledge that they possess. One way of doing this is to extend the range of lexical sentence stems (and lexical phrases) that they use. Other ways (Yorio 1989) include using more two-word verbs, fewer personal pronouns, and more collocations. This is an area where further research could usefully be done to characterize what native speaker idiomaticity consists of. For the moment, we can return to the claim made by Pawley and Syder (1983) that there is a real puzzle here, and while the answer may not be totally clear, everything we know is consistent with a lexical basis for achieving native-like selection.

Conclusion

The claims made at the end of Chapter 1 can now be expanded. At that point it seemed that an analytic system is often bypassed as a result of the pressures of real-time communication, but it was difficult to see what alternative knowledge system could be the basis for language. This chapter has argued that much of the time we rely, during rapid communication, on large chunks of memorized language. We rely on such chunks to ease processing problems, using them to 'buy' processing time while other computation proceeds, enabling us to plan ahead for the content of what we are going to say, as well as the linguistic form. Such planning, in turn, may consist of the retrieval of more language chunks or the shift to an analytic mode. The devices reviewed in Chapter 1—time creating devices, elliptical communication, reliance on comprehension and production strategies—are all of a piece with this analysis, since they too ease processing, and probably enable more effective lexical choices. The time so created may sometimes be channelled into the operation of the idiom principle, in fact, rather than the open-choice principle.

But this analysis is still concerned largely with performance, and language use. What is also important (although more strongly now because of the lexical dimension) is that second language *use*, in itself, does not reliably lead to second language *change*. So now we need to address the issue of what is likely to generate *change* in the interlanguage system, and indeed, what new perspective we need on the interlanguage system itself.

Regarding the issue of generating change, it is clear from the discussion in Chapter 1 that attention needs to be *drawn* in some way to language form. The difficulty is that what might be termed 'overt' methods of doing this, such as explicit rule presentation, have not been notably successful (Ellis 1994). Further, the hope that a focus on form would, through negotiation of meaning, be parasitic on communicative encounters (Long 1989; Pica 1994) appears equally discouraging (Aston 1986; Foster 1998). What is needed is to consider approaches which, in the context of meaningful communication, draw attention to form in more inductive ways, or raise consciousness. We need to develop pedagogic interventions where learners focus on form naturally, rather than artificially. We will consider these issues in Chapter 3, where we will review recent psycholinguistic accounts of how attention is handled in second language learning, as well as research from a general information-processing perspective.

The implications of a more prominent role for lexical processing within language use will be discussed in Chapter 4, where several models of second language acquisition will be reviewed. This chapter will argue that there are special considerations at issue when language development is concerned. So far we have only considered the relevance of a distinction between analyst's and user's models of language. As will be seen in Chapter 4, including the *learner's* model introduces another layer of complexity. The coexistence of analytic- and lexical-based systems will be shown there to be central to accounts of how learners can be induced both to develop fluency, on the one hand, and achieve sufficient focus-on-form, on the other. The main claim which will be made is an old one, but in a slightly different guise—the key to sustained progress is balanced development in the different areas of second language performance. In other words, excessive development in one direction may be at the expense of others.

3 Psycholinguistic processes in language use and language learning

The discussion in Chapter 1 demonstrated that strategies are implicated in language learning, while Chapter 2 showed how memory-based language plays an important part in such strategic choice. This chapter develops these ideas, and attempts to relate strategic behaviour to underlying psycholinguistic processes and to some more recent SLA research. In the first part of the chapter a series of models of increasing complexity are presented. These clarify the functioning of the three stages of information processing: input, central processing, and output, as well as the interaction between these stages, and the way material is represented in memory. The models show the way that, at each stage, there is a tension between attention to rule and form, on the one hand, and memory, on the other. In the second half of the chapter, relevant research studies from the second language field are reviewed which show how a psycholinguistically-based approach can provide an organizing framework which synthesizes much of the data in a meaningful way.

Attention, consciousness, and human information processing

We have seen that comprehension and communication strategies give the user greater ability to handle language successfully, but at the cost that syntax is de-emphasized, even temporarily sacrificed, to enable communication and meaning extraction to proceed. In the short term, while a language learner is engaged in actual communication, this is obviously beneficial, since it enables the learner to continue interaction. But in the longer term it may well be the case that the de-emphasis on syntax, when it occurs consistently, will have a negative effect on the process of interlanguage change and development. Learners may become effective communicators at a certain level of structural control, but not proceed beyond that level without considerable difficulty. This state of affairs can be represented quite usefully in terms of the constraints of the human information processing system, an approach that has the virtue that language development can be related to a much broader context.

Memory functioning

An influential model of memory functioning within cognitive psychology (Atkinson and Schiffrin 1968) suggested (at least) two major stages are implicated.

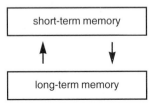

Figure 3.1: The operation of memory systems

The short-term memory system is considered to be limited in capacity, and to require conscious effort and control. It is also likely to be serial in operation. The long-term memory system, in contrast, is very large in capacity, can operate in parallel fashion, and may not be always susceptible to conscious control. This original model portrayed short-term memory as the gateway to long-term memory, with the transfer of material from the former to the latter effected by processes of rehearsal. The most quoted example of this is the rehearsal of a telephone number so that it can be slowly transferred to long-term memory (as well as be the basis for making an actual call). More recent formulations (for example, Gathercole and Baddeley 1994) have modified this interpretation. Short-term memory has been replaced by the concept of working memory, a system which still contains rehearsal 'loops' (both phonological and visual) and also a central executive component which is concerned with the allocation of a limited amount of attention. In addition, working memory contains those 'records' from long-term memory that are 'currently in a state of high activation' (Anderson 1995) and which may therefore interact with new material which has just been encountered. The interactions of these two systems is represented by the bi-directional arrows in Figure 3.1.

What this model does not do, though, is relate memory functioning in an effective way to the use of language. For that a slightly more complex version of Figure 3.1 is required, with short-term memory now changed to working memory.

Figure 3.1 proposes that when input is received, the person involved has only a limited-capacity memory system available, and that such a limitation places a fundamental constraint on how the (excess of) input is handled. Working memory has to extract from input (language input and other input, for example, visual, contextual) that which is relevant for ongoing comprehension. There are different views as to (a) how input and working memory interact, and (b) the extent to which (some) input is processed on-line, directly by long-term memory (see Gathercole and Baddeley 1994: Chapter 8 for discussion) with contextual knowledge from long-term memory mobilized ('activated') to enable this. But clearly when capacity limitations are important (as is likely to be the case in the second language context), working memory has an important role to play.[1]

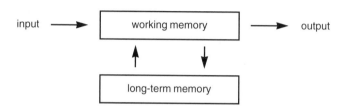

Figure 3.2: Memory systems and language

The interaction of working and long-term memory is also important for the production of speech. Here, material from long-term memory, concerned both with the propositions to be expressed as well as the linguistic means (knowledge of syntax, lexical elements, lexical chunks), has to be accessed and assembled. Gathercole and Baddeley (1994) propose that working memory can function as a sort of storage area while the different elements of a message are being orchestrated. So, as with the analysis of input, the central components of the information processing system have an impact upon the way language output is synthesized.

The representation in Figure 3.2 enables us to ask a series of more interesting questions which spotlight particular aspects of *language* functioning. For example:

Input

– What factors influence how input is processed?
– If capacities are limited, what reduces the efficiency of input processing?
– How can (less salient) features of input be made more likely to be processed?

Working memory /Long-term memory operation

– What role does awareness of the contents and operation of working memory play?
– Are language systems qualitatively different from other systems?
– How can the working memory/long-term memory connection produce change in long-term memory, rather than simply the transfer of information between these two areas?

- What types of analysis are performed on working memory material, and how useful are these?
- What is the nature of the long-term memory storage system—is it redundantly structured? parsimonious? modular?

Output

- Do all people use similar processing systems in similar ways?
- Can output be based on more than one system?

Recent developments in psycholinguistics suggest the beginnings of interesting answers to some of these questions—answers which have significant implications for both second language acquisition and language teaching. To address them, we will take the obvious route of working from input through central processing to output.

Input processing and second language acquisition

Earlier views of the role of input within second language research (for example, Long 1985) can now be seen to be unnecessarily limited. They suggested that 'quality' input in some way triggers the operation of acquisitional processes and drives interlanguage development forward. This process was sometimes required to draw on comprehensible input (Krashen 1985), to produce, unconsciously, the change in the underlying system— comprehensible input provided at the right stage of development is the catalyst for change. Given that little guidance was provided as to what 'the right stage' might mean, or of how the underlying processes work, little insight was provided, and, in any case, the conclusion that everything proceeded unconsciously, rendering irrelevant any control or structuring exerted by a teacher, was hardly appealing.

VanPatten and input processing

More recently, a number of researchers have drawn on work in cognitive psychology to reanalyse the functioning of input in terms of attentional processes (Gass 1991). VanPatten (1996) proposes three principles for input processing. These are:

Principle 1:
Learners process input for meaning before they process it for form.
- Learners process content words in the input before anything else.
- Learners prefer processing lexical items to grammatical items for semantic information.

– Learners prefer processing more meaningful morphology before less or non-meaningful morphology, for example, simple past regular endings rather than redundant verbal agreement.

Principle 2:
For learners to process form that is non-meaningful, e.g. third person -*s*, they must be able to process informational or communicative content at no or little cost to attentional resources.

Principle 3:
Learners possess default strategies that assign the role of agent to the first noun (phrase) they encounter in a sentence. This is the 'first noun' strategy, but:

– The first noun strategy can be overridden by lexical semantics and event probabilities.
– Learners will adopt other processing strategies for grammatical role assignments only after their developing system has incorporated other cues (case marking, acoustic stress).

For VanPatten (1996) there is a crucial contrast between comprehension-based and processing-based approaches to input. The former (for example, Krashen 1985) is dominated by the need to extract meaning, and may, as a result, not lead to any focus on form, since it is ongoing comprehension that takes priority (compare the discussion in Chapter 1). The latter is more concerned with the control of attention during comprehension, and the way different cues can be focused on, for example, through the development of appropriate and effective listening strategies (Clark and Clark 1977), such as exploiting the presence of past tenses and time adverbs to build propositions (with some focus on form) when language is used for past-time reference. VanPatten argues that the processing approach is compatible with some clear pedagogic goals. It suggests the usefulness of training language learners in effective processing, to make them more able to notice relevant cues in the input so that form–meaning links are more likely to be attended to.

VanPatten (1996) provides the following schematic model to show how such an approach fits into a wider acquisitional picture.

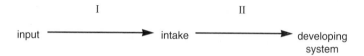

*Figure 3.3: VanPatten's model of processing and acquisition
(adapted from VanPatten 1996)*

The first arrow focuses on the stage where input is processed to make form more salient, so that rather than being satisfied with identification of (say) content words only (even though these may be sufficient to enable meaning to be extracted from the input) the learner can deliberately attempt to attend to aspects of form. The second arrow concerns explicit attempts by the learner to incorporate those elements in the input that have been attended to into a developing interlanguage system, to relate the forms extracted from the input to emerging hypotheses about the structure of the language concerned.

The focus for instruction in input processing is therefore at the input-to-intake stage. What such instruction aims to do is to maximize the efficiency of this stage in the information-processing flow. Then, with material to work on, acquisitional processes can work more effectively, and subsequently, output processes can have access to the product of such acquisition. The approach, as VanPatten (1996) claims, therefore does not compete with Universal Grammar (UG) explanations of acquisition, since that is more concerned with the intake-to-restructuring relationship, namely Stage II in Figure 3.3. Empirical research consistent with this model will be reviewed in the second half of this chapter.

Schmidt and noticing

In a similar vein, Schmidt (1990) proposes the crucial construct of noticing to start to account for the way in which (a) not all input has equal value and (b) only that input which is noticed then becomes available for intake and effective processing. Noticing, in other words, operates as a necessary but not a sufficient condition for effective processing to take place. In this respect, Schmidt is claiming, in contrast to Krashen (1985), that a degree of awareness is important before material can be incorporated into a developing interlanguage system. This analysis, though, if it is to go beyond the circularity and vagueness of earlier approaches (see, for example, Gregg (1984) or McLaughlin (1987) on Krashen), needs to specify what influences operate upon noticing. In an attempt to do this, Schmidt (1990) discusses six such influences.

Schmidt proposes that, other things being equal, the more frequent a form, the more likely it is to be noticed and then become integrated in the interlanguage system. Presumably this is simply because there are repeated presentations and greater opportunity for a form to have been noticed at some time or other. If attentional demands from elsewhere are fluctuating, there will be occasions when a form is not noticed, but because it occurs more often, there will be a greater number of occasions, other things being equal, when it is. Perceptual salience is a second influence. It concerns how prominent a form is in input. Again, other things being equal, the more a form stands out in the input stream, the more likely it is that it will be noticed. Correspondingly, the less perceptually salient a form, the less likely it is to be noticed (with clear implications for unstressed items). If attentional resources are variable, forms which call attention to themselves and are perceptually salient will have a greater chance of impinging on consciousness.

Third, in this respect, instruction may play an important role (Schmidt 1990; Schmidt and Frota 1986). Input contains many alternative features for processing, and the learner's task is to extract relevant features which can then be focused upon fruitfully. Frequency and salience are, in that sense, clear examples of bottom–up processing—what the learner 'extracts' from input is what is highlighted by its own qualities. Instruction can work in a more complex way by making salient the less obvious aspects of the input, so that it is the learner who does the extraction and focusing, but as a function of how he or she has been prepared. In a sense, learning is still input-driven (since the input is not being transformed) but it is the learner who chooses what to prioritize in the input. Schmidt and Frota provide many examples of this in Schmidt's own learning of Portuguese. The consequence of Schmidt receiving instruction was that what had been unstructured, undifferentiated input (but whose non-understanding had not impeded comprehension very much in the past) became noticeable and analysable, leading to future progress. In this view, the role of instruction is not necessarily therefore in the clarity or explanation it provides, but rather in the way it channels attention and brings into awareness what otherwise would have been missed. Equally, the ensuing noticing, provoked as it has been by instruction, does not cause learning to occur necessarily—it simply satisfies a first condition. The relationship between these additional influences and the earlier model of memory functioning is shown in Figure 3.4.

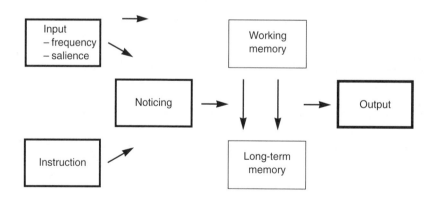

Figure 3.4: Influences upon noticing

The figure places noticing in a mediating role between input and the operation of memory systems. It also shows that certain factors make noticing more likely to occur, and therefore have an impact on the elements that a developing interlanguage system has to work with. So far, we have two such factors—one concerned with input properties (frequency, salience) and one concerned with how instruction can influence predispositions to extract particular material from the input. Note also that noticing impacts upon the memory systems in general. Some of the time working memory will be implicated, but on other occasions direct connection with long-term memory will reflect aspects of long-term memory in a state of high activation having an impact on what is currently being noticed.

One additional aspect of the figure needs clarification. It is difficult to represent time in figures of this sort. This is a problem of some importance since it is necessary to capture (a) the flow of time during an actual interaction, and (b) time elapsing during which an underlying interlanguage system may change and so come to process input differently, not to mention being the basis for language output. Although, for the sake of completeness, output is represented in the figure, the current discussion focuses upon the solid arrows which connect input to the actual memory systems, and the outline arrow reflects the output (at some later point) which has been influenced by current input and noticing.

Schmidt (1990) also discusses three other influences on individual differences (IDs) in processing ability, readiness, and task demands. Individual differences in processing ability concern the learner's capacity to deal with the range of forms in input. This seems, following Schmidt, to be an individual difference variable, in that some people will be more effective input processors than others, and be more able to notice, for given input, new forms which may then be integrated into their language development (compare the discussion of VanPatten, pp.46–8). This might be because some people have greater working memory attentional capacity, or because the analytic processes within working memory are carried out at greater speed. Skehan (1980) argues against the former, while work by Harrington and Sawyer (1992) is consistent with the latter interpretation. (Individual differences in aptitude and language analytic capacity are discussed more fully in Chapters 8 and 9.)

Schmidt's fifth influence on noticing is the current state of the interlanguage system, readiness to notice. In this case, noticing might be a function of what the internal structures or mechanisms are predisposing the learner to be ready to attend to. A variety of accounts offer suggestions about what 'readiness' might mean. For example, the Multidimensional Model (Pienemann 1984), based on cognitive processing principles, makes predictions about word order acquisition. In the acquisition of German, the model proposes that the capacity to place the verb at the end of a sentence in certain structures follows the capacity to place adverbs at the beginnings of sentences (a simpler sort of movement within the sentence). Schmidt's (1990) claim that noticing also depends upon readiness implies that a prediction can be made about what the learner can profitably notice in the sense that the product of such noticing stands a chance of being incorporated into the interlanguage system, because it is the 'next' thing to be acquired.

The last of Schmidt's influences on noticing is task demands which concerns what is expected of the language user at any given moment as a result of the activity he or she is engaged in. Schmidt (1990) argues that task demands may have processing implications, in terms of overloading the limited capacity system in such a way that noticing is less likely. Tasks based on familiar information with clear discourse structure, for example of a pair of students giving one another instructions to get to their respective homes, will probably have low task demands, while a task requiring imagination and abstraction, and a complex outcome, such as agreeing on the solution to a moral problem, will probably make much higher ones.

But there is another way in which task demands may exert an influence. Particular tasks may, through their characteristics, make certain language forms salient. Fotos and Ellis (1991), for example, use tasks which deliberately focus on adverb placement with the idea that task requirements will inexorably draw attention to such a grammar point. Tarone (1985) reports a study in which the same degree of constraint was not aimed at, but in which it could be seen that the discourse salience of the article system as well as direct object pronoun use was highlighted by a narrative task as opposed to a decontextualized manipulation task. So, a focus on a particular form may be associated with the nature of a particular task which, as a result, makes targeted noticing more likely to occur.

These additional influences can be incorporated into an extended version of Figure 3.4, shown here as Figure 3.5. Once again, noticing has a mediating role. Of the two boxes on the left of the figure, input qualities is unchanged, while 'instruction' from Figure 3.4 has been modified as 'focused input', comprising, besides instruction in itself (form-focused instruction), the selective effects of tasks (compare Fotos and Ellis (1991), and Tarone (1985)) which make particular forms salient because of their centrality to a particular task.

Schmidt's readiness and individual differences in processing factors are represented under the heading 'internal factors' and reflect the influence of long-term memory on what is likely to be, and can be, noticed. In other words, noticing is not simply a function of input, but is also affected by learner factors which influence how input is processed (compare Corder's 1973 discussion of the input to intake sequence). In this sense, the noticing is the result of existing knowledge systems and processing capacities (top–down processing) constraining what the learner can attend to effectively. 'Task demands' completes the boxes which have an impact upon noticing, and reflects, in a simple way, how demanding a particular language task is, and what free attentional resources are likely to be left over which could be directed towards noticing. Although represented separately in the above model, noticing must actually take place within short-term memory (Robinson 1995b), since the 'spotlight' consciousness which working memory provides is what is activated by the different influences upon noticing that we have covered. In this way, noticing becomes awareness and so the result of noticing becomes available for rehearsal, modification, and incorporation into long term memory (see the discussion on pp. 56–58).

As with Figure 3.4, the representation of time in Figure 3.5 is problematic. The figure emphasizes input processing and the interaction of input features, via noticing, with a current interlanguage system. The concern is with how processing current input may trigger change in the underlying system. Then, at a later stage, it is assumed that the consequences of any such change may have an impact on actual output.

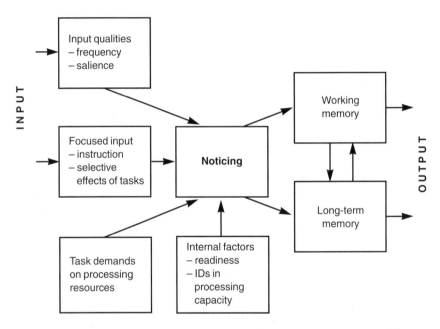

Figure 3.5: Types of noticing within the information-processing model

Representational systems and central processing

Next, having considered input processing, we need to examine what sort of system the input reaches and what happens to the input within the system. Four questions immediately arise:

– What sort of representational system is involved?
– What sort of processes operate upon such a system?
– How does the presentation of material influence learning? Are there 'better' forms of instruction?
– What role do the learner and learner awareness play?

Research relevant to these issues has mainly been conducted by cognitive psychologists. Although they may use language-like materials (artificial languages, for example), the focus is not on the language itself, but on a contrast between performance which reflects awareness of structured material and performance simply based on memory.

Rule-based versus exemplar-based systems

The debate on representation has been between proponents of generative rule-based systems (such as Reber 1989) and advocates of exemplar-based systems, i.e. accumulations of large numbers of formulaic items. In the former case, it is assumed that what is learned, although derived from actual instances (usually, in laboratory studies, of artificial language strings, for example, sequences of letters in permitted order) consists of underlying rules which have been induced from the stimulus material and then become the basis for generalization and transfer, for example, the sequence 'MV' must always be followed by a vowel. In the latter case, exemplars, learning is interpreted as the accumulation of chunks (also usually, in artificial languages, specific repeated sequences of letters—Schmidt 1995). These correspond to the formulaic units discussed in Chapter 2. Rather than relying on analysis and rule (compare the MV plus vowel sequence above) users of exemplar-based systems simply attempt to match current input with previous input which is known to be correct ('I've met the sequence MVA before.'). Judgements of well-formedness, or actual instances of production, are then based on direct access to such ready-made chunks. In the latter case, exemplars may contain structure but are actually learned as chunks (Carr and Curren 1994). The former interpretation regards development in terms of the growth and complexity of the underlying system involved, while the latter is more concerned with the accumulation of exemplars, and their utility in performance (Skehan 1996a). The former connects with Widdowson's (1989) discussion of analysability, of parsimony of rules and compactness of storage, while the latter connects with accessibility of a large-capacity, fast-access system. Most interesting of all in this regard is that Carr and Curren (1994), following Matthews *et al.* (1989), interpret findings in this area as being most consistent with a dual mode of processing, in which there is evidence for both structural learning and exemplar-based learning.

The connection with natural language learning here is clear. The rule-based interpretation would imply that interlanguage development would be the result of the restructuring that occurs with linguistic material (McLaughlin 1990), motivated by the continued operation of a Universal Grammar, or by other cognitive processes. The exemplar-based interpretation, in contrast, would argue for development as being the accumulation of useful chunks of language, language as formulaic items. This connects interestingly with the discussion in Chapter 2. There, motivated by linguistic analyses, increasingly based on corpus evidence, it was argued that formulaic language is more important than was previously realized. It was argued, following Bolinger (1975) and Pawley and Syder (1983) that rule-based accounts of the language system are not completely adequate. It was also argued, following Pawley and Syder (1983), Widdowson (1989), and Sinclair (1991), that language processing does not always follow a generative, rule-governed system, but that language users are adept at shifting in and out of an analytic mode.

In any case, the linguistic and psycholinguistic arguments coincide here—two systems co-exist, the rule-based analytic, on the one hand, and the formulaic, exemplar-based, on the other. In the former case, compact storage and powerful generative rules operate together to 'compute' well-formed sentences. In the latter, the central role is occupied by a very large, redundantly structured memory system, and (presumably) less powerful rules which operate on chunks much of the time, rather than on individual items. The memory-based system itself has to have some structure to make its items accessible, but we will assume here that something like the idiom principle (Sinclair 1991), and the combinatorial links between item sets which corpus-based work has revealed, will have a major role to play in the selectional and access procedures which are used. It also appears that language users can move between these systems, and do so quite naturally.

In addition to the nature of representation, we also need to consider the processes which operate upon such systems. Returning to the artificial language research, the major debate is the contrast between implicit and explicit learning of verbal material. As Schmidt puts it:

> ... implicit learning is incidental, does not involve selective attention to features of input that feed into the learning process, involves unconscious induction resulting in the establishment of abstract rules and representations, is the sole basis for spontaneous performance and is unaffected by instruction.
>
> (Schmidt 1995: 172)

In contrast, explicit learning does involve selective attention (to rules) and conscious induction of abstract rules, with such rules having a potential influence upon performance. A further complication in this debate concerns the relationship between these two learning systems. They may be distinct, non-interfaced, parallel systems (Curren and Keele 1993), or they may apply serially (Hayes and Broadbent 1988) with the implicit stage preceding the explicit. In either case, it is abstract rules which are at issue—what differs is the manner in which such rules develop.

Once again, there are parallels between such experimental psychology approaches and debates within language learning. An implicit rule-based view would correspond to the position argued by Krashen (for example, 1985), particularly in terms of the implicit system being the basis for communicative performance. An explicit rule-based system would correspond to the wide range of language teaching methodologies which rely on rule presentation, either before practice and production activities, or after communicative exploration, at which time they may have consciousness-raising and consolidating roles.

Given these interesting contrasts, there is still the issue of what psycholinguistic studies show regarding efficiency in learning. Three issues arise here: the interaction between types of learning and type of material; the phasing of explicit instruction; and the optimum relationship between implicit and explicit learning. Regarding the first of these, Ellis (1994) argues that with complex material, a limited number of variables, and some degree of saliency in the input, selective, rule-focused explicit approaches are superior, but with less structured materials, more variables, and less 'obvious' input, implicit approaches produce better results. With simpler material, both explicit and implicit approaches are possible. Even so, the generalization from such artificial, language-based studies to natural languages is unclear, a point developed, critically, by VanPatten (1994).

The phasing of explicit instruction, if there is any, is also a subject of debate. Matthews *et al.* (1989) argue that the most effective learning develops an implicit knowledge base, and then generates an explicit model of the material—this implies that explicitness is beneficial later. In contrast, Reber (1989) proposes that the earlier in training that explicit instruction is provided, the better. Ellis (1994) argues that this is especially important with more complex material, since the function of explicit instruction is to make aspects of the input salient (compare the earlier discussion of VanPatten's (1996) research on input processing and Schmidt's (1990) analysis of noticing). Ellis argues that such instruction can facilitate the way in which the patterns underlying exemplars can emerge. Schmidt (1994) proposes that this view of instruction—that it channels attention in selective and beneficial ways—has now reached the status of conventional wisdom. Developing this last point about the relative phasing of explicit and implicit instruction, Matthews *et al.* (1989) argue that the two forms of instruction have a synergistic relationship—there is additional benefit to having both which seems to go further than the simple 'sum of the parts'. This implies that issues of access are important here, and that dual forms of coding, explicit and implicit, may each have their uses. Although this research is based upon artificial languages, rather than second language material, the relevance is clear—instructional conditions which work for harmonious, balanced development may well be more effective. This point is developed in Chapter 4 when dual coding accounts are elaborated more fully.

Consciousness as awareness

So far, this section has discussed knowledge systems, whether analytic or memory-based, emphasizing analysability or accessibility (Widdowson 1989) as if they operated autonomously within the language user. But to relegate the user to such a bystander role is unsatisfactory. We also need to consider the user's own perception of how these systems operate, since such perceptions may themselves influence how processing systems operate and how learning takes place. In this respect, Schmidt (1990, 1994) discusses the role of consciousness in language learning. He distinguishes between several senses of this term, such as attention, awareness, and control. In this section, we will discuss consciousness as awareness, having already considered attentional factors above, with the discussion of fluency (control) to come below. For Schmidt consciousness has considerable importance in language learning. There is accumulating evidence (see the review in Carr and Curren 1994) that explicit learning of structured material is generally superior to implicit learning, suggesting that awareness of the learning itself, and of what is to be learned, confers advantages. Schmidt (1994) suggests that, for example, awareness enables more efficient solutions to the 'matching' problem (Klein 1986), noticing the gap between one's current language system and the language one encounters. Similarly, Schmidt proposes that awareness may enable learners to appreciate better the instruction they are receiving, especially the correction that is being given. Awareness may also make it easier to transform and recombine material as the structure of material is more available, and other organizational possibilities become clear (Karmiloff-Smith 1986). Finally, awareness may help learners operate the sort of dual-mode systems outlined above, where the learner/language user may need to combine rule-based systems during ongoing performance, and working memory may be the site where such orchestration occurs.

In this respect, one interesting possibility is that on occasions where rule-based systems are used for the generation of language, the products of such activity can themselves become exemplars and then be retrieved and used as exemplars on subsequent occasions. The 'first-use' may well be a first-principles generation of an utterance, but then the actual utterance, having come into existence, could be stored as a unit, and then used as a whole, facilitating processing demands when it is subsequently used. (All sorts of arithmetic rules and tricks function in much the same way, giving us a direct answer to a sum without the need to recompute on the basis of rules.) Clearly, consciousness as awareness would be of considerable help in this process, since it could ease the passage from one knowledge system to the other, providing the learner with a powerful means of developing the parallel knowledge systems (compare the discussion in Chapter 4 on relexicalization).

If we relate this discussion to the more complex model presented in Figure 3.5, we can now see that the processes which take place in working memory are themselves complex, as are the corresponding ones in long-term memory, not to mention the connection between these two representational systems. First of all, there are the issues of the speed and efficiency with which working memory material is processed. Essentially the 'consciousness assumption'

(Schmidt 1990) is that awareness of working memory operations adds to their efficiency. Further, we need to consider the related issues of the nature of representation as well as the connection with long-term memory. The discussion on rules versus exemplars suggests that conscious awareness would help in the focus on matching, feedback appreciation, and recombination, with each of these predisposing the learner towards a rule-based perspective which is more likely to lead to longer-term change. In addition, the greater the emphasis on these processes, the more likely it is that long-term memory *rule*-based representations will be accessed rather than exemplars, and the greater the likelihood of restructuring of the underlying interlanguage system and the consolidation of change. These issues are illustrated in Figure 3.6, which presents a more detailed representation of working memory and long-term memory than Figure 3.5.

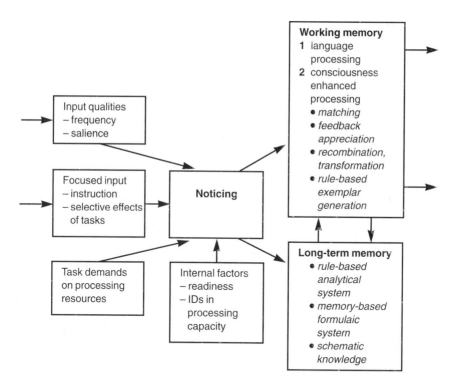

Figure 3.6: Influences on noticing and components of working memory and long-term memory

'Noticing' and 'input' function in a similar way to Figure 3.5, as 'task demands'. But the connection between 'internal factors' which have an impact upon noticing, and the functioning of 'central memory structures', working and long-term memory can now be described more clearly. Figure 3.6 suggests that long-term memory consists of a rule-based analytic system, a memory-based formulaic system, and general schematic knowledge. These interact, it is assumed, through the mediating action of working memory, whether engaged in ongoing language processing or not. Working memory, which is the basis for attention allocation, is the area in which (routine) ongoing language processing (comprehension and production) takes place, as well as metaprocesses which operate upon it, and which benefit from consciousness in the sense of awareness (Schmidt 1990). Such metaprocesses are the most effective way to cause the knowledge system in long-term memory to change, either when it becomes larger or when it becomes more complex, with changes in organizational structure, such as extension to or rearrangements of the rule-based system, or increases in the stock or inter-relationships of memory-based material.

An example of such processes in action comes from a recent series of studies by Swain (forthcoming). In the context of immersion education, with the sorts of limitations of output opportunities discussed in Chapter 1, Swain and Lapkin (1997) explored methods of giving learners tasks which drew them into (a) more syntactic processing, and (b) collaborative attentional focusing and construction of knowledge. Drawing upon the roles for output presented earlier, and supplementing them with (1) output as a device to cause learners to 'notice the gap', to realize where their interlanguage system is inadequate, and (2) output as a catalyst for metalinguistic analysis, Swain explored the utility of the dictogloss technique (Wajnryb 1991), students work in pairs to puzzle over the recovery of an item from an earlier dictation, as a device to engineer discussion between students which can enhance and focus attention. Through qualitative analysis of transcript data, she was able to show that:

- output caused a mismatch to emerge between the language which was known and that which was needed;
- the need to express meaning pushed learners to examine syntax as a means of achieving meaning;
- restructuring, a change in the underlying interlanguage system, occurred as the mismatch between current knowledge and required knowledge was resolved;
- the key to successful restructuring was the co-construction that followed from collaborative consciousness-raising and pooling of analytic capacities and previous knowledge.

In the context of a dictogloss that focused on present tense verb endings in French, Kowal and Swain (1994) report an example of two L1 English students who were troubled by the phrase they had transcribed as 'nous tracasse' (which they assumed initially to be a misrepresentation on their part of 'nous tracassons'). Collaboratively, they were able to puzzle their way to the realization that 'nous' was actually an object pronoun and that the verb ending they had originally transcribed was correct. In this way, they were able to develop a more detailed model of word order and verb agreement in French sentences.

To relate this to the model presented as Figure 3.6, it was the scaffold provided by collaboration which enabled the limitations of (individual) short-term memory to be overcome. Co-construction allowed the transformation of material to be achieved and its potential integration into long-term memory, when otherwise this would have been hindered by attention and memory limitations. In other words, a syntactic orientation to processing, which may not occur so naturally in communicative and immersion approaches, can be induced by giving learners tasks (such as dictogloss). Such tasks have to encourage hypothesizing, under conditions (collaboration, peer support) which enable restructuring to occur. Interestingly, Kowal and Swain (1994) report that restructuring of this sort, when measured by tests targeting material addressed in such collaborative interactions, was remembered well later.

Output

At the third stage in this information-processing model we need to make the link to output, and the ways in which some sort of underlying system can be the basis for producing language. This issue has been addressed by Schmidt (1992) in an examination of the psychological mechanisms underlying fluency and the way in which consciousness as control may operate. Drawing on his analysis, there seem to be three ways of accounting for the development of fluency: accelerating models, restructuring models, and instance models.

The development of fluency

The first approach, accelerating models, simply suggests that there is a natural sequence in which initial declarative knowledge (knowledge 'that') becomes proceduralized (that is knowledge 'how', Anderson 1989) or automatized (Schiffrin and Schneider 1977), so that essentially similar processes are used, but more quickly and with less need to use mental resources to control them. Instead, therefore, of knowledge or rules being laboriously mobilized and then applied, these knowledge sources, for example of subjunctives, are operated more and more quickly, and progressively less consciously. This model is easily illustrated through the acquisition of skills, such as driving a car, where procedures which initially dominate consciousness and consume all available attention, such as changing gear, recede in importance as they become routinized.

Restructuring approaches (Cheng 1985; McLaughlin 1990), in contrast, regard improved performance as the result of using better algorithms so that performance is better (and differently) organized, for example, sorting out the rule underlying tag forms, such as 'isn't it'. Following this approach one assumes that restructuring, when it occurs, is rapid, and immediately available to sustain improved performance (fluency in this case). Instance-based approaches, which were touched upon earlier (Logan 1988; Robinson and Ha 1993) regard fluency as the product of organizing performance so that it is based not on rules which are applied more quickly, or on rules which are more efficiently organized, but on contextually-coded exemplars, such as a particular example of a past tense form. These can function as units, which may have been the product of previous rule application now stored in exemplar form, and which require far less processing capacity, since such exemplars (which may be significantly longer than a word) are retrieved and used as wholes. In this view (Peters 1985; Schmidt 1992), learning is the result of instance creation, and performance (and the ensuing fluency) the result of instance use.

Each of these models has relevance for fluency, but in contrasting ways (Skehan 1996a). A restructuring approach (a reorganization of the rule-based analytic system from Figure 3.6) will have processing implications if the transformed system or sub-systems are better organized and easier to operate. One might imagine this happening with passivization in English, say as the generality of the rule is appreciated. The proceduralization model concerns an interplay between declarative knowledge and the fluency which arises from proceduralization, with the cost that less control is available over such material. The automatization of the regular past could be an example of this. Finally, instance theory portrays the relationship between the rule-governed knowledge system and the memory-oriented component differently, giving the latter a greater degree of autonomy, as more and more chunks become available for incorporation as wholes into language which is being planned.

The relevance of an instance-based approach

It is the third of these interpretations which will be developed here even though the other two make important contributions. This is so largely because an instance-based interpretation fits in more effectively with a dual-mode account of performance (see Chapters 2 and 4), where rule-based and memory-based systems coexist. Restructuring, in general, seems more important for interlanguage change and progressive extension and development. It is to achieve such development that the various pedagogic devices which contrive a focus on form are so important. However, it is assumed here that fluency is achieved either through the use of exemplars (memory-based chunks) or through the use of rule-based systems to generate future exemplars which then operate autonomously. In other words, it is unlikely that language output itself is mediated by restructuring, so much as the products of such restructuring. Proceduralization could indeed lead to greater fluency, to the extent that a rule-based system is operated more effectively, and it seems highly likely that some of the time exactly this situation will prevail. But in Chapter 2 it was argued that in native-speaker communication an exemplar–memory basis for language is required. So while proceduralization may be the consequence of an analytic knowledge system becoming more attuned to conversational realities, it would seem that this does not constitute the whole story, and that alternative bases are necessary to provide convincing accounts of fluency in actual performance (Robinson 1995b).

An instance-based approach also provides an interesting theoretical interpretation of the phenomenon of fossilization, in that one can now regard such an outcome as the premature product of a rule-based system which is then made available as an exemplar in future language use. In other words there is no requirement, in other words, that what are created as exemplars are correct. In beneficial circumstances rule-created exemplars may be supplanted by other exemplars which are created when the underlying rule-based system has evolved more. But if the underlying system does not so evolve, and if communicative effectiveness is achieved, the erroneous exemplar may survive and stabilize, and become a syntactic fossil. In this case, paradoxically, it is the usefulness in communication of a premature lexicalization that is the source of the enduring problem.

This analysis connects very clearly with the discussion of formulaic language presented in Chapter 2. What the exemplar-based studies claim is that, experimentally, instance-based learning can account for performance. This is entirely consistent with the analysis presented earlier. To cope with the problem of producing language in real time, that is, using exemplars based on previous rule generation or using formulaic language, is extremely practical as an attention-saving device. As a result, the overall load on the communi-cational system is reduced, and executive processes can distribute attention more evenly over the various components without any one of them disrupting the functioning of the others.

Summary

The three stages of information processing that we have reviewed in this section, input, central processing, and output, are simple to conceptualize, but have proved surprisingly useful as a framework. For input, the concept of noticing is central, since it then leads to an examination of the different influences upon noticing itself (Schmidt 1990), which were categorized as based on input qualities and input focusing, as well as internal factors and task demands. With central processing, the key factor concerns the existence of two representational systems, rule-based and exemplars. This, in turn, leads to a consideration of the processes (implicit and explicit) that operate upon these systems, and the optimum conditions (for example, phasing of explicit instruction; awareness on the part of the learners) under which learning can occur. The rule-based system is generative and flexible, but rather demanding in processing terms, while the exemplar (memory) system may be more rigid in application, but functions much more quickly and effectively in ongoing communication. The place of restructuring and collaborative hypothesis testing was illustrated to demonstrate a way in which memory limitations revealed by an information-processing model can be overcome. Finally, the implication of two such knowledge systems has an impact on output and fluency, since it is the memory-based system which is likely to be the system of choice, where communicative pressure and accessibility are paramount, so reducing the likelihood that the more open and generative rule-based system will be used.

But lying behind all three stages, and connecting with the discussion in Chapter 1, is the claim that meaning, for the older learner, takes priority (VanPatten 1996). Turning this around, one can equally propose that it is not a natural activity to focus attention on form, but that such a focusing has to be contrived in some way. At the input stage, noticing cedes priority to strategic processing. For central processing, the easier knowledge system to access is that based on memory. For output, similarly, unless form-enhancing processing conditions apply, instance-based performance (Skehan 1996a; Sinclair 1991) will be more natural.

Information processing research in second language acquisition

The discussion so far has drawn on both cognitive psychology research and some second language applications, although these have been mainly of a theoretical nature. We turn next in this chapter to examine relevant evidence for the operation of input, central processing, and output factors in the second-language field. The research brings out the importance of such feeder discipline research for the second-language field and will enable us (in Chapter 4) to go beyond characterizations of real-time performance, which have dominated discussion so far, and to start to consider issues related to learning and change. We shall look at studies which concern:

- the processing of input
- speech production.

The broader concern, in each case, will be to explore the impact of processing on interlanguage and longer term structural change.

Input-oriented research

The simplest processing-based way to look at input is in terms of system capacity and potential for overload. In this respect, VanPatten (1990) proposed that in most second-language processing, bottlenecks stretch available resources beyond capacity, and that the major priority for decision making is between form and meaning. In second-language processing VanPatten proposes that meaning will take priority, with the result that fewer resources will be available to attend to form. A consequence of this would be that for such processing, there will be less potential to extract useful aspects of the form of the input, with correspondingly less potential for effective solutions to what Klein (1986) has termed the 'matching' problem, i.e. a detection of a mismatch between the learner's variety of a language and the target variety.

VanPatten (1990) investigated this proposal in a study which centred on a comprehension task. A listening comprehension text was presented, and subsequently learners were required to reproduce the information that they had extracted. However, learners were put into several groups. In addition to a control group (which only had to listen to the text in the normal way), there were other groups given tasks such as listening for a particular lexical item, or for the definite article, or for a particular morphological marker. VanPatten reasoned that if processing resources are limited, and if meaning has a 'priority call' on such resources over form, then tasks which interfere least with processing, (for example, meaning-oriented tasks such as listening for a lexical item), would lead to higher comprehension scores than interfering tasks which emphasize form, (such as listening for the definite article, or listening for morphology). These predictions were borne out in VanPatten's study, indicating that processing capacity does have a constraining effect on what it is feasible to extract from input under real-time processing conditions. As a result, we cannot rely on useful aspects of form being extracted during ongoing language comprehension, and so the necessary input for the matching problem mentioned earlier is only likely to be forthcoming when there is little processing pressure.

Given that a focus on form is not naturally guaranteed through input processing, a number of investigators have explored what can be done to make it more likely that form in input will be attended to and even noticed. VanPatten and Cadierno (1993) contrasted two approaches to instruction. One was a conventional form of rule-oriented instruction which included an emphasis on output practice. The experimental treatment, in contrast, taught learners more effective strategies for the processing of input. The study focused upon word order aspects of the acquisition of Spanish by English L1 speakers. It capitalized upon the problem of the more flexible word orders that are possible in Spanish verb–subject–object (VSO) as well as subject–verb–object (SVO) in declarative sentences, and contrasted explicit presentation of rules with an approach based on strategies for input processing which emphasize implicit learning. VanPatten and Cadierno were able to show that the experimental group outperformed the traditional group when performance was measured by a comprehension test (with each of these groups outperforming a control group). More interestingly, the experimental group did not differ significantly from the traditional group when measured by a test of production (with each of these treatment groups outperforming the controls, yet again). VanPatten and Cadierno interpret these results to suggest that developing input processing skills is a feasible pedagogic strategy, and that input processing can be channelled towards form.

In a related study, Doughty (1991) compared three instructed groups, an experimental rule-oriented group, an experimental meaning-oriented group, and a control group. All groups were given instruction in the formation of relative clauses, with the focus of the instruction being the indirect object relative clause. In each case, instruction was via a computer program which presented material according to the appropriate methodology. In the rule condition there was explanation of the rule together with a computer-screen demonstration of the sort of movement required to form relative clauses. This was followed by practice. In the meaning condition there was easy access to the meaning of the texts being used through various screen support options. In addition, and crucially for the role of input processing, relevant aspects of the input could be highlighted on the computer screen, so that while no explication was provided, learners had their attention drawn to features of the input central to the relativization that they were learning.

As with the VanPatten and Cadierno (1993) study, the meaning-oriented group learned as much about the structure concerned (relativization, in this case) as the rule-oriented group, with both groups outperforming a control group. In addition, there was better comprehension on the part of the meaning-oriented group, and, very interestingly, greater generalization along both directions of the Noun Phrase Accessibility Hierarchy (NPAH) (Hyltenstam 1977). In other words, there was better performance both on relativization lower down on the hierarchy (easier, for example, relativization of subjects), and higher up (more difficult, for example, relativization of genitives). Doughty (1991) interprets these results to suggest that implicit learning can be comprehension driven, provided that there is adequate focus on form in the input materials.

Studies by Fotos and Ellis (1991) and Fotos (1993) can be interpreted similarly. Developing Schmidt's (1990) ideas on noticing and consciousness raising (tasks which draw attention to a particular form, but give no explicit information), the basic research design in the experimental group was to provide learners with consciousness-raising tasks targeted at particular structures (for example, indirect objects, adverb placement, and relative clauses in Fotos 1993). Such an instructional phase was followed one week later by an activity designed to reveal whether learners exposed to the grammatical consciousness-raising activities were more likely to notice the relevant structures in input. In addition, the research design contained a grammar lesson condition, as well as a control group. There was very little difference between the traditionally instructed group and those students who had been exposed to the consciousness-raising activities as far as the noticing measure was concerned, suggesting that traditional form-oriented instruction is not the only way in which noticing can be triggered and made more likely. In addition, there was no difference between the traditional and consciousness-raising groups as regards proficiency gains. Fotos also reports that gains in performance were maintained in a test administered two weeks after the noticing activity, a gain which Ellis (1994) attributes to the need to engage in the noticing activity.

These different studies, all concerned with input processing, produce a fairly consistent picture. Input processing is not naturally biased towards form, which suggests that unstructured input may not be particularly helpful. The VanPatten (1990) study shows that focus on form, in general, is a secondary consideration, and the processing priorities do not encourage much optimism that merely having to comprehend will cause learners to engage with form. On the other hand, provided that some sort of pedagogic intervention takes place, input can be exploited so that noticing, even of particular features, is possible. VanPatten and Cadierno (1993) suggest that processing priorities, at a general level, can be influenced, while Doughty (1991) and Fotos (1993) suggest that input can be processed beneficially for specific rules through the use of attention-structuring and consciousness-raising activities. These studies suggest useful avenues for future research as the comparative worth of different pedagogic interventions with different rules are explored, particularly with respect to the longer-term impact of consciousness-raising activities which sensitize learners to form while avoiding explicit focus. But what is of central importance is our greater understanding of the complexity of the form–meaning relationship. Contriving activities which are at once meaningful and provide scope for a focus on form and specific forms is an important challenge for the future.

The difficulties with the studies reviewed, though, is that they are still slightly limited in scope. What they do not show in any convincing manner is evidence that (a) the interlanguage change is enduring and (b) it has an impact on spontaneous language use rather than on the targeted tests which are given shortly after the experimental treatment. But a study which goes some way to remedying this problem is that of Schmidt and Frota (1986). This is essentially a diary study of Schmidt's learning of Portuguese in Brazil, over a nine-month period. Schmidt started his stay in Brazil by attending classes, but after a relatively short period decided that, after a change of teacher, he was not learning quickly enough, and so dropped out of formal instruction, intending to rely on informal learning contexts and the input and interaction opportunities they contained to drive his interlanguage forward. His progress was charted by regular monitoring sessions with his co-researcher, Frota.

The interest of this study is that Schmidt also kept a detailed diary of his progress, with the result that it was possible to check back to see what had been uppermost in his mind at various times during the research. In this way it was possible to make the longer-term links between input, noticing, and subsequent change that was not possible in the cross-sectional studies reviewed earlier. What this revealed was that Schmidt felt that a necessary prior condition for interlanguage development to take place was that noticing had occurred. In other words, what was important for him was to explore what sorts of things were more likely to produce noticing, since this might then lead to the incorporation of the newly noticed material into his evolving Portuguese interlanguage system. Schmidt was able to trace a number of these noticing-to-interlanguage change sequences, with the noticing, in turn, often facilitated by instruction (as well as saliency of form, frequency, and so on), the sorts of connections which it was not possible to establish in the earlier studies. It was these insights of Schmidt's which shaped the discussion of noticing presented earlier.

Influences on speech production

We see from these studies that input can lead to interlanguage system change, but that this change requires particular forms of input processing. But we also need to consider the connection between the interlanguage system (the central processing unit, so to speak) and the nature of the output system. In other words, if we are taking a processing perspective, we need to consider the processing conditions under which the central system can more effectively manifest itself in actual performance. A number of recent studies bear on this point, too. We will consider issues of attention paid to speech; the effects of planning on speech production; and the differential effects of these 'causes' on the measures of accuracy, complexity, and fluency.

Attention paid to speech

Tarone (1983) reviewed a number of studies which suggest that the amount of attention paid to speech has an impact on the accuracy of what is said. Following a Labovian paradigm (Labov 1972) she has operationalized attention through a variety of elicitation methods (for example, in decreasing order of attention: citation forms, reading, grammaticality judgements, narratives, and conversation). She has then shown how, for a number of forms, accuracy in performance changes predictably, suggesting that for redundant forms such as the third person -*s* the less attention available, the lower the accuracy.

In a different study Tarone (1985) has shown that attention to speech is not the only determinant of accuracy. Where non-redundant aspects of the language system are involved, i.e. elements which encode important aspects of meaning, with such elements having discourse significance, then accuracy does not vary simply as a function of attention. Discourse salience for forms such as the article system or object pronouns causes these to be used more accurately in narratives and interviews (the reverse effect to the attention to speech studies), suggesting that if we want to retain the crucial role of attention, we have to interpret these results by saying that discourse processing requires particular attention to be paid to forms which have unusual salience in communication.

The contrast between the two types of study reported by Tarone is instructive. In Tarone (1983), variable performance was conceptualized as due to differences in degree of attention, with this variable influenced simply by perceived degree of formality. The 1985 study, in contrast, views performance as a consequence of attention being drawn to aspects of language as a function of discourse demands. In this viewpoint, attention functions within a wider set of influences, of which we now recognize discourse pressure as one. It is also interesting to relate the influences on attention allocation to the earlier input-oriented studies. VanPatten (1990) reports a fairly generalized account, in which attention to (input) form is a consequence of spare capacity. The other studies all report factors which can serve to channel attention. In that respect they are similar to both the Tarone studies in that particular influences on attention allocation have been detected.

The effects of planning on speech production

We next consider the general functioning of planning prior to performance. The potential to prepare what is going to be said introduces a new element which may have interesting effects on a variety of aspects of language performance. Ellis (1987), for example, investigated the effect on performance of engaging planned versus unplanned discourse. He looked at the performance of learners on three related tasks, focusing on the use of different forms of the past tense. In Task 1, learners had to write a story from a picture series. In Task 2, the same learners had to speak a story to the same set of pictures that had already been written about. In Task 3 learners had to speak a story to a new set of pictures. Ellis proposed that the three tasks provided learners with progressively less planning time. He was interested in the performance of the learners on three forms of the past tense, which was produced with reasonable frequency, given the way the study was conducted. The three forms were the regular past, the irregular past, and the copula.

His results demonstrated that average accuracy of performance across all three past tense morphemes declined as a function of less planning time being available. This result is consistent with the sort of early research conducted by Tarone (1983), described earlier.

What is more remarkable is the picture that emerges when one looks at the past tense morphemes separately. Here the most interesting finding is that performance on the regular and irregular past tense forms differs markedly.

The regular past is severely affected by task conditions, declining in accuracy from 77 per cent (Task 1) to 57 per cent (Task 2) to 43 per cent (Task 3). In contrast, performance on the irregular past hardly declines at all. The comparable figures are 60 per cent, 57 per cent, and 55 per cent. Ellis (1987) proposes that the reason for this difference is that the irregular past draws upon a lexical basis for its production, the different irregular past tense forms are integrated, self-standing lexical units which are either known or not known. The regular past, in contrast, is constructed morphologically, on a rule basis, and so requires some available on-line processing capacity. Consequently, when planning time is reduced, as is the case when one moves from Task 1 to Task 3, on-line processing capacity becomes less available, and accuracy decreases. Since the lexical basis for the irregular past does not require this processing 'overhead', it emerges practically unscathed. This leads to the conclusion that manipulation of task conditions affects planning time, which in turn, influences the balance between lexical and syntactic performance. The connection with earlier discussion is striking. This seems an example of the importance of memory-based processing discussed in Chapter 2. It also illustrates the facility with which learners can switch between rule-based and exemplar-based representational systems, and shows how, if we want to promote the use of a rule-based system, the use of planned discourse should be supported.

The Ellis study has been extended on a longitudinal basis by Underwood (1990). Underwood used the same basic experimental design as Ellis but, in addition, he obtained data at two points in time, at the beginning and end of a 100-hour course of intensive instruction at the low intermediate proficiency level, where the students concerned were instructed in the use of the past tense. In this way he was able to calculate gain scores for each cell of a three-by-three matrix (three task conditions by the three past tense morphemes). Underwood discovered that the 'gain score' matrix, reflecting change after 100 hours of instruction, actually showed some decrements in performance, and these, too, involved an interaction between task conditions and morphemes. The irregular past showed improvement on all three tasks. However, although the regular past tense improved in accuracy level on Task 1, it decreased on Task 2 and Task 3. In other words, instruction seemed to be harmful. It is more likely, however, that what was happening to the regular past was an example of what Kellerman (1985) has termed 'U-shaped growth', in a process of restructuring what appears to be retrogression is a necessary step backwards, while a newer, and ultimately more robust and effective system is being constructed. Again, the implication is that task conditions can affect the balance between syntactic and lexical processing, but that this time there is a longitudinal learning dimension to add in to the equation.

Similar conclusions have been drawn by Bygate (1988) and Dechert (1983). Bygate found that in oral tasks, language learners tended to use units of expression which functioned as 'wholes'. The greater the processing difficulty that a task involved, the more likely it was that learners would use such units, since they seemed to 'buy the learners processing time', during which further utterances could be composed. Similarly, Dechert discusses the use of what he calls 'islands of reliability' in ongoing processing— formulaic language which functions, in mid-utterance, to allow the speaker to plan more creative language.

The next study to cover is that of Crookes (1989). Crookes, like Ellis, was interested in the issue of planning time, but from a slightly different perspective. Using information-gap tasks, he investigated the effect of giving learners ten minutes planning time, compared with learners being required to embark on the task immediately. He then compared the performance of the two groups of learners, planners and non-planners, on a wide range of measures. Interestingly, there was no significant difference between the two groups on accuracy measures (a finding which does not agree with the Ellis 1987 or Underwood 1990 studies). On the other hand, there was evidence that the planners used more ambitious forms of language. They used more complex sentences, and drew upon a wider variety of lexis.

It seemed that the planners in Crookes's (1989) study had channelled planning time not into achieving greater degrees of accuracy, but instead into complexifying the task itself, by taking more risks. In Ellis's (1987) case, a conservative strategy seemed to prevail, with the more controlled setting (the basic storyline given to the learners, with their problem being that of expressing the storyline) causing the effects of planning time to increase accuracy. Crookes (1989) proposes that the Ellis study suffers from the confounding of modality with planning, in that Tasks 1 and 2 were written, while Task 3 was oral. He suggests that, as a result of this, one cannot be sure that the changes in accuracy are due to modality or to planning time. This, though, does not really account for the essentially linear relationship that Ellis reports across all three tasks. In Crookes's case, the time available seemed to enable learners to use language closer to the 'cutting edge' of their language development, but at the cost of no greater accuracy being achievable. In these cases, a risk-taking strategy seems to have been employed which led learners to experiment, and not to rely on 'safe' forms. One can speculate as a result (a) that the consequences of a limited-capacity attentional system are apparent again, only this time the limited attention is directed to complexity, not accuracy, and (b) that different pedagogic goals can be associated with different methods of organizing language work in class, an issue we will return to later.

Foster and Skehan (1996) also explored the effects of planning time on task performance. Their study investigated two main factors: task design and processing conditions. The major discussion of task design will be in Chapter 5, but the processing conditions will be covered here. Foster and Skehan used three tasks: a personal information exchange task, a narration, and a decision-making task. All tasks were done by three groups of subjects.

Group 1 had no planning time. Group 2 were given ten minutes unguided planning time (as in the Crookes 1989 study). Group 3 were given ten minutes planning time, and guidance as to how they might use this time, with suggestions as to how language might be planned, and also suggestions as to how to develop ideas relevant to completing each of the tasks.

A number of different dependent variables were measured. First of all, fluency was indexed through pausing and total silence. This showed very large effects for both of the planned conditions. The unplanned group relied on many more pauses, and total silence was much greater, rendering their discourse unnatural and strange. A variety of measures of speech complexity were used, and these mostly demonstrated effects for planning. For example, there were clear relationships between amount of subordination and internal structuring of speech, and the three planning conditions. The planning conditions all generated subordination scores significantly different from one another, with the strength of the effect of planning being greater for the narrative and decision-making tasks than for the personal task. Essentially similar findings were obtained with two other complexity measures—range of verb forms used, and use of less frequent lexical items (Foster and Skehan 1996).

So far, the findings suggest a straightforward effect for planning. This situation is complicated, however, when we look at the findings for accuracy. Recall that one of the things that separated the Ellis and Crookes studies was the findings on accuracy. For Ellis there was an effect for this area, while for Crookes this was not the case. Recall, in addition, the Foster and Skehan (1996) study is much closer in design to that of Crookes. The accuracy results are presented in Table 3.1. The figures in the table represent the number of error-free clauses divided by the total number of clauses. The arrows show significant differences at .05 level. These measures are discussed in Foster and Skehan (1996).

These results are intriguing. There is a clear effect for planning since with one slight exception (narrative, detailed planning) the two planned conditions consistently produce more accurate performance. In this respect the results conflict with Crookes and agree with Ellis. But what is striking is that, in

	Personal	Narrative	Choice
No planning	.64	.61	.63
Undetailed planning	.76	.66	.73
Detailed planning	.69	.58	.71

Table 3.1: Proportion of error-free clauses

contrast with the results from the complexity measures, the highest level of accuracy shown here is for the undetailed planning condition. In other words, the consistently most accurate performance is when there is time to plan, but no guidance as to how to use that time. What seems to be happening is that simply having time leads learners to plan the language that they will use, and as a result their accuracy improves. When there is guidance as to how to use planning time, with some of that guidance suggesting a focus on the content of the messages which will be expressed, the consequence seems to be that accuracy suffers. It is as though there are limited processing capacities available here and a choice has to be made as to what to prioritize.

Results consistent with this interpretation are reported by Mehnert (in press). Within one study, she researched the effects of three different planning phases (one minute, five minutes, and ten minutes) as well as a no planning condition. She used two narrative tasks, one more structured than the other, with intermediate level learners of German in a university context. She measured task performance in terms of fluency, complexity, and accuracy. Data from this study are shown in Table 3.2.

	No planning	1 minute planning	5 minutes planning	10 minutes planning	Summary of significant effects (at .05 level)
% pause time (of total time for task)	52.1	36.4	29.9	27.3	0 > 1,5,10
Proportion of errors per 100 words	.31	.17	.21	.18	0 > 1,5,10
S-nodes per t-unit	35.8	31.0	31.4	48.6	0, 1, 5 < 10

Table 3.2: Results from Mehnert's study of the effects of varying planning time

The first measure, percentage of task time that was silence, shows progressive reduction as a function of greater planning time, but the significant effect contrasts the no planning condition (zero minutes) with the three other conditions (one, five, and ten minutes planning time respectively). The accuracy results (where accuracy is measured as the proportion of errors per 100 words) show a similar result for significance—the no planning condition is least accurate, and then no significant difference is found between the one, five, and ten-minute conditions. A contrasting pattern is found with the complexity measure, with no significant difference between the zero, one, and five-minute conditions, but with all of these significantly different from the ten-minute condition. The results suggest that, when faced with limited attentional resources for speech production, second language speakers are given planning time, they channel this resource initially to accuracy and fluency, and only later towards attempting more complex interpretations of tasks. In retrospect, it may be fortunate that previous researchers did, indeed, take ten minutes as the operationalization of planning time; anything less and we might not now have an interesting literature to discuss. The findings, in any case, are strongly suggestive of the need to explore exactly what happens during different planning periods, since it is clear that complex interrelationships between different language characteristics come into play.

In a related study, Skehan and Foster (1997), developing this processing theme, probed whether it is possible to influence the way attention is allocated during task completion. Following Willis and Willis (1988) and Skehan (1992) they reasoned that the knowledge, on the part of task participants, that they would have to engage in subsequent public performance of the same task, in front of other students and the researcher, would have an impact on the priorities that learners set themselves during task performance. In other words, whereas during tasks with no subsequent activities it is likely that all attentional resources will be allocated simply to task completion, awareness of a subsequent performance will highlight the need for greater accuracy even during the actual task. Consequently Skehan and Foster (1997) used a two-by-two research design in which two planning conditions (no planning versus (undetailed) planning) were related to two post-task conditions (no post-task versus public post-task).

Confirming the results of the earlier study, there was a clear effect with the planning group outperforming the non-planners on accuracy measures. The results for the post-task were more complicated, however, since there was an interaction between planning and post-task conditions. Having to do a post-task did not lead to greater accuracy with the planners, but it did lead to greater accuracy for the non-planners, suggesting that there are alternative means for achieving the same goal: devoting attention to accuracy. Either approach seems to work effectively, but it appears that there are no advantages in having two rather than just one influence focusing on accuracy. This is shown schematically in Table 3.3.

	No post-task	Post-task
no planning	–	✓
planning	✓	No stronger effect

Table 3.3: The effects of planning and post-task performance (adapted from Foster and Shekan 1997)

Beyond claiming that post-task activities can have some effect on accuracy, and how attentional priorities are allocated, it is too early to evaluate this result. The effect shown is rather weak, being neither additive nor general (the effect was found only for a decision-making task, and not on narrative and personal tasks). In addition, it may be, as Skehan and Foster (1997) argue, that the operationalization used to engineer a focus on accuracy, a general post-task activity, was not strong enough. Other options may need to be explored through further research before effective conclusions can be drawn.

Conclusion

We can now try to sum up the findings of the research presented in this chapter. We have seen how information-processing models are helpful in separating the different stages concerned (input, central processing, output), and in providing an organizing framework for more detailed discussion of the functioning of each separate stage. The first, and essentially fundamental, generalization which emerges is that attentional resources are limited, and that this constraint has far-reaching effects on second language processing and use. With input, VanPatten (1990) has shown that priorities are set, and that such priorities, other things being equal, contain a bias towards meaning— extracting meaning is seen as the primary goal, so that attention directed towards form is then a luxury, possible, under normal circumstances, only when other conditions are met. With output, the whole range of the research has shown how considerable attentional resources are required, with the result that a decision to prioritize one area necessarily de-emphasizes the nature of the processing elsewhere. The output research also suggests that the competition for attentional resources is fiercer than was appreciated, in that fluency, complexity, and accuracy are all desirable goals but compete with one another during ongoing communication. The linkage with strategic language behaviour from Chapter 1 is clear, since such behaviour eases the attentional burden.

This initial analysis reflects what may happen when there is no intervention. But in some ways the purpose of the research reported is to reveal ways in which attentional resources can be channelled to achieve pedagogic benefit. VanPatten and Cadierno (1993), Doughty (1991), Fotos (1993), and Fotos and Ellis (1991) have all shown how, despite any predilection for processing meaning first, conditions can be set up so that form is noticed, and that it is also possible to manipulate the conditions for maximizing the chances that such noticing can connect with underlying interlanguage development. These investigators have highlighted input strategy development, noticing, and consciousness-raising. The optimistic conclusion here is that each of these approaches seems to have paid dividends.

But it is not enough to influence input processing. This may indeed cause interlanguage change to be more likely to occur, but it is also important that any change which does occur can then be drawn upon during normal language use and production, and that the learner does not rely excessively on meaning-based lexical units. So the changes which occur also have to be available for output. And in that respect, several of the studies suggest how manipulations of processing conditions can be effective. The simplest effect is to use planning time to free-up on-line processing resources while a task is subsequently completed. The more that is planned, whether this is language, discourse, or content, the less computational work needs to be done during the task. Other things being equal, the result will be that more attention is available as a general purpose tool to achieve a variety of goals: greater fluency, complexity, or accuracy.

But the other general finding of these processing-oriented studies is that the priorities for the use of attention can themselves be influenced. To use planning, for example, can lead to greater complexity, either because more complex language is prepared, and/or because the planning time is used to formulate more ambitious content for messages. There is also evidence that, depending on the instructions given to the planners, different balances in priority can be established between complexity and accuracy. Finally, focusing on one specific structure, highlighting the classroom context, and using post-task activities to emphasize form can all channel attention towards accuracy. In general terms, that is, one is distinguishing here between planning and monitoring. Planning, most of the time, will predispose learners to try out 'cutting edge' language, or to be pushed to express more complex ideas. Monitoring is more likely to be associated with greater accuracy.

Drawing on this discussion of research following an information processing perspective, we can now examine current models of the psycholinguistics underlying second language development and performance. Chapter 4 will examine a number of relevant models. A greater coverage of these is necessary in order to develop some of the pedagogic insights reviewed in this chapter. We will return to task-based approaches and pedagogy in Chapters 5 and 6.

Note

1   Chafe (1994) speculates that the importance of discourse is partly explained by the need to circumvent the capacity limitations of working memory.

4 Models of language learning

So far, the discussion has emphasized aspects of strategy use, underlying memory systems, and second language processing. It has not really covered models of language development or considered ways in which the nature of the language system itself is important.

In the case of second language learning, we are dealing with a situation in which the following generalizations apply:

1 There is an existing knowledge system (the L1).
2 The L2 learner has considerably greater cognitive abilities and schematic knowledge than the first language learner.
3 A qualitatively different talent for learning languages is no longer available (see Chapter 9 for discussion of modularity and the critical period).
4 Ongoing performance may have an impact upon the nature of language learning.

The first two of these generalizations are self-evident (see Bley-Vroman 1989 for related discussion of generalizations on second language learning). The central issue is what implications they have for explaining second language data. The third is more contentious and is discussed more extensively in Chapter 9. In this chapter the claim is simply assumed, and so no automatic second language development is expected simply from exposure to input. The fourth generalization, expressed tentatively, is hardly controversial. But expressed more strongly, it has an important role in relation to the three other generalizations. Second language learners have cognitive abilities and schematic knowledge which give them important things to say, but they often have only rudimentary means for saying them. They have the tensions of the twin goals of wanting to solve current communicational problems while also increasing their command of a complex underlying system. Some early approaches suggested that the capacity to communicate should be deferred until a sufficiently complex and elaborate system was under control (compare Trim's (1980) *Gradus ad Parnassum*, wryly reflecting a view that patience and delayed reward are important in language learning). Now we accept that communication should be integral to language learning, even with formal instruction. The informal context places communication in a more 'driving' role, since interaction will be central to such learners.

This analysis raises difficulties for the distinction between models of second language learning and second language use. We are not dealing with a situation where these two activities can be neatly separated from one another, since learning is required to manifest itself through use throughout a language learning career, while performance may be the motor for learning (at least some of the time). As a result, in discussing the models in this chapter we will need to keep in mind four questions:

- What is the nature of the formal system, of the underlying competence, in each model?
- How does change occur in the underlying system?
- How is the system used to enable real-time performance?
- How do performance and change relate to one another?

These questions make the models more accountable to the generalizations given earlier, and bring out that it is not enough to be concerned with self-contained systems. In order to be relevant, such systems also need to make clear links with performance and change, and the way these two relate to one another.

Three models will be explored: Universal Grammar, the Multidimensional Model, and the Analysis-Control Model. This sequence starts with the most structural approach, and moves towards a progressively greater concern with processing. The chapter concludes with a proposal for the way processing influences need to be incorporated in any model of second language learning and performance.

Universal Grammar-based approaches

The Universal Grammar (UG) approach tries to account for the nature of language representation, the nature of language learning, and the nature of language use (Cook 1994). Essentially, a UG approach tries to characterize what structures and processes the child brings to the task of first language acquisition, drawing on the two central concepts of principles and parameters.

First language acquisition

Principles are invariant characteristics which are shared by all languages. One such principle is structure dependence, the fact that words are not simply strings of elements, but that they enter into structures, and that it is the structures which are the unit of organization. All languages exhibit this characteristic, and it is assumed that the child is equipped with the 'knowledge' that whatever language is encountered, it will have structure dependence. As a result, the nature of the 'unitization' problem, identifying the crucial units of the language concerned, and how they can be manipulated, is constrained very helpfully for the child learner. Parameters are features of language which can have more than one setting, such as pronoun positioning (before the verb, as in French, or after it, as in English), or pro-drop (whether a language allows subjects to be omitted, as in Spanish, or not, as in English).

This account changes the nature of learning in the case of first language acquisition. Rather than portraying it in terms of inductive generalizations which are hard-won as extractions from input-data (a colossally difficult task to undertake, given the complexity of language), 'learning' is the result of imposing structure on the input data as a result of the built-in expectations. Structure dependence functions clearly in this way—a whole range of empirical possibilities are instantly disallowed because they would not conform to such an underlying principle. Fruitless searching for generalizations would therefore be avoided. Similarly, the existence of parameters eases the acquisition task, in two ways. First, if parameters can be set in one of only two ways, once again a whole host of alternative generalizations and patterns in language do not need to be explored, rendering the task considerably simpler—input evidence simply needs to establish the choice between (say) A or B, converting language acquisition from an open-ended to a multiple-choice test with (usually) only two alternatives. Second, where parameters control more than one feature, the triggering of one aspect of the parameter can generalize to other features. So, triggering of the pro-drop parameter by means of subject omission (or presence) yields, 'at no extra cost', decisions on 'that' omission, 'dummy' pronouns ('it is raining', for example), and the like, thus multiplying the efficiency of language acquisition.

A UG interpretation has been used extensively to account for first language acquisition, where it has the strength to address theoretically the projection problem (the way in which learners know more than they could have learned from the input to which they have been exposed), the negative evidence problem (the way in which children learning their first language are exposed to primarily positive evidence, and do not generally receive feedback on their mistakes, or get told examples of incorrect sentences, even though such an approach is more helpful in general cognitive learning —White 1989). The UG approach, since it assumes that language is 'wired in' to the human brain in some way, can account for the speed of first language acquisition, achieved at a time when children are, in other respects, extremely limited in their capacity to learn all manner of things vital to their survival. In other words, children do not seem dependent on their environment for language (except that they need to receive triggering input), whereas in other respects they are dependent on caregivers for both learning experiences and for shelter and protection.

Second language acquisition

The next issue is whether a UG approach is relevant for second language acquisition. If it were relevant, one would have to accept that it is important for learners to interact directly with primary data, and that the development of an underlying system would be the result of such interactions. According to this view, it might be as irrelevant for teachers to instruct learners formally and in a rule-focused way as it would be for mothers to work doggedly through a language syllabus with their children.

Three general positions can be distinguished which reflect different types of involvement for UG:

- UG is still functioning, in the second language case, in exactly the same way as in first language;
- UG is completely unavailable for the second language learner;
- UG is essentially inoperative in the second language case as a system which can be newly engaged, but the effects from its operation in first language acquisition are still available.

The attractions of the first of these possibilities are considerable. If sustainable, it would make important links between second language acquisition and linguistic theory. It would portray the problem of second language acquisition, too, as one of the 'reinvention' of language (Wells 1985), where input is merely a foil for the powerful internal mechanisms and processes to operate upon, as parameters are reset, and principles adhered to. It would also provide a fairly precise model (at least in the eyes of Universal Grammarians) which could be the basis for bold predictions and hypothesis-testing research. So such an approach has to be considered seriously, since in many ways it is a parsimonious and preferable alternative.

Problems with a Universal Grammar approach to SLA

Although attractive, the UG approach will not be pursued here. There are several reasons for this. First of all, the attractions of precision are more apparent than real. Following certain assumptions, the model is meant to generate precise predictions which are testable, and which would therefore lead to progress in relating theory to evidence. In reality, however, there are few clear-cut studies which provide any sort of basis for unambiguous judgement (Schachter 1996). Generally, results fall some way between the alternatives which the three models above would lead one to expect. As a result, judgements have to be made to 'rescue' the starting hypotheses. An example of this is the body of research on the pro-drop parameter, reviewed in Cook (1994). Early hopes that bundles of features set by the operation of this parameter would lead to confirming evidence, i.e. that when, in the second language case, one feature of this parameter bundle is reset, there would be rapid evidence of the resetting of the others, have not been realized. Instead, while some predictions have been borne out, others have not, with discrepant results usually generating the need to provide post-hoc explanations with ever more complicated versions of the underlying linguistic theory.

Second, there is the problem that UG does not stand still. In many ways this is laudable, and a sign of the vitality of the field. The problem is that while researchers working within UG may be content with this state of affairs, 'consumers' who are interested not in developments in linguistic theory for their own sake, but instead in the explanatory value the account can provide in related areas, find themselves stranded since the version of the theory they are diligently testing proves to be abandoned by UG researchers themselves. We are currently having to deal with the rise of 'minimalism', with its likely profound implications for how SLA studies can be designed (Cook and Newson 1996). Given this state of affairs (and its likely continuation in the future, with even newer versions of the theory supplanting one another), the attractions of the approach wane considerably.

Third, there is the issue that UG researchers focus on what the underlying theory deems to be important; that is, the agenda is set from the fundamental discipline. So, in many ways, are the research methodology and the data collection methods. Each of these factors poses problems for second language acquisition and for language teaching. Schachter (1996) notes that many of the issues which the language teaching profession consider important do not receive high priority in UG studies. Similarly, methods of eliciting competence-oriented language seem a long way away from the concepts of proficiency that language teachers and second language researchers take for granted. As a result, there is a remoteness about UG studies as far as ongoing second language development is generally concerned, a lack of external validity which, quite apart from the experimental evidence, undermines the relevance and significance of the UG-based account.

Which brings us to the fourth reason why a UG approach will not be pursued here. Essentially it does not complement effectively the processing perspective which is fundamental to the current approach. There are two aspects to this claim. First, it is assumed here (see extensive discussion in Chapter 9) that a critical period for language development exists: that prior to the closure of the critical period the human brain is especially sensitive to language input, and processes it in a qualitatively different way; and that after the critical period is over, general cognitive modules are used as the basis for language development. After the critical period, that is, language development can be viewed as an example of the human-information processing system at work, in a way which resembles learning in other domains, such as a computer language, or a musical instrument, or some new area of knowledge. Second, the discussion earlier in this book has focused on the way in which for older learners, meaning is primary, strategic language use is pervasive, and processing-based generalizations have considerable utility in accounting for second language performance. In general, therefore, the approach emphasizes how noticing and attention have powerful influences, and how dual-mode processing and representational systems bear a closer relationship to performance itself. As a result, the prospect of using SLA studies as an arena which could shed light on underlying linguistic theory is not good. To return to the questions posed at the beginning of this chapter, UG is good at describing a formal, underlying competence (and possibly learning in the pre-critical period stage), but it is less convincing with second language learning, with real-time communication, and with the relationship between performance and change. For present purposes, therefore, the UG approach to language acquisition will remain pretty much in the background.

The Multidimensional Model

Pienemann (1984, 1989) and Pienemann, Johnson, and Brindley (1988) have proposed what is termed a 'Multidimensional Model' for second language acquisition. The two dimensions of the model are intended to address different areas of development. The first focuses on sequences of interlanguage development which are seen as invariant, while the second accounts for variation in other areas of language development, often features which have social relevance and which are less connected to language sub-systems. We will not pursue this more socially-oriented dimension here, instead focusing on the aspects of the model which emphasize constraints on language acquisition, since language processing is more clearly implicated in this area.

The first of Pienemann's dimensions, which is held to account for the sequence in which structures in the second language are acquired, is essentially cognitive in nature. It proposes the following stages that have to be passed through, cumulatively, during the course of development:

Stage
1   formulae
2   canonical order
3   adverb preposing
4   verb separation
5   inversion
6   verb final

Stage 1 learners rely on formulaic language, appropriate to a limited range of situations, but understood purely as chunks, so that no degree of manipulation of elements or adaptation to different circumstances is possible. Stage 1 is essentially non-syntactic. At Stage 2, the learner is able to produce utterances based on simple word order, with transparent meanings, generally of the S-V-O form. Knowledge of syntactic categories is still rudimentary, but the learner is able to vary this basic pattern to express meanings appropriate to

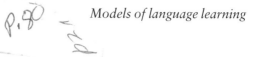

different situations. Stage 3 sees the first evidence of a capacity to manipulate material internally, although in this case the manipulation is rather limited. Learners are able to move a small range of elements, (such as adverbs, one-word negation), and place these only at the beginnings or ends of sentences. It can still hardly be said that true syntactic categories are being used.

By Stage 4 manipulation is no longer restricted to a small number of elements which have to be located at the beginnings or ends of sentences. The identification of internal elements of an utterance is possible, and some degree of manipulation of verb forms appears. At Stage 5 there are the first clear signs of operations on categories which can be regarded as syntactic. As a result, the degree of internal manipulation increases considerably. Finally, at Stage 6, internal analysis at the clausal level is possible, allowing some degree of subordination, and more complex syntactic manipulation.

A central attraction of Pienemann's account is the way it is based on processing operations. Progressive development through the six stages requires a greater degree of analysis at each point, and a greater capacity to manipulate the elements which have been identified. In other words, not only are emerging categories required, but also movement of the actual elements of such categories is involved. Compare the auxiliary and main verb in German and subject-verb inversion, again in German, when a sentence begins with an adverb. This, in turn, requires progressively greater short-term memory capacity to handle the computation needed to achieve the movement required to express the more complex meanings.

Given that this account stresses processing factors and memory limitations on the sorts of cognitive operations that are possible, Pienemann's account would seem ideally suited to function as the developmental underpinning of the approach taken. This may ultimately prove to be justified. After all, his model is unusually precise, and does have some supportive evidence. For all that, though, it will be taken as of marginal interest here, in that, broadly, it is seen as not yet ready to provide a complete enough account of language development to be viable. There are several reasons for this.

Problems with the multi-dimensional approach

First, although processing is fundamental for the model, there is little evidence to show that processing factors influence performance. The stages which need to be passed through are described in processing terms, but such descriptions come across as structural constraints, rather than connecting with the operation of a limited capacity system. Larsen-Freeman and Long (1991) also make the point that, despite the centrality of processing constraints, the model is not specific as to what allows learners to overcome such constraints and move on from one stage to another. A second problem concerns situational influences during speech production (and comprehension). We saw in Chapter 1 how older learners rely heavily on strategies of processing and draw upon contextual cues to make language more comprehensible. What was most important in this regard is that the exploitation of such cues could enable the learner to bypass a concern for syntax in ongoing communication. The approach taken by Pienemann assumes that internal processing forces will simply operate, and makes no real attempt to incorporate the limiting effects on syntactic development of the way language can be used meaningfully in real contexts. Third, there is the treatment of lexicalized language. We saw in Chapters 1 and 2 how important this area is, and how much of normal communication relies upon lexicalized chunks of language which are necessary for the speaker to keep up with real time, and for the listener to avoid having to deal with consistently new and difficult-to-process language. Pienemann (1984) seems to ignore these factors, preferring to regard the sequence of stages as inexorable in operation, and likely to replace peripheral lexicalized uses of language. This seems to emphasize acquisition itself excessively, and does not take adequate notice of the importance of ongoing language processing.

The literature contains a number of other criticisms of the Multidimensional Model. Cook (1994) claims, for example, that the simple cumulative nature of the model, complexification following a simple, one-dimensional path, is not consistent with linguistic theory. He argues that linguistic systems contain all manner of interconnections, and Pienemann's expectation that progress will always be forward is implausible. He proposes that current changes in a system may force learners to re-evaluate what seemed to be established features of the system, and change them, for example two steps back for three steps forward (Kellerman 1985). Tarone (forthcoming) argues that the evidence for the Multidimensional Model is not yet convincing (although it should be said that it is a considerable virtue of the model that it has generated a considerable quantity of data). She argues that it is still only a satisfactory account of the acquisition of German, with its emphasis on word order phenomena, and that the extensions to other languages have not been sufficiently successful. In addition, she suggests that the data collection has not produced evidence from a sufficient variety of language use contexts to enable the model to make general claims. Ellis (1994) makes the methodological point that it is difficult to know when formulaic language is being used.

It may be that the Multidimensional Model can overcome these criticisms, for example by developing a range of studies to cover a variety of language combinations which would then constitute more impressive confirmation of the operation of the universal processing principles. Similarly, other methodological problems could, in principle, be overcome. But the essential point here is that the model does not currently lend itself to functioning as a basis for the information-processing approach which will be taken in this book. The Multidimensional Model will be drawn on occasionally to illuminate, but will not otherwise be considered further.

The Analysis-Control model

A model which has a clearer processing dimension is that of Bialystok (1990). The model has developed considerably over the last fifteen years, although it, too, has always been portrayed in terms of two dimensions. Originally the two dimensions were described as knowledge and control (Bialystok 1981). More recently, the dimensions have been described as analysis and control, and it is emphasized that both of these dimensions represent a process. The analysis dimension concerns such things as the extent to which knowledge is more structured and differentiated, and the extent to which there is greater organization within the knowledge base. One assumes here that the more interconnections exist between the units of knowledge, the more analysed we can consider it to be. In addition, the analysis dimension concerns the extent to which knowledge is represented explicitly, with high levels of analysis associated with a greater ability to make more complex judgements, including metalinguistic judgements. High analysis and the ensuing greater explicitness are also seen as likely to facilitate more manipulation and restructuring of the material which has been analysed explicitly.

The control dimension concerns access to knowledge. Earlier versions of the model emphasized fluency and automaticity (at which time the knowledge–control contrast implied a type of competence–performance distinction). In contrast, Bialystok (1990) now proposes that control concerns the selection of items of knowledge, the capacity to attend selectively to those items which are relevant for a particular task, co-ordinate the items of information which are selected, and carry out these processes with automaticity. Given that the emphasis is on the processes of accessing information, fluency becomes merely the consequence of the above processes operating effectively, and is thus not so interesting in its own terms.

Bialystok's model has been the source of a great deal of empirical research. In the main this has explored how tasks can be related to the two-dimensional framework by analysing the demands they make for the processes of analysis and control (Bialystok 1990). The model has also been used as the basis for categorizing communication strategies, regarding them as principally analysis-based (concerned with manipulating the intended concept) or control-based (concerned with manipulating the means of expression) (Bialystok 1990).

Problems with the Analysis-Control model

Although there are a number of attractions in this model, it is not without its problems. First of all, there is the question of the nature of the representation involved. Analysis is seen as a process, implying that some sort of knowledge structure is being operated upon, and that the processes of differentiation, organization, transformation, and so on, produce some change in the underlying representational system. But this characterization of the role of analysis is not detailed in terms of the representational system itself, particularly when we consider that, in the case of second language learning, the system must be linguistic in nature, i.e. detail is lacking regarding the sorts of linguistic analyses which would need to be operative. A convincing account would need to be specific about interlanguage systems and their development. As a result, the concept of analysis seems detached and rather abstract—able to account for everything in principle, while not being detailed about specific things or making interesting predictions about the nature of language change. We need to know what structures the analysis operates upon, and what its products are, before we can effectively judge its usefulness.

A second difficulty is that the concept of analysis seems to incorporate two different areas. On the one hand it emphasizes the process of analysis and interaction with some underlying knowledge structure. With this account, to be high in analysis would imply having a more complex underlying system whose interrelationships have been fully established. On the other, there is a strong emphasis in Bialystok's model on the way in which high analysis is associated with more explicit knowledge representation and the capacity to make, for example, metalinguistic judgements. To be high in analysis implies the capacity to manipulate structures more efficiently because they are accessible explicitly. Two complications arise here. First, if this interpretation is correct, analysis seems to contain two different aspects whose interrelationship, and need for one another, is unclear. Why should explicitness go hand in hand with greater complexity? Why cannot the complex system happily operate on an implicit basis? Second, the implicit–explicit strand of the analysis dimension seems to involve the nature of the access to the knowledge structure itself. As such, this strand would seem to fit in more logically with the control dimension, since it would be implicated in such operations as the selection and co-ordination of items of knowledge.

The hybrid nature of the analysis dimension leads us to consider a third problem with Bialystok's model—the way in which it accounts for change and development. As was mentioned earlier, the model seems to take as its prime target the need to account for task performance in terms of the two dimensions posited. It is also implicit in the model that progress has to be from a state of low analysis and low control to one of high analysis and high control. But here we encounter problems. One would expect, particularly in the case of second language development, that as far as the underlying interlanguage structure is concerned, three different areas might be implicated. These are:

- size of underlying system;
- degree of complexity and analysis;
- explicitness.

The first of these, size of underlying system, is a function of the number of elements (syntactic patterns, lexical elements, for example) in the system, but does not in itself highlight organization. The second, complexity and analysis, is concerned with organization, and with the internal structure of the system. The simple past could serve as an example here. Size could grow simply through more exemplars (of both the irregular and irregular past) but complexity and analysis would come into play as generalizations are made reflecting the formation of the regular past and (perhaps) the identification of sub-classes of the regular past. Negation, relativization, and other systems could be viewed similarly. Finally, explicitness would concern whether the results of such analyses became available at a level of representation which allows them to be manipulated and articulated consciously.

We have seen that the Bialystok model addresses (rather uneasily, following the above account) the two areas of complexity and explicitness. But it does not deal in any clear way with how the system grows in scale, and how the degree of complexity relates to this increase in scale. As a result, there is no sense of what sort of path of development is likely to be followed, or of what forces will make it more likely for the system to grow, or to be made more complex internally. Occasional aspects of interlanguage development may be illuminated by the model, but it does not really have any means of addressing the range of concerns in the SLA field, or of findings related to the effects of instruction, or of structural sequences which emerge, and so on. Why would learners be pushed to develop progressively more complex systems for interrogation, for example? Why should particular sequences emerge? Which instructional alternatives are preferable?

Further, it is difficult to understand how the process of making knowledge structures more explicit fits into any sort of developmental framework. In the case of first language acquisition, the account is more convincing. One assumes that first language development is rapid, and largely complete as an implicit system by the age of (say) five. Then, coincident with the processes of schooling and literacy, one can understand how this existing implicit system can be made more explicit, and the progressively greater explicitness put to use. So in this context the movement from low explicitness to high explicitness makes sense because of the starting-point involved. What the learner is achieving, in many ways, is a new form of representation of the same thing he or she started with. But it is difficult to see the parallel in the second language field. The underlying system is what takes time to develop. It is unclear, therefore, how the process of 'making explicit' operates here. The assumption is that the implicit system is in place for the process of making explicit to start to operate. But for many learners the problem is precisely how the implicit system arises in the first place. Worse, many accounts of second language learning explore how the reverse sequence that Bialystok describes can operate, how knowledge which starts as explicit can become implicit. Such accounts try to explain how what happens in class can lead to the development of a system which can operate in real-time, and without the need for conscious awareness.

This brings us to the final problem we will address here—the relationship between the two dimensions. Earlier versions of the model were more easily understandable in terms of the competence–performance, or knowledge–process distinctions. But the current version stresses that both analysis and control are *processes*. In this respect, the issue of how the control dimension operates, *and what units it operates upon*, are not clear. Considerable selection and organization must take place during speech production. If we assume that the underlying knowledge system is rule-based, then we can start to propose assembly mechanisms by which speaking is possible. But we saw earlier that there are strong arguments for dual-mode models of processing, in which rules and exemplars (and exemplars created through previous rule application) co-exist. We have also seen how strategic processing is pervasive amongst older (post-critical period) learners. Finally, we have reviewed the literature on the importance of formulaic language. All of these factors pose serious problems for the way in which control mechanisms and the operation of attention combine in speech production. It is a virtue of the Bialystok model that the control dimension provides a framework within which such factors could operate. The problem is that it is not clear *how* they would do so. In that respect, 'control' seems a rather vague, cover term, which is not terribly illuminating as to what actually happens during processing. Once again it may provide a framework for describing what is happening, but it does not make predictions about exactly how processes coexist and interact. For that reason, the model will be treated here as relevant but only occasionally illuminating for the discussion.

Implications of a processing approach

We now need to sum up the discussion so far. Essentially, we can think of language use and language acquisition as constrained by the operations of a limited capacity information-processing system. This system:

- does not have the resources to process in an exhaustive manner all the second language input which is received (VanPatten 1990; Doughty 1991);
- is predisposed, at the input stage, to prioritize meaning, with the result that a focus on form has to be engineered in some way (VanPatten 1990; VanPatten and Cadierno 1993);
- represents (and learns) information in the form of rules or exemplars (Schmidt 1994; Skehan 1992; Carr and Curren 1994)
- benefits from some degree of awareness (Schmidt 1994; Fotos 1993);

– can produce language more effectively from lexicalized, exemplar-based representations unless beneficial processing conditions prevail (Ellis 1987; Crookes 1989; Skehan 1992; Foster and Skehan 1996).

We have also seen that 'structural' models do not address most of the issues raised by these points. Universal Grammar approaches tend to be selective in the aspects of the language system that they investigate (emphasizing areas of importance to theory, not necessarily of priority to language learners). They also (not unreasonably) de-emphasize the processing factors that are the focus for the current discussion. The Multidimensional Model (Pienemann *et al.* 1988), while emphasizing processing constraints, is in reality more concerned with the structural stages that learners pass through, and does not address mechanisms for change or how the processing limitations impact upon learning. Finally, the Bialystok model (1990), which seems closest to current interests, has the major problem that it, too, has little to say about the nature of change and development. It also has problems in separating the two dimensions on which it is based, and does not clarify the sorts of findings summarized above. Returning to the questions posed earlier, the strengths and weaknesses of the three approaches are summarized in Table 4.1.

	Universal Grammar	Multi-dimensional Model	Analysis-Control Model
What is the nature of the formal system, of the underlying competence, in each model?	strength	neutral	weakness
How does change occur in the underlying system?	neutral	strength	weakness
How is the system used to enable real-time performance?	weakness	neutral	strength
How do performance and change relate to one another?	weakness	weakness	neutral

Table 4.1: Strengths and weaknesses of the three approaches for second language learning

This summary brings out how difficult it is to have a model which gives a satisfactory account of representation, learning (change), and processing performance. Each of the models emphasizes one of the areas, somewhat at the expense of the others. Further, none of the models is good at accounting for the *relationship* between performance and change, i.e. *in accounting for ways communicative language use can lead to changes in the underlying system.* In view of this, what will be proposed here is not a model in any formal sense, so much as a series of processing principles, comparable in spirit to those proposed by Slobin (1973) for the first language case. The principles attempt to clarify how ongoing performance is compatible with some degree of focus on form. So what is presented is not a model of learning, or a model of performance, but a set of principles which can relate the two.

Towards a task-based approach

The following three chapters will examine how such principles can lead to a framework for the implementation of a task-based approach to instruction and testing. The basic distinction which needs to be made is between representation and process. The former is concerned with the nature of storage, the units on which it is based, the organization of such units, and the way in which such representations change. The latter is concerned with access to such representations and the way in which ongoing processing can take place in real time. And clearly there will be interfaces between representation and process, both during ongoing processing, when the representations are the basis for communication, as well as in terms of change taking place in underlying representations as a result of ongoing processing. As we will see, there are tensions between the competing systems which have to be resolved in some way. The purpose of the following chapters will be to see how instruction can make it more likely that these resolutions are productive.

The rule-based system

The basic issue is the proposal that representation functions by means of a dual-mode system, with access to rules and exemplars. Both are feasible, but how they exist, or rather, coexist, for any particular foreign language learner will depend on a range of factors—context of learning, nature of instruction, individual differences, and so on. The rule-based system is likely to be parsimoniously and elegantly organized, with rules being compactly structured. They will draw in turn upon lexical elements (themselves well organized in a lexicon) as necessary. Such a rule-based system is likely to be generative, with rules being creative in their application, and so precise in the meanings that they can express. It is also likely to be restructurable, with new rules replacing or subsuming old rules, and then functioning efficiently as an extended system. Such a mode of representation is also likely to be more sensitive to feedback since the precision and system which accounts for rule-organization will make the feedback more informative. In essence, then, the rule-based system prioritizes analysability (Widdowson 1989). But of course, all these gains are achieved at one considerable cost: their operation will lead to a heavy processing burden during ongoing language use. Rules need complex processes of construction to underpin their operation, in which the units from which they are composed are necessarily small, and require detailed attention during comprehension and assembly during production. This is resource draining (VanPatten 1994), and likely, in the case of the second language learner, to have capacity-stretching difficulties. As a result, this mode of communication may need supportive circumstances for it to be feasible.

The exemplar-based system

An exemplar-based system operates in more or less the opposite manner. It is heavily based on the operation of a redundant memory system in which there are multiple representations of the same lexical elements, because in each case the element functions as part of a unit longer than the word. In consequence, the system lacks parsimony, and has only a limited generative potential. In addition, given that relatively fixed phrases are involved, the potential for expressing new and precise meanings is more limited. But of course the gain of such a system is processing speed. Utterance units are now less numerous, since they are longer. In addition, they do not require excessive internal computation, since they can function as integrated wholes, with the need for analysis only coming into play for the point when the unit has been 'run off'. As a result, for the capacity-stretched foreign language learner, there are more attentional resources to devote to other areas, including the formulation of messages, and the conceptual content of what is being said (Levelt 1989). There is a danger (but see discussion below on the three-stage process of change) that an exemplar-based system can only learn by accumulation of wholes, and that it is likely to be excessively context-bound, since such wholes cannot be adapted easily for the expression of more complex meanings. It is also possible that since exemplars are not part of a structured system, feedback may not be so effective: there is not the same connection with a rule which can produce *general* change.

The dual-mode system

Clearly, neither the rule-based nor the exemplar system is ideal separately. The former emphasizes representation at the expense of processing, while the latter does the reverse. The former leads to the development of an open, form-oriented system, while the latter emphasizes meaning, and is less appropriate for underlying system change. The question then becomes one of exploring how the two systems might work harmoniously together.

In this respect, insights from first language acquisition and first language processing may be helpful. There is evidence that initial stages of first language acquisition are primarily lexical in nature (Bates *et al.* 1988; Nelson 1981). Contextually coded exemplars are used to communicative meanings in a direct manner. Then, at a later stage, strong processes of syntacticization come into play and operate upon the lexical repertoire that the child has developed. The result is that language which was available on a lexical base now becomes reorganized to be syntactically based, and the benefits of such a rule-governed system come into play. It is assumed, in the first language case, that this process is due to the maturation and operation of an inbuilt propensity to process language input in a manner qualitatively different from the way other material is processed, and that it is the operation of a LAD which produces this state of affairs.

However, this process of syntacticization, inexorable though it may be, is not particularly helpful as a basis for *processing*. (Nor is it consistent with the account of memory functioning given in Chapter 2.) It is proposed that what happens in subsequent first language development is that language which has been syntactized is then *relexicalized*. In other words, units are assembled to be wholes from language which has been analysable, and which can become analysable again, if need be. This connects very clearly with the discussion presented earlier (Carr and Curren 1994) in which rules may be used to create exemplars which have functional autonomy in their operation within ongoing language processing. The central issue is that the underlying system exploits rules to create the sorts of units described by Pawley and Syder (1983) and which are then available for access as units for processing with minimal computational demands (compare also Carr and Curren's discussion of exemplar-based learning). Lexical items may then appear in a number of different exemplars provided that each exemplar serves some communicative function. The sequence can be represented as in Figure 4.1.

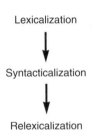

Figure 4.1: Sequence of exemplars of lexical items

Once language has been organized in this way, the user has available dual modes of processing, rules and exemplars, which can be mobilized as appropriate to different communicative contexts and goals. When time is pressing, and contextual support high, memory-based communication is appropriate. When there is more time, and precision is important, the rule-based system can be accessed. The first language user is then in the position of being adaptable to ongoing changes in communication conditions.

However, this has all been possible only because of the operation of a Language Acquisition Device during the critical period for language learning. Syntacticization occurred because it was programmed to do so following a maturational schedule (Pinker 1994). Once the critical period is past, this automatic engagement of a system designed to syntacticize is no longer an option. As a result, the primacy for meaning, in the context of a limited capacity information-processing system, means that there will be a greater predisposition towards the exemplar, memory-based system, and the internally-generated pressure for syntactization will not come into play. In other words, there is a danger that the second language learner will not progress beyond the first of the three stages mentioned above.

A system for second language learners

What this implies is that it is necessary to *contrive* the movement through all three stages, given that this will not happen by itself. Recall Klein's (1986) three problems for language learning, matching, analysis, and synthesis. What is required in such a three-stage system is that matching (and noticing and input processing) should be supported. More important, learners need to be led to engage in cycles of analysis and synthesis. In other words, if meaning primacy and communicational pressure make for exemplar-based learning, it is important that there should be continual pressure on learners to analyse the linguistic units they are using, so that they can access this same material as a rule-based system. Equally, it is important that when material does become available as such a system, learners should engage in the complementary process of synthesizing such language so that it will then become available in exemplar, memory-based form as well. If this is achieved, the second language learner will then be able to function in a way analogous to the first language learner and shift mode of processing to adapt to different contextual circumstances.

What is needed in language teaching is the sort of balanced and phased programme which will maximize the chances that such sustained and balanced progress will be made. The learner has to have a system which remains open to noticing and to change while at the same time making some gains in terms of fluency and real-time language processing. And here one must correct any possible mistaken impression that the three stages above are simply followed sequentially. The three phases describe what may be happening at different points within the language system at the same time: the relexicalization phase may be in progress in one area of language while the syntacticization phase is still predominant in another. In other words, the learner has to continually revisit two of the problems identified by Klein

(1986), analysis and synthesis. On the one hand the learner needs to be prepared to focus on structure, and to identify pattern. On the other, the identification of pattern is, in itself, insufficient, because the fruits of such analysis need to be reintegrated and synthesized into fluent performance with the patterns concerned. So the two processes are in constant dialectic, and one makes progress by judiciously analysing where this is profitable, and synthesizing where the appropriate bit of the language system is ready. The analysis is necessary to enable the learner to gain generativity and flexibility, and the synthesis is necessary to enable fluency and control to be achieved. But each must be ready to be used continually during an individual's course of language development.

One aspect of this account has implications for syllabus design. 'Knowing' a particular form is a multi-level affair. It is therefore futile to consider that something has been learned because it has been covered at a particular point in a syllabus, or because at some stage a learner gives evidence of being able to use it correctly. The problem is that the 'knowledge' that underlies language is at different levels, and that 'knowing' some aspect of the language at one level does not mean that one is able to use that knowledge at other levels. It is a case of reanalysing and resynthesizing constantly, so that what is newly relexicalized, for example, is reintegrated into the other areas which are already relexicalized, and can also coexist with what is still syntacticized. This implies that a cyclical syllabus is necessary. Such a syllabus would revisit aspects of the emerging interlanguage syllabus regularly to enable newly analysed or newly lexicalized material to be integrated into the developing system. The cyclical nature of the syllabus would avoid the situation of allowing only one chance for this to occur—learning and development are not so conveniently precise and packageable. To portray these issues in Widdowson's (1989) terms, the syllabus must make it possible to develop analysability and accessibility in maximum harmony. The analysable stage has to precede the accessible stage, but the learner must reach a stage where accessibility enables real-time communication. The former system is rule-based, while the latter is memory-based. As a result, the strength of the former is that the rule-basis enables flexibility and recombination of language elements, but at the cost of on-line computation which renders real-time communication difficult. The latter simply puts together fairly ready-made chunks of language and is not flexible, but it does enable the speaker to keep up with the speed of the ongoing discourse.

We have now reached the point where these more general processing considerations can be used to explore pedagogic issues. The next chapter attempts to provide a rationale for a task-based approach to foreign language instruction which takes account of the discussion presented so far.

5 A rationale for task-based instruction

The discussion in this book so far has suggested that psycholinguistic factors and processing conditions are highly relevant to second language learning and second language performance. The focus has been on research studies and theoretical discussions relevant to this perspective. Although there has been reference to pedagogy, this has mostly been indirect, and implications for second language classrooms have had to be teased out of the more fundamental discussion. In the next three chapters this emphasis is changed and pedagogy becomes the prime concern. I try to explore the implications of the previous chapters for language teaching, and in particular to demonstrate how a processing perspective can be important for a task-based approach to instruction. This chapter will explore the nature of tasks and review theorizing and research in this area. Chapter 6 will focus on the nature of performance on tasks, as well as how task-based instruction can best be implemented. Chapter 7 will apply the processing perspective to task-based testing.

The traditional presentation-based approach

A convenient starting point for a discussion of task-based approaches is to consider alternative, more traditional methods of organizing language teaching. The most influential such approach is that of the 3Ps: presentation, practice, and production. The first stage is generally focused on a single point of grammar which is presented explicitly or implicitly to maximize the chances that the underlying rule will be understood and internalized. This would essentially aim at the development of declarative knowledge. This initial stage would be followed by practice activities, designed to automatize the newly grasped rule, and to convert declarative to procedural knowledge. During the practice stage, the learner would not be expressing personal meanings so much as working through exercises which provide ready-made meanings (or no meanings at all). These exercises would be sufficiently straightforward so as not to strain the fragile and developing declarative knowledge system. At the production stage the degree of control and support would be reduced, and the learner would be required to produce language more spontaneously, based on meanings the learner himself or herself would want to express.

The durability of the 3Ps approach

Such an approach is now out of fashion with communicative language teachers (Brumfit and Johnson 1979) and acquisition theorists (Long and Crookes 1991), yet it is probably still the commonest teaching approach when judged on a world-wide basis. Communicative approaches have probably had only a marginal impact on the range of teachers operating in many school systems and so it is worthwhile reflecting briefly on some of the reasons for the durability of the 3Ps-based methods.

First of all, the approach has had an excellent relationship with teacher training and teachers' feelings of professionalism. It is very comforting, and places the teacher firmly in charge of proceedings. The 3Ps sequence is relatively easy to organize, and comes bundled with a range of techniques which, besides having the potential to organize large groups of students efficiently, also demonstrate the power relations within the classroom, since the teacher is the centre of what is happening at all times (Wright 1987). The techniques which enable the teacher to orchestrate proceedings so well are also eminently trainable, and lend themselves to perpetuation by means of a teacher training profession which passes on this one-directional view of how language teaching classrooms can be properly organized. The result is that a conservative profession, out of touch with language acquisition studies, has for many years simply transmitted essentially the same view of how teaching should be organized, and what teachers should be like. (See the critique in Willis and Willis 1996b.)

A second reason for the continued importance of this approach is that it lends itself very neatly to accountability, since it generates clear and tangible goals, precise syllabuses, and a comfortingly itemizable basis for the evaluation of effectiveness. Syllabus planning, that is, is seen as unconstrained by learner factors, and can be based on whatever units are convenient, and in whatever order for the units that the syllabus designer chooses (White 1988). The emphasis is on product, with the result that testing is seen as unproblematic, since it can focus on sampling whatever 'items' underlie the syllabus.

These reasons—secure teacher roles and teacher training, and clear accountability—go some way to explaining the persistence of what is essentially a discredited, meaning-impoverished methodology (White 1988). But in addition, a major contributory influence to this lack of persistence has been the lack of a clear alternative for pedagogy, not so much theoretically as practically, an alternative framework which will translate into classroom organization, teacher training, and accountability and assessment. Unless this is done, and teachers are provided with some means of designing classroom activities for their students, as well as devising methods of implementing syllabuses which are imposed upon them, alternative approaches will only appeal to those who are teaching in favourable circumstances, or who are unusually determined (or, it has to be admitted, are fashion victims). So the next three chapters will explore the viability of task-based teaching in this regard, as an approach to instruction which is theoretically defensible and practically feasible.

Task-based approaches: definitions and preliminary rationale

Instruction in which learners are given tasks to complete in the classroom makes the assumption that transacting tasks in this way will engage naturalistic acquisitional mechanisms, cause the underlying interlanguage system to be stretched, and drive development forward. At the outset, though, we need to examine basic issues relating to defining tasks and task-based instruction, and then try to understand why task-based instruction has gained such popularity, at least in some teaching contexts, despite the conservative power of the 3Ps approach.

Concepts and definitions of task

As a definition of tasks within task-based instruction, I propose, following Candlin (1987), Nunan (1989), Long (1989), and others, that a task is an activity in which:

- meaning is primary;
- there is some communication problem to solve;
- there is some sort of relationship to comparable real-world activities;
- task completion has some priority;
- the assessment of the task is in terms of outcome.

A complementary approach is to show what tasks are not, since it is often just as clarifying to specify what an alternative position represents. In this respect, and following Willis (1996), tasks:

- do not give learners other people's meanings to regurgitate;
- are not concerned with language display;
- are not conformity-oriented;
- are not practice-oriented;
- do not embed language into materials so that specific structures can be focused upon.

Applying positive and negative features in this way allows the following to be identified as task-based activities:

- completing one another's family trees;
- agreeing on advice to give to the writer of a letter to an agony aunt;

- discovering whether one's paths will cross (out of school) in the next week;
- solving a riddle;
- leaving a message on someone's answer machine.

In contrast, a number of other classroom activities would not count as tasks:

- completing a transformation exercise;
- (most) question and answer activities with the teacher;
- inductive learning activities where pre-selected material is conducive to the generation of language rules.

Of course, some of the time it may still be difficult to decide whether an activity merits the label 'task' since the two underlying characteristics of tasks, avoidance of specific structures, and engagement of worthwhile meanings, are matters of degree, rather than being categorical (Compare a 'for and against task' in which arguments on a particular issue are pre-packaged for learners; or an information transfer task of some artificiality and detachment from learners' lives). Such an approach to defining tasks will not deal with all situations unambiguously, since it is generally the case that skilled teachers (and 'aware' learners) can bring meaning to the most unpromising material (Bannbrook and Skehan 1990), just as the reverse can happen when a task with great potential is rendered mechanical through unimaginative implementation. But in the main the above characteristics will separate tasks from conventional language activities in which there is a much greater focus on structure, and the focus on structure itself may fit into a more extended sequence of form-driven activities.

Long and Crookes (1991) discuss a further quality of tasks: that they have a clear pedagogic relationship to real-world language needs. They believe that needs analyses should be conducted which identify target uses of language, allowing tasks which have a meaningful relationship to such language use to be designed for the classroom. In this way, the tasks themselves are meant to have pedagogic value. They are not reproductions of the real-world tasks but are adapted to make them more accessible while still retaining end-use qualities. I regard this as desirable, but difficult to obtain in practice. So while recognizing the attractions of such tasks, the emphasis here will be on the processing demands that are made by different sorts of task.

I will not be concerned either with the possibility that students can be involved in the negotiation of which tasks are used, and how they might be used (Breen 1987). This, too, I regard as desirable and interesting, but removed from the present emphasis on processing. I prefer to see what generalizations about task design and task implementation can be established more widely first, with the idea that any such progress can make task negotiation itself more meaningful. But later in the book I will consider the role of different learner types and also how learners can be supported to take on a more autonomous role within the classroom.

Justifying the use of tasks

Drawing on this characterization of what tasks are, it is now possible to ask the question *why* tasks would be used, i.e. what rationale underlies their role in instruction? At a general level, Long and Crookes (1991) propose that what is important is instruction that (a) enables acquisitional processes to operate, particularly by allowing meaning to be negotiated, and (b) maintains a focus on form, as opposed to a focus on form. As they put it:

> It is claimed that (pedagogic) tasks provide a vehicle for the presentation of appropriate target language samples to learners—input which they will inevitably reshape via application of general cognitive processing capacities— and for the delivery of comprehension and production opportunities of negotiable difficulty.
>
> (ibid.: 43)

In this way, Long and Crookes are advocating the use of analytic syllabuses (Wilkins 1976). These are syllabuses which present language in naturalistic units which then have to be operated upon, and broken down by the learner, with acquisitional processes then engaging with the input that has been received.

Up to a point, this justification for task-based instruction has been adequate—it establishes the general worth of such an approach. But it provides little guidance as to the precise ways in which tasks can be justified, something which is necessary if effective pedagogic principles are to be achievable (see discussion in Chapter 6). Consequently, and in keeping with the processing perspective of this book, two justifications will be offered here, the first concerned with general information-processing capacities, and the second with the selective channelling of attention that is possible.

Processing-based analyses of tasks are concerned with their information-processing load, and effectively focus on the difficulty of the task. The assumption is that more demanding tasks consume more attentional resources simply for task transaction, with the result that less attention is available for focus on form. As a result, the scope for 'residual' benefit from the task is reduced (compare the discussion of VanPatten's work in Chapter 3). So one goal in researching tasks is to establish task characteristics which influence difficulty. In this way pedagogically motivated task selection can be more effective. Where more demanding tasks are required, this can be achieved. In contrast, where easier tasks are needed so that spare attentional capacity can be generated for use with other pedagogical goals, for example focus on accuracy, this too can be attempted.

A selective-channelling rationale for tasks attempts to make links between desirable aspects of language performance during tasks and task characteristics which may predispose such performance. Here the focus is on the way the task itself leads attention to be used in particular ways. Such channelled use might be towards some aspect of the discourse, or accuracy, complexity, fluency in general, or even occasionally, the use of particular sets of structures in the language. Whichever of these applies, the intention is to go beyond saying that tasks are generally useful, or easy, or difficult, and instead to be able to claim that particular tasks may be appropriate to achieve particular pedagogic aims. In other words, more targeted selection of tasks is intended to enable instruction to foster the balanced language development that was discussed in Chapter 4, with development of fluency matched by development of accuracy and complexity. In this way, simply transacting tasks (and expressing meanings) is less likely to compromise longer-term interlanguage restructuring.

Investigations into task-based instruction

To enable us to gain a perspective on how feasible it may be to orchestrate task-based instruction, we will next review the range of investigations that have been conducted in the area. The review will first cover data-free proposals for dimensions underlying tasks which lead into earlier research into task difficulty. Then the effects of selective influences of task characteristics on particular features of language will be discussed, followed by a brief overview of research studies in the areas of participants within tasks and the familiarity of tasks.

Task dimensions and task difficulty

Candlin

Early attempts to characterize task difficulty were largely speculative. Candlin (1987) for, example, proposed a set of criteria by which tasks might be selected and graded. These are:

- *cognitive load*: this concerns the general complexity of the content of the task, including the naturalness of the sequence it may be required to follow and also the number of participants or elements;
- *communicative stress*: more stressful tasks are seen as those which involve pressure which comes from the interlocutor, either because he or she is a native speaker or because of superior knowledge or proficiency;
- *particularity and generalizability*: this concerns the clarity of the goal of the task, as well as the norms of interpretation;
- *code complexity and interpretative density*: the former concerns the complexity of the linguistic code itself, while the latter is concerned with the complexity of the operations which need to be carried out on such a code;
- *process continuity*: this derives from the familiarity of the task type as well as the learners capacity to relate the task to tasks they are familiar with.

Skehan

Interesting and influential though these criteria may be, they are difficult to relate in any transparent way to actual tasks of the sort that might figure in conventional communicative teaching, or to the elements of the definitions of tasks presented earlier (Long 1989). So, in an attempt to overcome this limitation, I proposed a three-way distinction for the analysis of tasks (Skehan 1992), based on code complexity, cognitive complexity, and communicative pressure. This groups some of the factors suggested by Candlin into slightly higher-order categories. The full scheme is:

1 *Code complexity*

- linguistic complexity and variety
- vocabulary load and variety
- redundancy and density

2 *Cognitive complexity*

Cognitive familiarity
- familiarity of topic and its predictability
- familiarity of discourse genre
- familiarity of task

Cognitive processing
- information organization
- amount of 'computation'
- clarity and sufficiency of information given
- information type

3 *Communicative stress*
- time limits and time pressure
- speed of presentation
- number of participants
- length of texts used
- type of response
- opportunities to control interaction.

The major contrasts here are between the language required, the thinking required, and the performance conditions for a task. Language is simply seen as less-to-more complex in fairly traditional ways, since linguistic complexity is interpretable as constrained by structural syllabus considerations, or developmental sequences. In other words, it is assumed that some tasks will be attempted with simpler language than others (although different schemes may have different views on defining simplicity).

A more interesting distinction is made between two aspects of cognition: the capacity to access 'packaged' solutions to tasks (cognitive familiarity), compared with the need to work out solutions to novel problems 'on-line' (cognitive processing). For example, one might compare the family tree task (comparing one another's family trees in pairs) and a riddle task (both taken from Willis and Willis 1988). In the former case, the task requires existing, well-organized 'chunks' of knowledge to be retrieved and mobilized for task performance. In the latter, elements of a task are easy to handle, but there is significant difficulty in manipulating them to achieve a solution that the task requires. It is assumed that in the former case attentional resources are not particularly stretched, and there is scope for a focus on form (VanPatten 1994). In the latter, where processing has to be directed at the cognitive problem involved, there is less attention left over to focus on form.

Cognitive familiarity is broken down further into topic familiarity and predictability, that is, the extent to which differentiated organized background knowledge is available (compare Bialystok's 1990 analysis). Familiarity of discourse genre is the extent to which 'easifying' macrostructures are readily available. Familiarity of task refers to jigsaw tasks, decision-making tasks, or riddles, where unfamiliarity of task type could make a task less predictable and less susceptible to previously developed communication strategies.

Cognitive processing deals with processing load during task performance. Information organization refers to the naturalness with which task-relevant information is structured—the extent to which narratives, for example, follow conventional temporal sequence. The amount of computation relates to the amount of transformation or manipulation of information that is necessary for a task to be completed—a riddle, for example, requires many items to be attended to simultaneously, and 'if-then' statements carried out. Clarity and sufficiency of information concerns the directness with which information is made available for learners, together with the extent to which inferences need to be made. Finally, information type is based on contrasts such as concrete–abstract, static–dynamic, contextualized–decontextualized (Brown *et al.* 1984).

The third major heading in this scheme, communicative stress, reflects the performance conditions under which the task needs to be done, and is once again concerned with implications for processing. The factors under this heading reflect the urgency with which a task needs to be completed, and the perception, on the part of the student, of how much pressure there is to complete the task under difficult conditions. When larger quantities of material are presented quickly, and when little time is available for processing, when more complicated responses are required, and there is little opportunity to slow down interaction to take account of processing limitations, it is assumed that it will become more difficult to give attention to form.

In a sense this three-part scheme flows from the definitions of tasks presented earlier. Rather than focusing only on one target, it assumes that a task, if it is to be worth the name, will make meaning primary, and have a relationship with the real world by giving learners something worthwhile to do under conditions which relate to real life. If this is the case, then it is inevitable that there will be a cognitive component to the assessment of task difficulty, since this generates the meaning and gives the task substance. Equally, a focus on communicative pressure captures another dimension of the real-world relationship—the way processing factors operate. So the three general components of the scheme focus on the different major influences on activities which qualify for the label 'task'.

Prabhu

Several other researchers have offered interesting characterizations of tasks. Prabhu (1987), in the Bangalore Project, attempted to develop a viable alternative language teaching methodology for use in difficult circumstances. The focus of the work was on task outcome, not form. Prabhu approached this problem by using a pre-task, whose purpose was to present and demonstrate the task, assess its difficulty for the learners in question, adapt the main task if necessary, and, very importantly, 'let the language relevant to the task to come into play' (Prabhu 1984: 276). Subsequently, the task proper would be transacted by students, with task outcome being the major goal that preoccupied the learners. Focus on error and on feedback would be explicitly avoided, and it was intended that language learning would be incidental to the transaction of the task itself.

As a result of experience in observing which tasks were most successful in generating useful language as well as being interesting to students, Prabhu recommended reasoning-gap tasks above all, in preference to opinion-gap and information-gap tasks. A typical task would be to plan a complicated itinerary of a rail journey across India, armed with railway timetables, or to complete a 'whodunit' story. Tasks were selected initially on the basis of such general criteria, and then, through classroom-based evaluation of the degree of success, they would be reused, adapted, or discarded.

Berwick

On a more empirical basis, Berwick (1993) used multivariate statistical techniques in an attempt to uncover underlying dimensions of tasks. Drawing upon previous research (Berwick 1988) and a wider literature on analysing educational activities (Cummins 1984; Mohan 1986), he proposed two dimensions as underlying tasks. The first concerns task goals, with contrasting educational and social poles at either end of the dimension. Educational goals have clear didactic function, while social goals require the use of language simply because of the activity in which participants are engaged. The second dimension is based on task processes, with extremes of experiential and expository tasks. Experientially oriented tasks seem to be more concrete in nature, and relate to participants' own experiences. Expository tasks are based on more abstract information which may be the basis for generalizations and decontextualized language use (Cummins 1984). Unlike Pica *et al.* (1993) and Duff (1986) who have clear ideas as to desirable bundles of task qualities, Berwick (1993) is more concerned to explore different types of language associated with tasks which contain different combinations of qualities. His previous research (Berwick 1988) suggested that experiential-social tasks produced more confirmation checks and referential questions, while educational-expository tasks generated more definitions and lexical uncertainty. There is value either way.

Berwick (1993) operationalized the contrasts by means of a task using 'Lego' toy building bricks (completed under two conditions: pair facing apart, and pair facing together); a pedagogic task which required instructions to be given about text location in the word processor of a laptop computer (again done under two conditions, with or without the computer present); and a discussion task. The computer task had didactic goals (and expository versus experiential processes, depending on the two conditions). The 'Lego' task had social goals (and contrasting processes, as with the computer task). The discussion task was seen to be social in goal orientation, and intermediate between expository and experiential for processes. Berwick used a large number of dependent measures to assess whether the tasks would pattern empirically in the way he predicted following the above dimensions. In fact, the results were not terribly supportive of the original predictions. A factor analysis yielded a three-factor solution, with the second factor providing some support for the experiential-expository dimension, and the third factor being consistent with the didactic-social dimension. But the main finding was that the first factor brought together, rather unhelpfully in terms of the initial hypotheses, the discussion and the 'facing-apart' 'Lego' task. Berwick interprets this factor in terms of foregrounding of information, though the logic of this interpretation is not entirely clear. What is more relevant, though, is the relative importance of the three factors. The first factor extracted is clearly of dominating importance, suggesting that to consider all three factors, as Berwick did, led to the over-interpretation of the data matrix. As a result, one cannot really take the results as supportive of the existence of the dimensions involved, although they remain interesting in themselves. It may be necessary to break them down into smaller sub-components to make progress in understanding them more fully.

Brown et al.

A series of data-based studies which influenced the scheme proposed in Skehan (1992) is reported by Brown *et al.* (1984). They investigated various task design features in an attempt to establish task difficulty on an empirical basis. From a number of studies which examined the effects on task difficulty of different types and different quantities of information, they proposed the following matrix:

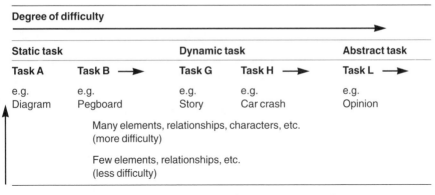

Table 5.1: Tasks of ascending difficulty (Brown et al., 1984)

The matrix proposes two dimensions which influence task difficulty. The easiest tasks on the first dimension, information type, are static tasks, in which the information does not change during the course of the activity. The examples given are diagramming and giving instructions about how to lay out a pegboard. In each case, visual information is involved, the task is essentially a one-way information-gap task, and the 'transmitter' simply has to explain how material is disposed in space. More difficult than this are dynamic tasks, in which elements change during the course of the task. In a car crash, for example, there is a narrative element, since not only has visual information to be communicated, but it also necessary to indicate the sequence of events, as well as the nature of the causality involved. Finally, the most difficult information type of all is considered to be the abstract task, since this contains decontextualized elements which have to be manipulated and expressed. The example given is that of expressing opinions.

If the first dimension is concerned with the nature of the information underlying each task, the other dimension concerns the scale of the task and the interrelationships between its elements. At the simplest level, this refers to the number of items or characters that are involved, suggesting, unsurprisingly, that more elements or characters make for greater task difficulty. Also important, but less developed, is the idea that the nature of the relationships between the elements contributes separately to task difficulty. This suggests that different sorts of relationship may lead to different degrees of difficulty.

Research reported by Foster and Skehan (1996) develops these findings. We were able to show that tasks based on personal, more immediate information were easier than those where less familiar and more remote information was involved. These studies are reported more fully below.

Selective effects of task characteristics

Pica et al.

Turning next to studies which show more selective influences of task characteristics, the major distinction is between researchers who have examined what might be termed discourse consequences of task features, and those who have looked at task effects on processing goals. In the former category, Pica *et al.* (1993) start from the assumption that acquisition takes place as a function of the learner engaging in interaction. This leads to the need to express meanings which may stretch interlanguage. It may also require learners to negotiate meaning (Long 1989), an activity presumed to be particularly helpful in bringing about language change. Consequently, Pica *et al.* analyse tasks in terms of their potential to lead to comprehensible input, As a result, their categorization system differs from that of Candlin (1987) in being more directly accountable to the SLA research tradition of interaction studies (see Pica 1994 for a review).

The basic distinctions that they make are:

1 *Interactional activity*
– interactional relationship
– interactional requirements

2 *Communicative goal*
– goal orientation
– outcome option.

Under *interactional activity*, interactional relationship concerns the information which different participants hold. One participant may hold all the information required, all participants may hold all information, or different participants may hold different information, with joint information being necessary for task completion. Interactional requirements concern expectations about how learners will participate in the encounter, and covers the degree of certainty with which learners will request and/or supply the information required. Goal orientation, under *communicative goal*, clarifies the nature of the task involved, proposing that tasks will either be convergent (all participants have the same goals as regards outcome) or divergent (goals will be different). Outcome options relate to how many options there are in attempting to meet goals, contrasting one possible option, or more than one. In most cases, tasks are analysed in terms of whether desired interaction qualities are certain, probable, or expected. The operation of this system is illustrated in Table 5.2, where three familiar tasks are analysed according to the Pica *et al.* (1993) scheme.

	Jigsaw	Information gap	Discussion
Interactional activity			
– interactional relationship	two-way	one-way or two-way	two-way or one-way
– interactional requirement	required	required	not required
Communicative goal			
– goal orientation	convergent	convergent	divergent
– outcome options	one-only, i.e. agreement	one-only, i.e. agreement	arbitrary, but probably more than one

Table 5.2: An analysis of tasks using Pica et al.'s (1993) framework

Pica *et al.* (1993) use this framework to evaluate tasks for their potential to generate comprehension of input, feedback on production, and interlanguage modification, and make the following recommendations for more effective tasks:

1 Each interactant should hold a different portion of the information which must be exchanged or manipulated in order to reach the task outcome.
2 Interactants should be required to request and supply this information to each other.
3 Interactants should have the same or convergent goals.
4 Only one acceptable outcome should be possible from their attempts to meet this goal (ibid.: 17)

On this basis, the jigsaw and information-gap tasks would be judged preferable to the discussion, since they have the desired qualities of balance of information distributed amongst participants, and focus encounters to maximize the chances that meanings will be negotiated. Even so, as Pica *et al.* themselves acknowledge, 'few studies have actually linked negotiation features found during task interaction with the acquisition processes themselves' (Pica *et al.* 1993: 27). In addition, it can be doubted how pervasive the negotiation features are at the individual level. Foster (1998), for example, reports research which, at the group level, reproduces the sorts of results typical of the literature. However, when results were examined at the individual level, she was able to show that these results were accounted for by a small number of extremely negotiation-oriented individuals (resembling Allwright's (1988) Igor, who dominated a class from an early classroom research study). Most of the participants in the tasks did not negotiate meaning at all in Foster's study, suggesting that the general tendency to report group scores may not give a true impression of typicality. Unless the negotiation set in motion by the small number of individuals then generated interactions which were vicariously helpful to the silent majority, the value of such interaction activities for interlanguage modification and readiness for change is debatable. In any case, research reviewed later will extend the set of features which it is desirable to build into tasks. For the moment, the important issue is not to lose sight of the important 'theory to classification scheme to research' nature of the Pica *et al.* (1993) approach.

Duff

In a study that was influential to the Pica *et al.* categorization scheme, Duff (1986) examined the contrast between convergent and divergent tasks. An example of the former category is the desert island game (a choice of six items from larger groups of items that you would like to have if marooned on a desert island), with the latter exemplified by a discussion on 'the good or bad effects of television'. In the former case, an arbitrary but agreed solution has to be arrived at collectively, whereas in the latter case, a range of opinions is unavoidable and indeed acceptable. Duff reported no overall difference in the amount of language produced with each task type, but did point to significant interactional and discoursal differences. The convergent tasks produced many more and shorter turns, while the discussion generated fewer but longer and more complex turns. Duff predicted that there would be a difference between the tasks in relation to negotiation of meaning indices in favour of the convergent task, since this would produce a need for precision and understanding on the part of the participants. In the main, this prediction was not fulfilled.

Robinson and others

In addition to the 'negotiation of meaning' studies, a significant proportion of the task-based research on the selective effects of tasks has taken a processing perspective. Generally, research studies of this sort can be linked to the competing processing goals introduced in earlier chapters, particularly Chapters 3 and 4. Robinson (1996), for example, has researched issues of task type and task complexity. In an overview paper, Robinson, Ting, and Urwin (1996) propose that task difficulty is influenced by the dimensions of cognitive load, planning time, and prior information. Regarding the first of these dimensions, and drawing on the work of Givón (1985), they propose that harder tasks will be less fluent, but more complex *and* accurate. In one study, the hard task involved a 'there and then' narrative, while the easy task was 'here and now'. Robinson *et al.* (1996) reasoned that the lack of immediate visual support (a cartoon strip) in the 'there and then' condition would represent a greater processing burden for learners (and so produce lower fluency) but would push learners to pay more attention to speech and to be more ambitious, so using more complex language. In a second study, a route-giving exercise based on a map, where the contrast was between a simple task which had a pre-drawn route, and a difficult task, where the route had to be invented, essentially similar predictions were made. In the first study there were no differences between the conditions for fluency, or for complexity when indexed by a subordination measure. There was, though, greater lexical density (a proposed complexity measure) on the more difficult task, and there was also greater accuracy, as indexed by target language-like use of articles, in line with the original prediction. In the second study, the prediction for fluency was confirmed, but not that for the other two dependent variables of accuracy and complexity.

Ting (1996) investigated the effects of planning on spoken and written description tasks. The planned oral descriptions were longer than the unplanned, but, in the main, no more accurate. Hypotheses in favour of an effect for planning were not confirmed for the writing task. Finally, in a series of studies, Urwin (1996) investigated the effect of prior knowledge on performance on listening comprehension tasks. She found that tests of listening comprehension were in favour of the prior knowledge condition for true–false inference questions, but not for multiple-choice questions aimed at detail.

Brown

Brown (1991) proposes three different dimensions for the analysis of tasks: tight–loose, closed–open, and procedural–interpretative. A tight task is one which has a definite set of questions or sub-tasks 'from which the group participants do not have the opportunity to stray' (Brown 1991: 4). With the second contrast, if the 'answers' to a task are drawn from a limited set, the task is regarded as closed. Finally, procedural tasks are those which involve getting things done, making decisions about given input, and so on, without any need for interpretation In each case, the other pole of the dimension is the opposite of the characteristics given.

Brown used three tasks which incorporated variety in terms of these dimensions (though not systematically). The first two tasks involved responding to poetry, and although one of these tasks was categorized as tight and closed, the other was judged loose and open. The third task involved preparation for a teaching practice assignment. Brown measured task performance in terms of fluency (repetition, prompts, rephrasings), repairs (negotiation of meaning), instructional input (when one participant explains something to another or gives an example), and hypothesizing (when a participant, through the task, is drawn into making a hypothesis). Brown reports that there were no differences between the groups for fluency or repair, but that the use of instructional language and hypothesizing (taken here to represent a specific aspect of complexity) were significantly greater for the two interpretative tasks than for the procedural (where, in fact, these qualities were non-existent).

Foster and Skehan

In two studies (Foster and Skehan 1996, 1997), Foster and I also investigated task contrasts (compare the discussion of this research in Chapter 3 on the role of planning). In the first of our studies, we used three tasks. The first was a personal information exchange task in which subjects were required to tell their partner, in pair work, how to get to their home to turn off a gas oven that had been left on. In a narrative task pairs of students had to construct a story based on a series of pictures with common characters but no obvious storyline. Finally, students were required to participate in a choice/decision-making task. They were provided with several problems in which they had to take on the role of judge, and decide upon the appropriate punishment for each of a series of crimes. The three tasks essentially opposed familiar with unfamiliar propositions, and clear structure for the information required with progressively less predictable structure and interaction.

Performance on the tasks was measured (see discussion in Chapter 3) in terms of fluency, complexity, and error-free clauses. The results are presented in Table 5.3, which shows results for the three measures, each broken down by planning condition and task. In this table accuracy is measured by dividing the number of correct clauses by the total number of clauses for each subject, and so represents the proportion of accurate clauses (a maximum of 1.00). Complexity is measured by dividing the total number of clauses by the total number of c-units for each subject, and so reflects the number of clauses per c-unit. The minimum value obtainable is 1.00. Fluency is measured by the number of total seconds of silence per subject per five-minute task. Table 5.3 shows that the different tasks have often subtly different effects upon performance. The personal and decision tasks lead to significantly higher accuracy than the narrative ones, while the personal task leads to lower complexity than the other two tasks. The narrative and decision tasks generate least fluency, very significantly so compared with the personal task.

	Personal	Narration	Decision-making
Accuracy			
unplanned	.64	.61	.63
undetailed planning	.76	.66	.73
detailed planning	.69	.58	.71
Average for task	.70	.62	.69
Complexity			
Unplanned	1.11	1.22	1.23
Undetailed planning	1.16	1.42	1.35
Detailed planning	1.26	1.68	1.52
Average for task	1.18	1.43	1.37
Fluency			
unplanned	32	120	91
undetailed planning	20	29	26
detailed planning	15	14	30
Average for task	22	54	49

Table 5.3: Accuracy, complexity, and fluency for three tasks and three planning conditions (Foster and Skehan 1996: 312–15)

There is also an effect of the planning condition (discussed in Chapter 3): for complexity and fluency the relationship is monotonic—the greater the planning, the greater the complexity and fluency. With accuracy, however, the highest values are found with the undetailed planning condition, showing, as argued earlier, that there are trade-off effects here, revealed by the attention allocation decisions made in the different planning conditions. But most interestingly of all here, there is a very clear interaction for complexity and fluency between planning condition and task. Complexity and fluency increase relatively little for the personal task whereas with the more demanding decision task and especially the narrative task, the changes in performance are dramatic, with very marked improvement when planning time is used effectively. It would appear, in other words, that planning time can magnify effects associated with characteristics of tasks, especially those requiring more difficult material and operations. Task characteristics alone, that is, are not the only story.

A second study confirms and extends these results (see discussion in Chapter 3 and in Skehan and Foster 1997 for further details). This second study used the same contrast in task types (personal, narrative, decision), but with each type represented by a different task. The personal information exchange required subjects to describe to a partner what had most pleasantly or unpleasantly surprised them about life in Britain. The narrative was based on two cartoon strips by the French humorist, Sempé, and pairs of students took it in turns to describe the story represented by their strip. Although in each case the storyline was quite unambiguous, whether the ending was funny or sad was clearly a matter of individual opinion. For the decision-making task, subjects were given three letters to a magazine agony aunt describing various personal problems with boyfriends, ex-wives, children, and so on. Each pair had to agree on the best advice to give to the letter-writers. The results from this study which relate to processing were presented in Chapter 3. Essentially, they were that planning (operationalized only as undetailed planning versus. no planning) had similar effects as in the first study, while the use of a post-task condition provided limited evidence of a selective effect on accuracy.

More interesting for this discussion of tasks, though, is that the two studies taken together enable more broad-ranging comparisons of tasks to be made. The two studies reported on so far have in common three task types, the planning variable, and measures of accuracy, complexity, and fluency. Given that each task type is represented by two different tasks, it is possible to look for generalizations about tasks and task types across the studies. Brief descriptions of the tasks are given in Table 5.4

Task type	Foster and Skehan (1996)	Skehan and Foster (1997)
Personal	'Explain to your partner how to get to your house so that an oven which has been left on can be turned off' (oven task)	'Compare with one another the things that surprise you about British life, including positive and negative surprises (surprise task)
Narrative	'Make up a story from a semi-related series of pictures' (*NB same characters, but no obvious storyline*) (weave a story task)	'Tell a story from a Sempé cartoon', (*NB there was a clear story structure and amusing punchline*) (Sempé task)
Decision-making	'Agree with your partner on the appropriate sentence for each of five crimes (*all crimes contained extenuating circumstances*) (judge task)	'Agree the advice that should be given in several 'Agony Aunt' situations'(*NB situations did not lend themselves to one simple piece of advice*) (agony aunt task)

Table 5.4: Comparison of tasks used in Foster and Skehan (1996) and Skehan and Foster (1997)

The exponents of each task type were intended to be broadly similar. However, when we compare performance on the two sets of tasks, some clear differences emerge, as shown in Table 5.5. See Foster and Skehan (1996) for a fuller explanation of how the dependent measures were operationalized.

	Accuracy			Complexity			Fluency		
	Personal	Narrative	Decision	Personal	Narrative	Decision	Personal	Narrative	Decision
Foster and Skehan (1996)	.70	.64	.68	1.14	1.32	1.29	31.8	76.8	59.5
Skehan and Foster (1997)	.67	.62	.69	1.38	1.30	1.65	85.8	26.4	51.7

Table 5.5: Task effects on accuracy, fluency, and complexity: collated results from Foster and Skehan (1996) and Skehan and Foster (1997)

Regarding accuracy, there is some consistency. The narrative task is the least accurate in each case (in the low .60s), with the other two tasks generating higher, but generally similar proportions of error-free clauses (in the high .60s). There is less stability, though, for complexity. Although the narrative task produces a remarkably consistent score across the two studies, this is not at all true for the other two tasks, where the second study task in both cases, generates a much higher level of complexity. With the personal task it is possible that since the first study task consists of a string of instructions, themselves clearly structured because of the underlying actions, it predisposes the speaker to use simple language. The second study personal task, in contrast, requires retrieval of less structured information, and the possible need to elaborate and justify the claims which are made. The result is greater subordination. With the decision tasks, the first study requires a (relatively) simple outcome (Pica *et al.* 1993), in that a prison sentence has to be agreed on, and. the decision can be represented by one answer. In contrast, the decision task from the second study leads to more complex outcomes, in that no simple solutions to the agony aunt problems are possible. Consider, for example:

Dear Sue,
My wife and I separated two years ago. Our three-year-old son lives with his mother, who now has a new boyfriend. They live in a house with other people and I am sure that many of them use drugs. I am very worried about the effects on my son of living in a place like this. Worse, the new boyfriend tells everyone that my little boy is **his** son.
   I love my little boy and I am afraid my wife will stop me seeing him. I don't want this to happen, so I don't say anything. But I am worried about my son living in this situation. What should I do?

Here, any action which is proposed may lead to some desirable but also to other undesirable consequences. The result of dealing with this more complex, differentiated outcome is greater linguistic complexity.

The fluency results add yet another dimension. The decision tasks produce consistency but there is a striking reverse in results for the other two tasks. The oven task, and the Study 2 narrative of a Sempé cartoon, each a well-structured task in macro terms, generate much the most fluent performances of all. In contrast, the Study 1 narrative, weaving a story which links an unordered set of pictures, and the Study 2 personal task, explain what has surprised you about life in Britain, are much less fluent, presumably reflecting different sorts of cognitive problems in each case. In the former, it seems more connected with the attention-consuming difficulties of imposing order on material which is inherently lacking structure, while in the latter the problem seems to be associated with the burden of having to retrieve and then express a range of ideas.

Two intriguing inferences follow from this joint review of the two studies. First, the findings corroborate conclusions one can draw from the separate studies that trade-off effects are operating very strongly. To improve in one area often seems to be at the expense of improvement elsewhere. Selective rather than across-the-board improvement seems to be more realistic. (The nature of trade-off effects will be pursued in Chapter 7.) Second, there are encouraging signs that task characteristics predispose learners to channel their attention in predictable ways, such as clear task macrostructure towards accuracy, the need to impose order on ideas towards complexity, and so on. Obviously, these interpretations are post hoc and need to be validated through further research. But they are suggestive, and imply that, if such results can be replicated, tasks may be chosen and implemented *so that particular pedagogic outcomes are achieved*.

Research into participants in tasks

There have also been a small number of studies of participants within tasks. Somewhat surprisingly, the focus of such studies has not tended to be on variables such as personality or ethnic background, but rather on the capacity of the researchers to engineer more effective task completion. Yule *et al.* (1992) for example, reported a number of studies probing 'hearer' effects, the consequences for subsequent task performance of having been in a listener role in a similar task in the past. The hypothesis is that working through such a role will make a subsequent speaker more sensitive to a listener's requirements, causing adaptation of the message to occur. Yule *et al.* report results partly consistent with this prediction.

Similarly, Plough and Gass (1993) have examined the effects on task performance of participants' familiarity with one another. They used two tasks, a 'spot the difference' task and a 'who will survive' task, with two groups of subjects: an unfamiliar group, and a familiar group where partners carrying out the pair work had known one another for 4–7 months. Performance in the task was scored to focus on interactional features, with the general prediction being that familiar subjects would use more interactional language, where this was defined as overlaps, sentence completions, echoes, and negotiation of meaning indices. Apart from a task effect, with most interactional features occurring more often with the spot the difference task, the results were mixed. A number of the predictions, such as for overlaps, sentence completion, and echoes, did not come out as expected. However, the negotiation of meaning indices did, with the familiar pairs using significantly more such indices than the unfamiliar pairs. To that extent, it would seem that there is a greater naturalness of discourse with pairs who are more relaxed with one another, and less constrained by unnatural formality (to the extent this is possible within any experimental design!).

Task familiarity

Plough and Gass (1993) also researched the effects of task familiarity. In this case, the tasks were, once again, a spot the difference task, and also a discussion task taken from Rooks's (1981) *Non-Stop Discussion Workbook*. The familiar group were defined as students who had done comparable exercises twice in class shortly before the actual data collection, while the unfamiliar group had not been exposed to such tasks before. The familiar group were therefore potentially affected by the familiarity of what was expected of them, but also the potential staleness of doing something they might find unchallenging. The results obtained were mixed, displaying no clear patterns. There was a tendency for the pairs familiar with the task to use more confirmation checks and for the unfamiliar pairs to use more interruptions. Plough and Gass take this latter finding to indicate that the unfamiliar pairs were more deeply involved with the task they were doing, with the possibility that the familiar pairs might have been bored. They interpret greater sentence completion on the part of the pairs familiar with the task as indicating a greater enthusiasm to get the task over and done with!

A contrasting study of familiarity is reported by Bygate (1996a, b). In this study, subjects were required to redo a narrative task (retelling a Tom and Jerry cartoon) after three weeks. Bygate (1996b) reports no fatigue or boredom effects, even suggesting that subjects provided positive feedback on the opportunity to redo a challenging task. Through qualitative analysis of the data, Bygate was able to compare specific performances at the two data collection points. He was able to show that redoing a task is associated with a number of changes in the nature of performance, all of which add to the density of the ideas which are expressed. Three aspects are noteworthy, as indicated in Table 5.6. What comes across from these comparisons is that the retelling is associated with greater organization and purposefulness, and it is clear that language complexity and underlying propositions are in a more ambitious relationship to one another. In addition, Bygate (1996b) reports that the repeated performance of the task seemed to engage a more syntactic mode, with subjects showing a greater tendency to self-correct. In some ways, the finding is comparable to those obtained in the studies of planning, and may also reflect Givón's (1985) claim that linguistic and conceptual complexity are correlated in performance, a claim also argued by Robinson (1995a) for the second language context.

	Examples from time 1	**Examples from time 2**
Greater precision and lexical search	a little film about a cat and a mouse and there was a board and she gave her erm touch her with her feet	I saw a very nice cartoon about Tom and Jerry mouse run up to a cupboard and she kicked the cat
More, and more complex, subordination	and thinks Tom's tail is starting to eat and pretend that this tail is another lure for the fish	so that the fish again thinks there's something to eat for him and what Jerry does is to make a lure out of Tom's tail
More complex argument structure in the verb phrase	and of course the fish chases behind him and the cat was afraid that the plates are break damaged	but the fish chases Jerry through the water because he had fear that the dish will get break

Table 5.6: Density of ideas and task repetition (Bygate 1996b)

Task-based research: summary and overview

A great deal of task-oriented research has been described in this chapter—on task difficulty, selective task effects, discourse features, processing-based outcomes such as fluency, accuracy, and complexity, and participants in tasks—and so there is a need now to summarize this research and take stock. It is also important to incorporate some of the more programmatic claims made by researchers such as Pica *et al* (1993). Table 5.7 attempts to provide just such a summary. Brief accounts of results are given, as are references to the supporting studies, and the interpretation and significance of the findings.

First of all, the table shows that there has been quite a lot of activity focusing on the different sorts of information that is used in tasks. One could generalize and claim that, other things being equal, tasks are more effective if they contain information distributed amongst the different participants, so that interaction is more likely, and may become of better quality. The strong version of this viewpoint would argue for the importance of negotiation of meaning as a major factor in catalysing acquisitional processes, but the reservations about the connection between such a basis for designing interaction and the actual engagement of acquisitional processes on the part of most learners have already been made (Foster 1998; Van Lier and Matsuo 1994). One could also generalize and claim that if information is of the right quantity (so that it represents a reasonable challenge, and does not overload learners) and is of appropriate interest level (so that involvement is promoted, and the task can be said to resemble real life), more natural discourse is produced which may relate to underlying interlanguage systems in a more dependable way.

It is not so easy to generalize about type, organization, and familiarity of information since wider pedagogic goals are involved. More familiar information will certainly be easier (possibly as well as more interesting) and is certainly associated with greater fluency, but the difficulty is that a continual diet of such information is not likely to extend proficiency in the language so effectively. A pedagogic plan in this respect would presumably go from the easy to the difficult, by moving from familiar to unfamiliar information. Similarly, concrete information as the basis for tasks is likely to be easier, but ultimately restricting, so that pedagogic sequencing again comes into play. Finally, the organization of information has particularly interesting and varied effects. Structured information seems to lead to greater accuracy and fluency, particularly where planning time is available. Less structured information, and disorganized information, especially where these connect with transformation operations, produce greater complexity, again especially when linked to planning. This may well be consistent with Givón's (1985) claims about a correlation between conceptual and linguistic complexity.

The findings on operations carried out in tasks are similarly two-edged. Clearly, more complicated operations, with many elements or relationships, and of an unpredictable nature (interactions which can develop in unforeseen directions), are going to be more difficult. But there are two factors which argue for balance and care in how a range of operations are desirable within the context of task-based instruction. First, once again, there is the pedagogic argument advanced in the previous paragraph, that learners will need to be able to handle tasks other than simple ones, and the pedagogic sequence which is designed will need to take learners through similar tasks at different levels of complexity in terms of the operations they contain. But there is also the factor of intrinsic interest of tasks. Prabhu (1987), in judging that reasoning-gap tasks were most effective, seemed to be saying that the need to compute during the task was both motivating and engaging for acquisitional processes. Clearly this is an area where research on achieving balance is necessary. Retrieval seems associated with fluency, while transformation leads to more complex language.[1]

The evidence on the utility of different types of task goals is equally intriguing. As we have seen, Pica *et al.* (1993), following Duff (1986), consider that convergent tasks are preferable to divergent tasks, since they trigger more negotiation of meaning sequences. The reservations here have been covered

Feature	Description/Finding	Studies	Language learning focus/ Explanation
Task			
Information			
Distribution: symmetric/asymmetric	Symmetric tasks generate more interaction and negotiation of meaning.	Pica et al. (1993)	More need for negotiation of meaning may lead to greater interlanguage malleability and capacity for change.
Type: concrete/abstract immediate/remote	Concrete/immediate tasks are easier, but evidence supporting this proposition is mixed.	Brown et al. (1984); Foster and Skehan (1996); Skehan and Foster (1997); Robinson (1996)	Concrete tasks ease information-processing load, releasing attention for accuracy and fluency.
Organization	Structured tasks produce greater fluency (unplanned) and accuracy (planned).	Foster and Skehan (1996); Skehan and Foster (1997)	Structured tasks reduce need for complexity and provide clearer macrostructure. Accuracy and fluency then benefit from more attention available.
Familiarity	Familiar information is associated with greater accuracy and fluency, but this is a tendency only, and is mediated by other factors.	Foster and Skehan (1996); Skehan and Foster (1997)	Familiar tasks ease information-processing load, thus releasing attention for accuracy and fluency.
Operations retrieval/transformation	Transformation leads to greater complexity of language, with lower frequency and accuracy.	Prabhu (1987); Foster and Skehan (1996); Skehan and Foster (1997)	Tasks involving transformation of material require attention and push learners to more complex language. Pressure for change is more likely, but at the expense of some control. Tasks requiring retrieval of organized information allow easy access to ideas, and reduce information load. Accuracy and fluency benefit from this.
few/many	More elements produce greater complexity.	Brown et al. (1984)	Numerous elements in tasks push learners to complex language use as they try to relate these different

Goals

arrange/decide vs. interpret	Interpretative tasks generate more complexity.	Brown (1991)	Such tasks lead towards hypothesizing and instructional language, which underlies the complexity.
open/closed vs. tight/loose	No effects found.	Brown (1991)	
focused/differentiated	Differentiated goals can lead to greater language complexity.	Foster and Skehan (1996); Skehan and Foster (1997)	Achieving task goals which have alternative viewpoints produces a greater need for justification and precision.
convergent/divergent	Agreed-outcome tasks favour short turns and less complex language; tasks allowing disagreement lead to longer turns and more complex and varied language.	Duff (1986); Pica et al. (1993)	Divergent tasks lead to elaboration and justification of positions generating more complex language. Convergent tasks require many 'local' agreements on specific issues, thus producing shorter turns.

Participants

relationship to one another	Familiarity might lead to more natural, interactive discourse.	Plough and Gass (1993)	The ease of interaction resulting from personal familiarity may cause the learners to be more willing to negotiate for meaning.
experience of different roles	Different roles explored.	Yule et al. (1992)	Experience of the hearer's role leads to greater sensitivity to appropriate discourse and alternative viewpoints.

Task familiarity

simple task, early repetition	More accessible, perhaps boring.	Candlin (1987); Plough and Gass (1993)	Repeated tasks cause learners to disengage attention and commitment.
more complex task, delayed repetition	Allows engagement of more organized, denser language and more syntactic mode.	Bygate (1996a,b)	Information-processing load is reduced. In addition, since the cognitive organization of the task is already available, the task provides scope for more ambitious language and greater precision.

Table 5.7: Summary of task-based learning research claims

ad nauseam, and will not be repeated. They do however connect with the need to establish a wider model of communicative competence against which to judge different tasks. The issue is that different goals may be appropriate for different aspects of competence. The convergent tasks, for example, produce more but shorter turns, with language which is necessarily more complex. This may, indeed, be fine some of the time, but there must also be opportunities to produce more complex discourse, involving longer turns (Brown and Yule 1983), so that learners have the opportunity to develop a more rounded set of communicational capacities. There is also the point that it seems difficult to separate a discussion of goals from a discussion of the interest that different goals have for different learners (Willis and Willis 1988). Divergent tasks of the sort described by Duff (1986), for example, with discussions on 'television' or 'age and wisdom' may be staples to lead learners to display some connected language, but there is no guarantee that the views that they have expressed are other than completely arbitrary to them. Santos Tambos (1992) proposes that the nature of the discourse produced by participants achieving goals where the meanings expressed are important to them (and the counter-arguments also important to disagree with) might produce a quite different sort of language. We have also seen that a transactional/interpretative distinction can be associated with similarities (repairs, interaction indices) and differences, with interpretative goals leading to conceptually-stretching language (Tizard and Hughes 1984).

Finally, the distinction between focused and differentiated outcomes offers promise, in that subtler, more differentiated outcomes appear to generate more complex language, especially when planned. In some ways, the three distinctions that have now been covered all capture a related contrast: between circumscribed tasks, on the one hand, (convergent, transactional, focused) and extendible tasks (divergent, interpretative, differentiated). The current generalization here seems to be that it is extendable tasks which generate complex, cutting-edge language in a more dependable way.

As was mentioned earlier, there is considerable scope for future research to find out more about the effects of such participant factors as age, gender, ethnic background, personality, and so on, on the nature of interaction in task and group work. Plough and Gass (1993) looked at participants' familiarity with one another, expecting to find more natural discourse in such circumstances. This prediction was only partially borne out. Possible different ways of assessing familiarity are warranted, as might be a different view of what dependent variables are likely to be most revealing. Van Lier and Matsuo (1994) suggest that indices which reflect asymmetry in discourse might be more promising. Regarding familiarity of task (an issue originally raised by Candlin 1987), two lines of research have shown promise. First, task familiarity has potential. Although Plough and Gass (1993) suggest that when boredom and repetitiveness are perceived, over-familiarity can be damaging, Bygate (1996a, b) has shown how such an outcome is avoidable. If fresh and additional challenges are seen, participants may exploit the greater task familiarity to produce more complex language. In such cases, task familiarity clearly resembles manipulation of planning time, since the earlier task completion could be viewed as a particularly effective way of structuring planning. Certainly the consequences for the language which emerges are similar. Second, there is promise in exploring the task participants' sensitivity to one another, and to the sort of interaction that would be most effective with one's partner. Yule *et al.*'s (1992) study of learners exchanging speaker and listener roles is a case in point, and, like Prabhu (1987) and Bygate (1996a, b), demonstrates the value of rehearsal, provided that the rehearsal introduces elements which are relevant but not repetitive. Second language learners, who may be operating at the limits of their competence, may have difficulty in co-constructing discourse: exchanging roles in the way Yule *et al.* have proposed may be an effective means of scaffolding such co-construction.

Conclusions

In Chapters 3 and 4 models of second language learning and performance were discussed which proposed that:

- because of limited attentional capacities, the construct of noticing has considerable importance, for it is central to the way a focus on form can be engineered;
- language use depends upon the coexistence of analysed and accessible systems, and performance is based on rule-based and lexically-based systems.

These proposals imply that second language development and second language use may enter into some degree of mutual tension since the priorities of real-time language use may siphon away attention from noticing and interlanguage change.

What this chapter has shown is that careful research studies can reveal generalizations about aspects of language use (fluency, accuracy, complexity) which enable both performance and development to be conceptualized within the framework of task-based instruction, and that attention can be channelled towards meaning or towards form. In this way, instructional decisions can be made more effectively both in immediate communicative teaching situations and in the longer term. The next stage is to relate these discussions of processing to actual pedagogic decisions. That will be the concern of the next chapter.

Note

1   There are frequently trade-off effects, for example complexity seems to be achieved at the expense of fluency and accuracy. These trade-off effects will be explored more fully in Chapter 7, where performance issues will be discussed in the context of testing.

6 Implementing task-based instruction

Most proposals to guide the nature of pedagogic intervention are judged more by their workability and pragmatic utility than by their connection with current acquisitional theory or research. This chapter takes a contrasting approach—it tries to clarify how the research findings reviewed in previous chapters can be related to instruction. The findings are incomplete, maybe partial, and may need to be supplemented part of the time by decisions which are not research-based. But at least they are a basis for action. This does not mean that research-based proposals should be adhered to slavishly, or that they provide a comprehensive basis for pedagogy. But to proceed only by imagination and seductive persuasion is to be prey to little but fashion and a blind commitment to change.

The chapter is organized into five main parts. At the outset, two contrasting approaches to using tasks are described. The two approaches, structure-oriented tasks and a very communicatively-oriented version of task-based instruction, have been chosen because they represent extreme positions and because they share the quality that they concentrate on one aspect of language performance at the expense of others. The structure-oriented approach emphasizes form to the detriment of meaning, while an extreme task-based approach focuses very much on meaning and not on form. In the second section of the chapter it is argued that an intermediate approach is necessary in which the central feature is a balance between form and meaning, and an alternation of attention between them. A set of principles is proposed which is meant to achieve just such a balance and alternation.

The main part of the chapter is concerned with two areas which are crucial to achieving such a balanced approach. The research discussed in Chapter 5 is drawn on extensively in the section on pedagogic approaches to task analysis and choice, while the rationale for processing and the associated research, covered in Chapters 3 and 4, is fundamental for the long section on task implementation which follows. The last section of the chapter is concerned with pedagogy beyond the level of the individual task, and considers how the achievement of balanced interlanguage development can be achieved by more careful task-sequencing decisions.

The pedagogy of tasks: current proposals

Two opposing methods of implementing tasks have been proposed, which differ in the way they relate tasks to specific language structures. The first 'traps' structures through task design, while the second advocates the use of communicative tasks on the assumption that transacting the tasks will drive forward acquisition. The first approach enables planning and systematic treatment of language, while the second maximizes the communicative attractiveness of tasks. We will examine two versions of each of these approaches before exploring a compromise proposal which draws on both of them.

Structure-oriented tasks

Some investigators have proposed that teaching activities can be designed which constrain language use in such a way that specific structures will be used. A programmatic version of this 'Machiavellian' approach has been proposed by Loschky and Bley-Vroman (1993). They distinguish between three structure-to-task relationships:

1 *Naturalness*: where the use of a structure during a task would be unforced, i.e. would not stand out, but where alternative structures would do equally well.
2 *Utility*: where the use of a particular structure would help the efficiency of the completion of the task, but could be avoided through the use of alternative structures or perhaps through the use of communication strategies.
3 *Essentialness*: where, in order to complete a task, a particular structure has to be used. Loschky and Bley-Vroman (ibid.) advocate this as the most difficult, but most desirable criterion to attain.

Tasks which satisfy the most stringent of these criteria hold out the prospect, according to Loschky and Bley-Vroman (ibid.) that they may trigger hypothesis-formation processes more effectively, and prepare learners to benefit from the feedback that is also more likely to occur. So what they advocate pedagogically is that tasks should be designed to meet this third, most demanding, criterion. Indeed, they argue against tasks unless there is a clear connection of this sort, a requirement which would seem to imply no central focus on meaning. The actual tasks which Loschky and Bley-Vroman discuss, for example an information-gap description task, and a 'Lego' arrangement task (ibid.: 164–7), do meet the criteria for task qualification outlined in Chapter 5. Clearly, they are optimistic that a range of structures can be reliably trapped inside a range of tasks without compromising primacy of meaning.

A similar approach has been taken by Fotos and Ellis (1991), who also advocate structure-oriented task-based instruction. They report on a study in which specific structures (dative alternation, adverb placement) were 'forced' by particular tasks, that is, there was no alternative but to use such structures as a result of task design. They compared this task-based approach with a more conventional explicit presentation (compare the discussion of a 3Ps approach in Chapter 5). Like Loschky and Bley-Vroman, Fotos and Ellis were exploring the possibility that learners who formulate their own hypotheses from structured materials are able to achieve the same generalizations, as efficiently as students receiving explicit presentation of language. In the main, the researchers' expectations were fulfilled, and they and Fotos (1993) conclude that such a version of task-based instruction is both effective and practical; it produces results and lends itself to adaptation to whatever structures it wants to focus on.

The proposals made by Loschky and Bley-Vroman (1993) and Ellis and Fotos (1991) can be related to the criteria for tasks outlined in Chapter 5. In both cases, but particularly with that of Fotos and Ellis, implicit learning materials are used with some emphasis on the artificial transformation of material so that particular structures become salient, that is, the tasks do not make meaning primary or have much of a real-world relationship. They also require regurgitation of pre-arranged meanings and are oriented towards display, conformity, and practice (Willis 1993; see discussion in Chapter 5). In addition, one might wonder at the feasibility of the approach for a wide range of structures, beyond those for which inventive materials have been developed. Willis (1993), for example, doubts that one can rely on the use of any particular structure when communication is in any sense natural. He gives the example, from pilot studies conducted with native speakers for the COBUILD course (Willis and Willis 1988), of tasks designed to elicit the second conditional, 'If I were you, I would …' naturally. A task attempting to achieve this goal was for the speaker to give advice to someone visiting a foreign country with which the speaker was familiar, so as to induce language such as 'If I were you, I'd visit …'. In fact, only a small number of conditionals were used and most 'advisers' used the simple present tense, saying things like 'When I'm in X, I like to visit the Y.' What seemed to be happening was that the simple present conveyed non-presumptuous advice, leaving the listener to make up his or her own mind as to whether this was a suggestion worth acting upon. The conditional form itself was presumably identified with too great a strength of suggestion, and so was avoided. Willis's point is that tasks cannot be contrived to trap structures without becoming unnatural. So, interesting as the proposals made by Fotos and Ellis (1991) and Loschky and Bley-Vroman (1993) are, by their very nature they fall outside the view of tasks presented here, and will not be pursued directly.

Communication-driven tasks

The contrasting position within a task-based pedagogy is to argue that giving learners tasks to transact will drive forward language development. The tasks themselves, it is argued, will create a need for language change and a means of fulfilling that need. This was the argument developed in Chapter 5 when a rationale for task-based instruction was developed. In practice, two versions of this position exist.

Willis (1993) is a strong advocate of a task-driven approach to instruction. He proposes that tasks which meet what might be termed a 'naturalness' condition, which are not conformity-based or display-oriented for any particular structure, will lead learners to develop language effectively. He does not argue directly for an acquisition-based approach to interlanguage development. Rather, in the context of a lexical approach to syllabus design, he suggests that transacting tasks will, in an unforced way, generate the most significant lexis of a language, and that learners will become able to use such lexis in syntactic patterns. He makes the point that the idiosyncrasies of lexis are being increasingly recognized, and so if learning involves a greater command of lexical constraints, rule-based formulations will be misleading or even non-existent for important aspects of language (compare Chapter 2). Basically, therefore, he proposes that approaches to instruction which are based on rules, explicitly or implicitly, are bound to be misguided. For him, in other words, tasks create the space for lexically-driven development to occur, and he is confident that natural tasks will enable important (and frequent) lexis to be used and learned.

A similar conclusion is reached, through a different route, by Long (1988), when he argues for a focus on *form*, as opposed to a focus on *forms*. Long argues that assessments of the effects of instruction, although positive, tend to be general and long-term rather than specific and short-term. He suggests that form needs to be important in the instructional materials, and in the learner's mind, and that without these conditions, fossilization and slower progress tend to be found. The evidence he reviews does not support the generalization that a concern for specific forms, whether these are traditionally covered or task-based, leads to their incorporation in the learner's interlanguage. Instead, he proposes that a task-based approach, in which real-world needs become the motivating force for task design, will generate interactions which engage acquisitional processes and lead to interlanguage development (Long and Robinson, forthcoming). The tasks will catalyse meaningful language use since opportunities to negotiate meaning and recast productions in a supportive environment can assist structural development in the target language.

The central difficulties with the position advocated by Willis and Long are that:

– it cannot deal with the problems addressed in Chapter 1—that over-emphasizing communication increases the risk of a greater reliance on communication strategies and lexically-based language
– there is no easy means of assuring systematic language development.

We saw, in terms of the first difficulty, that strategic behaviour and elliptical language are natural outcomes when communication is primary, and that reliance on such devices may move language structure out of focus, i.e. attention is directed to the communication itself. Further, Willis's proposal that tasks provide the arena for lexical development has to be set against the consequences of a dual-mode system of operation in which lexicalized items may be acquired directly and then become resistant to change and analysis—the sort of 'provoked' fossilization discussed in Chapter 4.

The problem of systematicity in language development is also important. A view that tasks will enable naturalistic processes to operate provides little scope for choosing tasks to push forward development syntactically and for effective monitoring of progress. Teachers and syllabus designers accordingly have an unsatisfactory passive role, not adequately supported at this time by knowledge of universal sequences in development. Further, a reliance on negotiation of meaning and recasting of output does not address this problem effectively either. Apart from the criticisms of how satisfactory and prevalent such negotiation is (Aston 1986; Foster 1998), there is the difficulty that such conversational behaviour is essentially local in character—an immediately relevant area of language receives beneficial attention, but it is not clear how this specific focus will leave a trace that relates to longer-term language development.

Exploring the middle ground: maximizing probabilities

As a result of such problems with the two contrasting approaches to task-based instruction—artificiality on the one hand, and lack of clear structure and control on the other—an intermediate position is argued here, in which naturalness of tasks still has importance, but attempts are made, through task choice and methodology, to focus attention on form, as advocated by Long (1988), to increase the chances of interlanguage development. Such an approach proposes that:

– engaging in worthwhile, meaningful communication may emphasize fluency at the expense of the focus on form that accuracy and complexity would require (see Chapter 2);

– attentional limitations constrain the capacity of the language learner to focus on a number of different areas simultaneously (see Chapter 3);
– different aspects of language performance, particularly accuracy, fluency, and complexity, enter into competition with one another (see Chapters 3 and 4);
– using (properly defined) tasks to generate communication means that the use of particular structures can be at best probabilistic, and is certainly not guaranteed (see the discussion in Chapter 5 and earlier in this chapter).

To be consistent with these proposals the challenge is to channel attentional resources so that there is balanced concern for communication on the one hand, and form at a general level on the other hand, so that neither dominates at the expense of the other. Two models for achieving such a balance are presented in this chapter. The first, from Willis (1996), emphasizes a methodology for using tasks to combine naturalness of communication with opportunities to focus on form. The second, my own, makes a similar attempt to show how balance between form and meaning can be achieved. In addition, it tries to link the methodology more explicitly to the information-processing framework which underlies this book, as well as the specific discussion of tasks presented in Chapter 5.

Willis and task-based instruction

Willis (1996) offers five principles for the implementation of a task-based approach. In general terms the principles provide input, use, and reflection on the input and use. They are:

1 There should be exposure to worthwhile and authentic language.
2 There should be use of language.
3 Tasks should motivate learners to engage in language use.
4 There should be a focus on language at some points in a task cycle.
5 The focus on language should be more and less prominent at different times.

In effect, the first of these points is proposing that input should be provided as an initiating force for language change. This, in turn, should be the basis for noticing (Schmidt 1990) and effective processing, which takes the input and directs attention to form. Clearly, the next two principles concern the ways in which language is actually used, with the motivation principle suggesting that tasks need to meet some criterion of engagement to be considered worthwhile. The remaining two principles are concerned with the ways in which form is brought into focus. Given that clear criteria argue for the naturalness of tasks, the requirements that a concern for form should be present and that the degree of prominence of a focus on form should vary at different stages and have cyclical qualities, suggests that pedagogic intervention needs to be artfully designed.

Willis's model for task-based instruction

Willis (1996) presents a model which is designed to meet these various needs (see Table 6.1).

Pre-task
Introduction to topic and task
Task cycle
Task
Planning
Report
Language focus
Analysis
Practice

Table 6.1:   Willis' model for task-based instruction (Willis 1996: 52)

The first stage is concerned with pre-task activities, and these are of three sorts. First, we have activation of whatever schematic knowledge is likely to make the task more interesting and more authentic (compare the motivation principle, on p.126). This reflects the way in which tasks have to be about something, to provide a reason for real communication. Second, there needs to be exposure to actual language samples, so as to provide opportunities for a focus on form to be set in motion, and for noticing to occur. This stage may involve the use of texts, or it may give learners opportunities to see/hear native speakers do parallel forms of the task to come. Third, there is the need to focus attention, by using activities which operate upon the texts and data, and which lead learners to direct attention to the form of what is said, and to maximize the chances that attention is focused in useful ways.

The second stage that is proposed consists of the task cycle itself. Within this stage there are the three sub-stages of (1) doing the task, (2) engaging in planning *post*-task, and (3) reporting. The task itself provides opportunity for language use (and the development of fluency, accuracy, and complexity), so holding out the prospect of interlanguage development, hypothesis testing, and the routinization of language. But it is also meant to sensitize the learner to the language which needs to be used. In this respect, it has an alerting function which is close to Swain's (1995) 'notice the gap' principle. But in the Willis approach the task itself is more prospective, in that it links with subsequent pedagogic activities which are intended to build upon the language task completion has sensitized the learner to (and the learner is aware of this). It also organizes the ways in which learners can plan a subsequent reporting phase by incorporating language whose relevance they have (it is hoped) established for themselves during the task. Hence, in this planning stage the learners can draft and rehearse their public performance, thus learning from one another (see Swain 1995 also on collaborative learning), while the teacher is at this stage in the permissible role of helper with the language, since the language which can then be supplied will be in response to perceived student need. In this role the teacher can help to ensure that there is a focus on form, and that learners' attention can be drawn to form–meaning relationships. At the end of the second general stage there is the reporting phase. This is the public performance which itself heightens attention to form and accuracy, and which also constitutes the validating activity for the previous planning. Interestingly, therefore, the role of planning is post-task, but pre-reporting, in contrast to the proposals made below.

Finally, Willis (1996) suggests that after the two preceding phases of pre-task activity and the task cycle, there should be some degree of language focus where a variety of activities can be engaged in. These may be of a consciousness-raising nature, where further input is provided and learners are required to process this input in a way which makes pattern regularities or features more salient. Alternatively, there may be some degree of explicit focus on a particular aspect of the language system. There may even, at this stage, be some degree of practice-oriented work. But, importantly, the focus on language comes after a task has been done (and even after the reporting has been done), with the intention that any language which is focused upon is relevant to learners and required for a communicative purpose, rather than introduced because a syllabus dictates that it should be covered at a particular point. In some ways, therefore, there are shared qualities here with a counselling–learning approach, in that support is provided to learners who want to express particular meanings. The approach that Willis suggests, however, is much more systematic and consistent with contemporary views on acquisitional processes.

Drawbacks to Willis's approach

The approach proposed by Willis (1996) provides useful guidance for the implementation of a task-based approach. It does, though, have some drawbacks. First, although it consists of a wide range of activities and guidance as to how instruction can proceed in such a way as to bring form into focus while natural communicative activities predominate, it does not link effectively with wider-ranging theory. Apart from accepting that there has to be a constant interplay between form and meaning (a considerable advance in itself from form-dominated or communication-dominated approaches), there is little clear connection with broader theorizing about second language acquisition, and the role of noticing, acquisitional sequences, information processing, and so on. Second, there is no explicit connection with research. There are loose connections with lexical syllabuses, but no clear way in which the pedagogic decisions which are made are an outgrowth of research findings, or, indeed, have been susceptible to empirical investigation. The suggestions are about pedagogic activities, based on experience, but not subjected to test, or grounded in other research. Although many of the claims which are made can be related to such research without much difficulty, such as the use of planning, or the principles which might underlie task selection, a research perspective has not been central to the development of the ideas expressed.

Related to this is a third problem. The approach does not clarify how specific aspects of performance can be focused on. That there is little detail regarding the nature of second language performance and the ways in which different pedagogic goals (fluency, accuracy, and complexity, once again) can be achieved. As a result, while there is guidance as to worthwhile activities the teacher might choose and implement, there is insufficient connection with the nature of interlanguage development. This brings us to a final criticism that there is insufficient detail as to how plans can be made and systematic teaching arranged. In other words, there is little guidance regarding task difficulty analysis, on the one hand, or syllabus specification, on the other. Once again, individual activities may be defensible; how they build into a more coherent framework is not.

An information-processing approach to tasks

To try to address these difficulties, I propose a set of five principles for task-based instruction. These principles are then followed by a model for the implementation of task-based approaches. The principles and the model are grounded in theory and research, and offer some prospects for the systematic development of underlying interlanguage and effective communicative performance. In this section the five principles are described, and in the next section key principles are related to pedagogic decision making. The five principles are:

1 Choose a range of target structures.
2 Choose tasks which meet the utility criterion.
3 Select and sequence tasks to achieve balanced goal development.
4 Maximize the chances of focus on form through attentional manipulation.
5 Use cycles of accountability.

Choose a range of target structures

It seems clear from acquisitional research that 'ordaining' a sequence of structures will not be effective, since the power of internal processing factors is simply too strong, so that learners do not simply learn what teachers teach. The result is that it is futile to fix on a particular structure and expect it to be learned. On the other hand, there is a need for systematicity in language development, and the only way to resolve this conundrum satisfactorily is to have some method of keeping track of interlanguage development, but not in narrow specific terms. Identifying a range of target structures therefore combines realism with the need to be organized. It also links with principles 2 and 5, as we will see.

Choose tasks which meet the utility criterion

Although Ellis (1994) and Loschky and Bley-Vroman (1993) advocate the more demanding criterion of tasks which meet the 'necessary' criterion, it is assumed here, following Willis (1991), that learners (and native speakers) are adept at evading the use of any particular structure, and to force them to conform is to render a task so unnatural as to make it of dubious value for acquisition. Consequently the teacher can only create appropriate conditions and hope that learners will avail themselves of the possibilities which operate. In this way, too, systematicity is being fostered, even though no guarantees exist as to which structures will actually be used in the ongoing nature of performance. Combined with principle 1, the intention is that tasks can be designed and relevant support activities can be chosen to make the use of structures easier without their being compulsory. The viability of principles 1 and 2 rests on the use of principle 5.

Sequence tasks to achieve balanced goal development

Giving learners tasks to do, even when these tasks are motivating and engage natural communicational abilities, is not enough: they also have to form part of a larger pedagogic plan. A milder form of this danger is that tasks may be used which are unfocused as far as long-term development is concerned. A more significant danger is that tasks may be chosen which, because of the communicational demands, their level of difficulty, or manner of implementation, may lead learners to deploy communication strategies, rely on lexicalized communication, or generally forget about any focus on form. The result will be that the focus on meaning will make it less likely that continuing interlanguage growth will occur.

To counter this, it is important that tasks are chosen which:

- are of the appropriate level of difficulty;
- are focused in their aims between fluency, accuracy, and complexity;
- have some basis in task-based research.

Principle 3, in other words, requires that proposals for task choice are accountable to research such as that described in Chapter 5, since such research should inform the nature of the pedagogic decisions which are made. A major portion of this chapter will expand on how such research connections can be made to support effective task sequencing.

Maximize the chances of a focus on form through attentional manipulation

All the approaches advocated here suggest that compelling the use of specific structures is not effective: what is needed is the provision of the most effective opportunity available for a focus on form in the context of meaningful language use. Specifically:

- at initial stages of task use, conditions need to be established to maximize the chances of noticing;
- in the task completion phase effective attentional conditions need to be engineered so that form is on focus. Specifically, this means that attentional demands which arise out of a task need to be of appropriate demand and level so as to ensure that simply transacting tasks does not consume all attentional resources;
- there must be opportunity for reflection and awareness so that whatever is accomplished during a task is not simply ephemeral, but can be processed more deeply and consolidated.

Principle 4 is the central principle in this information-processing approach, with all the other principles, in effect, dependent upon it. Later in this chapter, drawing on research discussions form earlier in the book, techniques will be covered which make possible the sort of attentional manipulation principle 4 requires.

Use cycles of accountability

Given the non-deterministic approach to how structure will be handled, a major problem remains as to how to make systematic progress in interlanguage development. We have seen that the use of specific structures cannot be guaranteed, and that what can be hoped for is a generalized focus on form in the context that a range of structures will have been targeted, and that the use of these structures will have been supported through task choice and task implementation conditions. The key to making progress here would seem to be to draw learners into consciously engaging in cycles of evaluation. In other words the goal of instruction at any one time would not be to require the internalization of a particular structure. However, periodically, what has been learned can be reflected upon and a stock-taking can be attempted by the individual learner.

The purpose of the stock-taking would be to chart what has been learned simply so that future plans can be made. It would also introduce an opportunity for systematization in the way progress is monitored, both by the teacher and the learner. This implies that a priority in task-based approaches to instruction is to mobilize the learner's own metacognitive resources to keep track of what is being learned, and what remains to be learned. In some ways this proposal connects with Breen and Candlin's (1980) arguments for retrospective syllabuses, except that a degree of planning and evaluation of progress in relation to aims brings a degree of structure to what otherwise might indeed be an 'aimless journey' (White 1988).

We can now restate the five principles:

1 Choose a range of target structures.
2 Choose tasks which meet the utility condition.
3 Select and sequence tasks to achieve balanced goal development.
4 Maximize the chances of a focus on form through attentional manipulation.
5 Use cycles of accountability.

The first, second, and fifth of these principles will not be developed further in this chapter. They constitute a fairly general framework. Choosing a range of target structures is something which should be informed by knowledge of second language acquisition research and syllabus design, but these knowledge sources cannot be deterministic: what is needed is some reasonable basis for being systematic, rather than a blueprint which has to be followed. Similarly, choosing tasks to meet the utility condition implies a role for the syllabus designer or teacher, but one whose function is again intended to create favourable conditions, rather than assure the acquisition of any particular item of language. In a sense, each of these principles can only function in a fairly loose way, and the fifth principle, the use of regular stock-taking to see what has been learned and what remains to be learned, is intended to cope with the lack of precision unavoidable in the first two principles. It enables a balance to be struck between the inevitable freedom that is necessary for acquisition arising out of communication, and the need to be able to track progress and develop plans for the future which are more precise than believing that any structure may emerge simply through interaction.

The principles which require elaboration are the third and fourth, selecting and using tasks. The discussion in Chapters 3, 4, and 5 now enables us to make research-grounded proposals on task selection and use. The final two sections of the chapter accordingly address each of these two principles, making links with the earlier coverage of research findings to justify the proposals which are made.

Principle 3: select and sequence tasks to achieve balanced goal development

Although research on the effects of task characteristics is far from complete (so that pedagogic decisions have to be judgements based on the integration of experience with research findings), there are areas where progress has been made. In particular, research into the negotiation of meaning, task difficulty, and selective influences of tasks can have an impact on instructional decisions. We will review each of these areas, providing a summarizing table of relevant results for each.

Research into the negotiation of meaning

The basic approach here is to propose that where tasks generate greater negotiation of meaning, conditions are more appropriate for interlanguage development to occur. Engaging in such negotiation is meant to produce better quality and more finely tuned input for language development (Long 1988). It is also meant to promote greater malleability in the interlanguage system and a greater willingness to explore language and try out hypotheses (Pica 1994). But we have also seen that the theoretical justifications for such research are rather weak, and have been challenged (Aston 1986; Foster 1998). None the less, findings in this area are extensive, and are relevant to decisions on task-based instruction. They are presented in Table 6.2. It should be noted that the first condition mentioned (in italics) produces a greater effect upon the negotiation of meaning.

Contrast	Source
Two-way tasks vs. one-way task	Long (1989)
Symmetric vs. asymmetric tasks	Van Lier (1996)
Convergent vs. divergent	Duff (1986)
Familiar participants vs. unfamiliar participants	Plough and Gass (1993)
Performance after taking hearer's role vs. direct performance	Yule *et al.* (1992)

Table 6.2: Influences upon negotiation-of-meaning indices

These findings suggest that it is possible to produce greater negotiation of meaning, so that, assuming this to be a desirable quality in task-based interaction, one can engineer a greater degree of active involvement, in order that clarification requests, confirmation checks, and so on are used more, with the possibility that they lead to better quality input and more malleable interlanguage systems.

Research into task difficulty

Knowledge of task difficulty provides the teacher or syllabus designer with information about the level of challenge that a task is likely to contain, a level which the teacher will then have to match with his or her knowledge of the students who will do the task. The rationale for needing and using such information is essentially twofold. First, tasks of appropriate difficulty are likely to be more motivating for learners as they feel that they are being required to respond to reasonable challenges (Willis 1996; Williams and Burden 1997) which are achievable if there is effort on their part. Second, given that attentional capacities are limited, tasks of appropriate difficulty imply that learners will be able to cope with the demands upon their attentional resources. This in turn leads to the most important consequence of all: if the appropriate level of task difficulty is chosen, there is much greater likelihood that noticing will occur, that balanced language performance will result, and that spare attentional capacity can be channelled effectively. In other words, learners will not be so likely to depend upon lexicalized language, communication strategies, and elliptical communication, since they will be able to cope with the informational demands placed upon them, and devote some attentional capacities to form, whether this is accuracy or complexity.

Task-based approaches, therefore, need to focus on task difficulty as a precondition for any task work. Table 6.3 summarizes the findings in this area. It should be noted that the second condition mentioned (in italics) produces greater task difficulty. Obviously, these contrasts do not represent all the different influences on task difficulty, but they are each supported by research findings. As will be discussed in more detail below, this information needs to be supplemented by teacher experience, since it will be used as part of a more complex picture to make pedagogic decisions.

Contrast	Source
Small number of participants/elements vs. *large number*	Brown et al. (1984)
Concrete information and task vs. *abstract*	Brown et al. (1984) Skehan and Foster (1997)
Immediate, here-and-now information vs. *remote, there-and-then information*	Robinson (1995a) Foster and Skehan (1996)
Information requiring retrieval vs. *information requiring transformation*	Skehan and Foster (1997)
Familiar information vs. *unfamiliar information*	Foster and Skehan (1996)

Table 6.3: Factors influencing task difficulty

Selective, goal-oriented influences upon task performance

The tensions between the performance goals of fluency, accuracy, and complexity have been discussed in earlier chapters. In Chapter 5 we saw that a number of selective influences on these goals have now been identified. The major factor, of course, is that all three goals—fluency, accuracy, and complexity—have to be achieved. The problem is that given limitations in attentional resources this is not feasible in any simple way, with the result that it is preferable:

- to have tasks which focus on particular goals;
- to implement sequences of tasks so that balanced development occurs as tasks which concentrate on different objectives follow one another in a planned manner.

In this way, ordered progress can be made, and the chances of unbalanced development, such as excessive fluency, which is difficult to convert into accuracy and complexity, can be minimized. Development in one area can be consolidated and integrated with other goals to ensure that solid foundations are constantly being built for the next stage of development.

As a pre-condition for such an approach to task selection it is vital to have a range of findings on which pedagogic decisions can be based. With the same caveat as in the last section, that current findings are not comprehensive or systematic, but that they are better than nothing, the following summary, drawing on Chapter 5, is possible, as shown in Table 6.4. The claims embodied in this table will be qualified in the next section when the effects of processing conditions will be discussed, since it will be seen that the effects of task characteristics can, to some extent, be modified.

Task characteristics	Source
Accuracy effects	
More structured tasks (especially when planned)	Skehan and Foster (1997)
Clear time line	
Familiar tasks	Foster and Skehan (1996)
Complexity effects	
Requiring more complex decisions	Skehan and Foster (1997)
Tasks requiring transformation of elements	Skehan and Foster (1997)
Tasks requiring interpretation	Brown (1991)
Divergent tasks	Duff (1986)
Interlanguage change effects	
Language focusing tasks, e.g. dictogloss	Swain (1995)
Fluency effects	
Structured tasks (unplanned)	Skehan and Foster (1997)
Familiar tasks	Foster and Skehan (1996)

Table 6.4: Selective goal influences from task characteristics

These findings have to be related to the principles covered earlier (see p. 132). Such goal-oriented findings do not add much to principle 1, 'choose a range of target structures' since the motivation for choosing such a set of structures has to be arrived at independently. But the findings are relevant to principles 2 and 5. A weakness with the use of the utility criterion (principle 2) is that it is only probabilistic in effect. But if tasks can be chosen which increase the chances of a focus on form, the utility condition may be more realistically attained. Findings such as those summarized in Table 6.4 show how fluency, accuracy, complexity, and interlanguage change are likely to be promoted. For example, if, through a teacher's assessment of a pedagogic situation accuracy is seen to be the currently important goal, then, other things being equal, structured and familiar tasks are to be preferred. On the other hand, if interlanguage needs to be stretched, and more ambitious language focused upon, complexity-oriented tasks with differentiated outcomes, transformations, interpretation, and divergent views are more desirable. There are no certainties here, but at least if task choices increase the chances of desirable outcomes, then instructional decisions are positive, even if not guaranteed, in their effects.

In this respect principle 5 is also relevant. Identifying task characteristics which, between them, identify conditions for the attainment of competing goals (principles 2 and 3) at least gives some basis for planning balanced development, with the result that if there are periodic cycles of accountability, such cycles can be used to assess whether unbalanced development has occurred and then make new plans accordingly which have some chance, through appropriate task selection, of remedying the imbalance. In other words, the capacity to choose tasks on a principled basis offers some prospect of translating the principles into some sort of effective action.

Taken together, the findings in Tables 6.2, 6.3, and 6.4 provide some guidance as to how tasks can be chosen with particular goals in mind, rather than simply because they work. The findings also show that an information-processing framework is useful since it highlights the pivotal role of task difficulty and the important functioning of the selective effects that tasks may have. Using these insights to choose tasks in a principled way can then enable the designer of instruction to plan that progress will be in desired directions.

Principle 4: implementing tasks to manipulate attentional focus

Once a task has been selected, there is still a wide range of choices as to how that task will be executed. The discussion in this section will be in three main parts:

1 What is done before the task proper is attempted.
2 What can be done during task completion.
3 What is done after the task.

The pre-task phase

As we saw in the Willis (1996) approach to task-based instruction, it is important to consider the activities which precede a task, and which are intended to make the task itself more productive. There are a number of reasons for engaging in pre-task activities, and it is useful to detail these at the outset.

Reasons for using pre-task activities

To introduce new language

Clearly the impetus for change has to come from somewhere, and the pre-task stage can be useful as one means of introducing new elements into the interlanguage system.

To increase the chances that restructuring will occur in the underlying language system

What has emerged with great clarity from second language acquisition research is that development is not simply a cumulative process of accretion in which, when something is learned, it is learned in all its complexity. Instead we have to accept that partial learning may occur: future input may have the function not of introducing new elements so much as of triggering a reorganization of existing structures (Sato 1988). Pre-task work is one way of achieving such reorganization.

To mobilize language

A development of the previous point is that where a repertoire of language is concerned, accessibility has to be distinguished from mere existence of a form or pattern. This is essentially an application, in the second language context, of Hymes's (1972) fourth feature of language: that it is done. In other words, part of the function of pre-task activity may not be connected with changing the underlying system so much as causing the learner to bring to prominence material which is stored, but which may not be active. This corresponds to Chafe's (1994) notion of a 'semiactive' level of consciousness. It is proposed here that very often the pedagogic challenge is not to focus on the brand new, but instead to make accessible the relatively new.

To recycle language

Very close to the previous point is the need to bring back to consciousness language which may not have used for a while, and which may need to be reactivated. The difference is that recycling language may be more specific in orientation, rather than creating conditions which enable the learner to mobilize whatever language seems relevant.

To ease processing load

So far the goals in pre-task activity have primarily concerned language. But part of the pre-task stage has to be an engagement with the content of a task. It may be important to use the pre-task phase to clarify ideas that will need to be expressed, either by retrieving relevant information into the foreground, or by drawing learners into composing themselves and thinking through task demands, such as by organizing things that they will need to say in such a way as to reduce the processing burden created when a task is actually being done.

To push learners to interpret tasks in more demanding ways

So far, we have been concerned with ways in which language can be brought into prominence and with how non-linguistic demands can be reduced. But there is also the issue of how pre-task work can lead learners to complexify a task, to think of more searching interpretations of the content of the task, with the result that they are pushed to the use of the more complex structures which are necessary for the more complex meanings they want to express. Pre-task work can also be effective in this direction, since it can cause learners to be more ambitious in what they try to say. This may well be crucial in pushing learners to try out new forms of language which they feel they do not yet control effectively but which are worth experimenting with.

Teaching

Pre-task activities of three major types will be covered here: teaching; consciousness raising; and planning. Teaching is clearly concerned with the introduction of new language, and perhaps with restructuring. It may be deductive and explicit (and of a more traditional sort), or it may be inductive and implicit, with material which is already structured, and in which learners need to search for generalizations. It can be speculated that deductive approaches introduce new language to the interlanguage system, while inductive approaches may be more effective to achieve restructuring of the underlying system, as the new elements of language which emerge inductively are related more effectively to the developing underlying system.

Consciousness raising

In recent years consciousness-raising activities have grown in importance in teaching, and now represent a wide range of choices that can be made (Sharwood Smith 1993). They connect with the earlier discussions of noticing, in that they attempt to raise awareness of language structure while providing learners with relevant language input and activity. Pre-task activities (compare Willis 1996), text exploration activities, for example with the task to find particular aspects of language or classify some corpus of language, exposure to parallel tasks, perhaps done by others, but with guidance as to what should be focused upon, exposure to material with some aspects highlighted (Doughty 1991) all constitute consciousness-raising activities. So do pre-task brainstorming activities and pre-task discussions. All of these change the learner's awareness of elements of the task before it is done, with the result that the task is then approached and performed differently. Although it is unlikely that new language will be introduced through consciousness-raising activities, they will make restructuring more likely, could mobilize and recycle language and might also change the processing load that the task contains.

Consciousness-raising activities can be used in several ways to reduce cognitive complexity. The cognitive familiarity of the task can be altered by pre-task activation sessions, where learners are induced to recall schematic knowledge that they have that will be relevant to the task they will do. (In this respect, what is happening is very similar to skills-based pre-reading and pre-listening activities, when the teacher helps learners to bring to consciousness knowledge relevant to a text that will be presented, and ask questions that they think the text might answer.) With task-based learning, the basic approach is similar, except that the foregrounding of relevant knowledge should also have a planning dimension, so that it has an impact on how the task is done (Foster and Skehan 1996). The cognitive processing load during the task to come can also be influenced by a number of procedures. Learners could observe similar tasks being completed on video, or they could listen to or read transcripts of comparable tasks (Willis and Willis 1988). Learners could similarly be given related pre-tasks to do (Prabhu 1987), so that they have clearly activated schemas when the real task is presented. Similarly, learners could be required to take roles in similar tasks (Yule *et al*. 1992) so that they could realize more accurately what is required without such a degree of support.

Planning

With planning we return to an area where recommendations for pedagogic practice can be based more clearly on research results. First of all, there is the issue of time. Mehnert (in press), as we saw, has shown that to achieve the different aims, the following uses of planning time seem optimal:

Fluency	Planning intervals of up to 10 minutes have a progressively greater effect, but the increase in the effect tends to diminish as more planning time is allocated.
Accuracy	The impact of planning on accuracy seems to come in the very early part of planning time. Periods as little as one minute lead to an effect, and this effect is not increased as more planning time is allocated.
Complexity	Planning time of 10 minutes seems optimal here, and time periods shorter than this do not seem to exert a very strong effect.

These findings provide guidance as to how the balance between accuracy and complexity can best be handled simply by manipulating the time available for planning.

An alternative method of addressing this same balance of pedagogic goals came out of the research reported in Foster and Skehan (1996). We were able to show that planning produced improvements in fluency, accuracy, and complexity but that there was a selective effect according to contrasting planning conditions. Telling learners that they had planning time but giving them no guidance as to how the time might be used led to a stronger accuracy effect. In contrast, giving learners guidance as to how they could use the planning time led to a higher complexity score. In other words, left to themselves, learners seemed to focus on form, and prepared language. Given suggestions (for both language and content), learners seemed to focus more on the content, and as a result pushed themselves to greater language complexity. An example of a task used and the 'detailed' instructions which accompanied it are given below.

PERSONAL TASK

Sending somebody back to turn off the oven!!

It is the afternoon, you are at school, and you have an important examination in fifteen minutes. You suddenly think that you haven't turned off the oven after cooking your lunch. There is no time for you to go home.

Explain to a friend who wants to help

- how to get home to your house
- how to get into the house and get to the kitchen
- how to turn the oven off.

You can make notes during the ten minutes, but you won't be allowed to use these notes while doing the task.

These are things you can do to help you prepare:

- think what problems your listener could have, and how you might help her
- think about how your listener can understand the order of the things she has to do
- think of ways to make sure your friend won't get lost
- think what grammar you need to do the task
- think what vocabulary you need to do the task
- think how to avoid difficulties and solve problems with grammar and vocabulary.

(Foster and Skehan 1996)

The various findings (Mehnert, in press; Foster and Skehan 1996) show that the effects of planning can be channelled, and so linked to particular pedagogic goals. Because of this planning can be incorporated in a principled way in decisions as to how to promote balanced development in second language performance, rather than occupying a constant and therefore more limited role in implementing task-based instruction.

The during-task phase

The usefulness of tasks, and the way they can be calibrated to achieve appropriate balance between the three goals (fluency, accuracy, and complexity), is certainly influenced by the specific manner in which a task is done. Unfortunately, this claim is not supported (or refuted) by empirical evidence, it is simply an under-researched area. As a result, most of the claims made in this section are programmatic and speculative rather than research-based.

Two general aspects of during-task activity will be covered:

- manipulations which influence the amount of attention available to the learner;
- pedagogic decisions which affect the focus of attention through a more extended task procedure.

Manipulation of attention

A number of choices which may influence attentional availability are available to the teacher. Following my analysis in Skehan (1996a), these will be considered to affect the communicative stress within which task performance operates. They are:

- time pressure
- modality
- support
- surprise
- control
- stakes.

Time pressure

Time pressure reflects the speed with which a task needs to be completed. With some tasks, participants are able to work at whatever pace they prefer, with the result that it is for the learners themselves to interpret how quickly they must work. Other things being equal (for example, not taking issues such as planning time into effect), it is assumed that greater time pressure will mean that there is less time for attention to form either in terms of accuracy or complexity.

Modality

Modality concerns whether a task is spoken or written. In effect, it functions in a similar way to time pressure, since it is predicted that spoken tasks (or tasks which have a substantial component of speaking) will permit less time to be allocated to on-line planning and attention to form. This is because once again the pressure of real-time performance will push learners to satisfy the need for adequate fluency, so that less attention is available elsewhere. In contrast, written tasks, or tasks with significant written components, will enable learners to marshal their resources to some extent, and as a result have some degree of choice in how they allocate their attention.

Support

Time pressure and modality are, in effect, teacher decisions as to how a task will be done. Similarly, the use of support while the task is being done is a choice available to the teacher to ease a task. In looking at task analysis, we saw that issues such as the amount of on-line processing and the degree of structure in a task can have an impact on attentional resources and a predisposition towards accuracy, respectively. In a similar way, if support is provided during the task, it can ease attention management, since in a direct way it can give the learner information which does not then need to be retained in memory. (Compare Robinson's (1995) research with 'here and now' versus 'there and then' tasks, or Brown *et al.*'s (1984) investigations of the effects of more abstract information.) The task can be completed by drawing upon the visual support (or any other sort of support) that is provided, with the result that the attention that is 'freed up' can be directed towards other goals. More specifically, support aimed at making a task more structured would possibly lead to less error following the research on structured tasks leading to more accurate performance (Skehan and Foster 1997).

Surprise

In contrast, it is possible for tasks to be modified mid-course by the provision of surprise information which modifies how the task is to be done. For example, in Foster and Skehan (1997), we used a decision-making task in which pairs of students had to make sentencing judgements for supposed crimes (just as in Foster and Skehan 1996), but where after five minutes of making such decisions some students were given additional information which modified the basis for the earlier judgements. For example, after originally being given the following problems to make judgements about:

---

1 The accused found her husband in bed with another woman. She took the bread knife and killed him.
2 The accused is a prisoner of war. Your country has just defeated his. He was a pilot. He dropped an atom bomb on your tenth largest city, killing 200,000 people and injuring many more.
3 The accused is a doctor. He gave an overdose (a very high quantity of a painkilling drug) to an 85-year-old woman because she was dying painfully of cancer. The doctor says that the woman had asked for the overdose. The woman's family accuse the doctor of murder.

4 At a party, these three teenage boys were having a fight with a fourth boy near a swimming pool. They threw him in the water and then stood on him till he drowned.

The learners were then told, for each of these cases, that:

1 It was discovered that for many years the husband had had a lot of girlfriends, and that his wife knew about these girlfriends. This was not the first time for her to discover him in bed with one of them. Also, he was a very violent man to his wife and children, and had hurt his wife several times.
2 First of all, the pilot refused the order to drop the bomb. Then, the general who gave the order said the pilot would be shot. Also, the general has not been punished.
3 Later, it was discovered that seven other old people in the same hospital had died in a similar way, through overdoses. The doctor refuses to say if he was involved.
4 The three boys (and the boy who died) were drunk. They cannot remember anything about the fight in the swimming pool. Another boy at the party said that the fourth boy started the fight.

Some of the learners in this study were given opportunity to plan, (both detailed and undetailed) and others, in the control group, were not. In fact, the results showed no effects for surprise, judged in terms of fluency, accuracy, or complexity. What seemed to be a stronger effect was that having to continue doing a task, and engage in spoken interaction, caused all learners to produce lowered performance. Further research is necessary here, with other task types and perhaps different methods of injecting surprise. But at the moment, although this sort of intervention could logically be expected to produce differences in performance, it appears that it does not.

Control

So far, we have considered influences on during-task performance which come from the interventions of the teacher. But it is also possible that learners themselves have a role to play here. For example, learners themselves may be more able, in some tasks to exert control over the way the task is done. This might be through their capacity to negotiate meaning. More ambitiously, it might be because they are able to influence the parameters within which the task operates, for example, by giving themselves more time to do the task, or by nudging the task to content which is easier for them to handle (Kumaravadivelu 1993). More ambitiously still, they might be able to negotiate the nature of the task itself, in a way called for by Breen (1987) in the context of process syllabuses, in which case the pressure the task entails, and the way the learner can respond to the task itself could be changed considerably (and unpredictably) but at least in a way which takes the task in interesting directions from the learners' point of view.

Stakes

Finally, regarding learners (or possibly through teacher intervention), there is the issue of stakes. Some learners may regard avoidance of error, or the use of a particular structure, as highly important and allocate attention accordingly. In other words, the issue may be one of learner goals, with some learners having their own views as to what they should be trying to do during a task. In such cases, learners may prioritize goals other than simply task completion, and may think that allocating attention to ongoing task content is not the only thing they should be doing. This viewpoint could be fostered by teachers who themselves induce learners to raise the importance attached to form, with the consequence that task completion itself is linked to wider pedagogic goals. We will return to this issue below when we discuss post-task activities.

Attention and more extended task procedures

We turn next to pedagogic decisions which influence how a task may be structured in a more extended manner. Two proposals have been made here, and as we will see after each of them has been presented, they share a number of features. Willis (1996, and see the discussion earlier in the chapter) suggests that the during-task phase consist of three parts:

– doing the task
– planning
– report.

Bearing in mind that, following the Willis approach, the task will have been introduced in some way, the first of these three phases gives the learners a task to engage with. At this stage the teacher's role is to circulate within the class and help learners formulate what they want to say, but not to intrude, and least of all to correct the language which is produced. In the planning stage, learners may prepare themselves for the coming report in which each group gives an account, to the other members of the class, of what they did as part of the group activity. At this stage, groups who are preparing are encouraged to draft, redraft, and rehearse what they are going to say and/or write. Finally, in the report stage, the results of the planning bear fruit, and one or more groups (but not necessarily all) make a report to the other class members.

Samuda *et al.* (1996) recommend an approach to tasks which interlaces meaning-based and form-oriented activities. Discussing what they term 'knowledge-constructing tasks', they contrast tasks in which there are samples of a target structure in the input with tasks which do not contain such 'seeded' structures. An example of the first type of task is one where an illustration of seven silhouettes seated or standing in three rows is given, accompanied by clues in the starting input, for example, 'The man who likes motorcycles is next to the person who likes fashion.' (The focus is on relative pronouns, in this case.) An example of the second type of task is 'things in pockets'. Students are provided with a bag of objects supposedly found in an overcoat which had been left on a plane. No specific structures are provided in the input, but the task is to speculate on the identity of the person who could have had these objects. To this end they are provided with a worksheet containing charts which requires them to assess the probability/possibility of each of the claims that they make. (Although not present in the input, the focus is intended to be on the use of language to express probability, such as modals and adverbs.) In the first case, the tasks are intended to exploit form–meaning relationships, while in the second the intention is to create a need to mean, but in such a way that there is a focus on the language which will be needed for the task to be completed successfully (compare Loschky and Bley-Vroman's (1993) 'natural' condition).

The intention is that both types of task create an opportunity for the teacher to supply form when learners feel they need it. To achieve this, as Samuda *et al.* (1996) claim:

> ... task design plays a critical role in structure-based tasks. Both Type A and Type B tasks are designed as a series of interlocking phases (or mini-tasks) within the overall task. The output of one mini-task serves as input for the next. Task design thus creates a scaffolding. This scaffolding can highlight relationships between form and meaning in various ways and at various points within the task. Task design also provides a scaffolding for focus on form that supports rather than impedes the communicative flow of the task.

This scaffolding can be illustrated through the two tasks mentioned earlier:

Who's who?	Things in pockets
• Group examine silhouettes, read input clues (see above), use accompanying chart, and speculate on possible positions for the different characters	• Group take out objects from bag, speculate about the identity, and use chart to assess probability of speculations on a number of categories
• Group complete cloze (containing high frequency of target structure)	• Group prepare oral presentation
	• Group give oral presentation
• Group create their own version of same task	• Group make poster summarizing their ideas about the identity of the mystery person

In each case one stage of the task feeds into the next, and each of the stages has slightly different functions, principally regarding the degree of focus on form and the degree of focus on specific form.

The approaches proposed by Willis (1996) and Samuda *et al.* (1996) have a number of features in common. Although each of them uses tasks which are purposeful, meaning-oriented, and so on, they also maintain the salience of form–meaning links. In addition, they have means of creating a need for language while at the same time providing methods of supplying that need without too heavy-handed a focus on form for its own sake. In addition, by following a more extended structure for task implementation, they make possible a lower degree of prominence for form since the requisite focus is cumulative rather than necessary at any one point. In addition, there is variation in the degree of prominence for form at different phases, and different amounts of communicative stress and support (compare the charts which 'ease' the tasks in Samuda *et al.* 1996). In this way, there is much greater scope for learners to reflect upon what they are doing, and as a result, to give some attention to form during the timespan of the task as a whole, while not being required to focus on form in an unnatural way at any particular time. As a result, the task structure promotes a greater degree of accountability for the individual learner without losing sight of the importance of meaning-based communication.

Post-task activities

We saw, at the end of the previous section, that the borderline which separates between-task and post-task activities is a fine one: both Willis (1996) and Samuda *et al.* (1996), in extending task-based work beyond simply transacting a particular task, show how what will happen next is important in considering the effectiveness of task-based instruction. Even so, with the caveat that particular activities may be equally locatable within or after actual tasks, it is useful to discuss what happens after the task proper to bring out the particular aims of this phase of work. Once again, the section has to be based on a mixture of research findings, generalizations based on practical experience, and speculation. The situation seems ripe for additional research to explore the assumptions which are made when data-based studies are not available.

Altering attentional balance

There are essentially two aims here. First, there is the issue of altering attentional balance while the earlier task was being done. Second, it is important, post-task, to encourage consolidation and reflection. Regarding attentional balance, the central problem is that one cannot interfere with the way the task is being done without compromising the central quality of a communicative approach, primacy of meaning. The result is that potential focus on form, which might be immensely helpful for longer-term development, cannot be made salient. As an alternative to within-task interference, the same goal may be achieved by requiring learners, post-task, to carry out activities which may cause them to allocate attention in different ways while they were doing the task, assuming that they were aware at that stage of the post-task activity to come. The goal, in such cases, would be to use post-task activities for which form is more important, and foreknowledge of which will lead the learners to allocate slightly more attention to form during the task, if such attention is thought to be useful as preparation for the task to come (the post-task activity). In this case, it is likely that if attention can be rechannelled towards form, the principal effect would be on accuracy, since standards of subsequent performance would be less likely to make more complex language prominent than to make correct use of whatever level of language was mobilized during the task.

Activities which can be argued to promote effective attention allocation during the task and a greater focus on accuracy are:

- awareness of an upcoming public performance
- awareness that task-based performance will be recorded and analysed
- tests.

We have already seen examples of how public performances can be embedded into the way tasks are done in the pedagogic proposals of Willis (1996) and Samuda *et al.* (1996). More accurately, perhaps, such public performances can be regarded as post-task activities. We saw earlier (in Chapter 3) that in Skehan and Foster (1997) we reported a selective effect on accuracy for such post-task public performance, but that (a) the effect was slightly weaker than was predicted and (b) it was confined, if one only looks at results which were statistically significant, to the decision-making task. These results are encouraging, but hardly conclusive.

So, instead of public performance, it may be more effective to require learners to have their task-based performances analysed either by themselves or by others. For example, performances can be recorded on video, and then learners, in their own groups or in larger groups, can analyse their performance for form or communicative effectiveness. Lynch (personal communication) advocates giving learners audio recordings of their own performances, and then requiring them to transcribe segments (of one minute or so, for example) of what has been said during the task.

These suggestions merit further research. The 'threat' of a public performance may be only an unfocused influence on the balance between fluency and accuracy, and so may not impinge on many learners—it may be perceived as remote (and also basically unthreatening by some). In contrast, the need to analyse one's own performance (or the anxiety that others may be going to do so) may be more galvanizing, and have a more direct effect on attention manipulation.

Reflection and consolidation

For the second aim, reflection and consolidation, the issue is to encourage learners to restructure, and to use the task and its performance as input to help in the process of 'noticing the gap' (Swain, forthcoming), and developing language to handle the shortcomings in the underlying interlanguage system that the noticing has revealed. Such post-task activities will make it more likely that form–meaning relationships and pattern identification are not transitory (as is the danger in meaning-oriented work) but are still available for attention and so are more likely to be integrated into a growing interlanguage system.

Willis and Willis (1996a) provide a number of examples of post-task activities which could achieve such an aim. They advocate providing learners with language input and focused tasks at this stage to enable them to relate aspects of language which have been made more salient, and, where gaps have been noticed, to realizations of how such gaps can be filled. They propose that learners can be given activities which require them to:

- identify, consolidate
- classify (either structurally or semantically)
- hypothesize, check
- engage in cross-language exploration
- search for patterns
- recall or reconstruct texts.

They give the example of how different uses of 'would', which was the focus of an earlier task, can be explored and reflected upon through the use of a set of examples. This could formalize insights garnered from the earlier activity and consolidate and extend them. Similarly, there is potential for the use of well-chosen (authentic or spontaneous) spoken and written texts to be the basis for analysis which illuminates earlier task activity. The development of user-friendly concordancing software might be especially useful in this regard (Murison-Bowie 1994). Johns (1991) has advocated the use of data-driven learning—the use of concordances to generate interesting examples of language use which may be helpful for the learner as the basis for inductive language learning activities. Such possibilities may be particularly effective in cases where previous task-based work has been able to highlight areas of language which would be ideal for further hypothesis testing. Concordances could then provide easily accessible data on precisely the hypothesis which was active in the learner's mind.

Devising effective instructional sequences

So far the discussion has essentially concerned the individual task, albeit with pre- and post-task activities included, as well as the possibility of more complex implementations of tasks (Willis 1996; Samuda *et al.* 1996). Tacitly, this has meant that the individual task is the unit of pedagogic choice. But it is also important to consider more extended sequences which are the basis for decision making, and which span more than the individual isolated task (compare principle 5, p.126). In other words, cycles of task-based activity can be an important component in any task-based implementation.

The simplest interpretation of this is to repeat the same task. We saw earlier, in the account of Bygate's work (1996a), that there are beneficial consequences in redoing a task provided that participants see adequate challenge in what they are asked to do. In such cases, the reworking of the task seems to lead to a greater focus on form, with respect both to accuracy and restructuring and more complex language. Hence, for tasks which lend themselves naturally to such repetition, there is potential to use a particular task more than once, and for good pedagogic reason.

This example leads to the first general reason for the use of cycles of tasks: the need to maximize the chances of balanced development of goals. It has been (repeatedly) argued that the three vital goals of fluency, accuracy, and complexity are in a state of mutual tension, and that achieving one may be at the expense of one or both of the other two. We have also seen that there is a wide range of influences which can lead to more effective prediction of the likely impact on performance of choosing a particular task (for example, structured tasks for accuracy) or of implementing it in a certain way (detailed planning for complexity, for example). It was also argued, in Chapter 4, that balanced interlanguage is a priority, since excessive and prolonged development in one area may not be easy to retrieve later, with the result that it is better to continually make small progress in one direction (such as restructuring, leading to greater complexity), and then see such progress matched in other areas (such as fluency or accuracy) as new language is integrated into a growing system. This perspective implies that in addition to having principles for the selection and implementation of individual tasks, sequences of tasks should also be examined for the cumulative impact that they will have. In this way, knowledge about task properties and implementation alternatives can ensure that the flow of tasks and their use is not going to make it more likely that unbalanced development will occur.

This, in turn, brings us to the fifth of the principles proposed earlier for task-based approaches to instruction: the need to engage in cycles of accountability. If balanced treatment of the goals of fluency, accuracy, and complexity is achieved, this maximizes chances that there will be an effective balance between a focus on form and a focus on meaning. But, although we have seen, through the work of Swain (1995), Willis (1996), and Samuda *et al.* (1996), that specific structures can be brought into prominence, there is no guarantee that they will be the structures which will be *internalized*. An attentional-based approach only maximizes the chances that form will be sufficiently salient for progress to occur.

This central dilemma is difficult to resolve. To require focus on particular structures would be to negate one of the central qualities of a task-based approach. But to be unable to probe whether specific areas of language have been attended to would seem to be a denial of a pedagogic role. The 'solution' proposed here is to suggest that monitoring cycles are used periodically. In these cycles, the attempt is made to assess which aspects of the language system have been attended to, and which of these have been internalized. Further, it will be important to assess the extent of the control over these forms, both in terms of fluency (the capacity to use them in real time) and accuracy (the capacity to use them correctly). This approach links with the first principle, creating a range of target language structures. In other words, it is not expected that those structures which may have been part of the instructional design will all have been learned—the expectation is that some of them, perhaps those that were the focus for noticing and attention, will be more likely to have been internalized. The need, therefore, is to identify which have been learned (and so will not be so important in future pedagogic planning), and which have not, since it will be these which will need to enter the next phase of pedagogic planning (and which should figure in future monitoring cycles).

Obviously one person who can initiate these monitoring cycles is the teacher. In this case the teacher can attempt to establish where there has been progress and what remains to be done. It is likely to be the teacher who can be more systematic in such assessment, since he or she will have been the one to make decisions in the first place, and also to keep records as the foundation for the monitoring cycle. But it is also important to involve the learner in the process of monitoring. To return to the central problem in communicative approaches: structures can be made salient, but their learning cannot be guaranteed. It is essential, therefore, to enlist the attention and involvement of the learner in periodic monitoring. It is only in this way that the learner will realize that accountability is not with the teacher but with the person actively involved, being the learner himself or herself. Since a block of instructional time will reveal that particular structures drawn from an original target range of structures have not been internalized, and therefore need to have renewed focus in the next block of instructional time, it is the learner who can direct future attention most effectively to ensure that the structures which have not been successfully learned in the past may be learned in the future. So the monitoring cycle has to be a collaborative activity and a joint construction of the teacher and the learner.

Conclusions

This chapter has been a key one in the sense that it contains a number of pedagogic applications which have only been possible through the analysis and discussion of research presented in the earlier chapters. Central to this have been the models which have clarified how a limited attentional capacity places a fundamental constraint on the way in which ongoing language performance can be the setting for longer-term language development. The natural predisposition of the older learner is towards meaning, with the result that noticing has to be contrived in some way in order that there is an attentional focus on form. Simply providing tasks to be completed runs foul of the dual-mode system the learners are adept at using, and which, under some circumstances, will over-emphasize a lexicalized approach to language performance.

By drawing on the research studies and models from earlier chapters, it has been possible to propose methods of organizing communicatively oriented instruction which balances a concern for form and a concern for meaning. This has been done by clarifying how what is known about task difficulty and the selective effects of tasks, coupled with the effects of task implementation conditions, can maximize the chances that a productive balance can be struck between form and meaning. It has been shown how this is possible at the level of the individual task, and also how sequences of activity have to take into account this crucial form–meaning balance. In this respect, what emerges is that pedagogic decisions, if they are not to compromise naturalness of communication, can only be probabilistic in nature, and so sequences of activities and careful monitoring are essential if continued development is to be nurtured.

Inevitably the focus in this chapter has been on relating processing influences to development and change. Performance has, of course, been central, since communication is still the engine for language change. But the main concern has been with how such change can be channelled systematically—performance has been treated only as a necessary component of this. In the next chapter, however, performance itself becomes the issue. The processing perspective that has been used is turned to another practical area, that of language testing, and it will be argued that once again, the underlying analysis of tasks and performance conditions is highly relevant to solving practical problems.

7 Processing perspectives on testing

In the past, the areas of second language development (the subject of previous chapters) and second language testing have remained remarkably separate from one another, and have been influenced by generally different perspectives. This chapter will argue that the processing perspective from these earlier chapters is relevant to how we conceive of models of language ability, as well as how we think language ability can be assessed. Once again, the discussion will point to task-based approaches as producing a valid and feasible basis for practical application, but this time to measurement.

Basic principles of testing

At the outset, though, we will look at the problems of assessment as they have been conceived by testers themselves. In general terms, a test is a systematic method of eliciting performance which is intended to be the basis for some sort of decision making, although this does not deny that many tests are not terribly systematic, elicit fairly questionable language performance, and do not lead to any decisions being made. Testers, in other words, argue for care and standardization in assessment in the belief that such methods of examining performance will have more to contribute to reliable measurement than informal assessment by people who may be very familiar with particular language users. Such teacher-assessors may have access to a wide range of evidence about the performance of their learners, but their standards may vary, and their focus of observation may also be unsystematic. So a more formal testing approach represents a belief in efficiency of sampling through systematic data collection, so that generalizations can be made to a wide range of contexts going well beyond the test itself.

Three underlying problems

In that respect, it can be argued that three underlying issues have particular significance:

- to infer abilities;
- to predict performance;
- to generalize from context to context.

The first of these, inferring abilities, contains a number of implicit assumptions. It is presumed, for example, that it is defensible to speak of competence-oriented underlying abilities. Further, it is generally assumed that such underlying abilities have some sort of structure, made up of different components, and with some sort of interaction and interrelationship between these different components (Canale and Swain 1980; Bachman 1990). It is also assumed that such abilities are indeed what underlie actual performance, with different performances drawing upon these underlying abilities in different but comprehensible ways (Bachman 1990). Finally, it is assumed that devising a language test which samples such underlying abilities in the most comprehensive and systematic manner will provide the basis for generalizing to non-testing situations. Once these assumptions are made, the focus of research activity then turns to establishing how such abilities are structured (for example, a skills-by-levels matrix—Davies 1977), and what methods there are of assuring systematicity of sampling by designing tests to achieve maximum coverage (for example a range of tests based on such a matrix, such as reading grammar, listening, phonology, and so on).

The second problem, predicting performance, focuses upon the way the abilities are actually used. The emphasis here is on how language users are able to cope (whatever their pattern of abilities) with the demands of using actual language in real time. The concern is not with generality or making the most accurate prediction for a range of undetermined potential situations, but instead with a test's potential to say something about how well actual performance will be handled. Factors such as time, acoustic conditions, communicative purpose, the relationships between participants, and so on would be important here. Abilities (such as an internalized grammar) might be a precondition for effective performance (Rea-Dickins 1985). However, such abilities cannot guarantee communicative effectiveness, and the need to incorporate performance conditions into test situations assumes much greater importance (Weir 1988).

The third problem, generalizing from context to context, is to be able to characterize features of contexts, so that one can identify what different contexts have in common (and conversely, how they differ), and how knowledge of performance in one area could be the basis for predicting how well someone would do in another. For example, one could investigate performance in a specialist area, such as a professional discussion, drawing on technical knowledge, and explore how such performance related to a capacity to engage in general conversation (Selinker and Douglas 1985). Or one could explore whether someone competent in more formal settings could also cope with conversation in more informal contexts.

Now it might be thought that discussing three problems separately in this way is simply to nit-pick. In some ways, it is obvious that what testing should do is find ways of solving the three problems simultaneously. The central difficulty with taking this approach is that each of the problems conceptualizes the underlying task of sampling language behaviour in a slightly different way. As a result, to follow one approach is, in practice, to downplay the importance of the others. An approach based on sampling abilities is likely to use some model of underlying competences, for example skills by levels, as mentioned earlier; or a model of communicative competence (Canale and Swain 1980). Consequently it will probably regard processing and contexts as things to be handled 'by extension' once the underlying pattern of abilities has been measured. In contrast, a processing approach will regard the capacity to handle real language use as the dominant factor, with abilities playing a subservient, servicing role. The emphasis in testing is then likely to be on establishing a sampling frame, not for abilities, but for the range of performance conditions which operate (for example mode of language use, opportunity to prepare, or degree of time pressure) so that generalizations can be made, in a principled way, to a range of processing conditions. Finally, contextually-driven approaches take as the major problem the differences between contexts. The result is that sampling has to find a defensible way of covering a range of contexts (such as familiar–unfamiliar or formal–informal), to enable claims to be made about what sort of performance is likely to be made in untested contexts.

Two responses

In practice, there have been two main responses to the abilities/performance/context conflict. One is to try to develop a model of underlying abilities (what Bachman 1990 has termed the 'interactive ability approach'). The other is to bundle together the performance and contextual problems, and to try to develop direct performance tests (the real-life approach, in Bachman's terms). The former approach emphasizes methods of identifying relevant abilities, and then hopes to find ways of saying something about performance and context. The latter concentrates on devising direct methods of gathering data, with relatively less emphasis on the abilities which they require for effective language performance, and then predicting to a limited range of situations on grounds of degree of comparability.

The first approach, which has been the more typical of language proficiency testers, has a lot to commend it. It is likely to be systematic in its portrayal of the underlying abilities and their interrelationships. It also connects, in well established ways, with the empirical methods that language testers use to evaluate models, for example, bivariate and multivariate statistical techniques, particularly factor analysis. In this way proposals are accountable to established methods of inquiry, holding out the prospect of cumulative progress in the development of ever more complex and accurate models. In addition, postulating underlying abilities highlights the problem that actual test formats have to be devised which measure such underlying abilities in as convincing a manner as possible. That is, the research methodology is the familiar one of starting with a construct, and then gathering data to assess whether the construct (a) has been well conceived and (b) leads to predictions about the real world which are confirmed. This leads, at a practical level, to the possibility (and possibility only) that the structure of abilities that is proposed can be used as the basis for a rounded and effective battery of actual tests which are the most robust means of predicting actual language use in a variety of situations.

Naturally, such a structurally-oriented approach has its problems. The emphasis is towards characterizing competence by using empirical methods which can lead to the reification of the underlying constructs as if they really exist and have psychological significance. Data, that is, is likely to be perceived in terms of the underlying structural model, and investigations are most likely to try to uncover ways in which the underlying structure requires further detailing, or maybe different arrangements of the component abilities (Gipps 1994). In addition, the approach tends to be static, providing a 'still picture' or snapshot of proficiency, rather than having a natural dynamic element, as in a 'movie film' which one could relate to learning and development.

The contrasting real-life approach achieves much greater success in predicting performance in the real world (see Weir 1988, for example). Since it aims only to predict performance in restricted situations, the test formats that it uses can simply simulate the desired situations fairly accurately, using realistic performance conditions as well as contextually-based material which is close to that which will be encountered in the real world (Bachman 1990). In general, this approach has emphasized content validity. Domains of language use are identified, and then these domains are sampled. The criterion for satisfactoriness of tests is how well they cover the domain in question. By pushing back the criterion to the domain of real-world use, the validation problem to be solved is made considerably easier, in that an effective needs analysis of the domain in question will provide a detailed target against which to judge the content of any particular test that is devised, and so provide a basis for assessment of the extent to which the test has content validity. Tests of this sort have become particularly popular in English for Specific Purposes (ESP), and with vocationally-oriented measurement.

The difficulty, of course, is that success is bought at quite a high price—the limited generalization that is possible beyond the set of performance or contextual conditions which the test is targeted at. If performance conditions vary, or if there are differences in contextual factors, it is very difficult to know if they are of minor importance or great significance. In the testing of ESP, there is the problem of knowing, for example, whether different sorts of medical specialization (for example general practitioner versus psychiatrist) are operating in the same context and under similar conditions, or need to have different sorts of test devised for them (Skehan 1984b). In such cases there is little underlying theory as to how a structure of abilities might link to different patterns of language use, and how such underlying abilities might relate to the different contexts and performance conditions. As a result, the initial attractions of such an approach to testing diminish all too rapidly (Messick 1988; McNamara 1996).

So in any comparison of the two approaches, the interactive ability and the real life, the former seems to have much more in its favour as regards prediction and generalization on a principled basis to a wide range of situations. For that reason, we will next examine some recent approaches that have been taken to characterize underlying abilities in a systematic manner, and then examine how the model which has been most developed currently can handle performance and contextual factors.

Models of communicative competence

The most influential formulation of the competence–performance relationship (Chomsky 1965) proposed an underlying rule-based knowledge system which is then implicated in actual language performance. Hymes (1972) criticized this (limited) Chomskyan account of competence and performance and their interrelationship. Most important, he proposed that there are competences which go beyond the linguistic domain discussed by Chomsky, specifically suggesting that we also have to take into account appropriateness of language use. But Hymes retained the idea of underlying competence, extending its scope to include contextual relevance, and so implying that appropriateness itself has an abstract element, is organized, rule-governed, and pervasive— qualities similar to those imputed to linguistic competence (McNamara 1995). So there was still a need to consider a competence–performance relationship. Problems in this area, though, would involve not only grammatical lapses, but also those of appropriateness, as when, for example, nervousness leads to a social gaffe which is instantly recognized as such by the perpetrator.

Components of competence: the Canale and Swain framework

Based on such work, Canale and Swain (1980) proposed a three component framework for communicative competence. Canale (1983) later extended this to four component competences:

- linguistic
- sociolinguistic
- discourse
- strategic.

The first of these derives from Chomsky's formulation of linguistic competence. The second is based on Hymes's (1972) work, which stresses appropriateness of language use, the individual's understanding of social relations, and how language use relates to them. Under some formulations it also includes knowledge which helps the language user to relate language to context and interpret and encode meanings. Discourse competence concerns the ability to handle language beyond the level of the sentence, to understand the rules of discourse (Canale 1983). These include an understanding of how spoken and written texts are organized and how to make inferences which recover the underlying meaning of what has been said and the connection between utterances. It is worth noting, in this regard, that one can speak more exactly of native-speaker norms for linguistic competence than for the two other competences—some native speakers do not distinguish themselves in the areas of sociolinguistic and discourse competences.

Strategic competence has a slightly different role (Canale and Swain 1980), since it comes into play when the other competences are unable to cope directly. In other words, strategic competence is compensatory in nature, drawn on when the developing language system of the second/foreign language learner is deficient in some regard, maybe because a word is lacking or an appropriate interlanguage structure has yet to be acquired. In such cases (compare Chapter 1), a range of devices may be drawn on to achieve the intended meaning or even to abandon the original meaning and resort to a simpler and more easily achieved goal (Færch and Kasper 1983). One final note in this area: we are still dealing with a competence, an underlying and pervasive system. The emphasis is not on what 'happens to occur' when difficulties arise and the learner's resourcefulness comes to the fore. We are dealing with knowledge about how to solve communication problems in general, which may then be activated when a particular problem is encountered. It is assumed that people vary in this respect, but that individuals are relatively stable in their capacity to solve such problems, and draw upon characteristic patterns of resourcefulness when faced with such difficulties.

An evaluation of the Canale and Swain framework

The Canale and Swain framework (1980; Canale 1983) essentially tries to subsume work such as that of Chomsky (1965) and Hymes (1972). The framework needs to be related to the three problems of testing mentioned earlier: inferring underlying abilities (the starting-point for the model), predicting performance, and generalizing across contexts. In this respect, Canale and Swain (1980) is clearly an interactive ability model, in Bachman's (1990) terms. As a result of its broader view of underlying ability, greater claims can be made that assessments based on the model can be the basis for generalization to a wide variety of contexts. That is, the constructs of linguistic, sociolinguistic, discourse, and strategic competences provide a more convincing characterization of someone's underlying abilities which can then be related more easily to contexts of actual language use. In addition, the framework allows the possibility of 'weighting' the underlying competences differently to allow more targeted focus on different language use contexts. For example, situations where interactional sensitivity is more important could be linked more clearly to sociolinguistic competence.

In reality, though, for the Canale and Swain (1980; Canale 1983) framework, linkages of this sort are only possible to a limited extent and the judgements which might be made are little more than intuitive. There is no direct way of relating underlying abilities to performance and processing conditions, nor is there any systematic basis for examining the language demands of a range of different contexts. As a result, it is not clear how different patterns of underlying abilities may be more effective in some circumstances than others, nor how these underlying abilities are mobilized into actual performance. Prediction and generalization are accordingly not advanced in any substantial way. In addition, strategic competence flatters to deceive. It does not really deal with how ongoing, ordinary communication is achieved, instead emphasizing characteristic language use only when there are problems. The discussion from earlier chapters is relevant to this. We have seen how the psycholinguistics of second language processing emphasizes the ways attention is used, how time pressure is handled, and how dual-mode systems facilitate effective real-time language use. A construct such as strategic competence now seems rather limited, only emphasizing the compensatory role of strategies discussed in Chapter 1, and not concerned with 'normal' communication in any convincing way. As a result, the Canale and Swain (1980) framework, though full of insights, cannot be considered either working (Cziko 1984) or comprehensive.

The Bachman model

The Canale and Swain approach has been further developed by Bachman (1990) and Bachman and Palmer (1996), who have proposed a similar, but more complex model. The Bachman approach contains several advances. First, the structure of the components has changed and become more detailed. Bachman (1990) discusses a tree structure for these components, as follows: Significant changes here are:

– the more complex layering of language competence, with its own internal organization, contrasting organizational (code) and pragmatic (contextual) competences;
– the movement of textual competence (to the extent that this bears a close relationship to Canale and Swain's discourse competence) to become part of organizational competence, seeming to imply that this is a part of a structurally-organized and somewhat autonomous knowledge base;

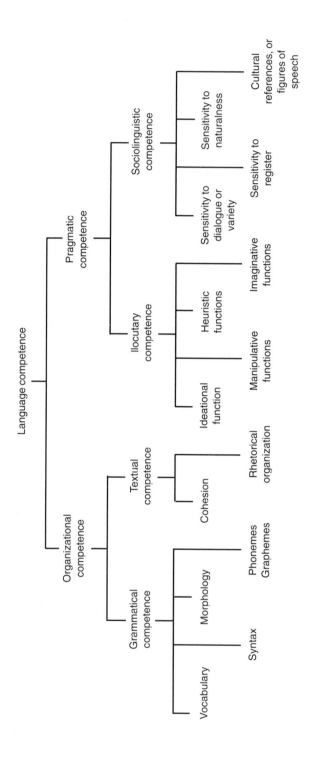

Figure 7.1: Bachman's components of language competence (Bachman 1990: 87)

- a more complex account of pragmatic knowledge, embracing illocutionary competence and sociolinguistic competence, and broadly concerned with knowledge of how to use language appropriately and effectively in different contexts;
- the greater status of strategic competence (not represented in Figure 7.1, but shown in Figure 7.2) since it is given some sort of equality to language competence.

These developments provide a more organized and detailed account of the underlying components of communicative competence. But despite the greater level of detail, and despite the way in which such a formulation can be linked to supportive (though not overwhelming) empirical evidence, the changes so far are simply ones of emphasis and detail. (See Celce-Murcia and Dörnyei 1996 for another modification of the original Canale and Swain 1980 formulation, different in detail, but following the same general approach.)

More radical is the change that Bachman proposes for the role of strategic competence. It is no longer seen as compensatory, only activated when other competences are lacking. Instead, it is central to all communication. It achieves this by carrying out a mediating role between meaning intentions (the message which is to be conveyed), underlying competences (those that have just been briefly examined), background knowledge, and context of situation. It carries out this role by:

- determining communicative goals
- assessing communicative resources
- planning communication
- executing this communication.

Bachman characterizes these capacities as metacognitive skills. They are cognitive because of the nature of the operations that they involve, and 'meta' since there can be self-awareness built into their operation. This analysis goes a long way to justifying the status of competence for these abilities. It implies that they are, indeed, underlying and generalized. They will have an impact upon all communication, simply operating in different ways as is appropriate on different occasions. One assumes, similarly, that they are stable, and the basis for characteristic methods not simply of solving communicational problems (compare Canale and Swain 1980), but also of engaging in 'normal' communication, for the native or the non-native speaker alike—goals are assessed, plans are made, and so on.

The most important factor, however, is that Bachman is redefining the relationship between competence and performance, since it now has dynamic qualities. This is shown more clearly in Figure 7.2, where the central mediating role of strategic competence between knowledge structures, language competence, and context of situation can be seen clearly. The functioning of strategic competence in this lynch-pin role (and its component processes of assessment, goal setting, and planning) underscores the point made above that what we are dealing with is a wide-ranging, underlying, and dependable competence.

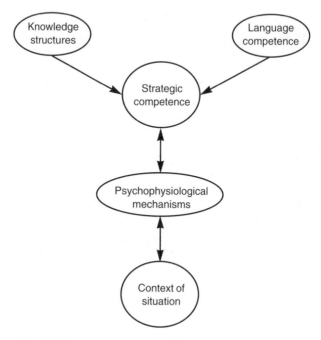

Figure 7.2: Bachman's components of communicative language ability in communicative language use (Bachman 1990: 85)

An additional development in Bachman (1990) is that it incorporates frameworks for analysing test method characteristics (TMCs) and target language use situations (TLUs). The former allows features of the test itself, such as the nature of the input received and the nature of the response, to be systematically examined. In this way a system is put in place for detecting (and replacing) test format characteristics which may generate measures of language performance which are an artefact of the format itself, and so not be an effective basis for prediction to real-world situations. The latter provides a framework for examining how language will be used in particular real-world situations. Then, most important of all, TMCs and TLUs can be linked. In this way, features of tests can be related in a principled way to features of language use so that the most effective matches can be found and the most worrying mismatches identified. This may allow systematic discussion of factors such as the inappropriateness of multiple-choice formats for some language use situations, or the degree of a format effect which intrudes when self-assessment is used as a testing technique, and, most generally, the authenticity of tests (Bachman and Palmer 1996).

Problems with the Bachman model

We need once again to relate the model we have discussed to our three previous questions of inferring abilities, predicting performance, and generalizing across contexts. In this respect there are significant differences between the Canale and Swain (1980) framework and the Bachman (1990) model. First of all, the Bachman model is:

- more detailed in its specification of component language competences;
- more precise in the interrelationships between the different component competences;
- more grounded in contemporary linguistic theory;
- more empirically based.

As a result, it is better equipped to reflect underlying abilities, form the basis for devising testing batteries which can claim to be comprehensive, and sample these abilities in a representative manner. If performance in a range of situations is thought to depend on such abilities, the scope to predict performance will accordingly be greater, and broader-based samplings of the abilities should generate more robust predictions. In addition, the development of the frameworks for analysing test method characteristics and target language use situations allows the 'weighting' of underlying abilities to be mapped onto specific language use contexts more systematically and selectively. So prediction of actual performance and even generalizations across contexts can be achieved more effectively.

Nevertheless these advantages, although significant, do not really confront the problems implied by the need to address processing and contextual issues. With respect to TLUs and TMCs, one can recognize that important progress has been made. These analytic tools enable the interactional authenticity of tests to be explored more systematically (Bachman and Palmer 1996), since important linkages are made with the operation of metacognitive strategies. In addition, TMC and TLU analysis has been applied to actual test use. Bachman *et al.* (1995) show how it can be used to compare two general purpose test batteries. Clapham (1996) reports applications of the framework to the analysis of tests of English for Specific Purposes, showing that the categories proposed can be applied to real contexts in an illuminating manner in such a way as to establish content validity on a principled basis. So such analysis, coupled with the sophisticated structure for communicative competence, allows more effective mapping of components of competence on to language use situations, as well as permitting more principled comparisons of the components of competence that are implicated to be made across situations. As a result, prediction of performance and generalization across contexts is enhanced.

There are, none the less, problems. The current status of the framework seems to be that it proposes categories which function as a systematizing checklist, but which do not give clear indications of significance, centrality, or relative importance. Headings such as testing environment, test rubric, input and output characteristics (sub-divided into channel, mode, length, and degree of speededness), the relationships between input and output (sub-divided into reactivity, scope, and direction of the relationship) are useful, and important not to forget, but cannot function if they all have equivalent weight in the scheme. An illustration of this is the difficulty in connecting to such an analytic framework the details of the findings in Chapter 5. That chapter showed how task difficulty influences performance and how task character-istics such as task structure and differentiated outcomes selectively influence performance, in areas such as fluency and accuracy (task structure) and complexity (differentiated outcomes). Findings such as these are difficult to incorporate in a list-based framework.

The processing perspective which has been argued in this book raises similar problems for the operation of strategic competence. Once again, despite the advance the Bachman (1990) account represents, particularly in the role that strategic competence has in orchestrating the contributions of other underlying competences during performance, there is the difficulty that the advantages are more programmatic than rooted in actual processing. Stages like assessment, goal-setting, planning, and execution are important conceptually, but what is vital is to relate them to researched processing constructs. Currently it is difficult to link them to the findings reported earlier on, for example the effects of different types of planning on different aspects of performance. Nor is it easy to see how the significance of dual-mode theorizing and lexicalized performance can be related to these programmatic stages.

Above all, the difficulty is that the account lacks a rationale grounded in psycholinguistic mechanisms and processes (and research findings) which can enable such a model to move beyond 'checklist' status and instead make functional statements about the nature of performance and the way it is grounded in competence (Chapelle, Grabe, and Berns, forthcoming). In an attempt to grapple with this issue, the next section will begin to explore how a processing perspective for testing can be articulated.

Analysability and accessibility: redefining the competence–performance relationship

One way of addressing this issue is to consider how linguistic competence may be represented psychologically and what processes are implicated in its use. In this respect, we can return to Widdowson's (1989) contrast between analysability and accessibility. This distinction, related to testing, connects with the nature of the psychological storage for linguistic material and the way performance in real time is coped with. Analysability implies elegant, parsimonious storage, with rules enabling the compactness of one-entry lexical systems. This requires the assumption that language production (and comprehension) operate at close to the lexical unit level, with computations based on the combinations of such units. In Chapters 2 and 4 it was argued that an exclusively rule-based system is implausible in face of the demands of real-time communication. For such communication units longer than the word have the considerable advantage in that they 'free-up' processing resources during language use because they do not require any internal attention, assembly, or decomposition. The redundant, larger storage system seems to be the price that has to be paid to enable speed of system operation (Bolinger 1975).

Above all, what is being emphasized here is Widdowson's (1989) accessibility, since this can take account of the actual operation of language. In so doing, it clarifies the fourth of Hymes's (1972) four charges on language: that it is done (the others, of course, being that it is grammatical, appropriate, and feasible). A rule-oriented, analytic view of language processing would treat all sentences as having equal likelihood of occurrence, as being of equal probability for creative generation. What Hymes's concept of 'done' implies is that there is some ranking of ease, usefulness, and relevance of the language that is used. This may partly reflect the individual (the psycholinguistically-motivated idiolect, as Corder (1981) might have termed it), and it may also reflect the speech community, which is likely to collectively value certain utterances more than others, a valuation which may also change over time. This might help to account for the way in which when one needs to speak a foreign language to native speakers but after an interval of non-use, one feels a couple of steps behind all the time, since one is clearly not using the sort of language the native speakers are now using.

These analyses force us to look at the competence–performance relationship in a new way, which has implications for the nature of language testing. For the first language case, a conventional view of the competence–performance relationship suggests that performance is based on competence, but that performance factors (fatigue, complexity of what is being said, emotional state, and so on) inevitably intrude. But we have also seen that a dual-mode approach has to be considered for first language performance, based upon analysability and accessibility, on rule and memory. In this view, communication can be based on a syntactic system, or a lexical/exemplar system, or a mixture of the two. This implies that competence will sometimes be influential, in the way in which traditional accounts would have us believe, but that when real time is a significant influence, a lexical mode of communication will predominate, with the result that performance will not be a pale reflection of competence, but will be subject to a range of processing factors. As a result, rather than looking at the ways in which an underlying system can come into play (components of communicative competence, for example), it may be more useful to examine the operation of these processing factors directly.

When we consider second language performance, the situation is rather different. Here we cannot so easily speak of an underlying competence in the sense of the product of the operation of a LAD. There may be a rule-governed system, but it will have developed in a radically different way—through conventional cognitive learning processes. Further, it is not so appropriate to think of language users 'switching down' to a syntactic system during communication. They may not have such a system to switch down to, since during their learning of the second language they may have lexicalized directly (see discussion in Chapters 2 and 4).

Strategic competence

This account clearly requires some revision to the competence–performance relationship. One possibility concerns the discussion presented earlier of the operation of strategic competence. It will be recalled that the major difference between the formulations offered by Canale and Swain (1980) on the one hand and Bachman (1990) on the other is in terms of the pervasiveness of the role of such a competence, with Canale and Swain restricting its operation to compensation and improvisation, a sort of proceduralized resourcefulness, and Bachman seeing such operations as simply special cases where difficulties are encountered. For him, strategic competence is implicated in all communication, since it discharges a mediating role between communicative competence, meaning intentions, context of situation, and knowledge of the world. It is in this respect that Bachman and Palmer (1996) speak of formulation of meaning, assessment of resources, planning, and execution as processes which must be gone through to achieve such communication. They characterize such processes as metacognitive abilities, which underlie the way in which competence is related to performance. Most of the time they will occur without undue need for attention, only revealing themselves more obviously when communication problems are encountered. But they are pervasive and unavoidable. Even if what we do is formulate meanings for which we easily have the appropriate communicative resources, and then plan the details of what we want to say and execute them, we are still following the same basic set of processes.

However, characterizing strategic competence in this way begs many questions. The most central of these, as mentioned earlier, is whether constructs such as assessment, goal-setting, and so on are more than programmatic labels for stages which may have a more conceptual than psycholinguistic role in actual communication. In this respect, if one is to take a more functional approach to understanding actual language use, it is necessary to ask what factors influence each of these stages—what has an impact on how a situation and one's own capacities are assessed, on how goals are set, and so on. This can be illustrated by relating task-based research to the two areas of planning and execution (Bachman 1990).

Pre-task planning and task performance

For pre-task planning, we have seen that:

- different lengths of time available for such planning influences performance features such as fluency, accuracy, and complexity (or range) in different ways;
- planning time available for complex tasks has a more dramatic effect than with easier tasks which draw on more familiar information;
- the effects of planning can be channelled through instructions, so that accuracy and complexity may be influenced selectively.

These results derive from studies of the time available before a task, and this is clearly not the same as ongoing planning during spontaneous communication. But they are suggestive, and indicate some of the dimensions which may influence aspects of speech performance.

The execution stage and research into performance priorities

The research from earlier chapters relevant to the execution stage concerns the trade-off effects found and proposals for dual-mode interpretations of performance. We saw in Chapter 5 that the effects of planning could be selective, sometimes favouring accuracy at the expense of complexity, and vice versa. This insight is clarified more directly from a testing perspective through an examination of a factor analysis of the datasets from Foster and Skehan (1996) and Skehan and Foster (1997). The pooled dataset, containing 72 subjects, included a measure of fluency (number of pauses per five minutes), accuracy (proportion of error-free clauses), and complexity (clauses per c-unit) for each of the three tasks (personal, narrative, and decision-making).[1] This generated nine measures in all. The factor analysis (principal components followed by varimax rotation) produced a three-factor solution, whose results are shown in Table 7.1.

These are striking results. One might have obtained proficiency-based factors (in fact, a single-factor solution) or a 'task' result (three factors each showing groups of loadings on the different tasks). What has emerged is a 'processing' solution. The first factor is clearly interpretable as based on the fluency measures, the second loads on two of the three complexity scores (with the narrative complexity score not loading so highly), and the third is a fairly clear accuracy factor. These results indicate that performance is complex and multidimensional, and that we have to consider the way in which there is

	Factor 1	Factor 2	Factor 3
Narrative: pauses	.73	−.38	−.19
Personal: pauses	.88	−.08	−.15
Decision making: pauses	.71	−.49	−.09
Narrative: error-free	−.18	.1	.83
Personal: error-free	−.52	−.06	.08
Decision making: error-free	−.24	−.02	.72
Narrative: complexity	−.50	.16	−.53
Personal: complexity	.03	.88	.12
Decision making: complexity	−.26	.81	−.08

Table 7.1: Factor matrix for datasets from Foster and Skehan (1996) and Skehan and Foster (1997)

competition for internal processing resources. The results are interpretable if we make two assumptions:

– performance in the three areas entails competition for attentional resources, such that committing attention to one area seems to be at the expense of the others;
– learners seem predisposed to prioritize particular areas consistently.

So 'execution', i.e. actual performance, is far from a straightforward, 'better-or-worse' affair—it reflects the priorities of the language learner faced with limited attention, a developing interlanguage, and performance pressures. To an extent, these insights could be incorporated into conceptions of strategic competence. But to take this approach would be limiting and force an attention-handling model into categories whose relevance is not at all obvious. For that reason, it is proposed here that dual-coding models of abilities, attention-linked tensions between performance goals such as fluency, accuracy, and complexity, and even an understanding of a redefined competence–performance relationship would be best handled within a construct of 'ability for use'.

Essentially, 'ability for use' is seen to mediate between underlying competences and actual performance. The advantages of the construct are that it can incorporate insights from psycholinguistically-motivated research. It also enables a dual-coding perspective to be addressed. That is, rather than draw upon a generalized and stable underlying competence, the second language performer adjusts to performance conditions by trying to allocate attention in appropriate ways. This enables real-time communication to become more feasible and some degree of fluency to be achieved. When communicative pressure is not so heavy, when precision is important, or when task demands emphasize form, a syntactic mode assumes greater importance. When pressure is greater and/or when effective communication is paramount, a lexical mode is used more. In this way, the learner, *essentially through a processing competence*, is able to handle the fluctuating communicative demands which operate, drawing on parallel coding systems which are available, and whose coexistence enables such flexibility to be used.

What this analysis suggests, therefore, is that different approaches to modelling performance are required which provide scope for such a processing competence to operate and so to be assessed. One method of achieving this is to use tasks as a central unit within a testing context. But if such an approach is favoured, it can only be feasible if we know more about the way tasks themselves influence (and constrain) performance. To explore how this might be done we turn, in the next section, to presenting a model of oral test performance which can incorporate the research discussed so far in this book.

A model to organize language testing research

The Kenyon-McNamara model

As a starting-point, a significant contribution to modelling the multiple influences on oral test performance comes from McNamara (1995, 1996). Following Kenyon (1992) he proposes the model, shown as Figure 7.3, to represent the interrelationships of these different influences.

Essentially, the model places performance in a central position, but influenced by a number of factors. These include the task which is the vehicle for performance, as well as the raters who observe the performance, and, equipped with scales and criteria, make judgements about it. The score which is used to assess the performance must therefore be seen as only partly a direct index of an actual performance. The model, through the interactants box, also allows us to see more clearly that the performance will be influenced by contextual factors, especially those concerned with the examiner (conventional oral proficiency interview) or other interactants (in group-based oral assessment). All these players may shape the nature of the interaction and the ensuing performance (see Van Lier (1989) for an interesting discussion of this point). Finally, there is, after all, a place in the model for the candidate and the way the candidate's underlying competence will influence performance. This is the most conventional part of the model. It assumes that the candidate draws on these competences (compare Bachman 1990) in a straightforward manner and that they have an impact on the task required, hence the performance, and the resulting assigned score. What is now clearer is that the candidate's underlying competence is only one amongst a number of other influences on the assigned score.

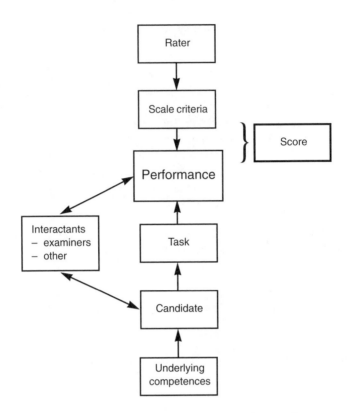

*Figure 7.3: Kenyon-McNamara model of oral test performance
(adapted from McNamara 1995: 173)*

The value of the model shown in Figure 7.3 is that it integrates a number of findings in the area of oral test performance, and becomes an organizing framework for research. The latter can be illustrated by mentioning a few representative studies. The nature of raters (for example, hawks versus doves, experienced versus inexperienced—Brown (1995); Lumley and McNamara (1995)) and the rating scales that they use (North 1996) have been researched in recent years, providing insight into the factors which systematically affect score assignments. Similarly, the interlocutor and the nature of the interactions may introduce important additional influences on performance and judgement. For example, McNamara (1996) argues that the co-construction of meaning which takes place in the interactions between examinee, interlocutor, and (possibly) other examinees, has been inadequately conceptualized within language testing. Similarly, Berry (forthcoming) argues that there are systematic and non-neutral outcomes from pairing particular types of examinees within group oral testing situations (such as introverts, when paired with introverts, being rated lower).

An expanded model

Although Figure 7.3 represents an important advance in understanding the assessment of oral performance, it does not centrally address the points discussed in the previous section, i.e. that:

- ability for use draws upon dual-coding capacities and organizes the way processing is adapted to performance conditions;
- tasks themselves are susceptible to finer-grained analysis, such that an effective distinction can be made between task characteristics and task implementation conditions.

To deal with these points, a modified version of the model is presented in Figure 7.4, which incorporates two extensions to Figure 7.3.

Regarding the first of these, Figure 7.4 shows that a second language learner's abilities require not simply an assessment of competences, but also an assessment of ability for use. To have competences which are unmobilized during performance does not confer much benefit. What is needed also is the capacity to translate these competences, through the ability to marshal analysed and accessible systems, so that good performance results. This goes well beyond the role of strategic competence (as discussed earlier), and draws into play generalized processing capacities and the need to engage worthwhile language use. Competences which do not connect to language use are meaningless, a point also made by Chapelle, Grabe and Berns (forthcoming) in their discussion of 'on-line processing assembly' within verbal working memory. Regarding the prediction of performance and generalizations across contexts, we see that tasks are central to this undertaking, and we can now start to make connection with the discussion from earlier chapters. Conditions of task implementation are likely to be a major influence upon how performance can be predicted. We saw in the last section how pre-task planning, for example, can have an impact upon performance, with different planning periods selectively affecting different aspects of performance, such as time periods of less than ten minutes not affecting complexity. Similarly, we have to consider how during-task and post-task factors influence performance. Task qualities, types, and characteristics will also be important in making generalizations across contexts. Tasks will influence difficulty and also have selective influences on different aspects of performance. By concentrating upon task design features, such as degree of inherent structure, it will be possible to base generalizations on task characteristics that are shared, or not, across the different contexts, and explore how selective effects operate, for example, degree of inherent structure and greater accuracy. In the next section these different components of the model which relate to processing research and which underpin the inclusion of the task qualities and task conditions boxes in Figure 7.4 are discussed more extensively.

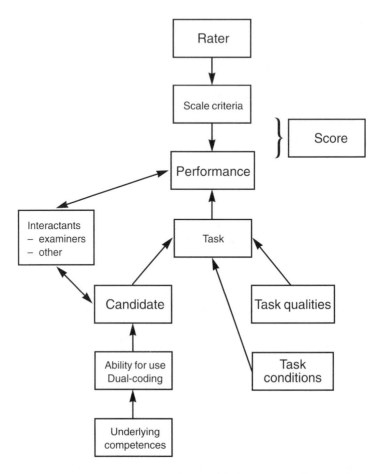

Figure 7.4: An expanded model of oral test performance[2]

Interactions between components of the model

Having briefly examined the different components of Figure 7.4 separately, it is now important to explore some interesting interactions between the components, in particular between the rating scales which are used and the other influences on performance. We saw earlier that rating scales are not 'neutral rulers', used in a simple manner to provide a measure of performance—rather, they can be an intrusion, a source of variance for scores which are assigned. The discussion in the previous section, linked to the interactions between the components of Figure 7.4, clarifies how this is so. The discussion on dual-coding, and especially, the discussion of the factor-analytic results (Skehan and Foster 1997) shows that there is competition between processing goals within performance. If fluency, accuracy, and complexity compete with one another for processing resources, and if scales used to rate performance address each of these areas, then the score used to characterize a performance may well be influenced by which processing goals were emphasized, since some language users may prioritize one or two areas at the expense of others, and this, if linked with rater priorities of particular areas, may influence the performance ratings which result. Consequently, some explicit concern for a performance dimension by rating scale interaction is required.

Similar considerations apply, perhaps even more clearly, to the interactions based on task qualities and conditions. Some tasks (see Chapter 5) seem to predispose higher levels of particular aspects of performance, for example, tasks with differentiated outcomes lead to greater complexity. Some task conditions—for example, detailed planning leading to greater accuracy—also have selective performance influences. Once again, since the scales which are used to assess performance may be selective in the aspects they value, it is clear that neither the choice of task nor the manner in which it is done is a neutral issue—each may influence performance selectively, and the manner of influence may have an impact on the performance rating which is assigned.

So the interactions that the model reveals bring out more clearly the complicated arena in which oral testing operates, and how this can be adjusted to. To put this succinctly:

– tasks and processing need to be understood if results are to be interpreted;
– tasks and processing provide guidance for the sampling that is necessary to enable generalization: we need to know what sorts of performances people are capable of.

The next section takes these rather programmatic statements and explores the evidence arising from processing and task-based research to survey the range of influences which have been proposed. In this way, the general insights from the model shown in Figure 7.4 can be translated into generalizations which impinge on the nature of effective performance testing.

Research bases for performance testing

This section summarizes processing and task-based research as it is relevant to performance testing. Three areas are discussed: tasks as elicitation devices, conditions for using tasks-as-tests, and methods of evaluating task-based performance. Research in these three areas shows clearly that although there is much still to learn, principled decisions are already possible to enable performance testing to be conducted in a more effective manner, so that predictions to actual language use as well as generalizations across contexts can be more readily achieved.

Tasks as elicitation devices

In Chapter 5 we discussed the factors which could have an impact upon task difficulty and task sequencing. The issues reviewed there are highly relevant to testing. One view of testing would be to assume that there is a scale of difficulty and that students with greater levels of underlying ability will then be able to successfully complete tasks which come higher on such a scale of difficulty. Such an approach underlies, for example, the postulation by item-response theorists of a unidimensional scale for language proficiency against which individual test takers can be located. The discussion of task difficulty presented earlier is, in many ways, targeted at the same place, except that it tries to achieve its aim by means external to the analysis of a set of test results. Such a 'task-analysis' approach underlies the work of Candlin (1987), Brown *et al.* (1984), Prabhu (1987), and Skehan (1992), reviewed earlier. The major factors which were identified as influencing task difficulty are listed in Table 7.2. (See also Chapter 6, Table 6.3). It should be noted that the second condition mentioned on each line (in italics) produces greater task difficulty.

Contrast	Source
Small number of participants, elements vs. *large number*	Brown et al. (1984)
Concrete information and task vs. *abstract*	Brown et al. (1984) Skehan and Foster (1997)
Immediate, here-and-now information vs. *remote,* *there-and-then information*	Robinson (1995a) Foster and Skehan (1996)
Information requiring retrieval vs. *information requiring* *transformation*	Skehan and Foster (1997)
Familiar information vs. *unfamiliar information*	Foster and Skehan (1996)

Table 7.2: Factors influencing task difficulty

In Chapter 5 we saw that familiarity of material was a very important factor in determining task difficulty. Task types which allow familiar material to be accessed easily from long-term memory and then used to achieve 'packaged' solutions to problems lead to easier tasks. Such tasks are less demanding on attentional resources, so leading to greater accuracy, fluency, and complexity and a lower susceptibility to task completion conditions (see pp.175–6). Similarly, more demanding reasoning, with more abstract material, had the opposite effect. It soaked up attentional resources with the result that performance was of lower standard. A similar analysis applied to the clarity and sufficiency of the material which was central to the task—the need to engage in extensive inferencing was a similar drain on attentional capacities which could otherwise have been directed towards qualities which would have been more likely to lead to higher test performance.

In addition, we saw that different task types seemed to predispose attentional allocation in particular directions (see Table 5.7 for greater detail). Tasks with inherent structure seem to provide some sort of scaffold which leads learners to emphasize accuracy. In contrast, tasks which require more differentiated outcomes, where simple convergence on one answer is inadequate for acceptable interactive task completion, produce more complex language. So do tasks where 'on-line' computation is involved, as learners have to attend to manipulating the content of what they are saying with the result that attention left over for accuracy is reduced. In addition, we saw that tasks which draw upon familiar material seem to support greater fluency.

Since raters of task performance (see below) are likely themselves to value some criteria over others, the choice of task, and its attendant influences on the nature of the resulting performance, may have a significant impact upon test scores. The conclusion one must draw here is that the nature of performance on a task is not something which is available for the tester's convenience, with one task being pretty much the same as another. Tasks themselves influence the nature of the performance which results, and so can have an impact upon someone's judged proficiency. In addition, task variation will clearly have a major impact on the effectiveness with which sampling is achieved, hence the importance of the task characteristics box in Figure 7.4, and the range of task-characteristic research which can underpin systematicity for the test tasks which are used in measurement contexts.

Conditions for using tasks as tests

Within the testing literature, there has been discussion of the way tasks may be implemented in testing. Morrow (1977), for example, discusses a number of qualities that tests need to be regarded as communicative. This approach has been developed by Weir and Bygate (1993), who include qualities such as:

- time pressure
- convincing reciprocity conditions
- setting
- role
- purpose
- appropriate interlocutors.

There are two problems with lists of conditions such as these. First, the conditions seem to make up a sort of threshold which must be met if a test is to be considered communicative. This position is hard to reconcile with the gradability of the implementation conditions for the use of tasks, for example the gradual nature of how, for example, time pressure varies as a performance condition. Second, lists such as these have an arbitrary 'magpie' quality, reflecting preoccupations amongst applied linguists at any particular time, rather than being based upon any solid empirical evidence or justified more theoretically. In that respect, there are significant omissions, such as many of the factors influencing task-based instruction which were covered in previous chapters.

The role of planning nicely illustrates the importance of testing conditions. At a general level, we saw in Chapter 5 that planning has a significant impact on the nature of performance, increasing fluency dramatically, leading to a wider range and greater complexity of language, as well as having interesting effects upon accuracy. More specific findings were that:

- different lengths of planning time impact upon fluency, accuracy, and complexity in different ways (Wigglesworth 1997; Mehnert, forthcoming);
- undetailed planning produced the highest levels of accuracy;
- detailed planning conferred an advantage relative to no planning.[3]

Since test performance will be rated on qualities such as fluency, complexity, and accuracy, it is important (see Figure 7.4) to relate assigned scores to conditions of task use such as these. Not to do so risks mistaking for a general effect a result which is, in reality, partly the artefactual consequence of the way the testing was conducted.

Other influences on performance discussed in the context of task-based instruction have not been researched so extensively. Even so, it is worth considering their likely impact during a test. We saw that these include:

- time pressure;
- modality;
- stakes;
- opportunity for control;
- 'manufactured' surprise;
- degree of support (principally visual).

Interpretations of these influences have to be more speculative, but at least the framework in Figure 7.4 allows us to conceptualize what sort of impact on performance they might have. *Time pressure* clearly makes a task more difficult, as well as changing the priorities that the language user is likely to operate. Greater time pressure, in other words, is likely to cause more lexicalized processing, and reduce concern with analysis, restructuring, and accuracy. An *oral modality* will probably produce comparable effects. *Stakes* concern the prominence for different goals, as when accuracy is accepted by all participants as being important. Possibly the activity of testing itself equalizes this factor, in contrast to what happens during teaching, where different perceptions may exist between learners of exactly what the stakes are. Greater *opportunity for control*, for example, to ask for clarification, delay, rephrase, modify (but not completely change) the task goals, and so on, is likely to make a test task easier in that difficulties are less likely to accumulate in impact, and the focus of the task can be closer to what the test taker would wish.

Surprise elements mean that original expectations will have to be changed, and new plans formulated (Harrison 1986). As such, the use of surprise elements by the test designer is most generally a way of making a test more difficult, even if more comparable to everyday speech. One can even regard the use of surprise elements as a means of counteracting the effects of planning and making it less likely that composed speech can be drawn on. The use of *visual support* can function to make a task easier, since the opportunity to refer to material which is important during the task is extremely useful, and more important, releases processing resources for use in other directions. In this case, the 'prop' provided by the visual (or other) support functions to save memory, and the constant need to re-access material from long-term memory.

What this discussion shows is that the conditions under which tasks are done and the way conditions interact with performance are a fertile area for research. Already we can see how, in areas such as pre-task (test) planning there are findings which clarify how conditions of task elicitation influence performance (as conceptualized in Figure 7.4). If we are to understand how testing conditions are to be standardized and/or how an adequate range of sampling conditions is to be identified, an understanding of this set of influences is essential. Unless research bearing on these factors becomes available, generalizations based on actual test performance will be a hazardous and chance-dominated undertaking.

Methods of evaluating task-based performance

Clearly, if spoken performance is elicited, the performance has to be evaluated in some way. A common approach within conventional language testing is to use analytic scales which are meant to enable reliable judgements to be made about different aspects of spoken performance. Such scales are likely to include areas such as grammar, vocabulary, fluency, appropriateness, pronunciation, and, sometimes, range. Representative examples are shown in Table 7.3.

Scales used in this way are an eclectic blend of convention in oral testing and theoretical justification. They may be abilities-driven scales (such as the ones for grammatical accuracy and general range) and processing-driven scales (the fluency scale above, for example). In slight contrast, in the previous chapter a variety of goals for task-based instruction were discussed. It was proposed that it was useful to consider separately:

- fluency
- breadth of language used and complexity (restructuring)
- accuracy.

Fluency[4]

Proposed level	Scale descriptors
Mastery	Can express him/herself fluently and spontaneously, almost effortlessly. Only a conceptually difficult subject can hinder a natural, smooth flow of language.
Intermediate plus	Can produce stretches of language with a fairly even tempo, although he/she can be hesitant as he or she searches for patterns and expressions. There are few noticeable long pauses.
Threshold	Can keep going comprehensibly, even though pausing for grammatical and lexical planning and repair is very evident, especially in longer stretches of free production.

Grammatical accuracy

Level	Scale descriptors
Expert	Good grammatical control; occasional 'slips' or non-systematic errors and minor flaws in sentence structure may still occur, but they are rare and can often be corrected in retrospect.
Intermediate	Does not make mistakes which lead to misunderstanding; errors occur but it is clear what he/she is trying to express.
Waystage	Can use some simple structures correctly, but still systematically makes basic mistakes.

General range

Level	Scale descriptors
Expert	Can express him/herself clearly and without much sign of having to restrict what he/she wants to say.
Threshold	Has enough language to get by, but lexical limitations cause repetition and even difficulty with formulation at times.
Waystage	Can produce brief everyday expressions in order to satisfy simple needs of a concrete type: personal details, daily routines, wants and needs, requests for information.

Table 7.3: Comparison of oral performance assessment scales

There are clear similarities between the two approaches (for example fluency, in both cases; grammar and accuracy; and complexity and range) but they each reflect different starting-points. The scales whose origins are in the practicalities of language testing reflect a need to achieve clarity of statements in each scale. In this way, it is hoped that reliable discrimination can be achieved along *separate* scales of measurement (fluency, grammar, and so on) under practical conditions, i.e. real-time rating or quick and efficient rating of recorded performance.

The processing approach which underlies the present chapter contrasts with the testing perspective in two major ways.[5] First, rather than include a range of scales or largely historical grounds, three areas are highlighted in a manner consistent with the processing discussion in the earlier chapters (represented in Figures 3.6 and 7.4, for example). The three areas oppose form and rule (accuracy and complexity) to meaning and real-time processing (fluency). Then, within form, the contrast is between conservatism and correctness (accuracy) and risk-taking and change (complexity). Hence scales are included for principled reasons connected to an underlying model, rather than being based simply on practicality or convention. This claim has a direct impact on the components of models such as Figure 7.3 and Figure 7.4, which incorporate raters, scales, and criteria as factors influencing scores which are assigned oral performances.

Second, and more important, what the testing-oriented analytic scales do not do is capture the competing demands on resources that the processing approach highlights. The task-based approach which has been elaborated in the last few chapters proposes that higher performance on one of the three scales may be achieved at the expense of one or both of the others. It has been argued that language users may choose to value one of these goals more than the others, and so compromise the balance of the performance that they produce. The factor-analytic evidence reported earlier in this chapter, for example, showed how central such performance trade-offs are, and how it is misguided to expect all aspects of performance to operate in unison.

Two consequences follow from this analysis. First, in practical testing contexts, it is not sufficient to include a range of analytic scales and then obtain scores on each of them which can be combined by some system of averaging. Instead, one must examine the dynamic interrelationship of the different outcome measures to make a judgement regarding the balance of language skills. Second, judgements of performance are partly a function of the way language is elicited, since task demands and processing conditions themselves alter the balance between achievement of the different goals. Planning in general seems to highlight complexity. But at a more specific level undetailed planning seems to be the most effective for achieving the highest level of accuracy, while detailed planning achieved the highest level of language complexity at the expense of a trade-off with accuracy, which declined somewhat. What language users are required to do influences the nature of the performance that is obtained. In more traditional testing terms, this would be regarded as a format effect, in that the nature of performance may reflect the way the measurement was obtained, rather than any pattern of underlying abilities. But, of course, following the present analysis, where the thrust of the investigation is towards processing, we would not really be dealing with artefact, so much as a demonstration of the range of elicitation methods we should use in order to obtain as effective a sampling of language as possible.

So what we need to do is not *avoid* effects such as these, but instead *design* testing procedures to probe as broad a capacity, on the part of the language learner, as can be used to cope with a range of realistic processing conditions. The basis for sampling would then not be (or not simply be) an abilities model, but instead a processing framework which would provide a more robust basis for generalizing to a range of performance conditions, as well as a surer basis for establishing construct validity.

Conclusions

Three broad conclusions follow from the discussion of testing presented in this chapter: that testing is central to applied linguistics; that a *weak* form of performance testing is justified, and that the methods used in language testing research need to be re-evaluated.

The centrality of testing

Regarding the first of these, it is often said in applied linguistics that testing is where the buck stops. Although most testing operates as a tool to solve practical problems, for example assigning students to levels, it is more interesting to reverse this relationship and to use measurement techniques and procedures *to explore the testability of theoretical claims which are made*, such as to use testing techniques to subject to scrutiny constructs from second language acquisition. In this respect, the argument for a more task-based approach to testing brings together contemporary theorizing and practical problem solving. As we have seen, proposals for a dual-mode approach to communication, which highlights processing factors, have significant implications for the measurement of a competence–performance relationship, since they argue that a reliance on lexicalized systems bypasses the need to engage competence in any conventional way. In such a case, accessibility assumes greater importance than analysability. As a result, there is limited value in taking abilities-driven approaches to measuring underlying competence—what is needed is some method of conceptualizing performance and processing influences directly.

A task-based approach to testing contains promise in this regard. It links naturally with research into information processing and task-based instruction. Such research is uncovering variables (planning, influences on processing within tasks, for example) which have systematic influences upon the nature of performance. In other words, if we take tasks as a relevant unit for testing, the research problem is to try to extend such systematicities as have been found and develop more refined measures of task difficulty. Such a processing-based approach could bring together practical testing concerns *and* acquisition- and performance-based research. If this were achieved, one advantage would be that testing and other research areas would be mutually beneficial, rather than the present situation, where testing research tends to be seen as isolationist and of lesser significance.

Weak versus strong forms of performance testing

A second implication of a processing approach concerns the distinction between strong and weak forms of performance testing (McNamara 1996). *Strong* performance testing duplicates real-world conditions for language *and cognition*. McNamara (ibid.) gives the example of a test for health professionals. When strong performance criteria are applied to a test encounter based on a typical medical consultation, there is a tension between the language tester's need to cause a worthwhile sample of language to be elicited and success in actual task outcome. For the latter, the best performance is one where the candidate speaks least, elicits most, and infers well through relevant schematic knowledge. In cases where relevant real-world (professional) knowledge is at issue, there is often a more limited, different, and very specific role for explicit language. In addition, the language specialist is often irrelevant for the evaluation of the effectiveness of what is said. It is communication which is at issue in such cases, rather than language display.

If, then, strong performance testing is a hazardous undertaking, the solution would seem to be a weak form of performance testing (language has to be produced, but not necessarily with reference to the knowledge base of the specialist), but one in which effective sampling can be achieved precisely through knowledge of how to choose tasks so that generalization is possible, and how to engage relevant processing conditions. Such an approach would seem an essential minimum for performance testing. In fact, a precondition for its viability is that testing decisions can be grounded in the sort of processing research covered earlier. As an approach it would have the weakness of not allowing easy incorporation of language use with specialist content knowledge. It would, however, have the strength of allowing performance generalizations based on principle, thus clarifying the limits of what language testers can contribute to specific purpose testing.

The need for re-evaluation of language testing research methods

To take such an approach brings us to the third conclusion, since it has clear implications for changes in how language testing research should proceed, and how construct validity should be established (Messick 1988). The model shown in Figure 7.4 compartmentalizes the influences on performance (and the test score) in such a way as to reveal the susceptibility to research of each of the different components. But if we ask how progress will be achieved, to refine what is currently only a schematic model, the most likely paths derive from focused *experimental* research, based on paradigms appropriate to fundamental disciplines. Any deeper understanding of *ability for use*, for example, is likely to be based on psycholinguistic research which tries to tease out which factors are most influential during speech production. Similarly, progress in understanding co-construction of meaning during oral test encounters has most in common with research in sociolinguistics and conversational analysis.

It may be, then, that a more hypothesis-testing approach to language testing and construct understanding is now appropriate. Studies can be framed in such a way that their results have an impact on how language is elicited, and how, then, it is evaluated. This may have the beneficial influence on testing of unlocking the difficulties (and the law of diminishing returns) in further multivariate studies of the structure of abilities.

Notes

1   The measures used were generated as a result of the information processing perspective underlying the research and the postulation that these three areas are important in performance and development. But measures of this sort are also highly relevant to testing. Typically, oral performance is assessed through the filter of rating scales (Alderson 1991; North 1996; McNamara 1996). There have been many debates about such scales in the testing literature. The approach taken here uses direct indices of performance rather than ratings by judges, and the time required to derive such indices would clearly not be justified in virtually all testing situations. But there is a clear resemblance between these research-based measures and scales that are typically used. Scales called 'grammatical accuracy', 'fluency', and 'range' are clearly related to accuracy, fluency and complexity measures as used in a number if task-based research studies, so the present measures can be taken as somewhat more objective versions of aspects of performance routinely included in rating scale approaches.

2   This model attempts to characterize influences on oral performance as these are relevant to testing. It is centrally concerned therefore with real-time processing and the contexts and tasks which confront test candidates. Figure 7.4 complements Figure 3.6, which was concerned more with input, noticing, and central processing as well as influences on interlanguage change. The current model, Figure 7.4, in a sense focuses on the output fluency components of the previous model in more detail and in ways more relevant to assessment.

3   A somewhat different aspect of planning within testing concerns the issue of task authenticity. Tasks need to contain a context and purpose if they are to be judged as communicative. But there is a distinction between a

tester's context and purpose (however plausible) and a test-taker 'authenticating' a task by relating it to their personal contexts and purposes. It may be well that planning makes such a linkage more likely to happen since the planning period can be used to identify how a particular task, such as the judge task from Chapter 6, may be given personal significance, for example by mobilizing one's own set of values. In this way the opportunity to plan may also increase the authenticity of the test tasks which are used.

4   The level descriptors are taken from North (1996), which in turn is based on Council of Europe work. It is an attempt to offer a criterion-referenced basis for the scale levels, which run (highest to lowest): Mastery, Expert, Intermediate, Threshold, Waystage, Beginner. See North (1996) for characterizations of these levels.

5   In the current discussion, the reliance on task-oriented research on careful measurement and objectively-derived indices is not taken to be the central issue.

8   Research into language aptitude

Limits of generality

In the previous seven chapters, the emphasis has been on universal factors in language learning. The main thrust has been to examine the effects of different processing constraints on learning and performance. The tacit assumption has been that learners are basically similar, and that the claims which are made apply to everyone. To be sure, different exposure to language may have different effects, as with learners whose pressing communication needs predispose them to lexical modes of communication. But in the main the assumption has been made that all learners bring the same basic equipment to the language learning task—an assumption consistent with the priorities of most contemporary second language acquisition research.

Chapters 8 to 11 will take a different approach. They will focus on the ways learners may differ from one another in their language-learning capacities. Such an approach has been unfashionable for a number of reasons. At a practical level, it introduces complexity to such influential parties as syllabus designers, textbook writers, and others, who would have to modify generalist approaches very considerably to take account of individual differences—a point returned to in Chapter 11. Theoretically, a concern for variation between learners threatens the power (and parsimony) of universalist accounts—it is, after all, a tempting research strategy to push generality as far as it can go, and only then examine what remains to be accounted for.

But there are dangers with such a strategy. One consequence would be that researchers minimize the extent of diversity because their attention is focused on the general. As a result, relevant evidence may not be gathered, or when it is gathered, it may be marginalized because it does not fit in well to an existing paradigm of inquiry. This, in turn, could lead to an inadequate integration of universalist and differential approaches (Cronbach 1957) to the disadvantage of each area.

In the main, this is what has happened in acquisition research. There are exceptions, of course. Nelson (1981) and Bates *et al.* (1988) have explored the consequences of different styles for the course of first language acquisition, while Pienemann *et al.* (1988) have proposed a two-dimensional model of second language acquisition, with the first dimension concerned with universal sequences in language development and the second with areas where there is a variation between learners. In addition, major texts in the area (such as Larsen-Freeman and Long 1991; Ellis 1994) contain coverage of areas such as aptitude, strategies, and style. But these books do not set themselves the task of providing a unified framework in which general and variational accounts are related to one another.

To attempt to address these issues, in the next three chapters we will explore cognitive aspects of individual differences, and try to integrate them within the information-processing viewpoint from the earlier chapters. This chapter and the next will examine the concept of foreign language aptitude, and will try to justify the usefulness of examining such an aptitude in terms of the three stages of input, central processing, and output. Then, Chapter 10 will explore the extent to which learning style can be brought within the same framework. In this way, some degree of integration between universalist and differential approaches will be proposed. Finally, Chapter 11 will explore some pedagogic implications which follow from this differential account.

Underlying assumptions, and critiques of aptitude

Generally, cognitively-based learner differences have been studied in terms of foreign language aptitude. Research into aptitude has attempted to discover whether there is a specific talent for learning languages, and if so, what the structure of such a talent might be. In general, researchers in this area have not been excessively influenced by other developments in second language acquisition and learning, and have not tried to locate their work within any such tradition. Instead, they have been more psychometric and test-based in orientation, and closer to the differential tradition in psychology, whose perpetual quest has been to identify the structure of human abilities (Carroll 1993). Accordingly, this chapter will examine the structure of aptitude, research results, research into the origin of aptitude, the context of teaching and aptitude relevance, aptitude and acquisition-oriented research, and pedagogic applications of aptitude research. Prior to this discussion, however, it is important to look at some of the conceptual issues fundamental to aptitude investigations.

Assumptions

There are two sorts of issues which need to be addressed in this section—the assumptions typically made by aptitude researchers and some of the general critiques that have been levelled against this type of research. Understanding the need to make assumptions helps us to see what the motivations behind aptitude research have been. Appreciating the critiques that have been made is necessary because aptitude research has not been popular, and examining the lack of substance in such criticism is an important stepping-stone to progress.

Assumption 1: the issue of specificity

The first assumption is that a talent exists which is specific to language learning. A strong contrasting viewpoint would be that abilities which facilitate language learning are the same as those important in any learning and simply operate on different material. Talented learners, in this viewpoint, will be talented learners of everything, a conclusion consistent with concepts of a general intelligence, or 'g' (Spearman 1927). A weaker version of this alternative viewpoint would be that within the area of cognitive abilities, people have strengths and weaknesses, and that these strengths and weaknesses (for example, in verbal skills, in spatial abilities, or in practical intelligence) equip individuals better for some areas than others.

Such a viewpoint—that there is no specific talent for language learning—implies that it is worth looking for the ability profile of the language learner, but that the place one should look for inspiration is the area of general intellectual functioning, with its range of models (implying general intelligence, multiple factors, hierarchical organization) and its relevant concepts (fluid and crystallized intelligence, for example Cattell 1971). This would also mean that language abilities, in the case of 'older' learners (beyond the post-critical period), are not distinct in any important way from general abilities. They would also imply that Universal Grammar, even if accepted as central to accounts of first language development, would no longer be operative. The contrasting perspective would be that a talent for languages is specific, and so different from any general mix of cognitive abilities. The claim, in other words, is that language has qualititive differences from other areas, and may represent an altogether different knowledge system. In this case it would be relevant to examine whether a Universal Grammar is still operative in the second language case.

We will return to this issue later, as the research on foreign language aptitude provides partial answers to a number of these issues. For the moment, we continue to make the assumption, for the sake of the discussion, that it is worth pursuing the separate nature of aptitude.

Assumption 2: stability and untrainability

The next assumption that is made is that such a language aptitude is stable in nature, is not susceptible to easy training or modification, and is not environmentally influenced, to any significant degree, at least after the early years. These assumptions imply that language aptitude is something we are endowed with as a set of cognitive abilities which are either genetic or fixed fairly early in life (Carroll 1981). Of course, it is not disputed that the environment can have some impact on one's language learning ability. This is because partly language learning itself gives a wider basis in experience for future learning, for example, learning a third language (L3) or having a more extensive L1 vocabulary. Similarly, learning a language will also teach the learner about the process of learning a language. But the central issue is that, although previous language learning is likely to bring into play beneficial changes for future language learning, there is still an underlying endowment which has not changed, and which acts as a constraint on what is possible in terms of the speed of future learning. (See Politzer and Weiss 1969 for evidence supporting this assumption.)

Critiques

In addition to the assumptions that aptitude researchers make, there have also been a number of criticisms of foreign language aptitude.

The 'everyone has aptitude' critique

Neufeld (1979) has been a consistent critic of aptitude research. In articulating a position which claims that individual differences in second language learning success should be ascribed to social factors, he makes two main points. First, after characterizing foreign language aptitude as different from first-language learning ability, he claims that there is very little variation in first-language learning ability. He argues from this that everyone possesses language learning ability and so it is invalid to search for differences in aptitude for second language learning. In this regard, he argues that critical period data (which leads to claims that adults are less effective learners than children, in all language domains, phonological and otherwise) is erroneous, and that 'exceptions' to the critical period hypothesis—people who successfully learn a second language to native-like levels—demonstrate that everyone has the potential to learn a second language.

The 'premature claim' critique

Neufeld's second major point about aptitude is that we do not understand sufficiently well what aptitude tests actually measure, particularly in terms of processes of learning, and whether language aptitude tests are cognitively or linguistically based. In this respect he suggests that 'I know no one, including the authors of the various modern language aptitude tests, who would categorically or even tentatively explain what language learning processes or strategies are.' Furthermore, in this regard, he speculates that 'hundreds of other seemingly irrelevant independent variables might conceivably have correlated as highly or higher, had they been examined' Neufeld (1979).

The 'relevant for formal learning only' critique

Krashen (1981) also criticizes foreign language aptitude work, but from a different perspective. In the context of his Monitor Model (Krashen 1985), which includes a distinction between acquisition and learning, he proposes that aptitude tests are methodology dependent, and work only when used in formal learning contexts. He suggests that only the achievements of learners exposed to methodologies which target conscious learning and focus on individual elements of language will be predicted by aptitude research. Krashen (1981) draws attention to the bulk of the validation studies with aptitude tests being conducted with such methodologies, thus constituting a limitation in the generalizability of aptitude constructs.

These assumptions and criticisms, together with the sort of evidence that would be important for their resolution, are shown in Table 8.1. We will refer to this table at relevant points during the discussion of language aptitude in this and the next chapter.

	Nature	Relevant evidence
Assumption 1	Specific talent	Relationship of aptitude measures and components to cognitive ability measures Evidence for the 'special' nature of language learning
Assumption 2	Stability, untrainability	Evidence of connection with first language learning Evidence of trainability
Critique 1: Neufeld	FLA=SLA no variation in FLA no variation in SL ability	Evidence of variation in first language learning ability Evidence of differences between first and foreign language learning ability Evidence of failure in second language learning
Critique 2: Neufeld	Lack of understanding of aptitude tests	Relevant construct validity arguments Arbitrary nature of such tests Greater understanding of 'failed' tests
Critique 3: Krashen	Aptitude is relevant to formal, conscious, learning contexts	Evidence that aptitude is relevant in naturalistic informal contexts

Table 8.1: Assumptions and critiques of aptitude research

Language aptitude research

In this section we will consider aptitude research under six headings: the structure of aptitude, aptitude research results, research into the origin of aptitude, context of teaching and aptitude relevance, aptitude and acquisition-oriented research, and applications of aptitude research.

The structure of aptitude

The simplest view of aptitude is the proposition that some people have greater levels than others, and that those who are blessed in this way are likely to make faster progress in language learning. Several research studies from the first half of this century took this approach, and attempted to develop tests of such a language aptitude. They enjoyed limited success, but seemed to be tied to the paper-and-pencil methodologies prevalent in language teaching at the time (Carroll 1981). When language teaching methodologies changed, and audio-lingualism become more widely used, these earlier tests seemed to lose their effectiveness.

The major development in the field of aptitude testing came with the work of J. B. Carroll, who directed a research programme which aimed to understand the nature of language aptitude, and then use this understanding to produce tests which would work in the context of the 'new' audiolingual methodologies. Carroll and Sapon (1959) generally researched by:

- constructing a large number of potentially useful aptitude tests;
- administering these to students of foreign languages at the beginning of a course of instruction;
- using factor analysis to examine the intercorrelations of the different aptitude tests to discover which of the aptitude tests duplicated one another, and were therefore redundant;
- examining the intercorrelations between the surviving aptitude tests and end-of-course performance on language achievement and proficiency tests. This stage established which of the 'predictor' tests matched their potential and which did not.

On the basis of this work, Carroll (1965) proposed that four factors underlie aptitude tests. These are:

1 Phonemic coding ability—the capacity to analyse incoming sounds in such a way that they can be retained.
2 Associative memory—the capacity to make associations between verbal material
3 Inductive language learning ability—the capacity to infer structure from a corpus of language material and make generalizations about how other linguistic material would be encoded.

4 Grammatical sensitivity—the capacity to see what functions words fulfil in sentences.

Carroll and Sapon (1959) published an aptitude test battery which operationalized the four underlying factors. The test, the Modern Languages Aptitude Test (MLAT), contains five sections, and provides a total score, as well as the potential for some detailed profile analysis. Interestingly, although the explanatory phase of Carroll's aptitude research emphasized the distinct contributions of each of the four factors of aptitude, the actual test battery consisted of sub-tests which were often not pure measures of each of the factors. Indeed one of the proposed factors, inductive language learning ability, is not measured at all.

In retrospect, this can be seen as unfortunate. The actual test battery was constructed for usefulness and general predictive power. The underlying four-factor account illuminated the actual tests, but was not represented in them in any pure form. No doubt, this was partly the result of prediction (the ultimate touchstone) being given overriding importance. Partly, also, it undoubtedly reflects the difficulty of producing 'pure' tests, since most language-related activities cannot avoid drawing on integrated abilities. Any test of inductive language learning ability, for example, will be benefited not only by this specific component of aptitude, but also by memory, since progression through verbal material, especially if there is a speed component, will be assisted by not having to look back to check the nature of emerging patterns and previous examples.

This tension in aptitude research between explanation and prediction (Skehan 1982) has pervaded almost all research in the area. At least the theory underlying the MLAT was recoverable since the connection between MLAT sub-tests and underlying theory was clear from the original research project (Carroll 1965). Subsequently, a major aptitude project, the Defense Language Battery Test (DLAB) (Petersen and Al-Haik 1976) prioritized prediction to such an extent that it led to little explanatory advance. The resulting aptitude battery, although it yielded better discrimination amongst higher aptitude students (the MLAT is prone to a plateau effect rather quickly, in this regard), did not add to our understanding of higher levels of aptitude. This state of affairs, prediction being highlighted at the expense of explanation, is obviously connected with Neufeld's (1979) Critique 2 (that we do not understand aptitude tests sufficiently well). Approaches such as that taken by the DLAB give the claim some justice. But we have seen that the theory underlying the MLAT is, in fact, clear, and, as we shall see below, justifiable in information-processing terms. Neufeld's critique is therefore seen as misplaced.

Aptitude research results

The MLAT (and a comparable language aptitude battery produced a few years later, the Language Aptitude Battery, Pimsleur 1966) were used in a considerable body of research during the 1960s and 1970s, and proved to be reliable and useful indicators of language learning success. They generally correlated at between 0.40 and 0.65 with end-of-course performance under conditions of intensive foreign language instruction with heterogeneous groups of learners. As such they have been a considerable success story in applied linguistics if judged in terms of the level of empirical relationship between a potential causal variable and the outcome variable of language learning success. In fact, the level of predictive success achieved exceeds that of any other proposed causal variable in magnitude of correlations found. (The only 'rival' predictor is that of motivation, although it can be argued that the levels of correlation here are not quite so high, in general, and less robust across studies.) So the neglect of aptitude research is a curiosity in itself, as researchers have pursued other potential predictors, for example personality, category width, even cognitive style, with remarkable zeal, despite the lack of underlying theory and empirical support.

Still, to return to the results themselves, they reinforce the rebuttal of Neufeld's claim that aptitude tests are not understood. Besides being empirically justified, the different sub-components make sense in terms of the skills that are necessary in language learning, in that phonemic coding ability concerns effective auditory processing of input. Grammatical sensitivity and inductive language learning ability concern more central processing of linguistic material, and memory concerns the acquisition of new information, and then its retrieval during processing. One aspect of this differentiated view of aptitude is that it implicitly proposes that people may vary in separate components, for example, high phonemic coding ability does not imply high memory ability. This has considerable significance, as we will see below, since it suggests aptitudinal strengths and weaknesses, rather than across-the-board winners and losers. The differentiated view also changes how we need to investigate the underlying abilities that comprise aptitude. These construct validity arguments will be developed below.

The research conducted using Carroll's views on aptitude has endured well (Carroll 1965, 1981, 1993). In particular, the constructs underlying phonemic coding ability and the two language capacity factors are still current, to some degree. The component which has stood the test of time least is that of memory. The MLAT studies were firmly based within an associationist tradition in psychology, and so were based on the stimulus–response format, operationalizing memory in terms of strength of bonding. Since then, conceptions of memory have changed, and some aptitude research has reflected this. In research conducted with British armed forces personnel (Skehan 1980, 1982), heterogeneous groups studying Arabic intensively for ten weeks were given a battery of aptitude tests at the beginning of their course, and then also took a battery of communicatively oriented end-of-course tests. The aptitude battery emphasized a range of memory tests, including but going beyond the associationist memory tests used by the MLAT. There were tests of short-term memory span, response integration (memory for material with very unfamiliar structure), memory for text and organized material, and memory for visual patterns. There were a number of high correlations between the aptitude measures and the end-of-course tests. Several correlated at above 0.50, for example the measure of response integration, indicating that a range of aptitude tests were predicting effectively in these circumstances. This allowed high levels of multiple correlation to be achieved, often above 0.70, accounting for half the variance in the end-of-course language tests.

In addition, the data was cluster analysed (Skehan 1986c). This statistical technique does not aim to identify underlying factors for the different tests used, but instead tries to group or cluster the subjects (the language learners), given their profiles on the different tests they have taken. This analysis revealed that successful learners achieved their success in one of two ways. Some successful learners achieved their success through high linguistic-analytic abilities, and seemed to be treating the 'problem' they faced as a linguistic puzzle-solving task. The other group of successful learners, in contrast, seemed to base their success on memory, and seemed to regard language learning as a task requiring the commitment to memory of vast amounts of material. Interestingly, there were few learners who were high in both verbal aptitude and memory aptitude; success seemed to come from just one of these sources. Nor did the two groups of learners differ in their profile of performance on the end-of-course tests (although it must be said that there was only limited scope for this to happen).

The parallel to the discussion in Chapter 3 is striking. There the discussion was presented as a contrast between rule-based versus exemplar-based learning. This line of argument suggests that, in post-critical period situations, the syntax–lexis tension is unavoidable when one has the simultaneous need for performance and development. The aptitude research now overlays this argument with yet further complexity since it suggests there are individual differences in the predisposition to view language learning as syntactic or lexical. That is, some learners seem to be more drawn towards a lexical, exemplar-based organization, and are readier presumably to apply rule-generated exemplars as the basis for performance. More syntactically-oriented learners, in contrast, are less drawn towards exemplars, and prefer to work with a rule-based system, compromising real-time performance, possibly, but keeping the rule-based system more open. We will pursue the implications of this congruence between information processing analyses and learner differences below.

Research into the origin of aptitude

Earlier, in discussing the assumptions that the study of aptitude makes, it was proposed that for aptitude to be of interest, it would need to be stable and (relatively) untrainable. If aptitude research can demonstrate this assumption to be justified, it suggests that a talent for foreign language learning will be fixed either at birth, or relatively early in life. In this respect Carroll (1973) speculated that aptitude might be the residue of a first language learning ability, and also that this ability fades at different rates in different people. In any case, the assumption is being made that aptitude for second language learning is connected to aptitude for first language learning.[1] Recently, it has been possible to investigate this question for the first time as a result of the existence of the Bristol Language Project (Wells 1981, 1985), which studied 125 children, born in the Bristol area between 1969 and 1972, a stratified random sample which covered the range of social classes.

Amongst other things, the project (Wells 1985) demonstrated that:

- systematicity in route of development, established by previous researchers (for example Brown (1973)) with small and not particularly representative samples, was confirmed and extended;
- development is influenced by the interactions that mother and child engage in, with mothers and children seeming to co-operate to ensure the delivery of relevant input for the child's current stage of development;
- some environments lead to more rapid developments than others, with 'extending' mothers (who accept topic nominations from the child and then help to develop them) having children whose progress is, other things being equal, more rapid, although the evidence in support of this claim is from only some areas of syntax.

But for present purposes, the most important finding was that there was very considerable variation between the children in rate of development, with the fastest children being considerable 'developmental' months (and even years) ahead of the slowest. This variation immediately questions Neufeld's Critique 1, since he is arguing that 'aptitude' is a misplaced construct, given that all native speakers become native speakers. While accepting that the course of language development is inexorable, the Bristol study demonstrates than not all native speakers progress at the same rate, suggesting that individual differences do exist (Bates *et al.* 1988), and thus that aptitude might connect with differences in rate of learning. (In passing, it should be mentioned that Carroll (1965) has always been careful to point out that aptitude tests do not predict that individuals cannot learn a language—their predictive scope is towards rate of foreign language learning.) As a result, the force of Neufeld's (1979) criticism is considerably weakened.

Another consequence of the existence of the Bristol study was that it opened up the possibility of longitudinal research, connecting the wide individual differences in rate of first language development with possible differences in foreign language aptitude. Accordingly, with considerable help from Gordon Wells, the Director of the Bristol Language Project, some 100 of the children from the Bristol study were contacted some ten to twelve years later, during the period 1983–4, and were then administered a range of aptitude tests. At the end of the school year, achievement test data was also collected using standardized measures constructed by a research team at the National Foundation for Educational Research (Dickson *et al.* 1985).

Despite the time interval involved, there were a number of significant correlations between the early first language measures and the later aptitude indices (Skehan and Ducroquet 1988). The Bristol Language Scale, a composite of a range of first language measures, produced correlations above 0.40 with subsequent aptitude, particularly with an aptitude sub-test measuring inductive language learning ability. Slightly higher correlations were obtained between more selective first language measures and aptitude. In particular, aspects of auxiliary development and the area of pronominalization correlated highest (Skehan 1989). In contrast, modality, noun phrase complexity, utterance length, number of clause constituents, and other such measures did not correlate so highly. The two higher correlating aspects of first language development, the auxiliary system and pronominalization, have been termed 'fragile syntax' by Goldin-Meadow (1982), since they are aspects that are most likely (a) to show environmental influence, i.e. to be susceptible to change in frequency of emergence and acquisition as a function of changes in input frequency, and (b) to be vulnerable to non-acquisition in extreme cases of language deprivation, such as that experienced by feral children. It is as though language aptitude connects most with non-central syntactic development. One assumes that learning a second language contains partly central aspects of language such as word order, recursion, and so on (what Goldin-Meadow termed 'resilient syntax') and partly less central aspects. It seems to be the latter which are most likely to connect with variation in aptitude and in subsequent differences in foreign language learning success. This implies that some aspects of language development do not atrophy while others do, but since the acquisition of a second language requires the whole of the system to be learned, the fact that some aspects atrophy influences the entire system.

In any case, the discovery of these connections is important for Assumption 2 (Table 8.1) regarding the stability of aptitude and its connection with first-language learning ability. Whatever seems to be implicated in foreign language aptitude does not appear to be simply the product of experience, but instead connects with underlying capacities. Although this finding does not rule out Carroll's (1973) proposal for differential fading of an initial endowment, it does render it less plausible, simply on grounds of parsimony—one can now take the initial variation and simply propose a constant value for fading to account for individual differences which are a reflection of original variation and a lower level of capacity to that which prevailed early in life.

Context of teaching and aptitude relevance

It will be recalled that one of the criticisms made of aptitude is that it applies only to formal instructional settings where there is a focus on isolated forms. The main proponent of this criticism, (Krashen 1981) draws attention to the way in which aptitude research, at the time he was writing, was almost exclusively carried out in formal settings. He concluded from this that aptitude was only relevant to such pedagogically-oriented contexts. Further, following his own proposals on the acquisition-learning distinction together with the operation of the Monitor Model, he relegated aptitude to influence only when conscious learning was concerned (and hence, to oblivion). But logically this conclusion is not warranted, since for it to be established, discriminant evidence is also necessary, that is, evidence that aptitude fails to function in informal settings.

Since Krashen's original claims, research has not been supportive of his position. In Skehan (1982) I reported on a formal context (instruction provided for army personnel), but one where the emphasis in the instruction was functional and communicative, and where the tests used to assess end-of-course performance were also communicatively oriented. As reported earlier, this research showed strong correlations between aptitude and achievement. More convincingly still, Reves (1982), researching in Israel, examined the effects of aptitude and other measures, including motivation, on a group of subjects who were studying English formally and Hebrew informally. She reported that aptitude was the strongest correlate of proficiency, exceeding all other measures, including motivation, in both contexts. Moreover, the predictive superiority in both contexts was similar, in that aptitude was just as superior in the informal context as in the formal. This suggests quite strongly that the capacities tapped by aptitude batteries are also relevant in naturalistic contexts.

This conclusion follows fairly naturally if one attends more to the componential nature of aptitude and relates it to an information-processing perspective (an argument that will be developed more fully later). Regarding the componential nature of aptitude, we have seen that phonemic coding ability is concerned with the processing of input and that grammatical sensitivity and inductive language learning ability are concerned with the organization and manipulation of linguistic material, and memory with the assimilation of new material. Broadly, instruction can be regarded as the structuring by 'experts' of the material/input which is presented and which is then to be internalized. In this view, aptitudinal capacities, faced with pedagogic material, have had their task simplified because material is being presented in a way designed to highlight its structure. One could conclude from this, using a reverse argument to Krashen's, that in these circumstances aptitude is less important because input has been organized to make its structure more accessible. In contrast, in informal contexts, where the ground has not been prepared to make generalizations and patterns salient, language learning represents more of a challenge, since it is incumbent on the learner to bring structure to unstructured material. In these circumstances, aptitude is likely to be more important. Following this analysis Reves's (1982) results are entirely to be expected.

Aptitude and acquisition-oriented research

Somewhat surprisingly, given the sheer quantity of acquisition-oriented research in recent years, investigations of the relationship of aptitude to acquisitional processes have been rare. As indicated elsewhere in this book, the emphasis has been towards establishing general findings which are meant to apply to all learners equally. Yet in principle, if development in a language requires a capacity to profit from input and restructure through the formulation of hypotheses about the structure of the target language, individual differences in aptitude could well have a major relevance to research in this area.

One study which is an exception is Robinson (1995c), who in a complex study wanted to investigate the effects of a number of independent variables. These were learning condition, difficulty of rule, and aptitude. Learning condition concerns four methods of the presentation of material: the implicit condition consisted essentially of a memory task; the incidental condition was portrayed to subjects as a comprehension task; the rule-search condition was explicitly presented as the need to induce the rule underlying some linguistic material; and the instructed condition involved teaching. The content in all of these cases was language which focused on two rules, an easy rule (subject–verb inversion with adverbs of location/movement) and a hard rule (pseudo-cleft location).[2] Finally, subjects took Parts 4 (words in sentences) and 5 (paired associates) of the Modern Languages Aptitude Test.

Two sorts of analyses were conducted of the results. Correlations were computed between the aptitude scores and scores on the criterion tests of learning which were used. Then, three ANOVAs (analyses of variance) were computed using a division of subjects into groups based on (a) whether a rule had been noticed (rule-noticers); (b) whether there was awareness of the rule (rule-aware); and (c) whether the rule could be verbalized (rule-verbalisms). These ANOVAs used aptitude scores as the dependent variable.

Results of the correlational analysis are shown in Table 8.2. Two generalizations emerge immediately from this table. First, the words in sentences scores have more significant correlations with criterion scores than the paired associates scores. Second, the presentational condition least influenced by aptitude is the incidental one. And perhaps particularly worthy of note is that the implicit condition (the memory condition) generates the highest correlation of all, but with the words in sentences aptitude tests, rather than the memory-based aptitude test. In Table 8.2 results are based on averaged correlations across easy and hard rules. Asterisks indicate significant correlations.

Presentational condition	Words in sentences	Paired associates
Implicit	.72*	.28
Incidental	.32	.23
Rule search	.49*	.47*
Instructed	.55*	.48*

Table 8.2: Correlations of aptitude scores and test results (adapted from Robinson 1995c: 321)

Clearly, aptitude is least implicated in performance where the focus is most clearly away from form and towards processing meaning (the incidental condition). The words-in-sentences sub-test enters into significant correlations with the other three conditions. What is interesting here is that all three of these conditions do have a concern with the formal elements in the rules (even the implicit condition, which led subjects to pay attention to the ordering of the elements in the stimulus material that was presented). So in all cases it was the capacity to identify sequence and organization which correlated with the more analytic component of aptitude, i.e. even when the task was portrayed as being memory-based, it was pattern identification which seemed to be the more operative ability—simple memory ability, as measured by the paired associates test, did not correlate so well. More research of this nature is needed, but these results already suggest that the language analytic aspects of aptitude may have wide-ranging and robust influences across a number of instructional conditions.

The ANOVA results, examining the tendency for rule-noticers, rule-aware subjects, and rule-verbalizers to differ in aptitude scores, corroborate these results. There were no differences in aptitude scores for the noticers/aware/verbalizers in the incidental (comprehension-based) condition, which is consistent with the lack of significant correlations which were found. The most likely condition to generate significant differences was the implicit condition (with four out of six possible results reaching significance), followed by the rule-search condition (three out of six), followed by the instructed condition (one out of six). What seemed to be happening here was that where more structure was provided, differences were less likely—the effect of instruction, in other words, was quite properly to negate the effects of aptitude. (See Skehan 1986a for an interpretation of this sort, drawing on Carroll's 1965 model of school learning.) At the other extreme, where a concern for form and sequence was associated with the least support and guidance for the learner (the implicit, memory condition), the effects of aptitude were the greatest. The learners had to draw most extensively on their own pattern-identifying resources.

These results are intriguing. They suggest that acquisitional processes do draw on aptitudinal components, and that such research may need, in the future, to be more precise as to the aptitudinal levels of the subjects who are studied. Unless this is done, considerable uncontrolled variance may question research findings. In any case, the study by Robinson (1985c) is pioneering: more research of this nature is urgently needed.

Applications of aptitude research

A worrying consequence of aptitude research is that it may reveal inequalities which teachers are powerless to alter, a conclusion which has doubtless been at the root of the distaste many have felt for such research. Perhaps as a result there is little research which tries to link aptitude to instructional method. This is a pity, since the structure of aptitude described earlier could link in very well with aptitude–treatment–interaction (ATI) research designs (Cronbach and Snow 1977; McLaughlin 1980), designs which probe whether different approaches to instruction are especially effective with particular types of learner. The assumption of such research would be that there is no single best method but that it is the combination of specific method type with specific aptitude profile which creates optimal learning conditions.

An unusual research study of this type is reported by Wesche (1981), completed within the Canadian Public Service Commission. Students were categorized according to aptitude profile. One group was identified as having particularly good memory abilities (relative to other abilities), and another group was identified as being high in verbal analytical abilities (again, relative to other areas). Some members of these groups were matched with appropriate methodologies (for the strengths concerned), and others were mismatched. Matched students did disproportionately better, and mismatched students worse. In addition, the mismatched students were unhappy about the type of instruction they were receiving. The high analytic students, for example, mismatched with a memory-oriented methodology, were bored and frustrated because they did not feel that the instruction they received was attuned to what they wanted. Wesche's findings indicate that aptitude research need not remain at an unrevealing, monolithic level, but that profile-based information could be vital for the design of effective interventionist techniques. The constructs underlying aptitude should, if they are important, connect with what goes on in the classroom, since such activities, if they follow the educational dictum of 'start from where the learners are', should try to identify how best to structure the presentation of information. An informed analysis of aptitude should be fundamental to such an endeavour.

Aptitude and processing

Carroll's four factors of aptitude

Earlier, we followed Carroll's (1965, 1991) claim that aptitude consists of four sub-components: phonemic coding ability, grammatical sensitivity, inductive language analytic ability, and memory. We can now try and relate this to some of the discussion in earlier chapters which took a processing perspective to second language acquisition. We can expand the description of the four factors as follows.

Phonemic coding ability

This is not just the capacity to make sound discrimination, but, more important, the capacity to code foreign sounds in such a way that they can be later recalled. Sound discrimination does vary between individuals, but this variation does not correlate with language learning success. What does correlate is the capacity to analyse sound in such a way that its representation enables it to be more than fleeting, allowing recall beyond immediate (and effortful) rehearsal.

Associative memory

This is the ability to make links or connections between stimuli and responses, for example, native language words and foreign language equivalents, and to develop the strength of such bonds. This interpretation of memory ability reflected the emphasis in psychology at the time the MLAT was produced, concerned as it was with relatively simple stimulus–response links, without particular concern for more complex memory organization or forms of representation. We have seen that more recent aptitude research (Skehan 1980) has expanded the conceptualization of memory considerably, to reflect some of the advances in contemporary cognitive psychology. Associative memory is now seen as one part only of this component of aptitude, and probably not the most important aspect. A capacity to memorize more auditorily complex material, together with the capacity to impose organization and structure on the material to be memorized are now seen as more powerful predictors of foreign language learning.

Grammatical sensitivity

This is the ability to understand the contribution that words make in sentences (as opposed to the ability to analyse sentences explicitly). There is a passive aspect to this ability, in that it emphasizes recognition of function, rather than explicit representation.

Inductive language analytic ability

This is the ability to examine a corpus of language material and from this to notice and identify patterns of correspondence and relationships involving either meaning or syntactic form. Basically this represents an ability to identify pattern, particularly in verbal material, whether this involves implicit or explicit rule representation. It is also a productive capacity in that the identification of pattern is seen as the prelude to being able to extrapolate from input material and go on to produce language on the basis of the pattern which has been identified.

Skehan's three factors of aptitude

In Skehan (1986a, 1989) I attempted to update the concept of aptitude and argued that it is more appropriate to view aptitude as consisting of three components: auditory ability, linguistic ability, and memory ability. Auditory ability is essentially the same as Carroll's (1965) phonemic coding ability (see the next chapter for a discussion of how this construct may be more widely applicable), and requires no more discussion at present. The second component of a three-factor view of aptitude, linguistic ability, draws together Carroll's grammatical sensitivity and inductive language learning ability. This melding is partly justified because the evidence requiring distinct factors here is not extensive (Skehan 1989). But on more logical grounds there seems no compelling reason to argue for separation so much as different degrees of emphasis. We can illustrate this by examining the component qualities of the aptitude sub-tests in this area. Three 'dimensions' seem to be operative, as shown in Figure 8.1.

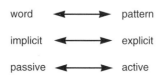

Figure 8.1: Dimensions of aptitude sub-tests

Grammatical sensitivity tends to represent the left-hand pole of each of these dimensions, while inductive language learning ability is more concerned with the right-hand side. Grammatical sensitivity allows concentration on one word (though in a larger structure), and only requires the test-taker to recognize, in whatever manner, the function the word fulfils so that it can be matched with another word. Inductive language learning operates upon longer structures and involves manipulation of a pattern at a greater degree of consciousness. But both sub-tests try to sample within the area of a general analytic ability, simply doing so in different ways, which, of course, could lead to slightly different patterns of correlation. For present purposes, though, there seems little justification in elevating what are differences in emphasis to the status of different constructs, and so the one language-related component will be used from now on.

The third component of aptitude, memory, is, in one sense, unchanged in its general nature. But we saw that there has been additional research which has complexified how memory is regarded, particularly in claiming that associational memory is only one sub-component here, and possibly not the most important one at that. Different memory abilities, for varied sorts of material, as well as memory of organized/structured material is also important. But the greatest change in how we look at memory as a component of aptitude is the result of developments outside aptitude research. It is commonplace in memory research to distinguish between coding, storage, and retrieval of material, with each of these implicating different aspects of memory. Most memory-linked aptitude research has been concerned with coding, what learners do to assimilate new material. The approach has assumed that the problem to explain is how learners can absorb the number of lexical elements that are needed to achieve communicative functionality in a language. It has been assumed that people vary in this regard, and that such variation is central to accounting for the memory sub-test correlations with foreign language proficiency tests.

We saw, though, in Chapters 2, 3, and 4 that there are changed views within cognitive psychology as to the nature of learning with structured material. In particular, the significant contrast is between rule-based and exemplar-based learning (Carr and Curren 1994). In the first case, rules are internalized and then used as the basis for 'computed' predictions. In the second, exemplars are learned directly and used for production as ready-made 'wholes'. But there is the additional possibility that rules may be used originally to generate productions, but their product then becomes an exemplar which itself is used for future production. This psychological view also complements the linguistic analysis put forward by people like Bolinger (1975) and Pawley and Syder (1983).

The significance of these changes in perspective is that within aptitude tests we now need to take the stage of retrieval much more seriously. What we need to investigate is the nature of the system which can support rapid access of a very wide repertoire of exemplars so that real-time processing is possible (see Schmidt 1992, and the discussion of fluency presented in Chapters 2 to 4). We saw, in the discussion of output and fluency, that exemplar models seemed preferable to automatization or restructuring models in that they allow different, more practical, and larger units to underpin the production of speech.

The consequence of this is that we need to consider whether there are, within aptitude, individual differences in retrieval skills which reflect the operation of memory systems. At present, we still have an encoding-dominated perspective, at least as far as the operationalization of memory measures is concerned. It may be that there are no significant differences within memory systems, so that good encoders are also good retrievers. We currently have to make this assumption. In the longer term, though, it is desirable that aptitude research explore the separate potential of more retrieval-based sub-tests. Provisionally, then, we have a reinterpretation of the role of memory within language aptitude. It is now not simply the capacity to assimilate and encode new material, it also implicates the capacity to retrieve exemplars (chunks) quite rapidly to support fluent speech production.

This three-component view of aptitude can be related to stages within a flow of information processing, as shown in Table 8.3. The table links with the models presented earlier, especially Figure 3.6.

Aptitude factor	Stage	Operations
Phonemic coding ability	Input	Noticing
Language analytic ability	Central processing	Pattern identification Generalization Restructuring Dual-coding organization
Memory	Output	Retrieval – 'computed' performance – exemplar-based performance

Table 8.3: Aptitude and processing stages

Phonemic coding ability

This is important in processing input (Skehan 1986b, 1989), handling the segmentation problem (Peters 1983), and coping with auditory material in real time, with its coding and analysis, so that it may be passed on to subsequent stages of information processing. Phonemic coding ability is concerned with the extent to which the input which impinges on the learner can become input that is worth processing, as opposed to input which may simply be an auditory blur or alternatively only partially processed. Such input processing will be important in classrooms where it is likely that structured input will be provided. But it may be even more important in informal contexts, where unstructured input, which may vary unhelpfully in acoustic quality, segmentability, and the acoustic salience of its components, will put an even greater premium on input-to-intake conversion. One can see that phonemic coding ability, in this sense:

1 is likely to be particularly important at beginning levels of language learning. At such points converting acoustic input into what might be termed processable input is crucially important, and failure in this area may mean virtually no input to deal with, and, in informal situations, the end of exposure to language learning opportunities;

2 is generally going to have a major impact upon how much comprehensible input is available for the next stage of processing. The more phonemic coding abilities succeed with the acoustic stimulus that the learner is presented with, the richer the corpus of material that will be available for subsequent analysis.

Language analytic ability

This concerns a central stage of information processing—the capacity to infer rules of language and make linguistic generalizations or extrapolations. It is here that rules develop, and restructuring occurs. The input to this stage is the product of the phonemic coding stage, and it is this material which is processed, examined for consistency of patterning, and then becomes the basis for rule formation. It is not clear exactly what structures and processes operate at this stage. If UG is still active, then we are dealing with an ability which is qualitatively different from general learning mechanisms. It may operate either directly with primary data or indirectly through the residue of its first language operation, when pattern extraction may reflect linguistic universal influences. If UG is not active, implying that language learning is not different from general learning, then more general cognitive processes of induction and deduction would be expected to play the prominent role. The correlations found in the Bristol follow-up research would suggest the former interpretation, while research to be examined in Chapter 9 would favour the latter.

Memory

Finally, as we have seen, memory, although traditionally associated with the acquisition of new information, is also concerned with retrieval, and with the way elements are stored, probably redundantly and formulaically. In this case the emphasis is towards how memory 'items' can be retrieved efficiently in real time to handle natural conversational demands. Fast-access memory systems, in other words, are what allow output to be orchestrated into fluent performance. We have also examined the proposal that people vary in the extent to which they rely upon such an accessibility-driven system. Some prefer to take a form-oriented 'computational' approach more clearly linked to rules, while others predominantly operate the meaning-based system. And in between, most people probably alternate between these two approaches, adapting to communicational conditions and task demands as appropriate. But in any case, what is implied is a form of dual-coding as the basis for language. One coding system is rule-based, creative, and flexible, but because of the processing overheads, slower. The other is memory-based, reliant on chunks, less flexible, and based on redundant storage (Bolinger 1975), but because of its basis in easy-to-assemble units, fast and convenient—the basis for native-like selection and native-like fluency (Pawley and Syder 1983). It is this retrieval side of memory that allows it to fit into a processing framework at the important output stage.

Conclusion

We started this chapter by examining the nature of the assumptions made by aptitude researchers, as well as the critiques which have been made of the concept of aptitude. Briefly, these were:

Assumption 1:	Specific talent for language
Assumption 2:	Stable, untrainable construct
Critique 1:	Everyone has aptitude
Critique 2:	Lack of understanding of aptitude tests
Critique 3:	Aptitude relates to formal contexts and learning only

We can deal with the critiques first. Regarding Critique 1, we have seen that despite the claim that everyone is the same in first-language learning ability (Neufeld 1979), there is, in fact, considerable variation in rate of acquisition (though not route, Wells 1986). In addition, there is considerable evidence of failure in second language acquisition (Bley-Vroman 1989), suggesting that there are important differences between the two areas. (See also the discussion in the next chapter on the critical period.) We have also seen that there is a relationship between the variation in rate that exists in the first language case, and foreign language aptitude test performance. In addition, we have reviewed evidence on the predictive successes of aptitude test batteries. Taken together, these points suggest that there is variation in first-language learning abilities, that there are similarities and differences between first- and second-language learning abilities; and that there is even greater variation in the second language case. Critique 1, in other words, is unwarranted.

We have reviewed, at length, the componential nature of aptitude and demonstrated that far from being a monolithic construct, its different-components make sense in relation to the nature of language learning, and can be related to an information-processing model of language. Critique 2 is thereby clearly attacked. Aptitude tests are not, in other words, simply predictive instruments which have no explanatory power. They have a rationale in relation to language learning processes, and then an even wider justification through general psychological processes. They are not arbitrary in any sense, even though the successful sub-tests from aptitude research have emerged rather inductively. We can now see, in fact, that the justification through construct validity which defends them simply required some time for the underlying theory to develop. Now that it has, we can understand their operation as well as use them predictively.

Finally, we have reviewed the only direct evidence that bears on Critique 3 (Reves 1982), and have shown that it does not support the critique. Further, on more theoretical grounds, if we take the components of aptitude to reflect different stages of the information processing of linguistic material, several factors argue for a greater involvement for aptitude in informal than formal ones. The need to process unstructured input, the need to extract systematicity and rule-governedness in non-pedagogic material, as well as the capacity to assimilate the large number of exemplars that underlie fluent performance, run directly contrary to the claim made by Critique 3 since they represent greater difficulty in informal contexts. Robinson's (1995c) acquisition-based research also questions the force of this critique.

An assessment of the two assumptions which were made is slightly more problematic. Assumption 2, though, is easy. The Politzer and Weiss (1969) evidence, together with the evidence from the follow-up research to the Bristol Language Project (Skehan 1986b) argues for stability and relative untrainability. The theoretical arguments about the meaning of the aptitude constructs and their connection with information processing add to this conclusion. However, we have not sufficiently addressed Assumption 1— whether foreign language aptitude represents a special talent for languages, unlike aptitudes for general learning. It is to that issue that we turn in Chapter 9.

Notes

1   Note that to speak of 'aptitude' for first language learning is to challenge Neufeld's (1979) claim (Critique 1, Table 5.1) that there is no evidence of variation in first-language learning abilities, variation which could manifest itself by differences in route of development or, less stringently, in rate of development.

2   The difficulty of these rules was established through careful empirical work. Even so, my reaction to them is that they are both fairly difficult, and that there is scope to base instruction on significantly easier rules than the 'easy' rule in the study.

9 Issues in aptitude theory: exceptional learners and modularity

Introduction

The previous chapter examined the nature and role of aptitude within fairly limited terms, essentially focusing on the relationship between aptitude and success in language study. In contrast, I will argue in this chapter that, far from having only a minor role, analyses of aptitude are relevant to some fundamental issues in applied linguistics, since aptitude can be seen as a rare window on the nature of the talent for language learning. Three issues, in particular, will be explored:

- The relationship between a putatively specific language learning ability, on the one hand, and general intelligence and cognitive abilities, on the other. (Is a talent for languages qualitatively different from other talents?)
- The capacity of aptitude to account for the performance of exceptional foreign language learners (as opposed to merely 'very talented' learners). (Are very talented learners simply high aptitude learners or do they have fundamentally different abilities?)
- Whether an aptitude for foreign language learning represents what is left after a first-language learning ability has faded in importance (in different rates in different people) or whether the nature of the abilities in first and foreign language learning cases is different. (Is there continuity in first and foreign language learning abilities?)

The final point brings out two other issues which will be central to this chapter: modularity in language organization, and the notion of a critical period for language learning. The central thesis of the chapter, as shown by the discussion of the above points, will be that there is modularity in the organization of first-language learning ability and foreign language aptitude, but that this modularity is differently organized. In the first language case, it is argued that the modular division is between syntax and semantics, while in the second language case it is argued that modules are most readily explicable in terms of stages of information processing, a framework which enables research into memory to be related to both aptitude and exceptional learners.

The close of a critical period, it is argued, is the point at which this changed pattern of modularity is established.

Aptitude and cognitive abilities

In the review of research in the last chapter it was argued that the construct of a specific aptitude is important in a range of language learning contexts and that it is componential, and theoretically justifiable, especially when an information-processing perspective is related to the three major aptitude components. But there is an alternative interpretation—that the correlations between aptitude tests and learning success are due not to a distinct aptitude, but instead to the operation of general cognitive abilities or intelligence (compare Assumption 1 from Chapter 8). Aptitude would correlate with proficiency because intelligence (what the aptitude tests are really measuring) is important in learning a language. It could also be the case that the correlations obtained in the follow-up study to the Bristol Language Project (Skehan 1986b, 1989) reflected the more intelligent children making faster progress learning their first language, and then making faster progress in learning a foreign language. The obtained correlation would then be accounted for by an underlying cause, intelligence, which affected both sets of measures.

Studies of the aptitude–intelligence relationship

Not surprisingly, there have been numerous empirical studies which have investigated the relationship between IQ (as the prime example of cognitive abilities) and language aptitude. The studies can be divided into those that are simply correlational, and those which use more sophisticated statistical techniques, principally factor analysis. In the former category, a typical study is that of Gardner and Lambert (1972) who reported a median correlation of 0.43 between IQ and aptitude in an unselected population of secondary (high) school children. Similarly, in Skehan (1982) I reported a relationship of 0.44 for a heterogeneous population of adult language learners. Both these figures suggest that while aptitude and intelligence are related, and indeed have a significant degree of overlap, they are not the same as one another and each makes separate contributions to the prediction of successful language learning. In each case, also, the aptitude measures generate higher correlations with the language proficiency measures than do the IQ measures.

In the latter category, Wesche *et al.* (1982) conducted a factor analytic study probing the aptitude–intelligence relationship, with a battery consisting of the Thurstone PMA (Primary Mental Abilities) sub-tests, and four of the tests from the MLAT. They (and see also Carroll 1983) found that a three-factor solution could account for their data, with the three factors labelled as verbal knowledge, general intelligence, and memory-within-aptitude batteries. Further analyses revealed evidence of a second-order, general factor which seemed to subsume all three more specific first-order factors. Wesche *et al.* (1982) label this a general intelligence factor.

A broadly similar result was reported by Sasaki (1991) who used confirmatory factor analytic techniques to investigate the relationship between aptitude and intelligence and the functioning of these factors in relation to second language proficiency. For the first of these research studies, she was able to establish that a second-order factor solution was the most satisfactory for her cognitive abilities data, with a general cognitive factor underlying three first-order factors, labelled respectively, aptitude, verbal intelligence, and reasoning. So, while these three first-order factors emerged separately, the hierarchical structure emerged at the next stage of the analysis, implying that the three first-order factors have strong relationships to one another. In relation to the second question she addressed, Sasaki found that the second-order cognitive ability factor correlated at 0.65 with second language proficiency, indicating that 42 per cent of the variance concerned was shared.

The different studies described in this section are reasonably consistent. All investigators have found significant relationships between aptitude and IQ, but the levels found have varied somewhat, from what might be called a low to moderate level of correlation (Gardner and Lambert 1972; Skehan 1982), to a moderate to strong relationship (Wesche *et al.* 1982; Sasaki 1991). It is also worth noting, in passing, that both Gardner and Lambert and I report data on fairly unselected groups, while Wesche *et al.* and Sasaki report on subjects who were streamed in one way or another, and are not so representative of the population in general. Perhaps those who are educational successes are more able to mobilize cognitive abilities to help in the task of language learning—metacognitive strategy management, so to speak. A further point to note is that the studies suggesting a stronger relationship between aptitude and intelligence require second-order factor analysis to bring this out, in each case reporting first-order factors which suggest some degree of separation. One can conclude, provisionally, that aptitude is not completely distinct from general cognitive abilities, as represented by intelligence tests, but it is far from the same thing.

A processing interpretation of the factor analyses

Things become more interesting when we regard foreign language aptitude as componentially structured. We can represent the factors extracted in the Wesche *et al.* (1982) and Sasaki (1991, 1996) studies as in Table 9.1.

Wesche *et al.*	Sasaki
First language verbal knowledge	Verbal intelligence
Abstract reasoning ability	Reasoning
Memory component of aptitude	Foreign language aptitude

Table 9.1: Factor-analytic studies of aptitude

There are clear similarities here, with reasoning appearing in each case, and aptitude also appearing twice, but with a greater emphasis on memory in the Wesche *et al.* study. The verbal area is represented on each occasion, although in Wesche *et al.* it links with first-language verbal knowledge, while Sasaki (1991, 1996) is concerned with verbal intelligence. So we can conclude that there is a certain degree of similarity in findings when a large number of cognitive and aptitude measures are factor analysed. In each case, there is evidence for some degree of separation for the aptitude construct and measures, but in the context of correlated factors, and a one-factor second-order solution.

What is most interesting in the Sasaki study, though, is how strongly the different aptitude measures relate to the relevant underlying factor. The measure representing language analysis is strongly implicated in the factor. In contrast, measures of paired associates (memory) and sound–symbol association (phonemic coding ability) are only weakly implicated. Essentially Sasaki's (1991) result, indicating three correlated first-order factors (and a one-factor second-order solution), which implies that aptitude is best situated within cognitive abilities, is only achieved at the cost of accepting weak involvement for measures of memory and phonemic coding ability. Similarly, in Wesche *et al.*'s results, the main measures of memory (paired associates) and phonemic coding ability (phonetic script) have amongst the lowest commonalties of the variables analysed, suggesting that while more cognitive aspects of aptitude have connections with general cognitive abilities, this is less true for memory and phonemic coding ability.

To return to the analysis presented earlier, what appears to be involved here is that aptitude and cognitive abilities seem to be closest to one another when one is dealing with central cognitive factors. They are more distinct when one is concerned with how input is handled in the first place (phonemic coding ability), and with how a memory system operates (paired associates). Further, when one looks at the central cognitive factors, the overlap between the two areas is very significant, but not complete, suggesting that the central processing component may draw upon general cognitive abilities to a large extent, but that there may be room for some involvement of a more specialized language faculty, potentially identifiable as the residue of Universal Grammar. To put this another way, the evidence from the research investigating the relationship between language and cognitive abilities provides support for both of the approaches we have discussed—the language-is-special viewpoint, and the language-is-the-consequence-of-general-ability viewpoint. We will return to this issue towards the end of the chapter, when the range of evidence on the issue of specialness versus general ability will be discussed. For the moment, the most striking (and new) conclusion to draw is that, in the case of foreign language aptitude, separation between specific and general abilities seems to be clearest where 'peripheral' processing factors are concerned. Drawing on the discussion from the end of Chapter 8, input and output each relate less to general cognitive functioning than do more central aspects of aptitude.

Exceptional learners

In this section we will look at a different source of evidence, that deriving from exceptional learners. This provides a different perspective on whether there is a separation between linguistic and cognitive abilities. The question which underlies this discussion will be whether there can be an exceptional talent for learning languages, qualitatively different from simply high aptitude. If there is, such a talent would suggest that there is something special about the nature of language learning, at least for some people some of the time. The evidence, as we will see, will extend and modify the conclusions drawn in the previous section, and demonstrate that we need to link language learning talent to the literature on neurolinguistics (Eubank and Gregg 1995), as well as recast modularity by relating it to earlier discussions of memory. We will look at exceptional L2 learners, relatively unsuccessful L2 learners, and then exceptional L1 users.

Exceptional L2 learners

There are five major studies to consider in this section, all of them focused on individuals or small groups of learners at the case study level. The first of these, CJ, a 29-year-old graduate student in education at the time of the research (Obler 1989; Novoa *et al.* 1988) had learned several languages post-pubertally, quickly, and to near-native proficiency (as confirmed by native-speaker judges). He had studied French and German at school, and evidently used the periods when he stayed in these countries to increase his proficiency very effectively. Subsequently, he learned Moroccan Arabic through formal and informal exposure, and then rapidly acquired Spanish and Italian during relatively brief stays in those countries.

Ioup *et al.* (1994) studied Julie, a British woman who emigrated to Egypt at 21 when she married an Egyptian. As Ioup *et al.* say, 'She has never had any formal instruction in Arabic, and therefore, can neither read nor write the language' yet she was judged by friends as having achieved native-like levels in about two-and-a-half years (Ioup *et al.* 1994: 77).

Schniederman and Desmarais (1988a, b) studied two learners, AB and XY, both selected because they had learned at least one language to native-like proficiency after puberty. AB was assessed (through native-speaker ratings and grammaticality-judgement tests) as native-like in French, and also fluent in Italian and German. XY had similar achievements in French, could pass as a native in Spanish, and was very fluent in German. Both AB and XY were interested in, and enjoyed learning languages.

Humes-Bartlo (1989) studied third- to fifth-grade children in New York, focusing on children who were judged to be fast or slow learners. Fast learners were those who, after being categorized as limited English proficiency students, were able to pass the screening procedure for entry to (non-supported) English classrooms after less than three years of schooling. Children who had had more than three years of schooling, but failed to pass the screening test, were assigned to the slow group.

Finally, Smith and Tsimpli (1995) studied Christopher, a young man who, despite being brain damaged and mentally retarded, demonstrated exceptional talent in second language learning. Christopher came to the attention of the researchers precisely because he had shown such talents (with knowledge of well over ten languages), and the researchers then probed the nature of the talent further by investigating how he dealt with new second languages as well as an artificial language.

Similarities between learners

Despite study-to-study variation in methodology, a number of themes emerge clearly. First of all, the outstanding learners did not seem to have exceptional intelligence and cognitive ability. Where IQ scores were obtained, they tended to be above average, but not markedly so. CJ, for example had an IQ of 107, while AB and XY had scores of 116 (although there was a verbal-to-performance IQ discrepancy of 15 points: verbal 121 to performance 106, in each case). The picture is less clear in Humes-Bartlo's research, with sub-test information only being available: fast learners were distinguished by their vocabulary knowledge and their performance on a verbal analogies test, while slow learners were the ones who performed higher on arithmetic and block design sub-tests, a result indirectly consistent with the verbal-performance IQ discrepancy reported by Schniederman and Desmarais (1988a, b). Other general cognitive tests are consistent with this picture of relatively ordinary IQ performance by the outstanding learners. CJ was not at all outstanding on verbal abstraction, and he only scored at the 50th percentile on the MLAT words in sentences sub-test, suggesting that he did not have any outstanding ability in the syntactic domain. Finally, Christopher did very poorly on performance and spatial tests of intellectual functioning, scoring at 75 or 76 on the Raven matrices, and achieving, at different times, scores of 42, 67, and 52 on the performance section of the Weschler Intelligence Scale for Children

(WISC). In contrast, he achieved scores on the verbal section of 89, 102, and 98.

In contrast, all the exceptional learners did outstandingly well in a number of areas of memory functioning. CJ, for example, did very well on all the MLAT tests involving memory. He was not simply good, but exceptional in areas such as the learning of new codes, simple pattern analysis and learning, and most notably of all, the retention of verbal material after a time interval. With the other memory tests, he generally performed at a high level in terms of published norms. With retention, he seemed in a class by himself, able to recall material to high levels weeks, after the original learning, and when there was no particular emphasis in the learning which would have allowed him to know that retention was going to be important. Interestingly, CJ performed at an average level on the Digit Span test, a test of short-term memory. AB and XY, faced with a slightly different collection of memory tests, also did very well indeed, performing extremely well (and above their IQ levels) on the Weschler Memory Test, the California Verbal Learning Test, and the Digit Symbol Test from the Weschler Adult Intelligence Scale (WAIS), and also very highly on the memory-linked MLAT sub-tests. Humes-Bartlo's (1989) fast subjects, too, were distinguished by their performance on an associative memory test, but not by a digit span test, or a memory-for-designs test. Julie, although not tested formally, reported very good memory and great ease in learning new vocabulary. Interestingly, her spoken Arabic was rich in conventionalized language, which as Ioup *et al.* (1994) point out, is claimed by Yorio (1989) to often distinguish the non-native speaker from the native at high proficiency levels. Christopher (Smith and Tsimpli 1995) as we will see, achieved high performance precisely because of his outstanding memory abilities. Despite the poor scores mentioned earlier on performance-based IQ measures, he achieved a score of 121 on the Peabody Picture Vocabulary Test.

These results, then, add up to a picture of the outstanding learner as being very good at assimilating new material. The emphasis does not seem to be on high analytic skills with language, but rather on dealing with relatively simple codes which can be learned and operated quickly, and which then can be the basis for the retention of material. Pattern analysis at a superficial level seems to be important, but the key seems to be the capacity to deal with large quantities of material to be memorized quickly and easily, abilities demonstrated clearly by CJ and Christopher, who, even amongst this group, seem to be the outstanding language learners, as indexed by their speed of language learning and the number of different languages involved.

Neuropsychological factors

An issue posed at the beginning of this section was whether there is any discontinuity between what might be termed the 'talented' learner, and the 'very good' learner, i.e. the learner with generally very high aptitude test scores. The previous investigators are essentially rejecting such an 'extension' interpretation of talent. In characterizing the talented learner as (a) achieving qualitatively different levels of success, (b) with relative ease and speed, and (c) on the basis of a very particular cognitive profile (crucially, outstanding verbal retentive memory), the claim is essentially that something different is at work. A number of the researchers appeal to neuropsychological factors, such as Geschwind and Galaburda's (1985) proposals on abnormal neuropsychological development which results from testosterone affecting a cluster of features localized in the cortex at a place susceptible to influence at a particular point during the course of foetal development. An excess of testosterone at this point leads to unusual cell development in certain areas of the left hemisphere, and in corresponding areas of the right hemisphere. Cells become more differentiated and have more complicated synaptic connections. In other words, Geschwind and Galaburda are proposing that, in the context of the human brain being involved, with the neurological sites underlying language ordinarily located in the left hemisphere, there are clear individual differences in the degree of lateralization that is possible, and also its nature. As a result, a range of behaviours for which the cortical sites in question are important, either directly or through their connections with other areas, develop abnormal potential.

Clearly, at this stage of the development of neurolinguistics we are in no position to understand the direct consequences for language (or any other area) of such different patterns of cell development. Instead, it is more meaningful, in the first instance, to follow Geschwind and Galaburda's proposal that the functional consequence of such an influence is likely to be that a cluster of features co-occur including an abnormal talent for language development. If consistent co-occurrences can be found, they offer supportive evidence for linkages between the different features from the cluster. As a result, researchers into exceptional learners have examined whether their subjects are unusually likely to possess more than simply the language-related feature from the cluster.

The complete set of features consists of:

- twins (in the family)
- left-handedness (in the family)
- problems with the immune system, leading to eczema, hives, allergies, and so on
- talent for languages
- correspondingly weak areas, frequently mathematical and spatial abilities
- possible schizophrenia (in the family)
- possible homosexuality (in the family).

CJ exhibited virtually all of these characteristics, while AB, XY, and to a lesser extent Julie, also matched the criteria to an unusual degree. So it would seem that if the Geschwind hypothesis on the influence of testosterone on patterns of cerebral lateralization and consequent behavioural function is valid, then a major determinant of foreign language learning talent is that the area of the left cerebral cortex which serves verbal memory, retention, pattern extraction, and simple code learning was in the process of development when unusual amounts of testosterone became available, for whatever reason, and influenced the nature of its structure. One assumes (Geschwind and Galaburda 1985) that the result was a different pattern in this area of cell assemblies which are particularly propitious for language development.

Even so, this is hardly a definitive account since it pieces together a reasonable interpretation from a number of different sources of evidence which then have to be assembled into a coherent picture. For example, what has been shown is that people identified as talented language learners show this cluster. It would also be important to identify individuals first because they manifest the cluster, and then examine whether people so identified are talented learners. So far, this has not been done. In any case, we can conclude this section by accepting that there is suggestive evidence that an unusual degree of language learning talent may be mediated by particular patterns of neuropsychological development. Further, such learners seem to be essentially memory-driven learners in terms of their capacities, but this is linked with an interest in the form of language. The exceptional learners do not seem to be exceptional in two of the three areas which have emerged from aptitude research (phonemic coding ability and language analytic ability), but seem to 'confine' their exceptional nature to the third. They seem to be an extreme and successful case of one of the learner types I proposed in Skehan (1986c). In the conclusion to this chapter, I will try to relate such unusual learners to the more general continuum of language learning ability that was the main focus in the first section.

Unsuccessful learners

In the previous section we examined learners so successful as to raise the question as to whether they were qualitatively different from people who are simply very good at languages. This section will examine the same basic idea, but at the other end of the ability range. Here the basic issue is to identify learners who, on the basis of their general abilities, ought, in theory, to be able to learn a language but in practice do not seem able to do so.

An early example of such research is that of Pimsleur (1968) who claimed that up to 30 per cent of children underachieved significantly because of inferior auditory abilities which prevented them from exploiting their cognitive and aptitudinal potential. Pimsleur *et al.* (1966) advocated the use of aptitude tests to screen such learners, coupled with the provision of remedial programmes. In this way, he thought that the relatively self-contained reason for the under-achievement could be removed, and the children could then perform at relatively normal levels.

Ioup (1989) was also interested in unsuccessful learners where there is no obvious reason for the lack of achievement. In a case study, she compared an unsuccessful learner (Jeanne) with a successful learner (Minh). She showed that the two learners did not differ from one another on a variety of cognitive tests, for example, in terms of IQ. The area which did separate them, however, was memory, particularly verbal memory, and more particularly retention after a time interval. This suggests that Jeanne was unsuccessful because she lacked the very abilities that made the talented learners such as CJ so successful.

Interestingly, Jeanne was also a poor speller, an ability linked to the phonemic coding ability component of aptitude. This, in turn, links up with some interesting recent work by Sparks and his associates (Sparks and Ganschow 1991; Sparks *et al.* 1992). Their basic research approach has been to examine populations of (a) unsuccessful learners and (b) dyslexics, by means of batteries of cognitive tests. Sparks and Ganschow propose that the two groups resemble one another to a striking degree, in that profiles of scores obtained by each group are indistinguishable from one another (a case of 'the null hypothesis strikes back') but clearly distinct from populations of normal language learners.

This leads Sparks *et al.* (1991,1992) to propose that the problems faced by the dyslexic in reading are close to those faced by unsuccessful language learners. It will be recalled, in this respect, that the phonemic coding ability component of aptitude was characterized as the capacity to make sound–symbol associations, and the capacity to code sounds in such a way that they could be retained for more than a few seconds. In addition, Carroll (1973) has speculated that native-language spelling ability is implicated in this area (one of the problems that Ioup's (1989c) Jeanne showed). This syndrome suggests that the capacity to exploit spelling correspondences (the coding system that literacy provides us with) to make units of verbal stimuli on the one hand, and the ability to process complex series of sounds on the other, are related. Put this way, the dyslexic's problems are that the words on the page do not easily form units (which could be retained), whereas the low aptitude student's problem is being unable to impose structure on sound so that it can be retained. Both the low-aptitude learner and the dyslexic are therefore unable to profit from print-mediated sound, and seem to lack any skills with which to process such stimuli and improve.

Sparks and Ganschow (1991) propose the Linguistic Coding Deficit Hypothesis to explain these findings, suggesting that the two groups in question have a fundamental processing problem. In terms of aetiology, one possibility is (Sparks *et al.* 1991, 1992) that dyslexics have a mild level of neurological impairment. This claim is based on evidence that cell structure in dyslexics has often been found to be slightly abnormal in certain left hemisphere areas, with the presumption being that these areas are particularly important in the sort of coding of sound that phonemic coding ability tests, and dyslexia assessment techniques measure. So here again the extreme end of the language learning continuum fits into a general conceptualization of aptitude, but at the same time suggests a qualitatively different level of performance which is constrained by patterns of neurological development.

Successful and unsuccessful learners and the nature of aptitude

We can now try to conclude the sections on successful and unsuccessful learners by offering a diagram, Figure 9.1, showing the relative importance of the different components of aptitude at different levels of language proficiency.

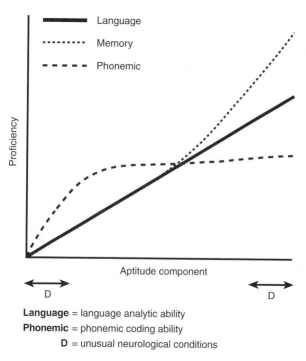

Figure 9.1: The relationship between aptitude components and proficiency level

The purpose of this diagram is to represent the discussion of the last few pages schematically. It is not based on clear evidence at all stages, since research has not been conducted which systematically probes the relationship between aptitude components and language learning success. But it tries to be consistent with the evidence that has been reviewed.

Basically, the diagram suggests that the Language Analytic Ability component (LAA) of aptitude has a monotonic, essentially linear relationship with success—this component of aptitude is equally important at all stages.

Importantly, though, the diagram in this form proposes that the relationship between LAA and proficiency is limited, at the 'top' end, to the 'very good' proficiency level, the highest proficiency level that LAA, in itself, will allow. So while every increase in LAA is helpful, it does not produce an exceptionally successful learner, comparable to CJ and Christopher. In contrast, Phonemic Coding Ability (PCA), which is the highest curve vertically in the early stages, is of greatest importance at that time. Subsequently, it plateaus, indicating that it functions as a threshold, and that, once it has served its purpose, its contribution to language learning success at higher proficiency levels is minimal.

Memory (M) is the most difficult component of aptitude to represent. It is important at all stages, in fact, and is hypothesized to have a reasonably linear relationship with success until an advanced level is reached. At that point, however, it becomes even more important, as shown by the steeper portion of the 'C' curve in the top right of the diagram. It clearly surpasses LAA in importance and becomes the determining factor for those unusual people who may achieve native-like command of a second language—those who solve Pawley and Syder's (1983) two puzzles of native-like selection and native-like fluency, and who satisfy Yorio's (1989) condition of using idiomatic language effectively. Finally, immediately below the x axis, the two D lines indicate the areas where unusual neurological conditions may have a strong influence on the level of language learning success that is attainable. They suggest that there is a normal distribution of aptitude between these points, but that beyond them qualitatively different neurological structures support exceptional second language learning at one end and constrain it at the other.

Far more research is, of course, needed to make this diagram more than a convenient schematic representation. It has been presented so as to be provocative of the sort of diagram it would be useful to have. When more direct research is available, especially with learners at the extremes, it may be possible to chart the relationships involved on more than a schematic basis. We will return to the issues underlying the diagram in the conclusion.

Exceptional language users

The previous section examined unusual second language learners. This section will look at exceptional first language users. These will provide a new perspective on the relationship between syntax and other cognitive abilities, since what the language users who form the case studies of this section have in common is, to use Curtiss' terms, a 'dissociation of language and cognition'. They each manifest grammatical acquisition in the context of severe cognitive deficit.

First of all, there is Antony, a six- to seven-year-old child who had an estimated IQ in the range of 50–56 (Curtiss 1977, 1982, 1988; Curtiss and Yamada 1981). What is surprising about Antony is that despite this very low cognitive level, many aspects of his language and language acquisition appeared normal. Speech emerged at one year, and by three years 'full sentences' were reported. His language was quite complex syntactically and morphologically, including, for example, pronoun use, complex complementation, relativization, and range of auxiliary development. Semantically, however, the picture was very different. He frequently made inappropriate lexical choices for example, 'We saw them on the *birthday*' (for 'cake') (Curtiss 1982: 295). He also had disruptive comprehension problems which were word-based. Nor was he good at making the correct inferences from what was said to him. The result of this was that Antony's speech seemed fluent and complex, but semantically unengaged. The implication seems to be that syntax, in his case, has developed fairly autonomously, and has not been integrated into a user system with any corresponding competence in semantics, the general expression of meaning, or communication.

A similar case is that of Laura (Curtiss 1989; Yamada 1981). Laura, too, is a retarded adolescent (IQ of 44) who none the less shows impressive verbal skills. She produces complex language (as with Antony, giving evidence of relativization, pronominalization, complementation, and so on). In addition, she uses richer lexical devices, but these are not really used appropriately: 'The police pulled my Mother an' so I said he would never remember them as long as we live'. She lacks number concepts. Her memory is extremely limited, and her logical reasoning is at a pre-operational level. So, once again, a wide range of complex syntax is available, but it does not link in any effective way with the expression of meanings, suggesting as before that the two areas can develop in dissociation.

Finally, Rick (Curtiss 1988), a 15-year-old mentally retarded boy, exhibited a very similar pattern of abilities to Antony and Laura. He, too, could produce complex syntax, but had only limited lexical abilities, and had difficulty in expressing propositional thought. He tended also to rely on a number of idiomatic elements in his conversation.

A comparable situation arises with two more general patterns of disability, Turner's Syndrome and Williams's Syndrome. In each case (Jackendoff 1993) there is severe cognitive retardation, with some specific areas of difficulty (for example, visual-spatial ability) but language development is either normal for the age of the child (Turner's) or even slightly more advanced (Williams's). In each case, then, language is able to develop with some independence from cognition. Comparable performance has also been reported for what are termed 'chatterbox' children (Cromer 1991) and hyperlexics (Cossu and Marshall 1986).

In contrast, there are also cases where there is specific impairment for language associated with normal cognition. Studies of aphasics come into this category (Karmiloff-Smith 1992), as do those of autistics (Frith 1991). But perhaps the most striking example of such a dissociation is the family studied by Gopnik (1994) and Gopnik and Crago (1991) who show a pattern of language deficit described by Jackendoff (1993: 114) as 'a classic instance of the inheritance of a dominant gene: those who have the gene are language impaired and have a 50 per cent chance of passing it on to their descendants'. In the most striking example, one member of fraternal twins was so afflicted while the other was not. Affected individuals, although able to cope with some aspects of language, have generalized difficulties with morphology, a problem which resists correction and instruction, and which is stable throughout the lifespan (Jackendoff 1993). As Gopnik and Crago say, 'apparent competence exhibited by the adults appears to be a result of lexical learning strategies rather than the construction of rules' (1991: 47), and further 'grammatical rule-processing and memorization are two psychologically, linguistically, and neurolinguistically distinct processes, one of which can be impaired relative to the other' (Gopnik 1994: 40).

We have now reviewed multiple sources of evidence for modularity in first and second language acquisition. In the first language case, the basis for modularity is the contrast between syntax and semantics. In the second language case, the opposition is between stages of information processing (input, central processing, output). The evidence is summarized in Table 9.2. (The asterisked cases are covered in this chapter.)

First language		Second language		
Independence of		Independence of		
Syntax	Semantics	Input	Central processing	Output
Antony*, Laura*, Rick*	Aphasics	Jeanne*		CJ*
Williams's children*	Autistics	Sparks's research*		XY*
Turner's children*	Gopnik's family*			AB*
Chatterbox children	Genie*			Christopher*
Hyperlexics	Chelsea*			Julie*
				Humes-Bartlo's research*

Table 9.2: Evidence supporting modularity in language acquisition

The first language data reveals the extent of the evidence that syntax and semantics can develop in independence of one another, and that a plausible interpretation is that a syntax module exists which can function independently. In most cases, fortunately, this dissociation is not significant since syntax and semantics can develop in harmony. But the potential is there, and this view is consistent with a 'pre-wired' interpretation of a human capacity for language in which there is a qualitative difference between acquisition of language and learning in other domains (Eubank and Gregg 1995).

The second language situation shows a marked contrast, in two ways. First, the evidence for modularity suggests that stages of information processing are fundamental (offering some support to the analyses of aptitude presented earlier). Second, the evidence is uneven, with a number of powerful case studies in support of memory, some research supportive of the input stage, and nothing to demonstrate the independence of unusual conditions for central processing. In effect, though, this is consistent with the 'normal aptitude' interpretation of the role of a language analytic capacity presented earlier, and the way specificity of foreign language aptitude (and separation from cognition) is more clearly seen in 'peripheral' areas.

The evidence in support of a memory-based interpretation of exceptionality and modularity in the second language case is particularly striking. To be exceptionally good at second or foreign language learning seems to require possession of unusual memory abilities, particularly the retention of verbal material. Exceptional L2 ability does not seem to rest upon unusual talent with rule-based aspects of the language, but rather on a capacity to absorb very large quantities of verbal material, in such a way that they become available for actual language use. As Smith and Tsimpli (1995) say, in relation to Christopher, the most striking case study in the group:

> ... we suggest that whereas in normal cases lexical learning is just one part of linguistic achievement, in Christopher's case it appears to predominate over all other domains. It could therefore be that the unusual speed which characterises his second language learning and the ease with which he switches from one language to another reflect a process of access and selection taking place entirely within the lexical component.
>
> (ibid.: 120)

and

> It ... highlights the mismatch between his lexical and morphological prowess on the one hand, and his syntactic and pragmatic limitations on the other. His lexicon is normal or, in some dimensions, enhanced; his other linguistic abilities are inhibited by problems of processing load.
>
> (ibid.: 188)

This is entirely consistent with the approaches to memory from earlier in this book. It has been argued that language itself is more memory-based than was previously appreciated (Bolinger 1975), an insight confirmed by more recent studies of corpus linguistics (Stubbs 1996). It was also argued that language performance, too, is also heavily memory and accessibility dependent (Pawley and Syder 1983, Widdowson 1989), with pressures of real-time communication (Bygate 1988). This was seen to be consistent with the research into task-based performance by second language learners (Skehan and Foster 1997) where tensions and trade-offs existed between fluency, accuracy, and complexity. In a sense, therefore, a prominent memory-based analysis in the second language case is almost inevitable—accessibility and fast access are integral to all 'older' language performance, first or second.

But this analysis requires one more piece in the puzzle—what, or rather when, is the discontinuity between 'younger' and 'older'? Or, to put this another way, one can ask whether there is a critical period for language development, and whether the close of such a period marks the separation between the two types of modularity.

The Critical Period Hypothesis

The existence of a critical period for language learning has enormous theoretical interest since it is central to obtaining any understanding of the human mind. It would be consistent with the existence of an LAD (Chomsky 1986), implying that humans are innately equipped for language. More important, it would suggest a genetically-influenced pattern for language development, and a qualitative contrast between language and cognition. But there are practical implications, too. We will review these briefly before going on to consider the theoretical and empirical issues.

Practical implications

There are three main practical implications. First of all, knowledge of the existence of a critical period, if this is associated with constraints on ultimate attainment in foreign language learning, should lead to a certain realism as to what is achievable in foreign language study. If the critical period is essential for the attainment of native-like competence, then later learning should be judged by objectives which are more limited. Second, if a critical period exists, this would support arguments for the introduction of language study early in the school curriculum, to take advantage of any special language learning talent that might exist. Third, to the extent that knowledge of a critical period is available, this might have implications for what are conceived as being appropriate instructional methodologies. It seems that at the ending of a critical period more general cognitive abilities are drawn on during the course of language learning, and so instruction should be attuned to such abilities. If a critical period did not exist, then we would not need to change approaches to language instruction so that they contrast with the conditions of first language development. If these conditions were effective with first language learners, and if the critical period has not disappeared, then similar approaches in the foreign language classroom might pay dividends.

The rest of this section will first survey the evidence on the existence of a critical period, then discuss explanations and theories which have been proposed for it.

Evidence on the Critical Period Hypothesis

Following the framework suggested in Long's (1990) extensive review of maturational constraints on language development, this section is organized to cover (a) first language development and (b) later language development.

First language development

One source of evidence for a sensitive period is the existence of maturational schedules of development in the first language. There are striking and well-attested similarities in speed and route of development, transitional structures used, error types, and so on. There is also a general lack of an effect for different types of environment, and a lack of correlation between IQ and first language development, suggesting that language and other cognitive developments take place independently. These factors suggest some process of unfolding, imperviousness to the environment, and learning 'coming from within'. While they are not direct evidence of a critical period, they are circumstantially supportive.

Against these arguments, though, one should discuss some evidence which does not fit so well. Wells (1986), for example, while confirming many claims on invariant developmental sequences from the general first-language development literature, also demonstrates that there is considerable variation in rate of first language development. While one can propose that the critical period does not need to be exactly the same age in every child (just as all children do not grow at the same rate or stop growing at the same time) it is interesting that there should be as much variation as there is. Wells (1985) similarly draws attention to environmental influences on the course of language development, suggesting that 'extending' mothers have children whose first language development is more rapid. Wells (1986) suggests that such mothers accept the conversational topics nominated by their children, and then 'say interesting things about the nominated topic'. In this way, meaningful interaction is associated with faster syntactic development, and so the environment counts for something. Other reviews of the effects of maternal speech are mixed in their claims, with some suggesting that the environment does have an effect (Barnes *et al.* 1983) and others not (Gleitman *et al.* 1984).

A different approach to variation in first language acquisition is to draw attention to styles of first language development. Nelson (1981), for example, discusses the way referential and expressive mothers may facilitate or hold back first language development in their children depending on whether or not the child is 'matched' to the mother's communication style. Best of all, evidently, for speedy first language development, is to be a referential child of a referential mother. Bates *et al.* (1988) similarly discuss different first language styles, drawing attention to the way some children seem more syntactically biased, while others are more lexical in orientation, but with all the children moving between stages where one then the other of these orientations predominates.

These sources of evidence suggest that, while a critical period for language development does exist, one must also take account of variation in rate of development (with this having some possible environmental linkage), and also different styles of development, although route of development still seems to be invariant. These would then be aspects of a critical period which would require explanation.

Pursuing the case of first language development, Lenneberg (1967), the most prominent advocate of a critical period, advanced two main sources of supporting evidence. First, he reviewed cases of recovery from traumatic aphasia in childhood. He reported that children affected by aphasia, and/or neurological insult prior to puberty had a good chance of recovery of language function. He proposed that plasticity in brain function prior to puberty, including the capacity of the right hemisphere to take over left hemisphere functions, made this possible. Second, he reported that, in the case of Down's syndrome children, in whom language development proceeds more slowly than with normal children, evidence of continued progress after puberty (for which there may still be scope) is not great. This, too, he takes as consistent with the claim that, once puberty is reached, neurological flexibility for language is lost.

Later language development

There are three main sources of evidence relating to language acquisition after the early years: second language acquisition; hearing impaired children and the acquisition of American Sign Language (ASL), and the case of feral children. As regards the first, there have been a number of studies which have examined the relationship between age and second language performance, for example, Oyama (1978) and Patkowski (1980), and the general consensus from such studies has been that there is reasonable evidence in support of a critical period, most clearly in the area of phonology (Long 1990). Even so, there are dissenting voices (Singleton 1989; Bialystok and Hakuta 1994; Kellerman 1996, for example) who suggest that the evidence is not strong enough to sustain the claims which have been made, and that other non-critical period explanations of the findings are possible. The most prominent recent empirical contribution is by Johnson and Newport 1991; Newport 1990; Johnson 1992), who report that there is a roughly linear relationship between age and language learning success until the onset of puberty. A typical set of findings is shown in Figure 9.2.

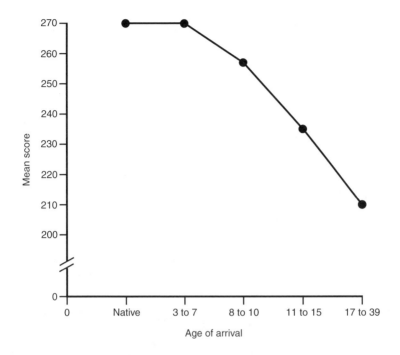

Figure 9.2: Age of arrival in US and correct score on a test of English grammar (from Johnson and Newport 1989)

The curve shows that between the age of seven or so and young adulthood there is an inverse relationship, a consistent decline in test performance. Looking at this data quantitatively, Johnson and Newport (1989) report a correlation of –.87 between age on arrival and performance in English for subjects in the age range three to fifteen years, and a correlation of –.16 for those between 17 and 39. In each case the older the age on arrival, the lower the performance in English. Prior to fifteen or so, age on arrival is the predictor of performance, whereas afterwards it has little significance since the correlation of –.16 represents a close-to-zero relationship which accounts for only a tiny proportion of shared variance.[1] Johnson (1992) also establishes consistency of results when performance was measured in the written mode. This study goes some way to countering Bialystok and Hakuta's (1994) claims that performance decrements for older learners might have been due to attentional and endurance factors which give younger test takers an advantage.

Johnson and Newport (1989) contrast two hypotheses to account for these data: the Exercise Hypothesis ('use it or lose it'), and the Maturational State Hypothesis (the Critical Period Hypothesis that humans possess a special capacity for language learning early in life). They conclude that their results support the Maturational State Hypothesis, so providing support for the contention that the waning of a special capacity has dire consequences for language learning after puberty. They make two additional and important points. First, the decline in abilities is gradual and not sudden, as is made clear by the shape of the curve in Figure 9.2. This means that the start of the decline occurs well before (say) the age of 15, but is not really affected by any sudden threshold—the capacity to learn languages diminishes slowly. In their critique of Johnson and Newport (1989), Bialystok and Hakuta fail to address this point, and as a result spend considerable time attacking what is essentially a straw man—the quest for sudden physiological changes which might correlate with the sudden close of the critical period. Second, language learning is still possible after puberty but it is less efficient and wider individual differences exist than in the case of first language acquisition (although in Johnson and Newport (1989) the reported individual differences in first language development reported by Wells (1986) are not particularly discussed).

In addition to their basic correlational study, Johnson and Newport (1989) also explore whether variables other than age could account for the inverse linear relationship found prior to age 15, and the lack of an age relationship thereafter. They are able to show that formal instruction is not an important factor, whether in the home or the English-speaking country. They report significant correlations between performance in English, motivation, self-consciousness, and American identification, but they also show that when the variance in these correlations which is associated with the age variable is partialled out, motivation no longer correlates significantly, and the two other variables generate much lower correlations. In addition, as they point out, there is the issue of causation, such that self-consciousness and American identification may be the consequence rather than the cause of success in learning English. Oyama (1978) confirms these results. So, by way of an assessment of these studies, the evidence that Johnson and Newport provide is very much in support of a critical period, and consistent with the findings of Oyama (1978) and Patkowski (1980).

Newport (1990) also discusses evidence for a critical period in the acquisition of American Sign Language. This is one of those cases of an unfortunate experiment provided by nature, since hearing-impaired children of hearing parents are likely to be exposed to ASL only on entry to residential schooling, which may take place early in childhood but may also occur at a later stage. It is possible, therefore, to study ASL acquisition across the school age range, and Newport reports studies contrasting native, early (4–6 years), and late (over 12 years) learners of ASL. Newport and Supalla (1990) (cited in Newport 1990) report that word order in ASL is not influenced by age whereas, in contrast, morphological aspects of ASL are strongly affected. There is, in fact, a correlation of the order of –.6 to –.7 between age and morphology scores, very similar to that reported by Johnson and Newport (1989) in the case of second language acquisition. ASL, now recognized as a language as complex as any other, thus shows the same sort of evidence of a critical period for certain aspects of language development.

Finally, we come to the case of feral children, another dreadful experiment by nature. Curtiss (1982, 1988) documents findings in this area, discussing cases such as that of Kaspar Hauser, Chelsea, and most important, Genie, the case we will discuss here. Genie was isolated from verbal contact from the age of 20 months until she was very nearly fourteen. Her disturbed father confined her to a room, and indeed to a chair, and deprived her of any verbal contact during any brief visits to her room by members of her family. She was finally discovered, hospitalized, and then looked after under more normal circumstances for some years. (See Curtiss (1977) and Rymer (1993) for accounts of these events, the first written by the academic researcher who was most closely involved, the second more recently by a journalist.)

Genie was studied intensively during the years after her discovery. She represents a human being exposed to her first language after the age of puberty, and so a terrible test of the Critical Period Hypothesis. For syntax to be still accessible to Genie would mean that the critical period does not exist, and that it is simply being exposed to one's first language that is the crucial issue. For Genie not to acquire syntax would strongly suggest that the part of the brain crucial for language development needs to receive input at a particular phase of the lifespan. So her case is a very important one, which accounts for the special nature of the research project she was at the centre of. She underwent a series of psychological tests and demonstrated a range of cognitive abilities, some of them, such as spatial operations, reaching (at least) the normal level. Genie's language development, however, even after a number of years, and despite adequate input and stimulation, was markedly deviant in many respects. Her acquisition of lexical elements was relatively good, and showed steady and continuous improvement. The development of her ability to produce sentences, in contrast, was severely limited. Her sentences were never more than long strings of simple elements. After eight years of 'normality' she still had not developed effectively in areas of the auxiliary system, of morphology, and of a range of syntactic operations. As Curtiss (1988: 370) says:

> The dissociation between acquisition of 'conceptual' aspects of language and acquisition of grammatical forms and rules reported in Kaspar Hauser's case, then, was a hallmark of Genie's language, too.

In addition, in Genie's case, language seemed not be located in specific left hemisphere regions (as is typical in the normal population) but instead seemed to be based in the right hemisphere in a more undifferentiated manner (Rymer 1993). So, many aspects of language, not having experienced the appropriate conditions earlier, did not develop. The timing of the interaction between genetically-programmed development and the necessary input was disturbed and seemed subsequently to become irretrievable.

The development of Chelsea, a hearing impaired woman misdiagnosed as retarded, shows a similar pattern (Curtiss 1994). On correct diagnosis it was discovered that an operation could correct Chelsea's hearing problems. However, after the operation was performed, Chelsea's pattern of language development was similar to Genie's—continuous vocabulary development but no capacity to acquire any range of syntax.

In a sense, Kaspar Hauser, Genie, and Chelsea are the reverse of Antony, Laura, and Rick, described earlier. In the former cases, such as Antony's, syntax was present, without effective semantic development. With Genie and the other feral children, the reverse is true, with considerable semantic development in contrast to impoverished syntax. But the conclusion this leads us to is similar to that from the section on exceptional language users—the development of one system does not automatically require the other. Once again, the implication is of an underlying modularity of organization, and the suggestion that the modules are fairly autonomous. Most of the time, with most people, there is an appropriate combination of genetic endowment and a normally beneficial environment to disguise this, as, for varying reasons, the two systems develop in tandem. But there are occasions, such as lack of exposure to appropriate input or unusual patterns of cognitive ability, which reveal the underlying autonomy. The critical period is, then, one aspect of this more general modularity, suggesting that the syntactic aspects of the LAD have to be engaged by a particular age.

Theory

The evidence we have reviewed—neurological insult, Down's syndrome children, second language acquisition, ASL acquisition, feral children—is consistent with the proposition that there is a critical period for language development which lasts until the early teenage years. Prior to this milestone languages are learned more readily. The evidence presented by Newport and associates (Newport 1990, Johnson and Newport 1989) also suggests that a gradual decline in language learning ability is involved, rather than a sudden reduction in potential. And, very important, the critical period is selective: it seems to affect most strongly the areas of accent and the structural, syntactic-morphological core of language.

This evidence prompts the need for explanation, and, not surprisingly, given such an important issue, many candidate explanations exist to account for the critical period in human language development. At the simplest level, all one has to say is that plasticity in cerebral potential is lost after puberty, with the process of lateralization being complete by that period (Lenneberg 1967) and the areas of the left hemisphere which underpin language being fairly fixed in their structure. This account would also imply that 'language', in this sense, is finite (Hurford 1991), in that whatever is to be acquired is so acquired by (well before) the age of puberty, despite an inherent level of complexity which still resists complete description by highly-trained grammarians. This is a significant contrast with most other cognitive abilities, where either cerebral potential still increases, or, more important, already-acquired cognitive abilities are important, in interaction with the environment, for further learning.

Even so, this is a rather vague and unsatisfying explanation. It does little more than use a complex label as if it accounted for a complex phenomenon. Worse, it does not really explain why language follows this particular path, while other abilities mature earlier or later, more quickly, more slowly, or whatever. There is not, simply in the term 'loss of plasticity', any account of what function a critical period serves so much as an acceptance of one more curiosity of nature. The argument, in other words, is one which simply pushes back the explanation one mystifying step. Not surprisingly, therefore, other accounts address the need to account for the critical period more directly.

A functional exploration

We will examine two such explanations here, one more functional, and one from evolutionary biology. In the more functionalist account, Bever (1981) proposes that in early language development, there is discontinuity between perception and production, and that grammar and morphology develop in order to resolve this discontinuity. Perception, it is assumed, is influenced by one set of processes and strategies, while production relies upon another. The child builds a grammar precisely in order to reconcile the divergences, and to be able to co-ordinate language use in the two domains. The grammar serves as an internal communication device or channel. Once this is achieved, the language learning system becomes 'decoupled' and is no longer available. As Bever says: 'The communication channel ... falls into disrepair because of disuse' (Bever 1981: 193).

Several problems, though, exist with this account. First there is the timing of the close of Bever's functionally-driven critical period. It is not clear why this should occur at puberty, rather than any other age, since there is no clear linkage to cognitive structures and processes which undergo any sort of drastic change at that point, and which could connect with language learning. Nor, come to that, is there any easy explanation of the *gradualness* of the level of achievement which is ordinarily possible. Why should the building of a mediating system take so long to achieve completion, and to *progressively* block subsequent native-like achievement?

Second, it is difficult to justify its detailed mechanisms—how the creation of such a system influences cerebral development and blocks the creation of any comparable system. Finally, we would like to know more about multiple early bilingual learners. What happens to such learners? Do they build mediating systems for each of the languages they are learning? If so, how are they able to do this without one system blocking the others prior to puberty, when such a consequence occurs afterwards?

An evolutionary explanation: early use of finite resources

An alternative perspective is to take a more clearly genetically-based line, and, while accepting the 'rigidity of lateralization' argument, try to explain *why* such a developmental course should come about. Hurford (1991) essentially takes this approach, attempting to account for the critical period through the perspective of evolutionary biology. The question that Hurford asks is 'What evolutionary value would there be for the critical period to exist?'. He assumes that, early in human development, language would have had evolutionary importance in terms of survival and reproduction. Given this starting premise, that possessing more language relative to possessing less language would have been associated with being alive longer and with being able to produce a greater number of offspring (who were 'gened' for language), Hurford uses a computer-based simulation to explore how such language learning potential would be used. He shows that in the context of regular but not extensive mutation the capacity to learn language will tend to move from (say) a starting-point equally distributed over the entire lifespan, through successive cycles of the computer simulation, until it is concentrated in early parts of the lifespan. In other words, if having language is a good thing for survival and reproduction, the earlier we have learned it, the better. So once language evolved, the advantage it provides for survival as early as possible in life will cause it to be a phenomenon which is acquired early—too many of the dilatory language learners, in (say) hunter-gatherer societies, would have been killed off in youth, and would not have had the chance to pass on their genes. Those people whose mutations had caused them to acquire language early would progressively become the dominant group.

Now the explanations of the critical period have to sustain two arguments—why the critical period starts early, and why it finishes early. In that respect, both Bever (1981) and Hurford (1991) seem slightly stronger on the former argument than the latter. Bever's position clearly requires a system to be built to solve a problem, but is not so precise as to why that system (or the mechanisms underlying it) are unavailable for reuse. Similarly, with Hurford the evolutionary advantage of early availability of language during the lifespan is clear. But then the movement of the critical period so that it is located early in the lifespan seems only to be the consequence of the assumption Hurford makes *that there is a fixed (finite) quantity of language learning ability*. In such cases, it will be advantageous that it is used as quickly as possible, since there is danger for the individual in waiting.

This, of course, requires us to ask why language learning ability should be fixed in this way. One possibility is that there is something in the nature of the system concerned that requires this. For example, Universal Grammar might have a structure that could, for some reason, only be activated once. But since this is an argument of considerable (current) vagueness, it will not be pursued here. Alternatively, one might say that if the normal need is to acquire one's own group's language early in life, then the lack of a functional need later will mean that there is no pressure for the retention of a language learning ability, and so it will atrophy, or the neurological space it draws on can be reused (Pinker 1994). These, too, are unconvincing explanations, simply describing what happens rather than accounting for it. Arguments which themselves have a motivated, evolutionary biology perspective would be more convincing.

An evolutionary explanation: constraining variability

An alternative account might be based on the degree of power that the LAD needs to have. A central requirement for the LAD is that it is able to guarantee effective first language acquisition with only minimal dependence on the environment for input. In other words, it has to cope with enormous variation in input (and the different linguistic circumstances in which children grow up) while producing a fairly constant output. In addition, it has to go beyond the information given because of the 'poverty of the stimulus' argument (White 1989). Evidence of this power is found in creolization (Bickerton 1981), where children of parents who do not share an L1 and who have created a pidgin language take the pidgin as input and transcend it, creating a new and more complex language of their own. Similarly, Goldin-Meadow and Mylander's (1990) work on the development of home sign in hearing impaired- children shows how a LAD, virtually deprived of input, nonetheless attempts to create language.

The need to possess such a powerful system which works for first language acquisition in all circumstances may then bring with it new problems. There is considerable evidence of variability in first (Labov 1972) and second (Tarone 1988) languages. There are clear contextual links between variation and situation in Labov, and it has also been argued that variation is the precursor for language change (Widdowson 1989). If, indeed, the variation in language can be exploited for the formation of in-groups and out-groups to enable markers of differentness to become more prominent, then there are social consequences. In the twentieth century, these choices do not tend to be species threatening, but instead simply reflect the complexity of present-day society, as some groups try to manufacture their distinctness from others, and use divergent language forms, while others converge to show their degree of belonging (Beebe and Giles 1984). In such cases, since members of the 'different' group are sufficiently bi-dialectal to achieve communication, there is no real problem of survival being jeopardized.

But in the context of much earlier societies, the consequences for survival of linguistic fragmentation and lack of mutual intelligibility could have been very severe. If a critical period for language did not exist, presumably the capacity for easy and fresh language learning would allow greater variability in language to occur throughout the lifespan, maximizing the chances that groups of hunter-gatherers would splinter into mutual incomprehension. There would also be the possibility that older members of groups (the repositories of knowledge) would not be able to communicate with younger group members, also threatening the survival potential of the group as a whole, and the individual members within it.

The existence of a critical period means that the essential core of language will remain relatively unmodified. Such a situation will, inevitably, place constraints on the capacity of language to change, but it will bring the very substantial reward that members of such a speech community will be 'guaranteed' successful communication with one another throughout their lifetime, ensuring that the process of language change will be relatively slow, spanning many generations before mutual comprehension is lost. The advantage of this argument is that, from an evolutionary biological perspective, there are *positive* reasons for bringing the critical period to a close because of the survival and reproduction advantages it would confer. It would be a case of the development of such a powerful acquisition device to guarantee success, on the one hand, and the need to limit the 'excessive' power which has been so created, on the other.

Summary

To sum up this section on the critical period, then, we can make a number of claims:

1 The evidence for a critical period is strong. It is based on multiple sources: second language acquisition, the acquisition of ASL, acquisition by the hearing-impaired whose problems have been corrected, and the problems that feral children encounter who are exposed to language after the onset of puberty. *None of these sources of evidence has to bear the explanatory burden alone.*
2 The evidence is consistent with a gradual decline in a language capacity which is complete by the onset of puberty.
3 Explanations for the onset and close of the critical period based on evolutionary biology are the most convincing, since they suggest reasons why a language learning ability would benefit survival chances.

Conclusion

This chapter has surveyed a wide range of issues connected with the nature of language learning talent, in the first and second language cases. By way of revision, six generalizations can be made to recap on the claims made in each section:

1 There is a range of evidence supporting modularity based on a syntax-semantics opposition in the first language case. The amazing syntactic development of the groups covered in Table 9.1, for example individual children such as Laura, and the various groups of children, for example Williams's syndrome, as well as the cases of semantic development without syntax, for example post-critical period learners and Gopnik's family, show that while the two areas will normally develop in harmony, they can, under special circumstances, operate with a considerable degree of independence.

2 The evidence in support of a critical period is strong, despite more recent counter-claims. The data on post-critical period second language learners, ASL learners, and post-critical period first language learners, such as Genie and Chelsea, does indicate that older learners proceed more slowly, and do not generally reach the same levels of accomplishment.

3 There is also modularity in second language acquisition, but the aptitude evidence suggests that this modularity is based on stages of information processing: input, central processing, and memory/output, and that the nature of a talent for learning second languages can be analysed into these three components.

4 Concerning the question of the existence of a *specific* talent for foreign language learning, it would seem that it is the more peripheral components of this second language aptitude, input and memory/output, which show most evidence of being qualitatively different from general cognitive abilities. Central processing does seem to have most in common with general learning abilities, with the evidence for a talent to deal with specifically linguistic material not being so strong.

5 Exceptionally successful foreign language learners consistently seem to be characterized by the possession of unusual memories, particularly for the retention of verbal material. Such exceptional learners do not seem to have unusual abilities with respect to input or central processing.

6 Very weak foreign language learners seem to lack input skills principally, as measured by aptitude tests such as phonemic coding ability.

Following from these generalizations, we can now return to some of the questions posed earlier. Most importantly, it seems clear that there is modularity in both first and second language learning, but the nature of the modularity is different in each case. In the first language case the contrast is between syntax and semantics, while in the second it would seem to derive from stages of information processing. The end of the critical period seems to be what separates these two bases for modularity.

The language–cognition relationship reflects this change. Prior to the critical period, language and cognition are, in principle, served by different modules or learning mechanisms. The fact that the environment generally causes them to develop in tandem should not disguise their mutual potential independence. Language, in other words, is qualitatively different from other areas of knowledge and learning. After the critical period, peripheral aspects of aptitude are separate from general cognitive abilities (Wesche *et al.* 1982; Sasaki 1991, 1996)—input processing and memory/output do seem to be distinct from general cognition, but central processing of linguistic material and general cognition do not seem so clearly distinct. The central components of second language learning, in this respect, are clearly close to general learning, a claim which has clear importance for the nature of second language instruction.

These are important conclusions to draw about the nature of modularity in first and second language learning, and about the language–cognition relationship in each case. But two more points also follow from the claims made in this chapter. First, once again, but now from an individual differences perspective, memory is central to an understanding of language acquisition. Earlier in this book, it was claimed that the importance of memory in language analysis, language learning, and second language performance has been vastly underestimated. The task-based research, for example, showed that fluency and accessibility implicate memory functioning in absolutely central ways. What we have seen in this chapter is the repeated evidence that exceptionality in second language learning derives from unusually developed memory capacities, and that the individual differences in this area suggest variation across a normal range (which has considerable functional importance), as well as a memory capacity above some threshold which seems to generate significantly greater second language learning capacities.

The second point concerns the nature of research into the critical period. Bialystok and Hakuta (1994) make the point that such is research often based on group differences. Certainly a key point in this research is the number of post-critical period learners who do very well. One can ask what proportion of all learners these make up, and, more searchingly, what it means for them to do very well. We have seen that memory is an important factor in succeeding with second languages, and from earlier chapters, that the nature of performance can involve trade-offs between difference performance characteristics. This would suggest a parallel research strategy to explorations of group differences. It would also be useful to explore, in the context of high achievers, whether there is any connection with superior memory abilities, in that such learners may well be more able to adapt to the constraints of a more information-processing perspective on learning. Coupled with this, it would be worth using a greater variety of tests to assess second language performance. In that respect, the tests used by Johnson and Newport (1989), grammaticality-judgement tests, may not be searching enough, in that they do not require real-time performance. The considerations discussed in Chapter 7 may be relevant here. We may need a range of performances, with a range of tasks, and under different processing conditions, to establish that high performers with judgement tasks can match pre-critical period performers. Only by using more relevant standards such as these, with individuals as well as groups, can we make convincing claims, either in support of or against the critical period.

Note

1   Bialystok and Hakuta (1994) dispute these correlations. On visual inspection of the diagram in Johnson and Newport (1989) they propose a different breakpoint and compute different results. These arguments are difficult to accept, however. There seems little motivation for the new breakpoint that they choose, other than subjective visual appeal (to them). My own comparable visual inspection of the data does not tally with theirs, but then subjective judgements of this sort are hardly likely to.

10 Learning style

Introduction

The study of aptitude, which was the main subject of Chapter 8 and a minor subject of Chapter 9, is often taken to imply that there are relatively stable qualities which confer an advantage for learning; some people are the lucky winners, while others are not so fortunate. This is likely to have been one of the reasons for the lack of enthusiasm for theorizing and research in this area. A contrasting perspective is to examine whether there is any evidence of variation in *style* of learning, the characteristic manner in which an individual chooses to approach a learning task. A style perspective contains two differences which render it more attractive. First, it implies that there may be some degree of disposition, so that the style someone adopts may partly reflect personal preference rather than innate endowment. In such a case, the 'fixedness' associated with aptitude would not apply. Second, there is the possibility that with style, even though there may be a continuum of some sort with more or less of an attribute being possessed, all the advantages may not accrue to only one end of the continuum.

Field dependence/independence

The main application of style to language learning has been through the concept of field dependence/independence (FD/I), developed in mainstream psychology by Herman Witkin (1962). Witkin *et al.*(1979) have proposed that a contrast can be made between analytic and holistic ('Gestalt') individuals. The former group, the analytic, faced with a situation in which decision making is necessary, are more able to separate a problem into components, and then focus on the components which have significance for decision making. They can, in other words, decompose a whole into constituent elements, and then focus on, transform, and generally manipulate the constituents independently of one another. But there is a downside to these qualities. Such people are also likely, in this 'style bundle', to be aloof and not oriented towards people, with the result that their relationships with others are less likely to be effective, and they are unlikely to be skilled operators within teams.

Field dependence/independence in language learning

In the field of language learning, this analytic style could manifest itself by an ability to analyse the linguistic material one is exposed to, identify its components, and then, perhaps, explore relationships between these components (a portrayal of style close to the central processing components of aptitude—Chapelle and Green 1992). Separating the essential from the inessential could involve an ability to focus on that data which would be most helpful at whatever level of interlanguage development one has reached, and to promote learning and development with maximum efficiency—an ability to avoid 'junky' data and the culs-de-sac which beckon. It is also possible to relate the FI construct to an input-processing dimension. In the case of auditory material, the learner has to extract what is important from the stream of incoming sound. This sound will contain a great deal of irrelevant information, and it will be advantageous to devote attention to features which help meaning to be recovered. In this respect, field independence would relate to the attentional capacities described earlier, with FI individuals having greater capacity to channel attention selectively and notice important aspects of language. They may then be more able to reflect upon the ways in which they have exploited their attentional system.

Field dependent people, in contrast, are likely to be less analytic, to perceive situations as wholes, rather than being analysable into components (some of which may be more important than others), and more likely to depend on external frames of reference for making judgements (rely on other people's opinions). For such people, the 'bundle' continues with some good news, in that they are thought to be sociable, person-oriented, and warm. To the extent that language development is aided by high-quality interaction, such people are more likely to be naturally drawn through their person orientation and their comfort in interaction situations to maximize encounters in which they are likely to receive good quality, relevant input, and have opportunities to use language to express meanings. As a result, their interlanguage systems should be stretched by the demands to communicate. This raises the possibility that such greater exposure could overcome the problem of a lack of an analytic orientation.

In sum, the FI individual benefits from the way he or she processes information but is seen to avoid situations in which language is actually going to be used for communication. FD individuals, while comfortable and sensitive in communication situations, are not seen to be effective information processors, and so, although provided with more information to work with, will exploit it less. From this one can infer that FI individuals should do better on non-communicative, more cerebral tests, while FD individuals should excel in more communicative situations, when what is assessed is language use rather than language-like use.

Clearly, this is a comprehensible and attractive 'package', whose lures have engaged the attentions of many researchers. Above all, there is the factor of style, mentioned earlier. What is being claimed is not that some people have greater ability than others, rather that there are differences in the way different people interact with the world and with the ways in which they perceive and organize information. Neither pole of the style dimension is regarded as being as 'better' but instead is simply seen to suggest alternatives. Further, each pole is seen as having advantages for different tasks. Some of the time an analytic predisposition will be an advantage, while on other occasions being person-oriented will be equally but differently advantageous, not least when it is other people who are more likely to have something useful to say about the solution to a problem. The first-principled, analytic, but aloof field independent might get there in the end, but a lot of time might be wasted when other people might be happy to pass on the fruits of their previous experience.

Three issues

In this formulation there are three slightly unclear issues which are worth mentioning. First of all there is the question of extremity. Most attempts to divide the world up into two types of people are good on the extremes but not so good on the (less interesting) people in the middle, who presumably do not pattern so clearly. Second, there is the issue of the 'fixedness' with which people can be located on the field independence/dependence continuum. One possibility is that the continuum manifests itself in a fairly fixed type of behaviour, with a person's position being relatively stable. Alternatively, people may have a range of styles that, so that different situations can be responded to variably and adaptably, with the individual responding in whatever way seems adequate to the task in hand. One would need to know not simply where someone is placed on the continuum but also how flexible they are—a point effectively made by Brown (1994).

Third, we need to consider the issue of measurement. In general, there are two ways to operationalize the FD/I construct, which we may regard as the hard way and the easy way. The hard way would use a measure like the rod and frame test (Witkin *et al.* 1979), in which subjects are seated in a tiltable chair and have to align a rod to vertical in a darkened room where there are no visual cues. The procedure is meant to provide a measure of the capacity to be independent from external referents, and to base the aligning judgement on internal cues. The procedure is individual, expensive in equipment, takes time to carry out, and is rather cumbersome. In contrast, the easy way to obtain a measure of field independence is to use something like the Group Embedded Figures test (GEFT). Subjects have to use a booklet in which simple visual figures are embedded inside progressively more complicated visual figures. Subjects then indicate where the simple figure is located within the more complex figure. The test is easy to administer, requiring only a normal room, and functions on a group basis. Not surprisingly, faced with the choice of constructing a special room in which to test subjects one at a time, or using a neat booklet in large quantities, most investigators have taken the latter option. The issue of measurement is a central one in discussing FD/I, and we will return to it later in the chapter.

The construct of field independence has had intermittent attention within second language research. It has generated positive but unspectacular results, with typical researchers publishing correlations between measures of field independence and language proficiency at around the 0.30 level. (One wonders how many additional research reports did not find relationships of even this size, and then were not submitted for publication because of such 'non-results'.) Correlations of this magnitude frequently attain significance, but do not indicate a major influence on second language learning success, since such correlations only account for about ten per cent of the variance in proficiency test scores. In addition, it is striking from this research that the selective theorizing from the bipolar nature of the construct has not been borne out in practice. Significant correlations are all with field independence, suggesting that the supposed advantages for FD students are more apparent than real.

The value of FD/I

This leads back to the distinction between style and ability. It can be proposed that the GEFT for measuring field independence is simply a disguised ability measure, and that it achieves its predictive power not from any style dimension, but because it contains, built in to its measurement procedures, scope for traditional intelligence to operate. In this case, the correlation between FD/I scores and language proficiency scores would be due to the way intelligence is measured, in surrogate fashion, by FD/I, and the way intelligence is helpful both in language learning and in performing well on language tests. The evidence on this issue is intriguing. When ability measures have been partialled out of the correlations between FI and language proficiency scores (Hansen and Stansfield 1981), the remaining correlation often fails to reach significance.

Drawing on such analysis, and the empirical data, I concluded some years ago that 'the field independence construct is one that has been mined for all it is worth' (Skehan 1989: 115), and suggested that investigators turn their attention to other issues. It is interesting to see, several years later, that the situation is nothing like so clear-cut. Since then, the stakes in FD/I research have got rather higher. Griffiths and Sheen (1992) criticized my assessment for being far too wimpish, and suggested that rather than researchers being advised to find more productive areas, they should be counselled to avoid the area because it is wrong-headed in principle. They contend that the series of

FD/I-motivated studies represent a classic case of a construct from one discipline being misapplied in another. In particular, they suggest that:

- FD/I has not been effectively measured in second language research, in that the typical measure, the GEFT, only correlates at 0.40 with the rod and frame test (Cronbach 1990), thus lacking convergent validity, while at the same time, it does correlate quite strongly with ability tests, thus providing the sort of convergent validity that is not wanted;
- FD/I was originally proposed as a visual or at least perceptual construct, and Griffiths and Sheen (1992) question how such a construct may be related to the second language area in any convincing way. One could similarly contend that the nature of the continuum which underlies the field independence construct is not clear. Currently, it is assumed that the opposite of field independence is field dependence, whereas it is possible that the opposite, in fact, is no field independence, i.e. that the poles of the construct represent a false opposition, in that each represents the end-point of distinct dimensions;
- Griffiths and Sheen (1992) contend that FD/I has been abandoned by serious psychologists, and so it represents a particularly clear example of an out-of-date construct applied outside its original context.

In a response to Griffiths and Sheen, Chapelle (1992) offers two reasons why the construct of field dependence/independence may still be worth examination. First of all, she agrees that FD/I has not been assessed appropriately. What is necessary, therefore, is for better measures of FD/I as a style to be used. Only if this is done, and unimpressive results still emerge, will it be possible to draw any conclusions about the usefulness of FD/I in SLA. In fact there are contemporary developments which hold considerable promise. Riding (1991), for example, has developed a computerized assessment procedure for measuring learning style. His procedure operationalizes a slightly different conceptualization of field independence. He proposes that two dimensions need to be considered, the visual and the verbal, and that separate testing procedures need to be used to identify each of them. Accordingly, the visual component of his testing procedure uses figural material, not dissimilar to the embedded figures test. In addition, however, he uses a verbal judgement task to establish style with language material. In this way, a more differentiated view of learning style can be used. Riding reports that such a measure is usefully predictive for a variety of learning tasks, as well as occupational decision making. We will discuss this work more extensively in the next section.

A new interpretation of FD/I

Second, based on Witkin and Goodenough (1981), Chapelle and Green (1992) discuss how the construct itself should be interpreted. They highlight three aspects of the construct that are important: reliance on internal or external frames of reference, cognitive restructuring abilities, and interpersonal competences. By separating out the different aspects of the construct in this way, they hope to provide greater clarity in the discussion.

Internally referenced people are more likely to make judgements based on their own interpretations of situations, and are likely to be confident of their own decisions. Externally referenced people are likely to want to justify the judgements that they make in the wider environment, and gather information to support what they decide. Such people are less likely to be confident. Cognitive restructuring abilities are those which allow a given set of components or ideas to be manipulated and transformed. They indicate flexibility with ideas, and a willingness to explore new arrangements. Finally, interpersonal competences, as discussed earlier, are concerned with the capacity to interact with other people comfortably and skilfully. It is assumed that people who have external frames of reference are more likely to appeal to and involve other people in their judgements.

A crucial aspect of this newer interpretation is that it allows a better perspective on the skill–ability tension from earlier discussions. Chapelle and Green (1992) propose that the restructuring component of the wider construct is the part which correlates with general intelligence, while the frame of reference is a typical 'style' construct, bipolar, with neither pole conferring a general advantage. Chapelle and Green go on to examine how this restructuring ability relates to other cognitive abilities, including that of foreign language aptitude. They draw attention to discussions within the psychological literature of a contrast between fluid and crystallized intelligence. The former is a sort of 'first principles' intelligence: a capacity to think through the solutions to problems in a fresh manner and be flexible, with an emphasis on reasoning, transformation, and general problem-solving skills. Crystallized intelligence, in contrast, concerns abilities to solve problems by emphasizing their similarity to previous problems, allowing previous learning to be mobilized, and where schematic knowledge is relevant. In the case of language learning, one would regard aspects of learning, or hypothesis formation, or inferencing which relate to the L1, as examples of crystallized intelligence at work, whereas what might be characterized as developmental or non-L1 approaches would implicate fluid abilities, with the further claim that such abilities are what GEFT measures.

Chapelle and Green (1992) propose that the sort of three-component structure for aptitude described in the last two chapters should be extended, with the language analytic component divided into a (crystallized) language analytic ability (the capacity to draw upon relevant knowledge of language in the current language learning task), and a (fluid) general analytic ability, (which is what would be drawn on to solve language learning problems but without reference to existing language knowledge). The former would account for the way the product of L1 learning facilitates, or interferes with, L2 learning, while the second would draw upon general problem-solving abilities.

Alternative views of style

Work such as Chapelle and Green's (1992) makes it clear that the attack by Griffiths and Sheen (1992) was overdone, and that the construct of field independence is richer and more promising than they allowed. This interpretation is supported by an examination of other researchers' work. What all these more recent investigators have in common, though, is that they work with two dimensions, not one, and then use the dimensions to characterize style preferences and characteristic modes of behaving. We will consider four such approaches here.

Emerging views of style from general learning contexts

Riding and Cheema

Riding and Cheema (1991) have proposed that there are two basic problems with the Witkin (1962) view of field dependence/independence. First, they argue that it does not represent each of the poles of the dimension positively. Second, they propose an additional dimension, contrasting visual and verbal representations. In terms of the first criticism, they echo the point made earlier that it is difficult to conceive exactly what is meant by Witkin's analytic–holistic contrast, especially when this is operationalized through a measure such as the GEFT, since the implication is that a holistic style is defined as no more than the absence of an analytic style. Holists, in other words, never get a chance to show their capacity to apprehend integrated, unanalysed perceptions as unified fields. The second problem that Riding and Cheema address is to posit an additional dimension, based around the visual–verbal contrast. It will be recalled that critics of the field independence construct have argued that it is excessively visual (see for example, Griffiths and Sheen 1992) at least in the way it is assessed, so that people who have strong visual skills have an automatic (and spurious) advantage. Riding and Cheema propose that if one considers the analytic–holistic approach to focus on style of processing, the visual–verbal contrast targets a level of representation, suggesting that while some people prefer to think in verbal terms, others prefer visual representations.

These contrasts would operate fairly directly with general knowledge structures, where, for example, there might be learning of content, and the issues would concern how material is analysed when presented, and then how it is organized to enable more effective retrieval. But one could also relate this analysis to language, and suggest that analytic learners prefer to search for the components of pattern in language and analyse a chunk of language into its component parts. This may well lead them to try to formulate rules, either implicitly or explicitly. One assumes these predispositions lead them to have a more flexible approach to patterns in language. Then they may represent the product of that process either verbally or visually. Holists, in contrast, would prefer to deal with language as chunks, and resist breaking down such chunks into sub-sections, but prefer to retain the larger unit of language, and look for ways of using it as it is. They, too, would then approach material verbally or visually.

Riding

Riding (1991) has developed computer-based procedures to measure these dimensions of style. He uses figures not dissimilar to the GEFT figures to assess analytic style. He also uses geometric figures to assess a holistic style, but in this case the requirement is not that people locate a simple figure inside a more complex figure (analyse into parts), but instead what is required is the perception of a whole figure, retaining its unity. In addition, Riding uses verbal judgement tests to make assessments of verbal–visual preferences, giving items like:

> *a banana is the same colour as a daffodil*   correct: visual

and

> *windsurfing is the same type as painting*   incorrect: verbal

(as well as incorrect visual items and correct verbal items). Crucially, since the test is computer-administered, it is possible to record latency of response, and Riding uses such measures to compare the facility with which judgements are made, allowing him, for example, to detect preferences for making verbal judgements or visual judgements. In this way simple items which everyone can actually do become the basis for discovering which areas are processed more readily.

Gregorc

Gregorc (1979) also uses two dimensions to describe style. He contrasts a serial–random dimension with a second dimension characterized as abstract–concrete. Regarding the first of these, serialists prefer to work their way through material sequentially and methodically, tacitly taking the approach that thoroughness will be the surest path to progress. Learners who prefer what is termed (maybe misleadingly) a 'random' approach prefer to see patterns emerge from data, and do not see methodical analysis as the key to ensuring that this will happen. Random learners are more likely to expect that if they try to apprehend a larger amount of initially unstructured data, the wider perspective will be more likely to create conditions for patterns to emerge. The second dimension focuses on the information which is being represented. Those who are oriented to abstractions are happy with generalities, detached from experience. Such people are able to cope with decontextualized material, manipulate it, and recall it with facility. A concrete approach, in contrast, requires material that is to be learned and processed to be close to reality, experience, and context. Such learners are mistrustful of abstractions, and want to relate material to their own personal experiences.

If we compare Gregorc's approach to that of Riding, we clearly see similarities and differences. The major similarity is that each posits a dimension which is concerned with processing material (Riding's FD/I contrast, and Gregorc's serialist–holist), and a second dimension which is concerned with representation (Riding's visual–verbal, and Gregorc's concrete–abstract). There are points of contact between the two views of processing. FIs or serialists seem to prefer to focus on elements, and then be concerned with the organization of such elements. FDs or random learners like to see a big picture, and then process this big picture as a whole. There are also points of contact between the two versions of representation. Riding's visual might connect with Gregorc's concrete, and verbal might relate more naturally to abstract. But this is not a convincing comparison when pushed to any great degree. Clearly it is possible to conceive of abstract visual and concrete verbal. But at least there is some probabilistic resemblance, suggesting that some degree of common focus is at work.

Kolb

We can continue this theme of similarity and difference by looking at the work of Lawrence Kolb (1976). Kolb characterizes learning style in dynamic and static terms. He proposes that the natural sequence for learning is a cycle containing four stages. These are shown in Table 10.1. The four stages of the cycle repeat in such a way that when the end of one cycle is reached, a new cycle can be started, that there is a need to constantly learn, but at progressively deeper and more complex levels.[1]

Kolb also suggests that a more static version of this sequence is possible to the extent that some learners have preferences for certain stages of the cycle at the expense of others. Some people prefer to rely excessively on a concrete approach, almost wallowing in experience, (and never distancing themselves from it). Another example would be learners stuck at the active-experimental stage, always changing things, but never really systematically observing the changes which have been provoked so that the benefit of change is appreciated. And so on, with inactive observers, and head-in-the-clouds theorists. Kolb then goes on to propose different responses that teachers may have to each of these four likely learning styles.

Stage	Transitional nature
Concrete experience	All learning should arise from one's concrete experience, since exposure to the real world is what provides the basis for other modes of thinking.
Reflection-observation	Drawing upon concrete experience, learners need to observe in a systematic manner, and reflect upon what they have observed to establish generalizations.
Abstract conceptualization	Following the process of data-based reflection, learners should theorize at a more abstract level to try to understand their experiences and to make sense of them.
Active experimentation	Theorizing should not be an end in itself: it should enable experiences to be understood more completely. As such theorizing is likely to provoke further questions which can best be addressed by going back to concrete experience, and acting upon it to produce change which then sets the entire cycle in motion again.

Table 10.1: Kolb's four stages of learning

Linking back with Riding and Gregorc, we see further change here. First of all, although Kolb portrays his ideas on style in terms of two dimensions, these dimensions do not have quite the same role as with the other two theorists. Kolb is more interested in using the poles of the dimensions to capture the more integrated qualities of people at the transitional stages. Second, he uses one dimension which is now familiar to us, (concrete–abstract), but another which is qualitatively different from what we have seen before, active experimentation versus reflection-observation. This dimension 'builds in' a sense of time passing. It also concerns how the individual interacts with the world, and as such, it is close to a personality orientation. In fact, if we reflect upon the nature of the two dimensions involved, representation (abstract–concrete) and interaction mode (active–passive), we can see that there is no concern at all for style of processing. In other words, Kolb is distinctly less cerebral in orientation, and more concerned with temperamental dispositions on the part of the learner to influence (or not) the information which will be collected and then processed. The processing itself is not in primary focus.

Emerging views of language learning style

Each of the approaches to style considered so far is general in scope, and not specifically addressed towards the language learning area. But more recently there has been an attempt to relate such style concepts to contemporary language teaching and learning. Willing (1987) interprets Kolb's (1976) abstract–concrete dimensions as field dependence/independence. The dimension is cognitive-perceptual in orientation. Consistent with the preceding discussion, Willing then interprets Kolb's other dimension in personality terms, contrasting a readiness to be proactive with a tendency to be accepting and take direction from others. Although there are points of contact between the two dimensions (compare the independence of the field independent person and the readiness to be active, and to impose structure on the environment of the 'active' person) there is sufficient separation for the more personality-based dimension to function independently.

The real value of Willing's reinterpretation of Kolb's work is that, on the basis of an empirical study with learners of English within the Adult Migrant Service in Australia, he attempts to characterize language learners in terms of the two-dimensional framework. This is shown in Figure 10.1.

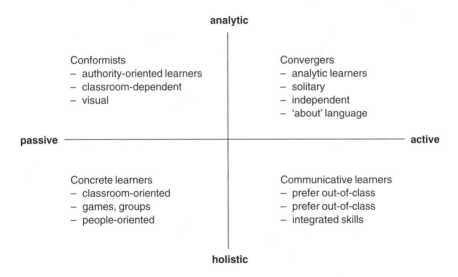

Figure 10.1: *Willing's two-dimensional framework of learning style*
(Willing 1987: 86)

Convergers

Figure 10.1 reveals four language learner types, corresponding to the types of general learner proposed by Kolb, with each of these defined by the relevant combination of the two dimensions. Convergers (field independent active) tend to be analytical learners who, when processing material, are able to focus on the component parts of such material and their interrelationship. Such learners respond to learning situations in characteristic ways. They are solitary learners who prefer to avoid groups, or even classrooms, altogether. They are independent, confident in their own judgements, and willing to impose their own structures on learning. These views also influence how they construe language. They are more likely to regard language as an object, not as something which enables personal values to be expressed. Such learners, in other words, are drawn more towards learning 'about' language than towards language use. They value efficiency, and tend to be cool, pragmatic, and detached. One sees these learners operating most comfortably in a self-access centre, where their capacity to plan, linked to the availability of materials and structure, would suit them very well.

Conformists

Conformists (field independent passive) provide an interesting contrast. They too have an analytic view of language, preferring to emphasize learning 'about' language rather than using language, and regarding language learning as a task susceptible to systematic, logical, and organized work. But they rely upon the organization of others, and are dependent on those they perceive as having authority. They are not so confident about their own judgements, in other words, and are happy to function in non-communicative classrooms by doing what they are told, following textbooks, frequently preferring a visual mode of organization for their learning, and taking an impersonal approach to learning. Such learners prefer well-organized teachers who provide structure, in the sense of classroom organization and plans.

Concrete learners

Concrete learners (field dependent passive) share some qualities with conformists. They, too, like classrooms and the imposed organization and authority that this can provide. But whereas the conformists like classrooms composed of individuals, concrete learners enjoy the sociable aspects of classrooms, and see them as composed of groups of interacting individuals. Such learners like to learn from direct experience, and are interested in language use and language as communication, rather than simply knowing about a system, since, as field dependents they are people-oriented. Their preferred activities in the classroom are organized games and group work, and a wide range of skills-based and communicative activities.

Communicative learners

Finally, we have communicative learners (field dependent active) who make up the fourth quadrant of the diagram. These learners are language-as-use oriented, but holistic in orientation. Their activity manifests itself in the way in which they are comfortable out of class, showing a degree of social independence and confidence as well as a willingness to take risks. Such learners are happy to engage in communication in real-life situations, without the support and guidance of a teacher, since they are mainly concerned with meaning. Their holistic learning orientation also shows itself as multi-skilled, in that they are not interested in an analytic approach, or in learning separately the different elements of a language. What they want to emphasize above all is general, unanalysed communicative ability, with this arising out of interaction with speakers of the language.

Clearly, these sketches of the four learner types are caricatures, in that they convey too neat and distinct a view of what learners are like to be convincing about real people. Most learners do not fall neatly into one or other quadrant, either occupying a range of space, or alternatively moving between quadrants when their behaviour is appropriately modified to take account of different sorts of learning contexts. The case studies provided in Stevick's *Success with Foreign Languages* (1989) illustrate this, as the individuals that he describes show a range of different approaches when faced with different learning opportunities. But it is useful to think of the extremes here, since they give a clear impression that the underlying dimensions separate out important aspects of learning style.

The need for further research

Even so, more empirical work is needed. Willing (1987) reports that in his study of immigrants to Australia, 10 per cent of learners are analytic, 30 per cent are authority-oriented, 10 per cent are concrete, and 40 per cent are communicative (leaving 10 per cent who do not fall clearly into any one of the quadrants). It would be interesting to discover what proportions would be found in other circumstances, with populations of learners drawn from different backgrounds, and when learning contexts differ also (when, for example, the language is not being learned in a country in which it is the native language). Similarly, research linking such learner types with actual experiences of learning, and information on the success of that learning, would also be welcome.

Looking back, the changes that Willing (1987) has made to Kolb's (1976) original characterization of learning style make for interesting comparisons with the work of other researchers. Kolb draws upon a personality dimension, relating to how people interact with the environment, cross-referenced with abstract versus concrete representations. The personality dimension then influences how data which operates upon the representational system is gathered. Willing, in contrast, although retaining the personality dimensions (but without the dynamic element from Kolb), then makes reference to a processing dimension, emphasizing how material is operated upon, rather than the material itself. Active people involve themselves with the world, and then if field independent, analyse it, while if field dependent process it holistically. Passive people do not interact in the same manner, watching rather than doing, and then either analyse or process in wholes. As a result there is little emphasis on the nature of representation.

Aptitude

Finally we can return to the discussion of aptitude as well as the discussion in earlier chapters in order to interpret language learning style in a way which contrasts with Willing's approach. We have seen that there is research to suggest that there are analysis-oriented learners and memory-oriented learners (Wesche 1981; Skehan 1986c). We could extend this insight and propose that there are two related dimensions, of degree of analysis and amount of memory. With the former, we would expect high analysis foreign language learners to develop differentiated, organized, and rule-based representations of language, with possibly, no great need to have more than a parsimoniously organized, single-representation lexical system. Such learners would engage in regular restructuring and complexification of the underlying interlanguage system. It is assumed, following the discussion in the earlier chapters, that such analytically oriented learners would value accuracy, and would strive to achieve it as part of a general orientation towards form. Low analysis learners, in contrast, would have smaller and less differentiated systems, and they might be less able to articulate anything about such systems.

High memory learners would have a wide range of lexicalized exemplars, considerable redundancy in their memory systems, and multiple representations of lexical elements. These exemplars, above all, would be highly accessible, and could be mobilized for communication in real time. Such learners might not need a complex analytic system to engage in communication. It is assumed that such learners would not value form highly, and so high memory learners might have some predisposition to fossilize and sacrifice accuracy and complexity for access. Low memory learners, in contrast, would not have such a repertoire of lexical elements, and might not have the multiple representations characteristic of high memory learners. As a result, they would have to make reference to other resources in order to cope with real-time communication.

Two dimensions: analysis and memory

We can represent these two dimensions as in Figure 10.2.

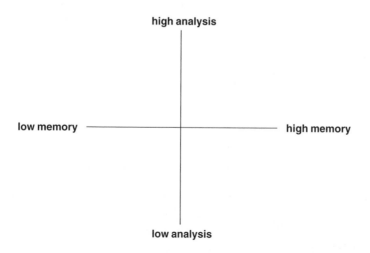

Figure 10.2: Analytic and memory dimensions underlying language learning

The figure shows that the two dimensions vary independently and each contains high and low poles. In consequence, one can imagine a range of different combinations from the two dimensions, such as high memory and low analysis, average placement on both, or even high analysis high memory.

The central question raised by this analysis is how learners' orientations to the two dimensions are to be accounted for. Three possibilities exist here: abilities, tasks, and style. A first interpretation would simply say that orientations towards analysis or memory are the result of abilities profiles. This, what might be termed the 'hard aptitude' interpretation, is essentially claiming that the approach a particular learner takes is constrained by his or her underlying aptitudinal strengths and weaknesses. Some learners, for example, will be doubly endowed, and so have available an effective analytic capacity and high memory abilities. Such learners can then operate an impressive dual-mode system, at both processing and representational levels, coping with both language-as-system and language-as-communication demands, leading to the development of a balanced interlanguage system at all stages. Others will manifest performance which is a reflection of poorer but balanced abilities. Still others will have characteristic approaches emphasizing memory or analysis, depending on aptitudinal profile. In all these cases, the concept of style would not be relevant, since the aptitude profile would be the dominant influence.

The second possibility is that task characteristics influence representational and processing outcomes. Here, and again drawing on the discussion from Chapters 5 and 6, if tasks or task implementation highlight form, then the analysis dimension will be more likely to be used. In contrast, if communication and pressure to handle real-time processing and fluency are the crucial factors, memory and access will be required. Careful pre- and post-task activity will lead to the former situations, and a priority for analysis, as will effective task choice, and a careful analysis of the task demands on attentional resources, on the assumption that if resources are not overloaded, the scope for form to be in focus is thereby enhanced (Schmidt 1992). Similarly, pedagogic intervention to ensure salience of instructional goals, and the importance of language will also increase the chances of more effective analysis. Conversely, a lack of salience of pedagogic norms, together with naturalistic processing conditions, may lead to greater reliance on memory and more lexicalized approaches to language use. In summary, then, one can sketch out ways in which task demands themselves will have significant influences upon the nature of processing and performance, and so constrain the functioning of the two dimensions concerned, analysis and memory, without having to implicate any concept of style.

In contrast, a style interpretation represents a predisposition, given one's pattern of abilities, and given task demands, to approach foreign language learning with a preference for analysis or for memory. Some learners, that is, prefer to concentrate their attention on form, pattern, rules, and systematicity. Others are less drawn to the organization of the material to be learned, and instead prefer to prioritize communication and the assembly of units of communication which are maximally accessible, partly no doubt because they are considerably longer than the orthographic word. Further, it is possible that there may not be exactly the same predisposition for representation as there is for processing. There may be those, that is, who focus on form, analysis, and rule in the longer term, when not engaged in ongoing communication, so that they value restructuring as a language learning goal, and accuracy over the longer term. But it does not follow automatically that such learners will operate exactly the same set of priorities when they engage in actual language use. In such cases, there may be a greater valuation of memory-based performance, and a willingness to highlight the demands of real-time language use. This, of course, raises the additional possibility that an important area for research might concern the connection between ongoing processing, and the willingness, perhaps through the operation of metacognitive abilities, to reflect upon one's learning and so draw upon one's direct foreign language learning experiences later in order to modify representational systems and restructure.

The place of style within an information-processing framework

We have now examined the work of several researchers with an interest in learning style. Their approaches are summarized in Table 10.2. Three of the positions (Riding, Gregorc, Kolb) contrast representation and processing quite clearly, one (my own) is relevant to each of these, but without major contrasts, and one (Willing) although using two dimensions, locates both relevant dimensions within processing. In addition, where there is a representation-processing contrast, it is the processing component in which style is emphasized. Two researchers (Riding and Willing) directly incorporate field independence as the construct underlying processing style.

Gregorc and I have comparable concerns to those addressed by the analytic–holistic contrast. Gregorc prefers to emphasize a serial–random contrast, suggesting that the sequential nature of processing is more important than the analysis into sub-components. I emphasize more the units which underlie processing, with size of unit altering the need to engage in analysis. Two investigators (Kolb and Willing) draw upon a personality disposition as a central part of style of processing, in each case suggesting that we must consider the extent to which operating upon the world constitutes an important influence, compared with waiting for material to be presented by others. The connections with a learning-through-interaction approach are very clear, but there may also be a relationship here to learners who are more inclined to test out hypotheses actively and provoke relevant feedback, rather than wait and hope that it will come. In any case, Kolb and Willing, by this personality emphasis, reveal the more cerebral orientations of all the other approaches.

An information-processing framework

Another way of making sense of these different approaches is to relate them to an information-processing framework. In this respect, Miller (1987) draws upon the three stages of:

Perception	pattern recognition
	attention
Thought	mode of reasoning
Memory	representation
	organization
	retrieval

At the first stage, perception (or input, in the terms used in this book), the emphasis is on the way in which individuals interact with information in the environment, attempting to recognize or impose pattern on material, while also allocating attention in focused and relevant rather than diffuse ways, i.e. noticing. The central component, thought, is concerned with the manipulation of the material which has entered the system, i.e. restructuring and its attendant processes. Finally, memory is concerned with mode of representation, the links and associations which give the long-term memory

	Representation	Processing	Area where style is emphasized	Relevance of style variation to language learning
Riding	verbal–visual	analytic–holistic (FI vs. FD)	Both representation and processing, but with an emphasis on processing for IDs	By extension from original work: largely focuses on pattern identification capacities.
Gregorc	abstract–concrete	serial–random	Mainly serial–random contrast in processing	Implies a contrast between the careful accumulation of patterns and insights based on larger language corpora.
Kolb	abstract–concrete	active–passive	Preferred stage from a cycle, e.g. active–experimental, with this preference reflecting how information is obtained and processed.	Mainly through the type of interaction with the environment, cf. current SLA, cf. also Chapelle and Green's (1992) person-. orientation.
Willing		FI–FD active–passive	Heavy emphasis on processing, both for linguistic material (FI/FD) and personality dimension (active–passive).	Clear connection with a range of typical and realistic language learning situations.
Skehan	analytic–memory	analytic–memory	Patterns vs. chunks – immediate – longer term	Targeted at language and the size of unit for representation, as well as the units for processing.

Table 10.2: Contemporary approaches to style

system organization (with this having a strong influence upon the manner in which central processing takes place), and retrieval of information from memory.

The parallel between this general purpose attempt to relate the information-processing stage to concepts of style and the preceding discussion is striking. It enables us to locate the concerns of the different researchers within a wider framework, and in so doing attempt to reduce the impression of confusion given as different people use different terms. The framework is shown in Table 10.3. (The table does not include the personality contrast of active–passive, since this is not centrally concerned with issues of information processing.)

	Processing	Representation
Perception *Input*	Holistic vs. analytic (R)	Visual vs. verbal (R)
Thought *Central processing*	Holistic vs. analytic (R, W) Assimilation vs. restructuring (S) Random vs. serial (G)	(Large) chunks vs. rules (S) Concrete vs. abstract (G, K) Visual vs. verbal (R)
Output *Retrieval*	Retrieval vs. computation (S)	Redundant vs. parsimonious (S)

G=Gregorc   K=Kolb   R=Riding   S=Skehan   W=Willing

Table 10.3: Stages of information processing and concepts of style

The table shows that different researchers have had different implicit emphases. Riding (1991) clearly emphasizes the first stages of information processing, and highlights the ways in which stimulus material is handled. It is interesting in this regard that accounts based on the construct of foreign language aptitude (which itself was discussed in terms of the three information-processing stages) emphasize phonemic coding ability at this stage, implying an ability concerned with imposing structure on sound. The emphasis is on combating fleeting memory with unfamiliar material, and this is given prominence over alternative processing perspectives which assume a dependable stimulus field to operate upon. In language learning terms, this is something of a luxury and a rarity.

At the other extreme, output retrieval, I have directly related representation and processing to the nature of language and its use (Skehan 1996a), and strongly emphasize the contrast between economical but computationally demanding structures, and redundant, large, but accessible memory systems. The contrast can then be seen as relevant for representation, the actual memory codings that are involved, and processing, how material in memory is accessed, in terms of rules which operate upon memory structures, and also the units of memory organization, ranging as they can from the minimal to the formulaic chunk.

But the widest range of interest is shown in the central processing stage. Regarding representation, Gregorc (1979) and Kolb (1976) concentrate upon the type of information which is preferred (abstract–concrete), as does Riding, though in his case the contrast is between verbal and visual. In contrast, I was more concerned with the nature of the organization of the material which is represented, and contrasted a rule-plus-lexis approach with a larger unit size beyond the level of word. Regarding processing—how the material which is represented is then operated upon—the major emphasis is on the holistic–analytic contrast (Riding, Willing), with Gregorc less interested in analysis of the material to be organized so much as a methodical style of working with such data. In discussing an assimilation–restructuring contrast, I was concerned with the methods by which organized structures can change, and was closer to the holistic–analytic dichotomy.

Implications of style research

Earlier it was mentioned that Griffiths and Sheen (1992), in criticizing concepts of field independence, argued that contemporary psychologists do not actively pursue research in this area. We have seen that this is not really sustainable. Riding (1991) and Miller (1987), themselves active researchers, also review considerable current activity. Moreover, much of this research is relevant to specific criticisms that have been made. As a result, several summary points can be made:

- there have been advances in overcoming measurement limitations;
- greater conceptual clarity has been achieved by separating ability and style;
- richer conceptualizations of style exist, all resting on two dimensions of variation;
- some of these conceptualizations are consistent with an information processing framework, and with a distinction between representation and process;
- the proposals by different investigators can be related to information-processing stages.

We now seem to be in a position where views of style are ready to underpin fresh research efforts. The positions that have been reviewed are either from outside language learning (Riding 1991, Gregorc 1979, Kolb 1976) and so need application and validating research in that specific domain, or they are largely untested (Willing 1987, Skehan, this volume) and so require urgent research effort. But in either case the area seems ripe for investigation. It is only by such work that we can discover whether style is both separable from ability and important for second and foreign language learners.

Note

1 Kolb characterizes learning in this way, but of course, a similar approach is taken from a number of different areas. Popper (1968) uses essentially these stages in the way he portrays scientific investigation, while action research in language learning also recommends basically the same four steps.

11 Learners, learning, and pedagogy

In earlier chapters of the book, the focus was on second language learning. Most of the discussion was research-based, but in Chapter 6 pedagogic applications of the processing perspective were covered, while in Chapter 7 practical implications for testing were explored. This chapter has a corresponding pedagogic role, only on this occasion the applications are based on the discussion of second language learners in Chapters 8 to 10, and they target broader themes, such as syllabus and methodology. The chapter is in three parts. First, to set the scene for the later discussion, the role of the learner in language pedagogy is explored, developing the central argument that the individual learner has frequently been ignored. Then, in the first set of applications, ability and style concepts are applied to traditional and procedural approaches to second language teaching. Finally, strategy use and style concepts are shown to be pre-conditional for process syllabuses (a topic of lively current debate) to work.

Influences on language teaching: the forgotten learner

Institutional constraints

Over the last quarter of the twentieth century, the (English) language teaching profession has undergone many changes. One interesting example of this is the role of materials, and in particular, in the nature of coursebook provision. The market for 'main courses' has grown enormously, and the top five coursebook series, in Britain alone, generate very large sales indeed. Responding to these greater rewards for producing successful courses, the series themselves have changed dramatically. Books now contain far more material, with 'multi' syllabuses (Swan and Walter 1984–87) as well as extensive accompanying material. In addition, the professionalism of the publishing process means that those series which are published have survived a rigorous monitoring and piloting schedule which is likely to have caused significant rejection of unsatisfactory material and revision of almost everything which remains.

All this, of course, represents a significant advance. It is difficult not to conclude that the materials which are now available are not simply more extensive but are also of better quality than their predecessors. In some ways these developments have rendered out-of-date an interesting exchange on the value of language teaching materials. Allwright (1981) argued that commercial materials are a juggernaut which are stifling for the individual and the mediating contributions that can be made by the teacher. In contrast, O'Neill (1982) argued that it is better to use professional materials than those produced under difficult circumstances by amateurs. The debate was nicely balanced, with each party making unanswered points, and the conclusion being a difficult one to draw. So it is all the more striking that since then the O'Neill position has seemed to prevail by default. Since the time of the debate we have seen an astonishing growth in accepted importance of a relatively small number of well produced coursebook series, with the result that the position that Allwright argued so cogently has been marginalized.

This, of course, leads us to consider the price that we have had to pay for such progress. Clearly, a central factor underlying publisher behaviour is to maximize profits and the simplest equation for doing so is to sell more units. The key to achieving this is to develop a product that targets the widest purchaser group possible. Most directly of all, it is in the publisher's interests to treat all learners as the same, in order that a coursebook series will not lose appeal to any particular group of buyers. As a consequence the scope to adapt material to learner differences is severely constrained.

But it would be wrong to think that publishers alone have created conditions which lead to such a situation. Syllabus designers, too, have taken a similar approach. The units and sequences of syllabus design are regarded as being equally appropriate for all learners, and no account is taken of styles or preferences or abilities which might make some approaches to organizing courses more appropriate for some learners than others. One could make very similar points about different approaches to classroom procedures. In general, different methodological approaches dispute principles with one another, but do not explore the more interesting question of how adapting a particular methodology for different learner types, or using different methodologies with different sorts of learner, might produce better results. In fact, methodology seems most comfortable when it is devising techniques by which large classes of learners may be organized efficiently. How else can we explain the success of thin rationales for the use of class activities such as pattern practice, drilling, and general lockstep teaching?

Other groups, too, participate in the conspiracy of uniformity. It is extremely convenient for administrators and educational authorities, for example, to assume that all learners are similar. A further factor in discouraging diversity of provision is accountability. Pursuit of such a goal is made much easier if one can assume that all learners are the same. One can also argue that the teacher training profession acts to consolidate many of these implicit power relations, by generally concentrating on how entire classes can be organized; by teaching teachers how to implement official syllabuses and coursebooks, and by testing in an approved manner. There is little emphasis, in most teacher training courses, on the development of techniques which serve to adapt material to the individual learner, or on ways of fostering individuality in learning. The teacher is usually equipped to be a pawn within a larger structure, rather than a mediator between materials, syllabuses, and the learners themselves.

As a result of this conspiracy of sameness on the part of many of the powerful agents in the field of second language instruction, we have the paradoxical position that those with most power lack interest in learner differences, whereas those with least power, teachers, have to confront mixed-ability classes on a daily basis. It is striking that those who have no choice but to deal with the reality of classes with palpable individual differences are not provided with tools which would enable them to deal with such diversity. Whatever the reason for these shortcomings, the teacher is placed in a strange position: having to improvise with the minimum of guidance.

Different views of curriculum and syllabus: a role for autonomy

Despite this trend to uniformity, there have been some moves which recognize the role of the individual learner, especially in terms of learner autonomy and learner responsibility. Within the area of curriculum development, there has been increasing recognition that we need less 'technical' and less élitist curriculum philosophies (Richards 1985). In particular, one can talk about cognitive development perspectives, and also what Richards termed 'self-actualization curricula'. The first of these de-emphasizes the transmission of a fixed body of knowledge and is more concerned to develop the capacity to learn independently, to develop effective thinking techniques, to learn how to learn. A self-actualization approach is similarly concerned with the individual, but instead emphasizes affective rather than cognitive development, and looks to the process of education to facilitate harmonious processes of personal growth. Such contrasting views of the curriculum elevate learner autonomy to central importance, since it is fundamental for learners to develop questioning attitudes, and to learn how to become independent and more self-aware learners (and people).

Relating these contrasting views of curriculum to contemporary discussion of syllabus reveals that the most common approaches to syllabus (structural, functional-notional) reflect the priorities and values of traditional, reconstructionist, or 'technical' approaches (Clark 1984). In contrast, newer approaches to syllabus construction (Breen 1987) are closer to the progressive curriculum philosophies. Procedural syllabuses (White 1988; Prabhu 1987) accept that it is the learner's own activities which are central to learning, and that it is by the learner engaging in communication and task completion that progress takes place. Even so, the basis for such syllabuses is still structural, and the person who 'calls the shots' is still the pedagogic expert, in that tasks are chosen by the teacher. So in this respect the approach is as authoritarian as the more traditional ones. What is different is that a sense of humility about learning means that while syntactic progression is the central aim of the syllabus, this aim is achieved by giving learners freedom in how they interact with tasks, although the tasks themselves are not of the learners' own choosing. The tasks are meant to engage acquisitional processes, and are chosen by the teacher, drawing on his or her previous experience (Prabhu 1987) or analytic capacities (Skehan 1996a), for their perceived effectiveness in this regard.

In process syllabuses, in contrast (White 1988; Breen 1987), the learner is given power not only to interact, but also to control the nature of the interactions which take place. The learner participates in the decision-making process and works with other learners and the teacher to decide what will be done in the language class and how it will be done. This is the only syllabus type, in other words, which can be justified in terms of the more progressive curriculum philosophies which were discussed earlier.

A central feature of process syllabuses is that learners and teachers discharge very different roles from those in all other syllabus types. Learners need to know how to be effective learners, since they are being given considerable autonomy and power, while teachers need to be able to accept a very different position with respect to their authority. Neither of these changes will occur easily. Learning how to become an effective learner is not an easy task (Oxford 1990) and requires careful preparation (Ellis and Sinclair 1989), something which was not fully appreciated in early proposals for process syllabuses. Similarly, teachers have to *learn* how to relinquish power, as well as how to provide useful information and advice to learners from their new role.

A central point here is that process approaches to syllabus construction (Breen 1987; White 1988) provide only a framework to enable learners to make more effective decisions about their own learning. Syllabus, in other words, is a 'shell' or general structure that facilitates the decision-making process for learners, helping them to become more effective, autonomous decision makers (see Table 11.1). The decision-making stages that this table shows structure the ways in which learners can have an impact upon their instruction, and show how, in principle, autonomy is achievable. But an assumption that they make is that learners are willing to, and capable of, playing a full part in syllabus negotiation. In practice, things are not so easy, and an important part of implementing a process syllabus concerns the issue of learner readiness, to which we turn in the next section.

Stage	Description
Goals	Learners and teacher need to discuss and agree upon what the language course should try to achieve.
Roles	Learners and teacher clarify what each expects of the other.
Plan	In some respects this is close to the syllabus aspect of traditional language courses, since it concerns the general shape of the lessons, and the sequence of events that will unfold.
Activities	The aspect of a process syllabus which is closest to methodology is the determination of the activities that learners and teacher will use. The activities which are used should reflect the wishes of the learners. Decisions will need to reflect what learners, perhaps after taking the teacher's advice, think will contribute most to their progress.
Evaluation	If learners are intended to have power, this power should manifest itself most crucially in decisions about what framework for evaluation and assessment will be adopted (Rea-Dickins and Germaine 1992)—it is their opinions which count here.

Table 11.1: A set of steps that teacher and learner need to negotiate at the outset of a language learning course (Breen 1987: 161)

Learner strategies and learner readiness

The area of learner strategy research has grown dramatically in importance over the last twenty years or so and holds out the prospect that it may enable process syllabuses to be more than simply theoretical curiosities. The first major development was the publication of the 'Good Language Learner' study (Naiman *et al.* 1975), which reported on semi-structured interviews with a number of very successful language learners. These interviews revealed that such learners attributed their language learning success to the use of five general strategies:

- an active learning approach;
- realization of language as a system;
- realization of language as a means of communication;
- handling of affective demands;
- monitoring of progress.

Other significant research into learner strategies was conducted in the 1970s and early 1980s, by Wong-Fillmore (1979), Rubin (1981), and Politzer and McGroarty (1985). With hindsight, much of this earlier learner strategy research foreshadowed the second language acquisition literature. The active learning approach would generate exposure to considerable quantities of input as well as many interaction opportunities. Similarly, the judicious balance that good learners were thought to strike between language as system and language as communication parallels the arguments put forward in this book for a balance between analysis and synthesis, and a focus on form, as well as a concern to put that form to use. The capacity to monitor in general suggests a learner who is sensitive to restructuring and the progressive complexification that interlanguage development requires.

The early strategy research was a revelation, consistent with a wider appreciation of the role of strategies in psychology more generally, and insightful in the results that it delivered. It was also a source of inspiration for those who argued for process syllabuses, since it seemed to hold promise for how learners might be better understood, and then be better equipped to handle the sort of autonomy that such syllabus types required. So one of the first inferences to be drawn from such research was that if one could identify the strategies adopted by good language learners and then teach poor language learners to use such strategies, these less effective learners would become more able to handle language learning demands. It was this inference which lay behind research studies which tried to assess the worth of strategy training (O'Malley *et al.* 1985b) and attempts to develop learner training materials (Oxford 1990). Ominously, those studies which were completed were not especially encouraging in their results—O'Malley *et al.* found only marginal gains, at best, and in some areas no gains at all when comparing students who had received such instruction with those who had not. Later findings, in fact, suggested that all learners use strategies, and that the crucial issue is whether strategies are used flexibly and appropriately (Chamot and Kupper 1989).

Still, such findings did not discourage an explosion of activity in the production of materials to develop strategies. There have been some actual coursebooks, such as Ellis and Sinclair (1989) which structure the way in which learner training is done. Willing (1987) similarly provides stand-alone learner training materials, although the intention is that from a wide range of materials the teacher will simply select those that are appropriate at any particular time. There are also manuals to prepare teachers to train strategies, such as Oxford (1990) and Wenden and Rubin (1987). Finally, there have been attempts to produce what are termed 'integrated' learner training materials in main coursebooks, such as *Flying Colours* (Garton-Sprenger and Goodall 1989).

The proliferation of materials for learner training is encouraging, but the lack of a corresponding empirical justification for their use is disturbing, and requires some principled response if strategies are to be incorporated into language teaching. One approach is to explore how not all strategies are equivalent, and in that respect the distinction made by O'Malley and Chamot (1990) between three strategy types is useful. Social-affective strategies concern how learners engage in social interactions more effectively, use their fellow learners and interlocutors to help them solve problems, deal with affective problems; give themselves encouragement; and deal with anxiety. Cognitive strategies are concerned with the direct activities that are engaged in to promote learning. They would include such things as memorization techniques, inferencing, and so on. They represent what learners actually do to process the material that needs to be learned, and would correspond to Rubin's (1981) direct learning strategies.

Finally, we have metacognitive learning strategies, such as goal setting, planning, monitoring, evaluating, channelling attention, and so on. Metacognitive strategies are broader in application than the more direct repertoire of cognitive strategies, and may indeed subsume them. Above all, they are concerned with two things, reflection and flexibility. Reflection represents the learner developing some degree of self-awareness in learning, and shows how a given learner may appreciate his or her strengths and weaknesses. Flexibility arising from effective metacognitive strategy use organizes and gives purpose to the way cognitive and social-affective strategies are used, and increases the likelihood of appropriateness of strategy choice (Chamot and Kupper 1989). Rather than engage in activity for its own sake, the good learner is more able, through metacognitive awareness, to select strategies appropriate to a particular problem.

For process syllabuses to work, some capacity on the part of the learner to apply such metacognitive strategies is essential. If flexibility and reflection are the key aspects of strategy use, then inculcating learners into such use, through metacognitive strategies, is essential for process syllabuses. Such strategies are the tools which learners must have if they are to be ready to assume the autonomy that process syllabuses imply. Equipped with such tools, learners can benefit from such independence—without them they are likely to flounder.

Learners, procedural and process syllabuses

So far, we have examined how institutional forces have downplayed the role of the individual learner, how some curriculum and syllabus developments have started to provide a wider learner role, and how learner strategy research may be productively applied to bring about more effective language teaching. We now need to tie up some loose ends, and also summarize a range of learning and learner issues to prepare for the pedagogic issues covered in the rest of the chapter.

Procedural syllabuses

We can start by contrasting the assumptions that are made about learners by the two sorts of syllabus that were discussed in an earlier section, procedural and process syllabuses. Procedural syllabuses expect that interlanguage development will occur as a result of the way learners have to transact tasks.

But all learners are treated as the same, and it is assumed that a diet of tasks, properly implemented, will bring about better fluency, restructuring, and accuracy. The way the individual learner fits into this is unclear, and the types of learner differences discussed in the last few chapters are not addressed—a serious limitation for task-based approaches. To remedy this, teachers need to know:

– what learning strengths and weaknesses as well as preferences different students have;
– how tasks can be selected and implemented to take account of these factors.

The next section of this chapter will relate ability and style concepts from Chapters 8 to 10, as well as some of the earlier discussion of tasks, to traditional and procedural approaches to language teaching.

Process syllabuses

There are also questionable assumptions behind the process approach to syllabus construction:

– that the teacher has knowledge about learners and learning which can help learners to make better decisions;
– that the teacher is able to induce learners to take on progressively more responsibility;
– that the teacher can lead learners to clarify their own pedagogic aims so that the learners themselves can be induced to make better pedagogic decisions.

Similarly, it is assumed that learners can make effective decisions for themselves, can articulate their own language learning needs, and can work effectively with a 'facilitating' teacher. Portrayed in terms of Breen's (1987) five stages, the assumption is that learners are able to participate in meaningful discussion about goal setting, role allocation, the planning of learning, the activities to be used, and the forms of evaluation.

Problems can occur if these assumptions are not met. Learners may not accept the degree of independence required for process syllabuses to function, either because they are unfamiliar with such an approach or because, for style or personality reasons, they are not attracted to the degree of independence and decision making involved. In such cases, process syllabuses may fail at the first hurdle. One can also imagine situations where the general idea of a process syllabus is accepted, but it is put into practice in an unsatisfactory manner. Learners may simply not have the range of skills and strategies that a process syllabus presupposes. A process syllabus needs learners who are able to plan, direct attention, and set goals. If these strategies are not present, dissatisfaction may result. Learners may have power, but feel frustrated because they are not able to use it effectively. Similarly, the capacity to monitor and evaluate is crucial. Without such a capacity, progress is likely to be fragmented into a number of unconnected skills which the learner can deploy, but which do not easily form any connected system or whole.

The final section of the chapter explores how style concepts and strategy use can be applied to process syllabus implementation, particularly through project work. It argues that without detailed integration of such individual differences, such syllabuses can easily lead to failure and frustration.

Aptitude and procedural syllabuses

An introductory model

Figure 11.1 provides a general model to incorporate many of the issues that have been discussed so far. It draws upon Skehan (1989) and Willing (1989). The model contains four individual differences. Modality preferences refers to the general predisposition to use visual, auditory, or 'action' approaches to learning. This concerns the preferred input channel and relates to research by Reid (1987) which suggested that 30 per cent of learners preferred auditory input, 40 per cent visual, and 30 per cent kinaesthetic.

Aptitude was covered in Chapters 8 and 9. Besides the three aptitude components, (phonemic coding ability, language analytic capacity, memory), the contrast is made between two preferences: an analytic predisposition and a memory predisposition. Style concerns the material covered in Chapter 10, and brings in the cognitive dimensions of holistic versus analytic processing, and the contrast between visual and verbal representations. In addition, the personality aspect of style, active versus passive (Willing 1987), conveys the impression that style is not simply cerebral. Finally, the discussion of learner strategies from earlier in this chapter is represented, showing the distinction between metacognitive, cognitive, and socio-affective strategies.

The left-to-right movement in Figure 11.1 reflects progressively greater degrees of malleability for the learner difference concerned. Strategies, that is, are seen as the most capable of change. Style is seen as less malleable, but to the extent that individuals command a range of styles, they can move along a sort of style continuum as is appropriate given different instructional and communicational demands (Brown 1994). The next box, aptitude, would then represent a more fixed endowment of abilities, so that while learners may learn to exploit their aptitude profile to the best degree possible, it still represents a limiting factor in their speed of language learning. Finally, research such as that of Reid (1987) suggests that modality preferences may also be fairly fixed in nature and reflect generalized processing preferences.

Using this model, we can more easily examine the appropriateness of language instruction for the individual learner as well as the scope for instructional adaptation. We will look first at the scope for adaptation in traditional methodologies and then focus on task-based and procedural approaches.

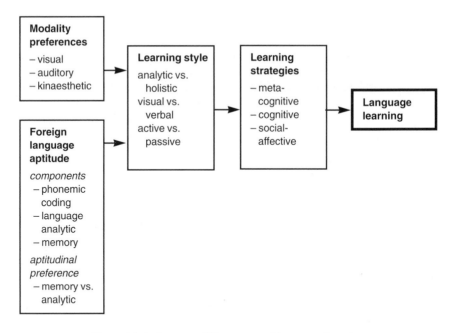

Figure 11.1: Learner differences and language learning

Adapting instruction for learner differences

Traditional approaches

There are two ways in which adaptation can be achieved in traditional methodologies: diagnostic approaches, and matching learners and methods through aptitude-treatment interactions. Regarding the first of these, in the testing literature four test types—aptitude, achievement, proficiency, and diagnostic—are distinguished. It is, in fact, more helpful to oppose the fourth test type to the other three, in that it is easy to imagine diagnostic proficiency tests (which identify weaknesses in proficiency profile), and diagnostic achievement tests (which identify areas of non-learning). Following this line of reasoning, diagnostic aptitude tests are also possible, with the aptitude tests used to identify areas of likely weakness in future learners, so that profile information can be available before a course starts, and then instruction can be adapted pre-emptively in light of this knowledge. In Chapter 9, for example, the relative contribution of different aptitude components at different proficiency levels was discussed. It was claimed that phonemic coding ability is particularly important at earlier stages of learning, but decreases in importance at later stages. The danger is that auditorily weaker students get left behind and lose out cumulatively as the general pace of learning at initial stages proves too great. Advance knowledge about low phonemic coding ability could be turned to advantage here. Auditorily weaker learners can be provided with the 'pre-emptive remedial action' that will enable them to overcome what seems to be a specific and relatively short-lived area of weakness. In other words, the diagnostic interpretation of aptitude can help to avoid penalizing learners whose potential may not otherwise be realized.

A second way in which instruction can be profitably adapted is to modify instruction to take account of aptitude profiles and consequent preferences; compare the Wesche (1981) study exploring the consequences of matching and mismatching learners with methodologies. Wesche discovered that matching learners with methodology led to both higher levels of achievement and more satisfaction, suggesting the general utility of such aptitude-treatment interaction research as well as the appropriateness of the particular contrasts which were researched. There has been little empirical research which has built upon Wesche's report, although theorizing in this area has indeed extended the analytic-memory contrast that was the basis for her study: the time would seem ripe for more work of this sort.

Procedural and task-based syllabuses

Drawing on the discussion in Chapters 5 and 6, the basic assumption here is that learners vary in the extent to which they prioritize analysis versus synthesis. In other words, a dual-mode system is envisaged, with different learners being predisposed to emphasize restructuring and accuracy, on the one hand, or fluency and exemplar-based learning, on the other.

We can represent extreme forms of this scenario (consistent, thoroughly analytic learners versus invariantly exemplar-based learners versus balanced learners) in the form of a graph, shown in Figure 11.2) which portrays contrasting paths of interlanguage development.

Path A represents learners who balance attention to form and meaning throughout their learning careers. Such learners switch attention judiciously so that their interlanguage system is more likely to be regularly reviewed (leading to a more 'open' and permeable system in general) but attention is also devoted to integrating language, on an exemplar-base, so that natural communication is achieved. The other two paths suggest learners whose progress is not so balanced, and for whom a particular aptitudinal profile or processing preference (analytic versus memory, from Figure 11.1) is associated with characteristic predominance of formal goals over communicational goals, (path B) or vice versa (path C). Path B learners, for example, may not complete the final part of their learning curve because they are excessively rule-oriented, and although they may achieve complexity of language knowledge, may not be able to translate such complexity into actual language use. Path C learners, in contrast, may have acquired communicative fluency too early, with the result that fossilization makes later progress difficult (compare the discussion in Chapters 2 to 4) as a result of strategic competence and lexicalized communication becoming too effective.

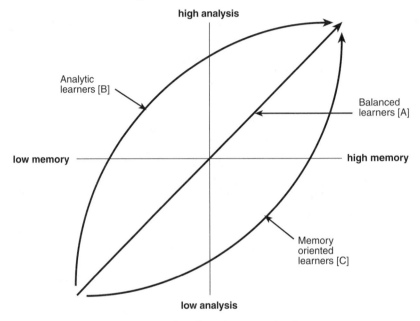

Figure 11.2: Paths of interlanguage development

We now need to ask how the paths shown in Figure 11.2 come about. One interpretation, consistent with the last paragraph, is that the paths represent the consequences of the aptitude profiles of the learners concerned, that interlanguage development is determined by aptitudinal strengths. It is more realistic to view such paths as the trace of what has happened in the learning histories of individual learners, the product of the interaction between learning opportunities and aptitudinal profile. So here we are concerned with the way in which, for example, path B comes about because we have an analytic learner who has not had any instructional (or generally environmental) pressures to take a more communicative, memory, and exemplar-oriented view of language learning. Similarly, path C would be that of a learner whose predispositions are towards fluency, synthesis, and integration, and away from analysis, and for whom the environment has also pushed more towards communication than analysis, either through a one-dimensional diet of task-based instruction or perhaps the urgency of actual, real-world communicative encounters. This leaves path A. Such a path may represent a learner whose aptitude profile balances analysis and memory, and who is naturally equipped, therefore, for balanced development. Alternatively, it may be a learner whose natural processing predispositions are more towards analysis or synthesis, but for whom environmental or instructional pressures have had a corrective role. In this case, the balanced, desirable path will have been created because of the appropriateness of the environment, or more probably, instruction.

We next need to consider how instruction can be adjusted to take account of the problematic developmental paths. This can be illustrated by applying the model for task-based instruction presented in Chapters 5 and 6 to adapting instruction for individual differences. Recall that the earlier model advanced five principles for the implementation of task-based learning:

1 Choose a range of target structures.
2 Choose tasks to meet Loschky and Bley-Vroman's (1993) utility condition.
3 Select sequence tasks to achieve balanced goal development.
4 Maximize the chances of a focus on form through attention manipulation.
5 Use cycles of accountability.

The third and fourth principles are central here. The third principle involves selecting tasks of appropriate difficulty level and also choosing tasks which predispose learners towards particular processing goals (for example structured tasks for accuracy, tasks based on familiar information for fluency). The fourth principle suggests how the nature of the task can be changed by the conditions under which it is done. It was argued in earlier chapters that pre-task planning can be channelled towards restructuring and change in the interlanguage system. Post-task activities can highlight the importance of accuracy. So the five principles, together with the three-phase implementation model, are concerned with manipulation of the focus of attention without losing the primacy of communication. Through effective task choice, appropriate pre-task activities, and careful task implementation, followed by high priority being attached to post-task reflection activities, a great deal of variation in the focus of attention is possible.

In earlier chapters these pedagogic devices were presented as if all learners are the same. The preceding discussion questions this viewpoint, and argues strongly that knowledge of learner predispositions should be input to the pedagogic choices which are made, balancing the different processing goals which are operative. Faced with analytic or memory-oriented learners, tasks can be chosen and implemented to induce learners to address aspects of performance and developmental course which might not come naturally. This approach is illustrated in detail in Table 11.2, where suggestions are made for each learner type at the different phases of a task-based approach.

The overriding aim in each case is to build an emphasis into task-based instruction which counteracts what may be natural tendencies to take unbalanced paths towards language development. In the case of analytic learners, the intention is to build in a greater concern for fluency, and the capacity to express meanings in real time without becoming excessively concerned with a focus on form (which is assumed to be a natural processing inclination anyway). In the case of memory-oriented learners, the intention is

Stage	Analytic learner	Memory-oriented learner
Pre-task linguistic	Not required	Emphasis on planning and preparation Appropriate use of detailed and undetailed planning
Pre-task cognitive	Some planning to drive towards more complex meanings to tasks based on familiar information	Some planning, to lighten the attentional burden during the task
During task: task choice	Slightly more difficult tasks Tasks based on familiar information	Slightly easier tasks Tasks containing structure Tasks with differentiated outcomes
During task pressure	Increased pressure – less time – oral modality – less control	Slightly easier tasks – no time limits or pressure – opportunity for control
Post-task	Focus on communication No obsession with accuracy	Analysis of language Stress on public performance

Table 11.2: Pedagogic alternatives with contrasting learner types

to set limits to the natural tendency to prioritize communicative outcome above all else, and to focus attention on both or either of restructuring/ complexity or accuracy. This is achieved either by reducing cognitive load, or by increasing language focus. Although actual implementations are unlikely to be so one-sided as this, the fundamental point is that the framework introduced in Chapters 5 and 6 can be adapted in a fairly straightforward manner to make it appropriate for decisions influencing the individual learner, and as a result provide the teacher with a principled basis for what will inevitably be difficult decision making.

Equipping learners for autonomy

So far we have looked at instructional adaptations based on a relatively unchanging aptitude. With style and strategy the situation is different, in that not only can such qualities be modified but it is also crucial the learner should have a stake in achieving such change. Indeed, it becomes the responsibility of the learner to work towards beneficial change, rather than solely the responsibility of the teacher to make benevolent decisions. In this way, the learner will rely on the teacher far less, and, as a result, increase the amount of time spent learning, since such learning is not constrained by a requirement for the teacher's presence. Only by such achievements is it likely that process syllabuses will be practically feasible.

It will also be recalled, from the earlier discussion, that process syllabuses are rich in assumptions made about the readiness of learners to take on the new roles, and to play their part in formulating plans and organizing their own learning activities. In general, the conclusion was reached that simply 'announcing' a process syllabus is likely to produce confusion, as learners may not be ready to make the necessary decisions, or have the skills that are prerequisites for effective learning to proceed. To address these issues, the remainder of this chapter (a) examines the suitability of project work as a vehicle for actual implementation in process syllabuses, and (b) explores how the individual learner can be equipped to make such syllabuses work. The claim will be that project work enables the gradual development of autonomy with progressively greater responsibility being taken by learners, and that it is an excellent structure for preparing learners to approach learning in their own way, suitable to their own abilities, styles, and preferences.

The suitability of project work

Haines (1989) suggests that projects are student-centred activities, with students choosing which topics to do and how topics will be approached. He proposes several types of project which reflect different ways in which student-centredness manifests itself, including information and research projects (for example, finding out about pressure groups in the UK, or Fried-Booth's (1986) example of students choosing and working on a *Good Wheelchair Guide for Bath*, both of these projects suitable for a *second* language context), surveys (such as attitudes towards native speakers of the language, or from Fried-Booth (1986) again, a language survey, which researches the extent to which a target language is spoken in a particular country, both of these projects being appropriate for a *foreign* language setting), production projects, such as developing a radio programme, and performance projects, such as arranging an American evening, where the project aims at the 'performance' itself.

Projects are also likely to be collaborative, avoiding competition, and tending to lend themselves to analysis of global goals into sub-components which are then delegated to sub-groups, who take responsibility for completing them. This in turn leads to the possibility of specialization within a project and a clearer structure for individual contributions. Projects are also likely to integrate skills, since the sub-goals which are likely to be specified will require balanced and realistic use of language, as sets of activities need to be accomplished. Finally, projects tend to contain a tangible end-product. On the one hand, this makes the project meaningful and purposeful. On the other, it operates as a sort of public record of the project, of which the participants have ownership, and which will give the project some durability. This last quality has a clear relationship with the public performance argued for in task-based instruction. There the justification was that knowledge of a public performance during a task would change the way in which attention was controlled, and insinuate a greater focus on form. The same argument can apply, although perhaps not quite so strongly, to the end-product nature of project work. Students will regard such end products as public documents and as a result take their formal accuracy more seriously. It is likely that they will bring about a greater concern for form throughout, to the extent that learners perceive (and can be led to perceive) the connection between ongoing project activity and final outcome (compare discussion of post-task activities in Chapter 6).

Sequences in project work

Given this discussion of project types and project characteristics, the issue becomes one of how such potential for involving students can be realized most productively. In this respect, Fried-Booth (1986) suggests the sequence shown in Figure 11.3 for the gradual implementation of projects, which enables progressively greater responsibility to be taken by learners. Introductory activities (not elaborated here) are sufficiently close to what happens in more cosseted classrooms so as not to provoke anxiety, but contain moves towards more independent learning situations. The next stage is represented by what are termed 'bridging' activities (Fried-Booth 1986) or 'lead-in' activities

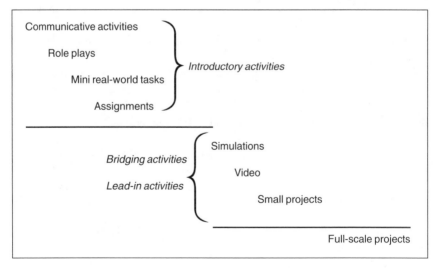

Figure 11.3: Stages in the implementation of project work

(Haines 1989). These provide less structure and support, and push learners to greater independence and the need to take responsibility and analyse problems. It is the teacher who decides upon topics, so the autonomy that students enjoy is more concerned with how they set about the tasks, rather than in choosing which tasks they should do. Once these stages of introductory and bridging activities have been successfully completed, learners are ready for full-scale projects, in which they take on much wider responsibility for topic choice as well as topic execution. We next need to consider the stages which have to be followed in the culmination of the above sequence—the full-scale project. Fried-Booth (1986) suggests that the following three stages have significance (with each of the stages having sub-stages):

Classroom based

- provision of stimulus material
- definition of project objectives
- analysis and practice of language skills
- design of written materials

Carrying out of project

- group activities
- collation of information

Review/monitoring

- organization of material
- final presentation.

In all these stages the teacher can have an important role. During the classroom-based stage, he or she can make thematic suggestions at the stimulus stage, assist organization and realism at the objectives stage, provide specialist advice and knowledge of resources at the skills and design stages, and so on. During the execution stage, the teacher can offer solutions to problems, act as a referee between disagreeing groups, provide gentle evaluation, and so on. Then, at the final product stage, the teacher can continue to help in the way material is organized, delegation between groups is achieved, and the final presentation is prepared for. Through the different stages, then, there is a move from analysis and preparation to less structured action, to a phase where reflection and accountability are brought to bear as the fruits of the action phase are put to some use.

Developing the skills of individuals

Now that we have examined the nature of project work in general and have seen how it would be implemented, we can explore the extent to which specific things can be done to develop the language learning skills and achievement of individuals. In this respect, it is clear that a greater degree of intervention is assumed on the teacher's part. Where conventional project work is attempted, the teacher should occupy a facilitative, responsive role, with autonomy given to the learners. What is argued here is that, in order to foster the development of individuals, teachers may need to be more pre-emptive. Wherever possible this should be attempted at the bridging or lead-in stage, but on occasions it seems inevitable that if the teacher wants to achieve improvement with individuals, he or she will have to direct what specific students do and also, possibly, raise consciousness within the group regarding the individual students themselves and how they may each have slightly different learning-to-learn goals. We will examine two methods of adapting project work for the individual learner, the development of more effective strategy use, and the accommodation of different learner types (Willing 1987).

We can start by examining the potential projects have for the development of strategy use. There are three main stages within project work, with pre-project activities, bridging activities, and then full projects linked to the different forms of strategy training that would be most appropriate at each stage. The strategy training itself targets metacognitive strategies, with the three major categories of arranging one's own learning plan (AOLP), controlling attention (CA), and evaluation (E).

Pre-project work

Communicative activities

Communicative activities could be used to develop learners' capacities to mobilize resources and existing knowledge so that the activity could be done better. They can also be used to help learners centre attention on the task at hand (CA). Such activities can also be used to develop limited self-monitoring and self-evaluation, since learners can be encouraged to reflect upon the nature of their own performance (E).

Role plays and mini real-world tasks

In contrast, role plays and mini real-world tasks can draw learners into structured opportunities to engage a planning capacity, giving them the chance to analyse problems, assess their own strengths and weaknesses, develop methods of self-management, plan, and set appropriate goals (AOLP).

Bridging and lead-in activities

Bridging and lead-in activities, such as the use of simulations and small projects, are an excellent area to build in strategy training, since the degree of teacher control is greater. They provide focused and systematic opportunities to use metacognitive strategies.

Giving a short talk

Giving a short talk (Haines 1989) provides ample scope to help learners analyse a problem, work out what their strengths and weaknesses are, how the talk could be planned, and what the speaker aims to accomplish with the talk (AOLP).

Conducting an interview

Besides enabling a wide range of AOLP strategies, conducting an interview (Haines 1989) would allow learners the chance to mobilize resources and existing knowledge, to prioritize and organize what would be accomplished, to foresee problems, and to devise methods of centring their attention in the face of the near-simultaneous need to listen and extract meaning from responses, while also formulating new questions (themselves linking with lines of preparation for the interview), so that considerable attention management would be needed (CA).

Expressing information in different ways

This focuses upon a component skill for subsequent projects, since many project types (for example, information and research, surveys) presuppose competence in this area (Haines 1989). Here the basic intention is to present the information which has been collected in different ways to achieve a greater degree of variety in project presentation. Such a lead-in activity could also have a self-evaluation dimension, in that not only would students be encouraged to be creative in the ways they explore pie-charts versus tables or case-studies, etc., but they would also be encouraged to reflect upon the effectiveness of these different choices. In this way, they could be led to go beyond activity for its own sake, and to develop the confidence to question their own achievements so that they might be improved.

Full-scale project work

Stimulus and objectives

The stimulus and objectives phases lend themselves very well to the general strategy of arranging one's own learning plan (AOLP). A problem needs to be analysed, and then broken down into different sub-sections. The objectives need to be specified and related to language skills. There is considerable scope here for clear views of the language required to emerge, for individuals to see who would be required to develop which skills, to plan how the project will be done and how individual contributions will be assembled into a coherent whole, and for strengths and weaknesses of individuals to be built into the planning. Learners can be encouraged to support one another, and to devise strategies which then capitalize upon the sub-groupings of students so produced. Objectives can include tangible outcomes (for example, the production of a video), and individual-based outcomes in terms of strategies developed and the weaknesses overcome.

Analysing and practising skills

The main focus here is that students should develop effective strategies for centring attention (CA). Later, they will have to engage in language use situations, and the purpose of the skills phase is to prepare themselves for such situations. They will need to develop the strategies that will enable them to do this, such as relating what is required to what they already know, using attention effectively, and identifying communication problems and devising methods of overcoming them. In this respect, there is scope not only to develop specific repertoires of useful language behaviour, but also to encourage learners to analyse their strategic use so that it can be applied more readily in new situations. An important secondary focus of this stage is to develop self-evaluation and self-monitoring (E).

Group activities

In this phase, teams or groups of learners will go outside the classroom to work on the main part of the project—the gathering of relevant information to implement the plan that has been made. The emphasis, as far as strategy use is concerned, is to focus attention effectively (CA) and to evaluate what has been accomplished so that (a) completion of the project sub-goal is recognized and (b) there is useful learning about learning (E).

Learners have to develop skills to make decisions during actual language use and develop effective metacognitive strategy use, so that their interactions are not overly planned, but instead respond more spontaneously and modify goals, use repair strategies, etc. as interactions unfold. Learners will also need to strike an appropriate balance between form and meaning, so that they make the same sorts of links as do learners in task-based instruction, and do not prioritize meaning excessively at the expense of form. However, in line with the importance of metacognitive strategies, it is not the capacity to carry out particular procedures that is important so much as the capacity to reflect upon one's own language use, in such a way that it can be modified and made more effective. Hence it is the link between assessment of situation, planning, and goal setting, on the one hand, and the evaluation of effectiveness and quality of outcome on the other, that are important.

Collating information and organizing material

The collation of material is the prelude to making reports and presentations, and so the form in which information is collated may start to have implications for the language of the final report. That being the case, there will be an emphasis on the role of formal accuracy and structural complexity, in that learners can be encouraged to plan and to use appropriately ambitious language for the task to come. In other words, there is still scope for the use of attentional strategies (CA) as well as a new arena for the operation of evaluation and monitoring strategies (E).

Final presentation

It is important for learners to appreciate the significance of the final presentation, since to do so is more likely to galvanize them to be more purposeful at the earlier stages. So there is considerable scope for planning, analysis, and preparation of the final reporting back. The learner must think how everything that has gone before can be channelled into the public performance (AOLP), and centre attention effectively in the contribution that he or she makes to the presentation itself (CA). This is also the stage when evaluation is most relevant, since such evaluation is motivated by a clearer awareness of the audience for the presentation (E).

Project work should, through a process of gradual planning and withdrawal of support, wean learners away from excessive teacher dependence. The aim, in other words, has to be to equip learners to take responsibility for their own learning in a skilled manner, an aim which requires:

- a capacity to think ahead about what is needed, to analyse, and plan;
- a capacity when using language to do so effectively, and in a way that balances immediate communicational demands with longer-term pedagogic goals;
- a capacity to reflect upon one's learning and to assess the effectiveness of what has been done with a view to modifying one's approach in the future to make it more effective.

Learner style differences

This detailed breakdown demonstrates how strategy work can be integrated into projects and how, in fact, such integration, at the pre-project and bridging stages, is vital if full-scale projects are to be viable. But, in fact, project work lends itself to still further adaptation for the individual. In particular, learner style differences can be accommodated within such an approach. To return to the learner types (Willing 1987) discussed in Chapter 10 (convergers, communicators, concrete learners, and conformists), each of these learner types contains strengths and weaknesses and, to the extent that style is to some degree malleable, there is the possibility that skilful use of the project work format can induce learners to retain the advantages of their learner type while dealing with their weaknesses.

Convergers

Convergers will be able to plan effectively within project work and will not lack confidence in going outside the classroom to implement the activities that the project requires. So they are likely to come up with goals and suggestions for sub-group activities which will fit in with what the project is trying to achieve. The problem is that they may lack a corresponding enthusiasm to engage in communication and actual language use—they may be good at finding out about things, but not through direct language use with speakers of the language. It may be useful, therefore, to use bridging activities which require such learners to develop social skills and to work in groups, so that they take their part in a team and also learn how to interact more effectively with learners who are different from themselves. They could also benefit from practice in the sorts of direct language use activities which will certainly come later, and which they might otherwise try to avoid. (It is, of course, a paradox of autonomy that learners may use the freedom so given in order to avoid the very areas they would benefit from addressing!) Then, in project work itself, such learners could be encouraged to take on less cerebral projects (for example moving away from always doing information, research, and survey projects, and towards production and performance projects), steered towards language-involving activities, and assigned roles which do not permit them simply to gather information.

Concrete learners

Concrete learners will need the converse treatment. They may well feel comfortable with actual language-use situations but tend not to approach them with adequate planning. Their interpersonal and interactional skills may be fine but their capacity to approach problems systematically may not be so advanced. As a result, bridging activities could be directed more profitably at the capacity to set goals, plan, and analyse (at the pre-activity phase), and then organize their attention, switching more effectively between goals rather than always emphasizing the same one of communicative fluency. They will need to develop the capacity to reflect upon form and monitor in a more focused way, so that attention is paid to accuracy as a goal, and risk taking is more likely to occur and produce more complex language. With such learners, there may be a greater need to propose more structured topics, so that information and research projects as well as surveys may draw such learners into areas they might not otherwise explore. It is likely that they would benefit also from being required to take charge of the final stages of the project, the collation and organization of material, as well as the final presentation.

Conformists

Conformist learners are those learners who feel most comfortable within classrooms which are directed and organized by the teacher. Yet the central quality of project work is that it transcends the bounds of the classroom, with the result that passive learners are likely to be the most threatened by what is required. They will need to develop a greater willingness to take on responsibility and become more autonomous in their approach to learning. They may benefit from the structure of mini real-world tasks (Fried-Booth 1986), in which there will need to be work outside the classroom but following a structured plan from the teacher. Similarly, not only could such learners be required to participate in simulations (within class) but they could also be required to plan for them, so that they develop more confidence with their analytic capacities and their ability to take on individual responsibility. The alternative to taking these approaches would be that such learners, when pitchforked into autonomy, would find the lack of structure very threatening and take to evasion rather than involvement.

Communicative learners

Basically, the remaining category, communicative learners, do not require a great deal of adaptation in project work—they seem to be the learners who are most naturally inclined to thrive in such an organization. They are not afraid of going outside the classroom, and will be willing to engage in natural conversation. The difficulties that might be faced here are more connected with whether the learner involved is analytic or holistic.

Conclusions

The general themes of this chapter have been that there are clear implications for pedagogy from the study of learning and learners, that these implications, for a variety of reasons, have had surprisingly little attention, and that there is scope now to explore just how instruction can be adapted to take account of the person who is most involved, the actual learner. Even so, it has to be admitted that the claims which have been made have had to be largely extrapolated from the research literature rather than attested by actual research studies. This has been largely the result of the *lack* of research that is available. What we have now is more theory and research on the nature of second language learning which can be applied to adapting instruction, as well as a little research on more malleable learner differences. It is important that such research is extended, so that we have a more principled basis for examining why not all learners will benefit in exactly the same way when provided with a given set of instructional conditions. Only in this way will we be able to put research in second language acquisition and language learning to proper use.

12 Conclusions

This concluding chapter tries to restate, in a more condensed form, the central issues discussed in the book. It is organized into three sections. The first (and longest) reviews the ideas and claims that have been the driving force of the book, focusing on a cognitive basis for language learning, the importance of dual-coding approaches and memory, and the tension between learning and performance. The second section summarizes the implications of these basic ideas and how they can be the basis for pedagogic intervention and application. The main themes of the section are instruction, individual differences, and assessment. The final section outlines areas where additional research would be beneficial.

Fundamental concepts and claims

Second language learning is cognitive and linked to aptitudinal components

A precondition for the claim that second language learning is cognitive is that a critical period exists for language learning. Prior to the end of this critical period language learning proceeds through the automatic engagement of a Language Acquisition Device (able to cope with impoverished, inadequate input, and so on). Subsequent to the critical period such pre-wired capacities are no longer available, with the result that other approaches to second language learning have to be used (Bley-Vroman 1989). The evidence (Johnson and Newport 1991) is also consistent with a gradual, rather than abrupt end to the critical period, such that the scope to engage a Language Acquisition Device gradually diminishes, so that by the age of 14 to 17 or so, direct primary processes no longer apply.

Prior to the closure of this critical period, there is modularity in language learning, but the most significant aspect of this modularity is a contrast between syntax and semantics. Subsequent to the critical period, there is also modularity, but organized on the basis of information-processing stages: input, central processing, and output. In other words, the end of the critical period is the point at which the nature of language learning changes from being an automatically engaged process to one in which it becomes yet another cognitive activity. From this point on, the search is for cognitive abilities which support the different aspects of second language learning. This book takes the line that these abilities are best understood if they are linked to the stages in which information is processed.

One perspective on these abilities is through the study of foreign language aptitude. Evidence reviewed from this area has suggested that a talent for foreign language study has three general components: phonemic coding ability, language analytic ability, and memory. These three components of aptitude can be linked to the stages of information processing, in that phonemic coding ability connects with the input processing stage, language analytic ability with the central processing one, and memory with the output stage to the extent that this links with fluency and with the retrieval of information to enable real-time communication. An implication of this analysis is that there are individual differences between language learners which are based on abilities relevant to building blocks in information processing, that it is possible to regard aptitude components not as fanciful extractions from factor analyses of test batteries, but rather as integrally based in a cognitive view of the process of post-critical period foreign language learning.

Given the move in the study of second language acquisition in recent years towards more cognitive interpretations, these linkages have significant advantages. Recent research into the input stage has set great store by concepts such as noticing (Schmidt 1990), focus-on-form (Long 1989) and notice the gap (Swain 1995), while VanPatten (1996) has emphasized the value of training learners in input-processing strategies. Clearly there are strong cognitive components here, and it is striking that studies of aptitude which were carried out forty years ago (Carroll and Sapon 1959) had already identified a relevant ability, phonemic coding ability, in this area. At the central processing stage the connections are clear, even if more complex. SLA researchers have emphasized processes such as hypothesizing, (over)generalizing, making inferences, and so on, as the ways in which interlanguage development, restructuring, transfer, and change are more likely to occur. The alternative processes may be numerous, but one clear claim does emerge from this work—the construct of language analytic ability within aptitude may be essentially a cover term for this range of cognitive processes which collectively underpins the process of language change and development.

The advantage of viewing second language learning through information-processing stages continues when we consider output. There has been regular discussion of fluency in the second language field (Brumfit 1984) and also in linguistics (Fillmore 1979), but it has rarely been conceived of as a problem integral to and significant for processing accounts. In a discussion from a psycholinguistic perspective, Schmidt (1992) showed that fluency has to be understood in all its complexity, and that, crucially, simply viewing greater fluency as the development of greater automatization is of limited use. What is now possible, through work such as Bolinger (1975), Peters (1983), and Pawley and Syder (1983), is to view fluency as partly dependent on the role of memory in performance, and the way in which the unit of performance may vary, sometimes functioning at the morpheme level, but often drawing on larger units beyond the level of the word, and including very large numbers of ready-made phrases. The consequence of this is to recast the performance problem not simply as a computation problem (that underlying rules are applied in interaction with simple lexical elements) but also as a retrieval problem, where chunks of language are orchestrated, in real time, to achieve fluent performance. In this way, the third component of language aptitude, memory, can be reinterpreted as relevant not simply to the acquisition of new information, but also as relevant to the coding, organization, retrieval, and use of existing information. In this way, an aptitude component has a direct relationship to the effectiveness with which output is organized.

Dual-coding and memory are critical

This discussion of the role of output leads naturally into the area of memory functioning. Drawing on the distinction made by Widdowson (1989) between analysability and accessibility, the claim is that language use can emphasize precision and 'computed' complexity (analysis) or speed linked with ease of processing. Normally (native) language users are adept at combining analysed and accessibility modes, shifting between them as communicational circumstances make appropriate. If performance demands are high, it is likely that accessibility will become a more important mode, while if performance conditions are not so pressing, and/or if precision in communication is important, the analysis mode will dominate.

The emphasis on accessibility in this view derives from the much greater importance linguists now give to memorized, familiar, idiomatic language. Although the language system contains the potential to generate an infinite number of sentences, in practice a restricted set of choices is routinely made (compare Hymes's 1972 concern for language which is 'done', i.e. ratified by the consistent choice of a speech population). Language users are more comfortable speaking about the familiar, and are able, by drawing on a capacious memory system, to produce a great deal of language quickly by means of routinized phrases. (Language comprehenders, too, have such a bias towards the familiar.) This recasts our view of how language functions. A powerful generative system exists, but may be bypassed most of the time. This bypassing, reflecting preferences for the familiar and reassuring, also eases processing demands and enables real-time communication to proceed.

But this state of affairs, although very functional in the native language case, leads to some penalties in the case of the second language learner. Language as communication emphasizes familiarity, meaning, and memory rather than originality, form, and computation. The second language learner, who may aspire to performance which is similarly memory- and meaning-biased, has a problem to the extent that the focus on form which is also desirable as the basis for underlying change and development is not naturally connected with processes of communication. Performance is likely to be shaped by the familiar and the routinized. The second language learner, deprived of a LAD, has in some way to cope with the performance bias towards meaning while also extending and controlling the complex system that the second language consists of. This is a conundrum that it is very difficult to solve. It requires either a learner who is especially sensitive to form, or instructional conditions which themselves artfully juxtapose the demands of form and meaning in effective ways. It is to concerns of this nature that we now turn.

Tensions between learning and performance

So far, an explicit distinction has been made between form and meaning, and it has also been argued that post-critical period learners emphasize meaning, a factor which has significant and potentially harmful consequences for the nature of second language development. This implies that second language learners need to handle a conflict of goals in these two areas. But implicit in the previous discussion has been a further contrast, between form which emphasizes control and conservatism, and form which emphasizes risk-taking and interlanguage change. The former implies a learner willing to rely on less ambitious communicative aims and less ambitious form, but form which is adequately controlled and where error can be avoided. The latter suggests a learner willing to take on complex form and respond to challenges, but who may not have control over such formal elements as are involved, and so will make more errors.

These tensions, between form and meaning (fluency), first of all, and then within form between accuracy and complexity-restructuring, exist at any moment of time, and are resolved by the second language learner during particular communicative events. But the real issue, in the wider context of second language development, is how these three goals, fluency, accuracy, and complexity, coexist over more extended periods of time. The ideal situation, easy to describe but difficult to achieve, would see the three goals in some sort of productive harmony. Progress in one would be accompanied by development in the others. Complexity-restructuring would see growth in the underlying interlanguage system matched by the development of control over the (relatively) newly acquired form, the progressive elimination of error in its use, and the integration of the form into fluent performance through its dual-coding, where appropriate, as an accessible memory-based unit. In this way, second language development would be balanced in nature, and situations would be avoided where (say) fluent but limited and inaccurate learner proficiency would result, or alternatively complex and/or correct but painfully slow performance would be characteristic. Given this potential state of affairs, the challenge facing pedagogy is to establish principles which enable instruction to foster balanced development. In other words, teaching decisions need to be informed by developments in second language acquisition research, but be practically usable within realistic educational contexts. We will return in the next section to the ways in which a task-based approach to instruction may satisfy these conditions.

But there are also consequences for assessment which derive from this same tension between learning and performance. Essentially, to introduce notions of memory-based performance and dual-coding is to redefine the competence–performance relationship. If performance can be based on access-oriented systems used directly, drawing upon lexicalized chunks and exemplars, then actual real-time language use may be able, at least for some of the time, to bypass what might be termed a complex, rule-governed, acquired system. Performing language, in other words, may go well beyond simply using an underlying rule-based system.

This analysis raises the issue of what sort of assessment is deemed appropriate in the context of second language testing. Prevailing views have tended to propose that abilities models should underlie testing procedures, and that while performance conditions are necessary for satisfactory and valid test procedures, it is the underlying abilities which are the central target for the testing which is being done, and which are also the basis for the most effective generalizations. The view argued in this book, in contrast, suggests that performance itself is far more interesting and important than it has been given credit for within testing, and that it is essential, if effective assessment is to proceed, that a range of processing conditions are built in to the test formats which are used. If such variation in processing is not built into assessment, it will be very difficult indeed to sample language in such a way that generalizations can be made to a range of performance conditions. It is inadequate, in other words, to devise sampling frames for underlying abilities, however principled and defensible such sampling frames might be. There is no alternative to testing performance directly, and as a result, confronting the issue of how such performance can be sampled. Although alternative methods exist (for example a situational approach through discourse domains), it has been argued here that the only way forward is through tasks, themselves analysed for processing demands. Only in this way can effective sampling be accomplished, and a robust basis for generalization established.

Implications of the processing approach

The next section takes the underlying ideas from the previous few pages and attempts to summarize their relevance for pedagogic applications.

Instruction

Given the prioritization that occurs with older learners towards meaning, the central pedagogic problem is to contrive, in the context of convincing communication, an adequate focus on form. The problem, in other words, is to manipulate attention in such a way that it does not always target the same goal (fluency, accuracy, complexity) but is allocated to each in turn, maximizing the chances that balanced foreign language development will occur. At the input stage, it is important to create conditions to make it more likely that noticing will occur. This will cause new elements to be salient for the interlanguage system, and so create the conditions under which change may occur. At the central processing stage, the main aim is to ensure appropriate division of attention and adequate concern for form within the context of meaning-based activities. Finally, at the output stage, the need is to create a balance between rule-based performance and memory-based performance, in such a way that the latter does not predominate over the former and cause fossilization.

To achieve this set of pedagogic aims two general approaches were discussed. First, five general principles were proposed as the basis for pedagogic planning and design.

1 Choose a range of target structures.
2 Choose tasks which meet the utility criterion.
3 Sequence tasks to achieve balanced goal development.
4 Maximize chances of use of a focus on form through attentional manipulation.
5 Use cycles of accountability.

The principles fundamentally accept that particular forms cannot be taught in any guaranteed way, but that in contrast, fertile conditions can be set up which maximize the chances that development will occur. These require a range of target structures which may be made salient in attentional terms, and which can then be monitored at regular intervals. But there is no compulsion, and the intention is simply to create favourable conditions rather than require particular aspects of language form to be internalized.

The second and more specific approach to pedagogy was to develop a system for analysing tasks and implementing them. The analytic system is intended to enable tasks of the appropriate level of difficulty to be chosen, and/or tasks to focus on particular aspects of language performance. In this way, tasks of appropriate difficulty level provide a fair challenge for the learner's attentional resources (so that some attention can be devoted to form without a concern for meaning being compromised), while targeted tasks can increase the chances that particular aspects of performance which need to develop are focused on in an efficient manner (allowing, say, complexity and restructuring to be selectively supported). Regarding task implementation, the three-stage system which was described (pre-, during-, and post-task manipulations) is intended to help the teacher achieve the same goals as the task analytic framework, to influence attentional load and enable selective targeting of goals. We saw how pre-task activities can ease the processing load when a task is being done. We also saw how pre-task planning can be influenced to be selective in its effects, such as with particular types of planning, targeting accuracy, and other types of planning complexities. Similarly, there are during- and post-task choices which can have an impact on the nature of the performance that results, a claim of some significance since it goes some way to clarifying how teachers have scope to influence language use in desired directions.

Individual differences

In Chapter 11 it was alleged that the English Language Teaching profession has been obsessively concerned with the teacher, very much at the expense of the language learner. As a result, there has been remarkably little enthusiasm, in materials or methodology, to cater for the individual learner, about whom the convenient assumption has been made that the classroom teacher can accommodate sufficiently through flexible classroom teaching techniques (although little guidance is provided in teacher training as to how this could be done). In fact, there are a large number of ways in which the instruction can be made more sensitive to the individual learner, and this book has only considered those which arise from the (rather restricted) study of cognitively-based individual differences (see Williams and Burden 1997 for an interestingly different account). But even so, it was argued that there are implications for pedagogic intervention which become clearer when one locates the study of individual differences within an information-processing perspective.

First, individual differences in processing preference were related to the course of development within task-based instruction. If balance between fluency, accuracy, and complexity restructuring is important *in general* such that language instruction over time needs to ensure that learners do not consistently prioritize one of these at the expense of others, balance over time *for particular learners* becomes even more important. Learners who might prefer to emphasize fluency (say) would then need to be treated slightly differently from learners who prioritize form, either for accuracy or complexity. Learners, that is, may prefer to do what comes naturally to them, even though this may have unfortunate consequences for longer-term development. It may therefore need to be part of a teacher's expertise to assess what is appropriate for individual learners so as to avoid extended unbalanced development, which may be difficult to retrieve. The teacher, in other words, may have the difficult task of having to induce learners to address areas which they find more difficult, or which their styles of processing predispose them to avoid, such as the fluency–meaning-oriented learner needing to confront issues of form.

The second area for pedagogic intervention concerned the way project work constitutes a wonderful opportunity to take account of individual differences. In the context that project work, although an appealing general framework to encourage learner responsibility and involvement, requires considerable preparation on the learner's part if the potential of independent work is to be realized, there is scope to exploit knowledge of stylistic preferences to guide the way in which preparation is accomplished for any individual learner. In this way, how individuals are nurtured and supported so that they become more willing to take responsibility for their own learning (and so be able to continue to learn without needing to rely on a teacher) will depend on learner styles and preferences. The proposals made in this book have been brief and exploratory, but it is clear that there is enormous scope for much more research in the area. Only if such research is accomplished will it be possible for project work to be adopted with a wide range of learners, and for process syllabuses to become more than theoretical curiosities because of the practical difficulties in attaining them.

Assessment

Until recently, performance testing has functioned at a fairly superficial level. Communicative tests have been seen as those which meet a set of performance conditions, but there has been little attempt to conceptualize the dimensions of performance in any convincing way. As a result, abilities-based approaches 'clothed' by communicative tests have been regarded as the most effective way to assess. What was claimed in Chapter 7 is that this approach is inadequate. Figure 7.4 showed that performance assessment is the result of a number of interacting factors. These include the nature of the raters of the performance, as well as the rating scales that they use. They also include the nature of interactional conditions which generate performance. But most important for present purposes, they include (a) the tasks and task conditions which elicit language and (b) the dual-mode system that the candidate draws upon to actually use language. It is only meaningful to assess performance when each of these influences is operative in ways which can be described systematically.

As claimed earlier, this analysis has a major impact on how the competence–performance relationship is conceptualized, since it demonstrates that performance itself has to be considered independently, and is not there simply as a convenient method of accessing underlying competence. But the analysis also has fundamental importance for the nature of assessment and testing. In order to say anything worthwhile about the nature of a second language learner's proficiency, some clear view is necessary about how dual-mode systems are engaged, and how language is elicited through the tasks which are chosen, and how those tasks are elicited. The method of assessment, in other words, is not a technical problem at the level of format effects whose intrusive influence needs to be eliminated—it is *the* central problem in testing, since it is how language is elicited, and how performance is engaged that is the crux of the matter and the basis for any generalization on language ability that is made. To that end studies of task characteristics and of task conditions such as planning or the introduction of surprise elements are essentially studies into testing as much as they are studies of communicative performance and development. Only in the context of such research can defensible decisions be made about the composition of assessment batteries. Without such research the development of 'communicative' approaches to testing will only be a veneer, based on intuition and hunch, rather than founded on principle.

Additional research

This book has attempted to develop a coherent view of second language performance, second language development, and second language assessment, as well as the nature of individual differences in second language learning based on cognitive approaches. The aim of the book has been to show that this perspective can have a unifying effect on much research, and that it exists in some opposition to an approach based on linguistics and Universal Grammar. As a result, the arguments have attempted to reinterpret much of the research which exists and ignored much research which, although high quality, did not fit within the framework adopted. Although there has been an interpretative element to virtually every chapter, it is also the case that the claims which have been made have been linked to research wherever possible, often synthesizing through an information-processing framework areas of research results which have been regarded as essentially separate.

But inevitably there has been a need to go beyond existing research results to enable a wider framework to be described. While the framework is not inconsistent with existing research, it does now require some greater empirical underpinning, and it is to areas where more research is most urgently needed that this final section briefly turns.

The role of memory

One essential area that merits further research is that of the role of memory in second language processing. Earlier chapters have reviewed evidence of an indirect nature that memory is central in language use. Processing research has shown how exemplars have an important role in verbal learning experiments. Performance research has shown how the 'units' that the learner draws on go beyond the orthographic word, and individual difference research shows that memory ability is an important component of language aptitude. All this is consistent with views such as those of Bolinger, (1975), Pawley and Syder

(1983), and Sinclair (1991), reviewed earlier. But what is needed now is direct research into corpora of foreign language performance, possibly using modern text analysis software, to show that the 'units of language production' (Peters 1983) are indeed lexical in nature, and reflect, in ongoing speech, the underlying existence of a dual-mode system. Postulation of the importance of such a system is too much of an inference at the present time; some extensive corpus-based research in the second language field is required.

Research is also needed into the way attention operates in second language learning and performance. The current situation is that a number of researchers have shown that attention has considerable functional importance, and that viewing the second language learner as a limited-capacity information processor is a productive approach to take. It enables the study of pre-task influences such as planning and consciousness-raising, as well as during-task influences and post-task effects. In these cases it is useful to draw on simple models of attention which view it as an undifferentiated, limited resource which underpins ongoing performance and is also the gateway into long-term memory. What are needed now are more sophisticated models of attention (Robinson 1995b), which can be the basis for more selective predictions of attentional effects and a greater level of understanding, which says more, for example, than that detailed planning leads to a greater emphasis on complexity while undetailed planning prioritizes accuracy more. Such complex models could build on the findings currently available, and attempt to extend them more selectively. The goal of such work would be to clarify how balance can be achieved, within language performance, between the response to ongoing real-time processing (achieving fluency), the capacity to extend the underlying system (through the use of more complex language and the restructuring of the underlying interlanguage system), and the capacity to use such an underlying system with control (producing more complexity and restructuring). Models which enable greater understanding of the specific functioning of attention in these areas while performance unfolds will give us a much better basis for understanding how instructional interventions can be more effectively designed, and how tasks and task conditions can be selected to provide more generalizable assessments of performance.

A further development from research into attention from a model-building perspective would be additional research into pedagogic applications, especially as they relate to a task-based implementation of communicative language teaching. Studies of attention manipulation can, as the earlier chapters have shown, have an impact on the pedagogic choices that are made. But there is something of a gap between attentional manipulations with tasks at a particular time and sustained, longer-term change in the underlying interlanguage system. So far the assumption has been made that success in introducing a focus on form *at a time* will have a beneficial impact on interlanguage development *over time*. But this is very much an assumption. What is needed is a way of bridging the gap between ongoing performance and sustained development. The set of five principles proposed in Chapter 6 were an attempt to deal with this issue. But a much more satisfactory approach would be to engage in more longitudinal research which is more directly able to show how contriving a focus on form during instruction will have effective cumulative influence. Current research is almost entirely based on cross-sectional designs from which inferences are made about more extended change. But now, on the assumption that methods of engineering a focus-on-form are better understood, we can justify the greater commitment of resources and time that is required for more longitudinal research. Unless this is done, the claims made by second language acquisition researchers will always have only limited conviction.

The book has also discussed the role of cognitively-based individual differences in second language learning ability, and tried to integrate such concerns within the more general information-processing framework. Two lines of research are clearly required in this area. First, we need an updating of foreign language aptitude tests. In some ways, it is astonishing that the aptitude tests that we have, largely developed as they were some 30 to 40 years ago, are interpretable in terms of the stages of information processing. They were developed by using a range of starting hypotheses for the sorts of tests that would be predictive of language learning, and then refined and distilled through factor analysis. So their 'modernity' is pleasing. But it would now seem timely to review the tests that are available, and perhaps develop new versions of tests in the three information-processing stages which are more theoretically grounded and which reflect more modern data elicitation techniques. Such redeveloped aptitude tests might not lead to significant revisions of our understanding of aptitude, but they might be more effective predictors, since they would be likely to be better representations of the three underlying abilities concerned.

There is also scope for research into how instruction can be adapted to take account of individual differences. The book has reviewed evidence that there are cognitively-based learner differences for aptitude and style which relate naturally to an information-processing framework. In addition, Chapter 11 contained suggestions as to how such differences might be catered for both with task-based approaches as well as within the context of project work. Essentially, connections were made between research and instructional areas which followed from the analysis of language learning that had been presented. But what are essentially speculations need to be matched by research studies which do not simply assume that there ways in which instruction can be made more sensitive to the individual learner—the suggestions should form the basis for research studies which gather data on learner performance and learner satisfaction in situations when different pedagogic alternatives are chosen which reflect such differences. Currently, 'learner autonomy' and 'learner-centredness' are fashionable terms, but they are still not grounded sufficiently in research results. The frameworks and suggestions made here should go some way to guiding the manner in which aptitude–treatment interaction studies could be most fruitfully designed so that learner-centredness in future will reflect an effective combination of theory and research findings.

Bibliography

Alderson, J. C. 1991. 'Bands and scores' in J. C. Alderson and B. North (eds.): *Language Testing in the 1990s*. London: Modern English Publications and The British Council.

Allwright, R. 1981. 'What do we want teaching materials for?' *ELT Journal* 36/1: 5–18.

Allwright, R. 1984. 'The importance of interaction in classroom language learning'. *Applied Linguistics* 5: 156–71.

Allwright, R. 1988. *Observation in the Language Classroom*. London: Longman.

Anderson, A. and T. Lynch. 1988. *Listening*. Oxford: Oxford University Press.

Anderson, J. R. 1989. 'Practice, working memory, and the ACT* theory of skills acquisition: a comment on Carlson, Sullivan, and Schieder'. *Journal of Learning, Memory, and Cognition* 15: 527–30.

Anderson, J. R. 1992. 'Automaticity and the ACT* theory'. *American Journal of Psychology* 105: 165–80.

Anderson, J. R. 1995. *Learning and Memory: An Integrated Approach*. New York: Wiley.

Asher, J. J. 1977. *Learning Another Language Through Actions: The Complete Teacher's Guidebook*. Los Gatos, Calif.: Sky Oaks Publications.

Aston, G. 1986. 'Trouble-shooting in interaction with learners: the more the merrier?' *Applied Linguistics* 7: 128–43.

Aston, G. 1995. 'Corpora in language pedagogy: matching theory and practice' in G. Cook and B. Seidlhofer (eds.).

Atkinson, R. C. and R. M. Schiffrin. 1968. 'Human memory: a proposed system and its control processes' in K. W. Spence and J. T. Spence (eds.): *The Psychology of Learning and Motivation*, Vol. 2. New York: Academic Press.

Bachman, L. 1990. *Fundamental Considerations in Language Testing*. Oxford: Oxford University Press.

Bachman, L., F. Davidson, K. Ryan, and I. Choi. 1995. *The Cambridge–TOEFL Comparability Study: Final Report* Cambridge: University of Cambridge Local Examinations Syndicate.

Bachman, L. and A. Palmer. 1996. *Language Testing in Practice*. Oxford: Oxford University Press.

Bannbrook, L. and **P. Skehan.** 1990. 'Classrooms and display questions' in C. Brumfit and R. Mitchell (eds.): *Research in the Language Classroom*. London: Modern English Publications and The British Council.

Barnes, S., M. Gutfreund, D. Satterly, and **G. Wells.** 1983. 'Characteristics of adult speech which predict children's language development'. *Journal of Child Language* 10: 65–84.

Bates, E., I. Bretherton, and **L. Snyder.** 1988. *From First Words to Grammar: Individual Differences and Dissociable Mechanisms.* Cambridge: Cambridge University Press.

Beebe, L. and **H. Giles.** 1984. 'Speech accommodation theories: a discussion in terms of second language acquisition'. *International Journal of the Sociology of Language* 46: 5–32.

Berry, V. (forthcoming) 'An investigation into how individual differences in personality affect the complexity of language test tasks'. Ph.D. thesis, Thames Valley University.

Berwick, R. 1988. 'The effect of task variation in teacher-led groups on repair of English as a Foreign Language'. Ed.D. thesis, University of British Columbia.

Berwick, R. 1993. 'Towards an educational framework for teacher-led tasks' in Crookes and Gass (eds.). 1993a.

Bever, T. 1981. 'Normal acquisition processes explain the critical period for language learning' in K. C. Diller. (ed.). 1981.

Bialystok, E. 1981. 'The role of linguistic knowledge in second language use'. *Studies in Second Language Acquisition* 4: 31–45.

Bialystok, E. 1990. *Communication Strategies: A Psychological Analysis of Second Language Use.* Oxford: Blackwell.

Bialystok, E. 1991. 'Attentional control in children's metalinguistic performance and measures of field independence'. *Developmental Psychology* 28: 654–64.

Bialystok, E. and **K. Hakuta.** 1994. *In Other Words: The Science and Psychology of Second Language Acquisition.* New York: Basic Books.

Biber, D. 1988. *Variation Across Speech and Writing.* Cambridge: Cambridge University Press.

Biber, D., S. Conrad, and **R. Rippen.** 1994. 'Corpus-based approaches to issues in applied linguistics'. *Applied Linguistics* 15/2: 169–89.

Bickerton, D. 1981. *Roots of Language.* Ann Arbor, Mich.: Karoma.

Bley-Vroman, R. 1989. 'The logical problem of second language acquisition' in S. Gass and J. Schachter (eds.): *Linguistic Perspectives on Second Language Acquisition.* Cambridge: Cambridge University Press.

Bolinger, D. 1961. 'Syntactic blends and other matters'. *Language* 37: 366–81.

Bolinger, D. 1975. 'Meaning and memory'. *Forum Linguisticum* 1: 2–14.

Bourne, J. 1986. ' "Natural acquisition" and a "masked pedagogy" '. *Applied Linguistics* 9: 83–99.

Breen, M. 1987. 'Contemporary paradigms in syllabus design: (Parts 1 and 2)'. *Language Teaching* 20: 91–2 and 157–74.

Breen, M. and **C. Candlin**. 1980. 'The essentials of a communicative curriculum in language teaching'. *Applied Linguistics* 1: 89–112.

Brown, A. 1995. 'The effect of rater variables in the development of an occupation-specific language performance test'. *Language Testing* 12: 1–15.

Brown, G., A. Anderson, R. Shilcock, and **G. Yule.** 1984. *Teaching Talk: Strategies for Production and Assessment.* Cambridge: Cambridge University Press.

Brown, G., K. Malmkjær, and **J. Williams.** (eds.) 1996. *Performance and Competence in Second Language Acquisition.* Cambridge: Cambridge University Press.

Brown, G. and **G. Yule.** 1983. *Teaching the Spoken Language.* Cambridge: Cambridge University Press.

Brown, H. D. 1994. *Principles of Language Learning and Teaching* (3rd edition). Englewood Cliffs, N. J.: Prentice Hall.

Brown, R. 1991. 'Group work, task difference, and second language acquisition'. *Applied Linguistics* 11: 1–12.

Brown, R. W. 1973. *A First Language.* London: George Allen and Unwin.

Brumfit, C. 1984 *Communicative Methodology in Language Teaching.* Cambridge: Cambridge University Press.

Brumfit, C. and **K. Johnson.** 1979. *The Communicative Approach to Language Teaching.* Oxford: Oxford University Press.

Bygate, M. 1987. *Speaking.* Oxford: Oxford University Press.

Bygate, M. 1988. 'Units of oral expression and language learning in small group interaction'. *Applied Linguistics* 9: 59–82.

Bygate, M. 1996a. 'Effects of task repetition: appraising the developing language of learners' in J. Willis and D. Willis (eds.).

Bygate, M. 1996b. 'The effect of task repetition on language structure and control'. Paper presented at AAAL Conference, Chicago.

Canale, M. 1983. 'On some dimensions of language proficiency' in Oller (ed.).

Canale, M. and **M. Swain.** 1980. 'Theoretical bases of communicative approaches to second language teaching and testing'. *Applied Linguistics* 1: 1–47.

Candlin, C. 1987. 'Towards task-based language learning' in C. Candlin and D. Murphy (eds.): *Language Learning Tasks.* Englewood Cliffs, N.J.: Prentice Hall.

Carr, T. and **T. Curren.** 1994. 'Cognitive factors in learning about structured sequences: applications to syntax'. *Studies in Second Language Acquisition* 16: 205–30.

Carroll, J. B. 1965. 'The prediction of success in intensive foreign language training' in R. Glaser (ed.) *Training, Research, and Education.* New York: Wiley.

Carroll, J. B. 1973. 'Implications of aptitude test research and psycholinguistic theory for foreign language teaching'. *International Journal of Psycholinguistics* 2: 5–14.

Carroll, J. B. 1981. 'Twenty-five years of research on foreign language aptitude' in K. C. Diller (ed.).

Carroll, J. B. 1983. 'Psychometric theory and language testing' in Oller (ed.).

Carroll, J. B. 1991. 'Cognitive abilities in foreign language aptitude: then and now' in T. Parry and C. Stansfield (eds.): *Language Aptitude Reconsidered.* Englewood Cliffs, N. J.: Prentice Hall.

Carroll, J. B. 1993. *Human Cognitive Abilities.* New York: Cambridge.

Carroll, J. B. and **S. M. Sapon.** 1959. *Modern Languages Aptitude Test.* New York: Psychological Corporation.

Carter, R. and **M. McCarthy.** 1995. *Language as Discourse: Perspectives for Language Teaching.* London: Longman.

Cattell, R. 1971. *Abilities: Their Structure, Growth, and Action.* Boston: Houghton Mifflin.

Celce-Murcia, M. and **Z. Dörnyei.** 1996. 'Communicative competence: a pedagogically motivated model with content specifications'. *Issues in Applied Linguistics* 6: 5–36.

Chafe, W. 1994. *Discourse, Consciousness, and Time.* Chicago: University of Chicago Press.

Chamot, A. U. and **L. Kupper.** 1989. 'Learning strategies in foreign language instruction'. *Foreign Language Annals* 221: 13–24.

Chapelle, C. 1992. 'Disembedding "Disembedded figures in the landscape …": an appraisal of Griffiths and Sheen's "Reappraisal of L2 research on field dependence/independence"'. *Applied Linguistics* 13: 375–84.

Chapelle, C., W. Grabe, and **M. Berns.** (forthcoming) *Communicative Language Proficiency: Definitions and implications for TOEFL 2000.* Princeton: Educational Testing Service.

Chapelle, C. and **P. Green.** 1992. 'Field independence/dependence in second language acquisition research'. *Language Learning* 42: 47–83.

Cheng, P. W. 1985. 'Restructuring versus automaticity: alternative accounts of skill acquisition'. *Psychological Review* 92: 414–23.

Chomsky, N. 1965. *Aspects of the Theory of Syntax.* Cambridge, Mass.: MIT Press.

Chomsky, N. 1986. *Knowledge of Language: Its Nature, Origin, and Use.* New York: Praeger.

Clapham, C. 1996. *The Development of IELTS: A Study of the Effect of Background Knowledge on Reading Comprehension.* Cambridge: Cambridge University Press.

Clark, H. H. and **E. Clark.** 1977. *Psychology and Language.* New York: Harcourt, Brace, Jovanovitch.

Clark, J. 1984. *Curriculum Renewal in School Foreign Language Learning.* Oxford: Oxford University Press.

Cook, G. 1989. *Discourse.* Oxford: Oxford University Press.

Cook, G. and **B. Seidlhofer.** 1995. *Principle and Practice in Applied Linguistics.* Oxford: Oxford University Press.

Cook, V. J. 1994. *Linguistics and Second Language Acquisition*. London: Macmillan.

Cook, V. J. 1996. 'Competence and multi-competence' in Brown *et al* (eds.).

Cook, V. J. and M. Newson. 1996. *Chomsky's Universal Grammar* (second edition). Oxford: Blackwell.

Corder, S. Pit. 1973. *Introducing Applied Linguistics*. Harmondsworth: Penguin.

Corder, S. Pit. 1974. Lecture, British Council, Paris.

Corder, S. Pit. 1981. *Error Analysis and Interlanguage*. Oxford: Oxford University Press.

Cossu, G. and J. C. Marshall. 1986. 'Theoretical implications of the hyperlexia syndrome: two new Italian cases'. *Cortex 22*: 578–89.

Cowie, A. P. 1988. 'Stable and creative aspects of language use' in R. Carter and M. McCarthy (eds.): *Vocabulary and Language Teaching*. London: Longman.

Cromer, R. F. 1991. *Language and Thought in Normal and Handicapped Children*. Oxford: Blackwell.

Cronbach, L. 1957. 'The two disciplines of scientific psychology'. *American Psychologist* 12: 671–84.

Cronbach, L. 1990. *Essentials of Psychological Testing* (fifth edition). New York: Harper and Row.

Cronbach, L. and P. E. Meehl. 1955. 'Construct validity in psychological tests'. *Psychological Bulletin* 52: 281–302.

Cronbach, L. and R. Snow. 1977. *Aptitudes and Instructional Methods*. New York: Irvington.

Crookes, G. 1989. 'Planning and interlanguage variation'. *Studies in Second Language Acquisition* 11: 367–83.

Crookes, G. and S. Gass. 1993a. (eds.): *Tasks in a Pedagogical Context: Integrating Theory and Practice*. Clevedon, Avon: Multilingual Matters.

Crookes, G. and S. Gass. 1993b. (eds.): *Tasks and Language Learning: Integrating Theory and Practice*. Clevedon, Avon: Multilingual Matters.

Cummins, J. 1984. *Bilingualism and Special Education: Issues in Assessment and Pedagogy*. Clevedon, Avon: Multilingual Matters.

Curren, T. and S. W. Keele. 1993. 'Attentional and non-attentional forms of sequence learning'. *Journal of Experimental Psychology: Learning, Memory, and Cognition* 19: 189–202.

Curtiss, S. 1977. *Genie: A Psycholinguistic Study of a Modern Day 'Wild Child'*. New York: Academic Press.

Curtiss, S. 1982. 'Developmental dissociations of language and cognition' in L. Obler and L. Menn (eds.): *Exceptional Language and Linguistics*. New York: Academic Press.

Curtiss, S. 1988. 'The special talent of grammar acquisition' in L. Obler and D. Fein (eds.).

Curtiss, S. 1994. 'Language as a cognitive system: its independence and selective vulnerability' in C. Otero (ed.): *Noam Chomsky: Critical Assessments*. Vol. 4. London: Routledge.

Curtiss, S. and **J. Yamada.** 1981. 'Selectively intact grammatical development in a retarded child'. *UCLA Working Papers in Cognitive Linguistics* 3: 61–91.

Cziko, G. 1984. 'Some problems with empirically-based models of communicative competence'. *Applied Linguistics*. 5: 23–38.

Davies, A. 1977. 'The construction of language tests'. in J. P. B. Allen and A. Davies (eds.): *Testing and Experimental Methods: Edinburgh Course in Applied Linguistics*. Vol. 4. Oxford: Oxford University Press.

Dechert, H. 1983. 'How a story is done in a second language' in C.Færch and G. Kasper (eds.).

De Keyser, R. 1994. 'How implicit can adult second language learning be?' *AILA Review* 11: 83–96.

Dickson, P., C. Boyce, B. Lee, M. Portal, and **M. Smith.** 1985. *Foreign Language Performance in Schools: Report on the 1983 Survey of French, German, and Spanish*. London: Department of Education and Science.

Diller, K. C. 1981. (ed.). *Individual Differences and Universals in Foreign Language Aptitude*. Rowley, Mass.: Newbury House.

Doughty, C. 1991. 'Second language instruction does make a difference: evidence from an empirical study on SL relativization'. *Studies in Second Language Acquisition* 13: 431–69.

Duff, P. 1986. 'Another look at interlanguage talk: taking task to task' in R. Day (ed.): *Talking to Learn*. Rowley, Mass.: Newbury House.

Ellis, G. and **B. Sinclair.** 1989. *Learning to Learn English*. Cambridge: Cambridge University Press.

Ellis, R. 1984. *Classroom Second Language Development*. Oxford: Pergamon.

Ellis, R. 1987. 'Interlanguage variability in narrative discourse: style shifting in the use of the past tense'. *Studies in Second Language Acquisition* 9: 12–20.

Ellis, R. 1994. *The Study of Second Language Acquisition*. Oxford: Oxford University Press.

Eskey, D. 1988. 'Holding in the bottom' in P. Carrell, J. Devine, and D. Eskey (eds.): *Interactive Approaches to Second Language Reading*. Cambridge: Cambridge University Press.

Eubank, L. and **K. Gregg.** 1995. '"Et in Amygdala Ego"?UG, (S)LA, and Neurobiology'. *Studies in Second Language Acquisition* 17: 35–58.

Færch, C. and **G. Kasper.** 1983. *Strategies in Interlanguage Communication*. London: Longman.

Fillenbaum, J. 1971. 'On coping with ordered and unordered conjunctive sentences'. *Journal of Experimental Psychology* 87: 93–8.

Fillmore, C. J. 1979. 'On fluency' in C. Fillmore, D. Kempler, and W. S-Y Wang (eds.): *Individual Differences in Language Ability and Language Behaviour*. New York: Academic Press.

Fodor, J. 1983. *The Modularity of Mind*. Cambridge, Mass.: MIT Press.

Foster, P. 1998. 'A classroom perspective on the negotiation of meaning'. *Applied Linguistics* 19/1.

Foster, P. and P. Skehan. 1996. 'The influence of planning on performance in task-based learning'. *Studies in Second Language Acquisition* 18: 299–324.

Foster, P. and P. Skehan. 1997. 'Modifying the task: the effects of surprise, time and planning type on task based foreign language instruction'. *Thames Valley Working Papers in English Language Teaching*. Vol. 4.

Fotos, S. 1993. 'Consciousness-raising and noticing through focus on form: grammar task performance versus formal instruction'. *Applied Linguistics* 14: 385–407.

Fotos, S. and R. Ellis. 1991. 'Communicating about grammar: a task-based approach'. *TESOL Quarterly* 25: 608–28.

Fried-Booth, D. 1986. *Project Work*. Oxford: Oxford University Press.

Frith, U. 1991. 'Asperger and his syndrome' in U. Frith (ed.) *Autism and Asperger Syndrome*. Cambridge: Cambridge University Press.

Gardner, R. and W. Lambert. 1972. *Attitudes and Motivation in Second Language Learning*. Rowley, Mass.: Newbury House.

Garton-Sprenger, J. and S. Goodall. 1989. *Flying Colours*. London: Heinemann.

Gass, S. 1988. 'Integrating research areas: a framework for second language studies'. *Applied Linguistics* 9: 198–217.

Gass, S. 1991. 'Grammatical instruction, selective attention, and learning' in R. Phillipson, E. Kellerman, L. Selinker, M. Sharwood Smith and M. Swain (eds.): *Foreign/Second Language Pedagogy*. Clevedon, Avon: Multilingual Matters.

Gass, S., C. Madden, D. Preston, and L. Selinker. 1989. (eds.): *Variation in Second Language Acquisition: Psycholinguistic Issues*. Clevedon, Avon: Multilingual Matters.

Gass, S. and J. Schachter. 1989. *Linguistic Perspectives on Second Language Acquisition*. Cambridge: Cambridge University Press.

Gass, S. and E. M. Varonis. 1994. 'Input, interaction, and second language production'. *Studies in Second Language Acquisition* 16: 283–302.

Gathercole, S. E. and A. Baddeley. 1994. *Working Memory and Language*. Hove, Sussex: Lawrence Erlbaum.

Geschwind, N. and A. M. Galaburda. 1985. 'Cerebral lateralisation: Biological mechanisms, associations, pathology: I, II, III'. *Archives of Neurology* 42: 428–59, 521–52, 634–54.

Gipps, C. V. 1994. *Beyond Testing: Towards a Theory of Educational Assessment*. Brighton: The Falmer Press.

Givón, T. 1979. *Syntax and Semantics, Vol. 12: Discourse and Semantics*. New York: Academic Press.

Givón, T. 1985. 'Function, structure, and language acquisition' in D. Slobin (ed.): *The Crosslinguistic Study of Language Acquisition*. Vol. 1. Hillsdale, N. J.: Lawrence Erlbaum.

Givón, T. 1989. *Mind, Code, and Context: Essays in Pragmatics*. Hillsdale, N. J.: Lawrence Erlbaum.

Gleitman, L. R., E. L. Newport, and **H. Gleitman**. 1984. 'The current status of the motherese hypothesis'. *Journal of Child Language* 11: 43–79.

Goldin-Meadow, S. 1982. 'The resilience of recursion: a study of a communication system developed without a conventional language model' in E. Wanner and L. Gleitman (eds.): *Language Acquisition: The State of the Art*. New York: Cambridge University Press.

Goldin-Meadow, S. and **C. Mylander**. 1990. 'Beyond the input given: the child's role in the acquisition of language'. *Language* 66: 323–55.

Gopnik, M. 1994. 'Impairment of tense in a familial language disorder'. *Journal of Neurolinguistics* 8: 109–33.

Gopnik, M. and **M. B. Crago**. 1991. 'Familial aggregation of a developmental language disorder'. *Cognition* 39: 1–50.

Gregg, K. 1984. 'Krashen's Monitor and Occam's Razor'. *Applied Linguistics* 5: 79–100.

Gregorc, A. 1979. *An Adult's Guide to Style*. Columbia: Gregorc Associates.

Grice, H. P. 1975. 'Logic and conversation' in P. Cole and J. Morgan (eds.): *Syntax and Semantics 3: Speech Acts*. New York: Academic Press.

Griffiths, R. and **R. Sheen**. 1992. 'Disembedded figures in the landscape: a reappraisal of L2 research on field dependence/independence'. *Applied Linguistics* 13: 133–48.

Haines, S. 1989. *Projects for the EFL Classroom*. London: Nelson.

Hansen, J. and **C. Stansfield**. 1981. 'The relationship of field dependent-independent cognitive styles to foreign language achievement'. *Language Learning* 31: 349–67.

Harley, B. and **M. Swain**. 1984. 'The interlanguage of immersion students and its implications for second language teaching' in A. Davies, C. Criper, and A. Howatt (eds.): *Interlanguage*. Edinburgh: Edinburgh University Press.

Harrington, M. and **M. Sawyer**. 1992. 'L2 working memory capacity and L2 reading skill'. *Studies in Second Language Acquisition* 14: 25–38.

Harrison, A. 1986. 'Assessing text in action' in M. Portal (ed.): *Innovations in Language Testing*. Slough: Nelson.

Hayes, N. and **D. E. Broadbent**. 1988. 'Two modes of learning for interactive tasks'. *Cognition* 28: 249–76.

Higgs, T. and **R. Clifford**. 1982. 'The push toward communication' in T. Higgs (ed.): *Curriculum, Competence, and the Foreign Language Teacher*. Skokie, Ill.: National Textbook Company.

Humes-Bartlo, M. 1989. 'Variation in children's ability to learn a second language' in K. Hyltenstam and L. Obler, (eds.): *Bilingualism Across the Lifespan*. Cambridge: Cambridge University Press.

Hurford, J. 1991. 'The evolution of the critical period for language acquisition'. *Cognition* 40: 159–201.

Hyltenstam, K. 1977. 'Implicational patterns in interlanguage syntax variation'. *Language Learning* 27: 383–411.

Hymes, D. 1972. 'On communicative competence' in J. Pride and J. Holmes (eds.): *Sociolinguistics*. Harmondsworth: Penguin.

Ioup, G. 1989. 'Immigrant children who have failed to acquire native English' in S. Gass *et al* (eds.).

Ioup, G., E. Boustagni, M. El Tigi, and M. Moselle. 1994. 'Re-examining the critical period hypothesis: a case study of successful SLA in a naturalistic environment'. *Studies in Second Language Acquisition* 16: 73–98.

Jackendoff, R. 1993. *Patterns in the Mind: Language and Human Nature*. Hemel Hempstead: Harvester Press.

Johns, T. F. 1991. 'Should you be persuaded: two examples of data-driven learning' in T. F. Johns and P. King (eds.): *Classroom Concordancing*. Special issue of *ELR Journal* 4: 1–16.

Johnson, J. S. 1992. 'Critical period effects in second language acquisition: the effects of written versus auditory materials in the assessment of grammatical competence'. *Language Learning* 42: 217–48.

Johnson, J. S. and E. Newport. 1989. 'Critical period effects in second language learning: the influence of maturational state on the acquisition of English as a second language'. *Cognitive Psychology* 21: 60–99.

Johnson, J. S. and E. Newport. 1991. 'Critical period effects on universal properties of language: the status of subjacency in the acquisition of a second language'. *Cognition* 39: 215–58.

Karmilloff-Smith, A. 1986. 'From meta-processes to conscious access: evidence from children's metalinguistic and repair data'. *Cognition* 23: 95–147.

Karmilloff-Smith, A. 1992. *Beyond Modularity: A Developmental Perspective in Cognitive Science*. Cambridge, Mass.: M.I.T. Press.

Kellerman, E. 1985. 'If at first you do succeed ...' in S. Gass and C. Madden (eds.): *Input and Second Language Acquisition*. Rowley, Mass.: Newbury House.

Kellerman, E. 1996. 'Age before beauty: Johnson and Newport revisited' in L. Eubank, L. Selinker, and M. Sharwood Smith (eds.): *The Current State of Interlanguage*. Amsterdam: John Benjamins.

Kenyon, D. 1992. 'An investigation of the validity of the demands of tasks on performance-based tasks of oral proficiency'. Paper presented at the Language Testing Research Colloquium, Vancouver, Canada.

Kess, J. E. 1992. *Psycholinguistics*. Amsterdam: John Benjamins.

Klein, W. 1986. *Second Language Acquisition*. Cambridge: Cambridge University Press.

Kolb, D. 1976. *Learning Styles Inventory*. Boston: McBer.

Kowal, M. and M. Swain. 1994. 'Using collaborative language production tasks to promote students' language awareness'. *Language Awareness* 3: 73–91.

Krashen, S. 1981. 'Aptitude and attitude in relation to second language acquisition and learning' in K. C. Diller (ed.).

Krashen, S. 1982. *Principles and Practice in Second Language Acquisition.* Oxford: Pergamon.

Krashen, S. 1985. *The Input Hypothesis.* London: Longman.

Kumaravadivelu, B. 1993. 'The name of the task and the task of naming: methodological aspects of task-based pedagogy' in Crookes and Gass 1993a.

Labov, W. 1972. *Sociolinguistic Patterns.* Philadelphia, Pa.: University of Pennsylvania Press.

Larsen-Freeman, D. 1986. *Techniques and Principles in Language Teaching.* New York: Oxford.

Larsen-Freeman, D. and **M. Long.** 1991. *An Introduction to Second Language Acquisition Research.* London: Longman.

Lenneberg, E. 1967. *Biological Foundations of Language.* New York: John Wiley and Sons.

Levelt, W. 1989. *Speaking: From Intention to Articulation.* Cambridge: Cambridge University Press.

Logan, G. D. 1988. 'Towards an instance theory of automatisation'. *Psychological Review* 95: 492–527.

Long, M. 1985. 'Input and second language acquisition theory' in S. Gass and C. Madden (eds.): *Input and Second Language Acquisition.* Rowley, Mass.: Newbury House.

Long, M. 1988. 'Instructed interlanguage development' in L. Beebe (ed.): *Issues in Second Language Acquisition: Multiple Perspectives.* Rowley, Mass.: Newbury House.

Long, M. 1989. 'Task, group, and task-group interaction'. *University of Hawaii Working Papers in English as a Second Language* 8: 1–26.

Long, M. 1990. 'Maturational constraints on language learning'. *Studies in Second Language Acquisition* 12: 251–86.

Long, M. and **G. Crookes.** 1991. 'Three approaches to task-based syllabus design'. *TESOL Quarterly* 26: 27–55.

Long, M. and **P. Robinson.** (forthcoming) 'Focus on form: theory, research, and practice' in C. Doughty and J. Williams (eds.): *Focus on Form in Classroom SLA.* Cambridge: Cambridge University Press.

Loschky, L. and **R. Bley-Vroman.** 1993. 'Grammar and task-based methodology' in Crookes and Gass 1993b.

Lowe, P. Jr. 1982. *ILR Handbook on Oral Interview Testing.* Washington, D.C.: Defense Language Institute.

Lumley, T. and **T. McNamara.** 1995. 'Rater characteristics and rater bias: implications for training'. *Language Testing* 12: 55–71.

Lyons, J. 1968. *Introduction to Theoretical Linguistics.* Cambridge: Cambridge University Press.

Lyster, R. and **L. Ranta.** 1997. 'Corrective feedback and learner uptake: negotiation of form in communicative classrooms'. *Studies in Second Language Acquisition* 19: 37–66.

Matthews R. C., R. R. Buss, W. B. Stanley, F. Blachard-Fields, J. R. Cho, and B. Druhan. 1989. 'Role of implicit and explicit processes in learning from examples: a synergistic effect'. *Journal of Experimental Psychology: Learning, Memory, and Cognition* 15: 1083–100.

McLaughlin, B. 1980. 'Theory and research in second language learning: an emerging paradigm'. *Language Learning* 30: 331–50.

McLaughlin, B. 1987. *Theories of Second Language Acquisition*. London: Edward Arnold.

McLaughlin, B. 1990. 'Restructuring'. *Applied Linguistics* 11:113–28.

McNamara, T. 1995. 'Modelling performance: opening Pandora's box'. *Applied Linguistics* 16: 159–79.

McNamara, T. 1996. *Measuring Second Language Performance*. London: Longman.

Mehnert, U. (forthcoming) 'The effects of different lengths of time for planning on second language performance'. *Studies in Second Language Acquisition*.

Messick, S. 1988. 'Validity' in R. Linn (ed.): *Educational Measurement* (third edition). New York: American Council on Education/Macmillan.

Miller, A. 1987. 'Cognitive styles: an integrated model'. *Educational Psychology* 7: 251–68.

Mohan, B. 1986. *Language and Content*. Reading, Mass.: Addison Wesley.

Morrow, K. 1977. *Techniques of Evaluation for a Notional Syllabus*. Centre for Applied Language Studies: University of Reading.

Murata, K. 1994. *A Cross-cultural Approach to the Analysis of Conversation and its Implications for Language Pedagogy*. Tokyo: Liber Press.

Murison-Bowie, S. 1993. *MicroConcord: Concordance Programme Handbook*. Oxford: Oxford University Press.

Naiman, N., M. Frohlich, H. H. Stern, and A. Todesco. 1975. *The Good Language Learner*. Research in Education Series, No. 7. Ontario: Ontario Institute for Studies in Education.

Nattinger, J. R. and J. S. DeCarrico. 1992. *Lexical Phrases and Language Teaching*. Oxford: Oxford University Press.

Nelson, K. 1981. 'Individual differences in language development: implications for development and language'. *Developmental Psychology* 17: 170–87.

Neufeld, G. 1979. 'Towards a theory of language learning aptitude'. *Language Learning* 29: 227–41.

Newport, E. 1990. 'Maturational constraints on language learning'. *Cognitive Science* 14: 11–28.

North, B. 1996. 'The development of a common framework scale of language proficiency based on a theory of measurement'. Unpublished Ph.D. thesis, Thames Valley University.

Novoa, L., D. Fein, and L. Obler. 1988. 'Talent in foreign languages: a case study' in L. Obler and D. Fein (eds.).

Nunan, D. 1989. *Designing Tasks for the Communicative Classroom*. Cambridge: Cambridge University Press.

Obler, L. 1989. 'Exceptional second language learners' in S. Gass *et al* (eds.).

Obler, L. and D. Fein. 1988. (eds.): *The Exceptional Brain: Neuropsychology of Talent and Special Abilities.* New York: Guilford Press.

Oller, J.W. 1983. (ed.). *Issues in Language Testing Research.* Rowley, Mass.: Newbury House.

O'Malley, J. M. and A. U. Chamot. 1990. *Learning Strategies and Second Language Acquisition.* Cambridge: Cambridge University Press.

O'Malley, J. M., A. U. Chamot, G. Stewner-Manzares, R. Russo, and L. Kupper. 1985. 'Learning strategy applications with students of English as a second language'. *TESOL Quarterly* 19: 285–296.

O'Neill, R. 1982. 'Why use textbooks?' *ELT Journal* 36: 104–11.

Oxford, R. 1990. *Language Learning Strategies: What Every Teacher Should Know.* Rowley, Mass.: Newbury House.

Oyama, S. 1978. 'The sensitive period and the comprehension of speech'. *Working Papers in Bilingualism* 16: 1–17.

Patkowski, M. 1980. 'The sensitive period for the acquisition of syntax in a second language'. *Language Learning* 30: 449–72.

Pawley, A. and F. Syder. 1983. 'Two puzzles for linguistic theory: nativelike selection and nativelike fluency' in J. C. Richards and R. Schmidt (eds.): *Language and Communication.* London: Longman.

Peters, A. 1983. *The Units of Language Acquisition.* Cambridge: Cambridge University Press.

Peters, A. 1985. 'Language segmentation: operation principles for the perception and analysis of language' in D. Slobin (ed.): *The Crosslinguistic Study of Language Acquisition, Vol. 2: Theoretical Issues.* London: Erlbaum.

Petersen, C. R. and A. Al-Haik. 1976. 'The development of the Defense Language Aptitude Battery (DLAB)'. *Educational and Psychological Measurement* 36: 369–80.

Pica, T. 1994. 'Research on negotiation: what does it reveal about second language learning, conditions, processes, outcomes?'. *Language Learning* 44: 493–527.

Pica, T., R. Kanagy, and J. Falodun. 1993. 'Choosing and using communicative tasks for second language instruction' in Crookes and Gass 1993b.

Pienemann, M. 1984. 'Psychological constraints on the teachability of languages'. *Studies in Second Language Acquisition* 6: 186–214.

Pienemann, M. 1989. 'Is language teachable?' *Applied Linguistics* 10: 52–79.

Pienemann, M., M. Johnson, and G. Brindley. 1988. 'Constructing an acquisition based procedure for assessing second language acquisition'. *Studies in Second Language Acquisition* 10: 217–43.

Pimsleur, P. 1966. *Pimsleur Language Aptitude Battery (PLAB).* New York: Harcourt, Brace, Jovanovich.

Pimsleur, P. 1968. 'Language aptitude testing' in A. Davies (ed.): *Language Testing: A Psycholinguistic Approach.* Oxford: Oxford University Press.

Pimsleur P., D. M. Sundland, and R. D. McIntyre. 1966. *Underachievement in Foreign Language Learning.* Washington, D. C.: Modern Language Association.

Pinker, S. 1994. *The Language Instinct.* Allen Lane: The Penguin Press.

Plough, I. and S. Gass. 1993. 'Interlocutor and task familiarity: effect on interactional structure' in Crookes and Gass 1993b.

Politzer, R. and M. McGroarty. 1985. 'An exploratory study of learning behaviours and their relationship to gains in linguistic and communicative competence'. *TESOL Quarterly* 19: 103–23.

Politzer, R. L. and L. Weiss. 1969. *An Experiment in Improving Achievement in Foreign Language Learning through Learning of Selected Skills Associated with Language Aptitude.* Stanford, Calif.: Stanford University (ERIC Document Reproduction Service ED046261).

Popper, K. 1968. *The Logic of Scientific Discovery.* London: Hutchinson.

Postovsky, V. 1977. 'Why not start speaking later?' in M. Burt, H. Dulay, and M. Finocchiaro (eds.): *Viewpoints on English as a Second Language.* New York: Regents.

Prabhu, N. S. 1987. *Second Language Pedagogy.* Oxford: Oxford University Press.

Rea-Dickins, P. 1985. 'Language testing and the communicative teaching curriculum' in Y. P. Lee, A. Fok, R. Lord, and G. Low (eds.): *New Directions in Language Testing.* Oxford: Pergamon.

Rea-Dickins, P. and K. Germaine. 1992. *Evaluation.* Oxford: Oxford University Press.

Reber, A. 1989. 'Implicit learning and tacit knowledge'. *Journal of Experimental Psychology: General* 118: 219–35.

Reid, J. 1987. 'Learning style preferences of ESL students'. *TESOL Quarterly* 21: 87-111.

Reves, T. 1982. 'What makes a good language learner?' Unpublished Ph.D. thesis, Hebrew University of Jerusalem.

Richards, J. C. 1985. 'Language curriculum development' *University of Hawaii Working Papers in English as a Second Language,* 4/1.

Riding, R. 1991. *Cognitive Styles Analysis.* Birmingham: Learning and Training Technology.

Riding, R. and I. Cheema. 1991. 'Cognitive styles – an overview and integration'. *Educational Psychology* 11: 193–215.

Robinson, P. 1995a. 'Task complexity and second language narrative discourse'. *Language Learning* 45/1: 99–140.

Robinson, P. 1995b. 'Attention, memory, and the noticing hypothesis'. *Language Learning* 45/2: 283–331.

Robinson, P. 1995c. 'Aptitude, awareness, and the fundamental similarity of implicit and explicit second language learning' in R. Schmidt (ed.).

Robinson, P. 1996. (ed.). *Task Complexity and Second Language Syllabus Design: Data-based Studies and Speculations.* Special Issue of University of Queensland Working Papers in Language and Linguistics.

Robinson, P. J. and **M. A. Ha**. 1993. 'Instance theory and second language rule learning under explicit conditions'. *Studies in Second Language Acquisition* 15: 413–38.

Robinson, P. S., C-C. Ting and **J-J. Urwin**. 1996. 'Investigating second language task complexity'. *RELC Journal* 26: 62–79.

Rooks, G. 1981. *The Non-Stop Discussion Workbook*. Rowley, Mass.: Newbury House.

Rubin, J. 1981. 'Study of cognitive processes in second language learning'. *Applied Linguistics* 117–31.

Rubin, J. and **A. Wenden**. 1987. *Learner Strategies in Language Learning*. Englewood Cliffs, N. J.: Prentice Hall.

Rymer, R. 1993. *Genie: Escape from a Silent Childhood*. London: Michael Joseph.

Samuda, V., S. Gass, and **P. Rounds**. 1996. 'Two types of task in communicative language teaching'. Paper presented at the TESOL Convention, Chicago.

Santos Tambos, P. 1992. 'Types of convergent and divergent task: the effects of personal opinion'. Term Project, Thames Valley University.

Sasaki, M. 1991. 'Relationships among second language proficiency, foreign language aptitude, and intelligence: a structural equation modelling approach'. Unpublished Ph.D. thesis, University of California at Los Angeles.

Sasaki, M. 1996. *Second Language Proficiency, Foreign Language Aptitude, and Intelligence: Quantitative and Qualitative Analyses*. New York: Peter Lang.

Sato, C. 1988. 'Origins of complex syntax in interlanguage development'. *Studies in Second Language Acquisition* 10: 371–95.

Schachter, J. 1996. 'Learning and triggering in adult L2 acquisition' in Brown *et al* (eds.).

Schiffrin, R. M. and **W. Schneider.** 1977. 'Controlled and automatic information processing II: perceptual learning, automatic attending, and general theory'. *Psychological Review* 84: 127–90.

Schmidt, R. 1983. 'Interaction, acculturation, and the acquisition of communicative competence' in N. Wolfson and E. Judd (eds.): *Sociolinguistics and Second Language Acquisition*. Rowley, Mass.: Newbury House.

Schmidt, R. 1990. 'The role of consciousness in second language learning'. *Applied Linguistics* 11: 17–46.

Schmidt, R. 1992. 'Psychological mechanisms underlying second language fluency'. *Studies in Second Language Acquisition* 14: 357–85.

Schmidt, R. 1994. 'Deconstructing consciousness: in search of useful definitions for Applied Linguistics'. *AILA Review* 11: 11–26.

Schmidt, R. 1995. (ed.): *Attention and Awareness in Foreign Language Learning* (Technical Report No. 9). Hawaii: University of Hawaii Second Language Teaching and Curriculum Center.

Schmidt, R. and **S. Frota.** 1986. 'Developing basic conversational ability in a second language: a case-study of an adult learner' in R. Day (ed.): *Talking to Learn*. Rowley, Mass.: Newbury House.

Schniederman, E. and **C. Desmarais.** 1988a. 'The talented language learner: some preliminary findings'. *Second Language Research* 4: 91–109.

Schniederman, E. and **C. Desmarais.** 1988b. 'A neuropsychological substrate for talent in second language acquisition' in L. Obler and D. Fein (eds.).

Scott, M. 1996. *Wordsmith*. Oxford: Oxford University Press Multimedia Publishing.

Selinker, L. and **D. Douglas.** 1985. 'Wrestling with context in interlanguage theory'. *Applied Linguistics* 6: 190–204.

Sharwood Smith, M. 1981. 'Consciousness-raising and the second language learner'. *Applied Linguistics* 2: 159–69.

Sharwood Smith, M. 1993. 'Input enhancement in instructed SLA: theoretical bases'. *Studies in Second Language Acquisition* 15: 165–80.

Sinclair, J. McH. 1988. (ed.): *Looking Up*. London: Collins.

Sinclair, J. McH. 1991. *Corpus, Concordance, Collocation*. Oxford: Oxford University Press.

Singleton, D. 1989. *Language Acquisition: The Age Factor*. Clevedon, Avon: Multilingual Matters.

Skehan, P. 1980. 'Memory, language aptitude, and second language performance'. *Polyglot* 2: Fiche 3.

Skehan, P. 1982. 'Memory and motivation in language aptitude testing'. Unpublished Ph.D. thesis, University of London.

Skehan, P. 1984a. 'On the non-magical nature of foreign language learning'. *Polyglot* 5: Fiche 1.

Skehan, P. 1984b. 'Issues in the testing of English for Specific Purposes'. *Language Testing* 1: 202–20.

Skehan, P. 1986a. 'Where does language aptitude come from?' in P. Meara (ed.): *Spoken Language*. London: Centre for Information on Language Teaching.

Skehan, P. 1986b. 'The role of foreign language aptitude in a model of school learning'. *Language Testing* 3: 188–221.

Skehan, P. 1986c. 'Cluster analysis and the identification of learner types' in V. Cook (ed.): *Experimental Approaches to Second Language Acquisition*. Oxford: Pergamon.

Skehan, P. 1989. *Individual Differences in Second Language Learning*. London: Edward Arnold.

Skehan, P. 1992. 'Strategies in second language acquisition'. *Thames Valley University Working Papers in English Language Teaching* No. 1.

Skehan, P. 1995. 'Analysability, accessibility, and ability for use' in G. Cook and B. Seidlhofer (eds.).

Skehan, P. 1996a. 'A framework for the implementation of task based instruction'. *Applied Linguistics* 17: 38–62.

Skehan, P. 1996b. 'Implications of SLA research for language teaching methodologies' in D. Willis and J. Willis (eds.).

Skehan, P. and **L. Ducroquet**. 1988. *A Comparison of First and Foreign Language Learning Ability*. Working Documents No. 8, ESOL Department, Insitute of Education, London University.

Skehan, P. and **P. Foster**. 1997. 'The influence of planning and post-task activities on accuracy and complexity in task-based learning'. *Language Teaching Research* 1/3.

Slobin, D. 1973. 'Cognitive prerequisites for the development of grammar' in C. A. Ferguson and D. Slobin (eds.): *Studies of Child Language Development*. New York: Holt, Rinehart, Winston.

Smith, N. and **X. Tsimpli**. 1995. *The Mind of a Savant*. Oxford: Blackwell.

Sparks, R. E. and **L. Ganschow**. 1991. 'Foreign language learning differences: affective filter or native language aptitude differences'. *Modern Language Journal* 75: 3–15.

Sparks, R. E., L. Ganschow, J. Javorsky, and **J. Pohlman**. 1992. 'Test comparisons among students identified as high-risk, low-risk, and learning disabled in high-school foreign language courses'. *Modern Language Journal* 76: 142–58.

Spearman, C. 1927. *The Abilities of Man*. New York: Macmillan.

Spolsky, B. 1985. 'Formulating a theory of second language learning'. *Studies in Second Language Acquisition* 7: 269–88.

Spolsky, B. 1989. *Conditions for Second Language Learning*. Oxford: Oxford University Press.

Stevick, E. 1989. *Success with Foreign Languages*. New York: Prentice Hall.

Stubbs, M. 1995. 'Corpus evidence for norms of lexical collocation' in G. Cook and B. Seidlhofer (eds.).

Stubbs, M. 1996. *Text and Corpus Linguistics*. Oxford: Blackwell.

Swain, M. 1985. 'Communicative competence: some roles of comprehensible input and comprehensible output in its development' in S. Gass and C. Madden (eds.): *Input in Second Language Acquisition*. Rowley, Mass.: Newbury House.

Swain, M. 1995. 'Three functions of output in second language learning' in G. Cook and B. Seidlhofer (eds.).

Swain, M. 1997. 'Collaborative dialogue: its contribution to second language learning'. *Revista Canaria de Estudios Ingleses* 33.

Swain, M. and **S. Lapkin**. 1982. *Evaluating Bilingual Education: A Canadian Case Study*. Clevedon, Avon: Multilingual Matters.

Swain, M. and **S. Lapkin**. 1997. 'Task-based collaborative dialogue'. Paper presented at the AAAL Conference, Orlando.

Swan, M. and **C. Walter**. 1984–7. *The Cambridge English Course*. Cambridge: Cambridge University Press.

Tannen, D. 1989. *Talking Voices: Repetition, Dialogue and Imagery in Conversational Discourse*. Cambridge: Cambridge University Press.

Tarone, E. 1981. 'Some thoughts on the notion of communication strategy'. *TESOL Quarterly* 15: 285–95.

Tarone, E. 1983. 'On the variability of interlanguage systems'. *Applied Linguistics* 4: 143–63.

Tarone, E. 1985. 'Variability in interlanguage use: a study of style-shifting in morphology and syntax'. *Language Learning* 35: 373–403.

Tarone, E. 1988. *Variation in Interlanguage*. London: Edward Arnold.

Tarone, E. (forthcoming) 'Research on interlanguage variation: implications for language testing' in L. Bachman and A. Cohen (eds.): *Interfaces between SLA and Language Testing Research*. Cambridge: Cambridge University Press.

Ting, S. C-C. 1996. 'Planning time, modality, and second language task performance: accuracy and fluency in the acquisition of Chinese as a second language' in P. Robinson (ed.).

Tizard, B. and M. Hughes. 1984. *Young Children Learning*. London: Fontana.

Towell, R., R. Hawkins, and N. Bazergut. 1996. 'The development of fluency in advanced learners of French'. *Applied Linguistics* 17: 84–119.

Trim, J. 1980. *Developing a Unit/Credit Scheme of Adult Language Learning*. Oxford: Pergamon.

Underwood, M. 1990. 'Task-related variation in past-tense morphology'. Unpublished M.A. thesis, Institute of Education, London University.

Urwin, J-J. 1996. 'Prior knowledge, pre-tasks, and second language listening comprehension' in P. Robinson (ed.).

Van Lancker, D. 1987. 'Non-propositional speech: neurolinguistic studies' in Ellis A. (ed.): *Progress in the Psychology of Language* Vol. 3. Hillsdale, N. J.: Lawrence Erlbaum.

Van Lier, L. 1989. 'Reeling, writhing, drawling, stretching, and fainting in coils: oral proficiency interviews as conversation'. *TESOL Quarterly* 23: 489–508.

Van Lier, L. 1996. *Interaction in the Language Curriculum: Awareness, Autonomy, and Authenticity*. London: Longman.

Van Lier, L. and N. Matsuo. 1994. 'Variation in interlanguage conversation'. Manuscript, Monterey Institute of International Studies.

VanPatten, B. 1990. 'Attending to content and form in the input: an experiment in consciousness'. *Studies in Second Language Acquisition* 12: 287–301.

VanPatten, B. 1994. 'Evaluating the role of consciousness in SLA: terms, linguistic features, and research methodology'. *AILA Review* 11: 27–36.

VanPatten, B. 1996. *Input Processing and Grammar Instruction*. New York: Ablex.

VanPatten, B. and T. Cadierno. 1993. 'Explicit instruction and input processing'. *Studies in Second Language Acquisition* 15: 225–43.

Wajnryb, R. 1991. *Grammar Dictation*. Oxford: Oxford University Press.

Weir, C. 1988. *Communicative Language Testing*. Exeter: University of Exeter Press.

Weir, C. and **M. Bygate**. 1993. 'Meeting the criteria of communicativeness in a spoken language test'. *Journal of English and Foreign Language* 10: 27–43. Central Institute of English and Foreign Languages, Hyberabad.

Wells, G. 1981. *Learning Through Interaction*. Cambridge: Cambridge University Press.

Wells, G. 1985. *Language Development in the Pre-school Years*. Cambridge: Cambridge University Press.

Wells, G. 1986. 'Variation in child language' in P. Fletcher and M. Garman (eds.): *Language Acquisition* (second edition). Cambridge: Cambridge University Press.

Wenden, A. and **J. Rubin**. 1987. *Learner Strategies in Language Learning*. Englewood Cliffs, N. J.: Prentice Hall.

Wesche, M. B. 1981. 'Language aptitude measures in streaming, matching students with methods, and diagnosis of learning problems' in K. C. Diller (ed.).

Wesche, M. B., H. Edwards, and **W. Wells**. 1982. 'Foreign language aptitude and intelligence'. *Applied Psycholinguistics* 3: 127–40.

White, L. 1989. *Universal Grammar and Second Language Acquisition*. Amsterdam: John Benjamins.

White, R. 1988. *The ELT Curriculum*. Oxford: Blackwell.

Widdowson, H. G. 1989. 'Knowledge of language and ability for use'. *Applied Linguistics* 10: 128–37.

Wigglesworth, J. 1997. 'An investigation of planning time and proficiency level on oral test discourse'. *Language Testing* 14: 85–106.

Wilkins, D. 1976. *Notional Syllabuses: A Taxonomy and its Relevance to Foreign Language Curriculum Development*. London: Oxford University Press.

Williams, M. and **R. Burden**. 1997. *Psychology for Language Teachers*. Cambridge: Cambridge University Press.

Willing, K. 1987. *Learning Styles in Adult Migrant Education*. Adelaide: Adult Migrant Education Programme.

Willing, K. 1989. *Teaching How to Learn: Learning Strategies in ESL*. Adelaide: Adult Migrant Education Programme.

Willis, D. 1991. *The Lexical Syllabus*. London: Collins.

Willis, D. 1993. 'Syllabus, corpus, and data-driven learning' in C. Kennedy (ed.): Plenaries from the 1993 IATEFL Conference, Swansea, Wales.

Willis, J. 1996. *A Framework for Task–based Learning*. London: Longman.

Willis, D. and **J. Willis**. 1988. *COBUILD Book 1*. London: Collins.

Willis, D. and **J. Willis**. 1996a. 'Consciousness-raising activities in the language classroom' in J. Willis and D. Willis (eds.).

Willis, J. and **D. Willis**. 1996b. (eds.). *Challenge and Change in Language Teaching*. London: Heinemann.

Wilson, D. 1996. 'Context and relevance' in G. Brown, K. Malmkjær, A. Pollitt, and J. Williams (eds.): *Language and Understanding*. Oxford: Oxford University Press.

Winitz, H. 1978. 'A reconsideration of comprehension and production in language training'. *Allied Health and Behavioural Sciences* 1: 272–315.

Witkin, H. 1962. *Psychological Differentiation*. New York: Wiley.

Witkin, H. and D. Goodenough. 1981. 'Cognitive styles: essence and origin'. *Psychological Issues Monograph* 51. New York: International Universities Press.

Witkin, H., D. Goodenough and P. Oltman. 1979. 'Psychological differentiation: current status'. *Journal of Personality and Social Psychology* 37: 1127–45.

Wong-Fillmore, L. W. 1979. 'Individual differences in second language acquisition' in C. J. Fillmore, W-S Y. Wang, and D. Kempler (eds.): *Individual Differences in Language Abilities and Language Behaviour*. New York: Academic Press.

Wright, T. 1987. *The Roles of Teachers and Learners*. Oxford: Oxford University Press.

Yamada, J. 1981. 'Evidence for the independence of language and cognition: a case study of a "hyperlinguistic" adolescent'. *UCLA Working Papers in Cognitive Linguistics* 3: 121–60.

Yorio, C. 1989. 'Idiomaticity as an indicator of second language proficiency'. in K. Hyltenstam (ed.): *Bilingualism Across the Lifespan*. Cambridge: Cambridge University Press.

Yule, G., M. Powers, and D. Macdonald. 1992. 'The variable effects of some task-based learning procedures on L2 communicative effectiveness'. *Language Learning* 42: 249–77.

Index

Note: page numbers in italics refer to figures or tables; *n* refers to footnote.